Grand Excursion

UPPER MISSISSIPPI *by John Frederick Kensett, oil on canvas, 1855.*
(Saint Louis Art Museum, Eliza McMillan Trust)

Grand Excursion

ANTEBELLUM AMERICA DISCOVERS THE UPPER MISSISSIPPI

STEVEN J. KEILLOR

AFTON HISTORICAL SOCIETY PRESS

Afton Press is grateful to the
Katherine B. Andersen Fund of The Saint Paul Foundation
for helping to fund the publication of
GRAND EXCURSION: Antebellum America Discovers the Upper Mississippi.

Copyright © 2004 by Steven J. Keillor

Edited by Michele Hodgson

Designed by Mary Susan Oleson

Production assistance by Beth Williams

Printed by Pettit Network, Inc.

Library of Congress Cataloging-in-Publication Data

Keillor, Steven J. (Steven James)
Grand excursion : antebellum America discovers the Upper Mississippi / by Steven J. Keillor.— 1st ed.
p. cm.
Includes index.
ISBN 1-890434-63-9 (hardcover : alk. paper)
1. Mississippi River Valley—Description and travel. 2. Mississippi River Valley—History—1803-1865.
3. United States—History—1815-1861. I. Title.

F353.K45 2004
973.6'6--dc22
                          2003024709

Printed in China

Afton Historical Society Press publishes
exceptional books on regional subjects.

W. DUNCAN MACMILLAN   PATRICIA CONDON JOHNSTON
President   *Publisher*

Cover painting: DAVENPORT AND ROCK ISLAND CITY *by Henry Lewis, oil, 1855.* (Collection of the Muscatine Art Center, Muscatine, Iowa)

To Will and Sonia

May your journey together be as happy
as that of the excursionists

CONTENTS

FOREWORD

ANNIVERSARIES INVITE US to reconnect our past with our present. They encourage us to reflect on how yesterday's actions shaped today's world, and to rediscover the power of history in guiding our aspirations for tomorrow. The sesquicentennial of the Grand Excursion of 1854 is one such anniversary. The 2004 reenactment of the Grand Excursion reconnects us not only to a time of exploration and expansion in our young nation, but also to a greater understanding of the vital role of the Mississippi River in the development of our country.

In *Grand Excursion: Antebellum America Discovers the Upper Mississippi,* Steven Keillor retells the story of that one-week, three-thousand-mile roundtrip adventure launched in June 1854. Seen through the eyes of a historian of our age, the journey comes alive once more as we follow eastern scientists, clerics, politicians, and financiers as they head west by train to Rock Island, Illinois, and travel north by steamboat to St. Paul, Minnesota.

Entwined with the travel diary itself are Keillor's profiles of notables of the day, including historian George Bancroft, scientist Benjamin Silliman, writer Catharine Maria Sedgwick, and former U.S. president Millard Fillmore. Each profile represents a significant aspect of 1850s society: history's literary and religious biases, science's pre-Darwinian beliefs, women's changing roles, and politics' partisanship. Our country's two-party system,

and, in particular, the westward expansion of slavery, followed on the heels of the contentious Kansas-Nebraska Act of 1854, which reawakened the slavery issue in the United States and became the decisive (and divisive) moment that ultimately led to the Civil War.

Key to westward expansion was the nation's railroad-driven economy. All of the Grand Excursionists were guests of the railroads, whose owners had orchestrated the excursion for their own purposes. With completion of track from Chicago to Rock Island, Illinois—and, therefore, completion of the first line from the Atlantic Ocean to the Mississippi—far more vigorous trade between the river and the rest of the world was at last possible. The heart of North America was ready to do business, and the Grand Excursion was the railroads' calling card. True, the excursion introduced passengers to the beauty of the Midwest and its majestic river. But thanks to dozens of enthusiastic newspaper journalists aboard the flotilla, it also introduced a nation's worth of entrepreneurs to a region rich in resources and ripe for settlement, commerce, and wealth.

Those of us on the Upper Mississippi who are celebrating the 150th anniversary of the Grand Excursion are doing so for our own purposes as well. Ten years ago dozens of the river cities touched by the original Grand Excursion—from the Quad Cities of Iowa and Illinois to the Twin Cities of Minnesota—

began sharing ideas about the sesquicentennial, and how it could serve as a catalyst for rediscovering the river's importance in the lifeblood of our communities. Over the last decade at the annual Millard Fillmore Dinner in St. Paul, for instance, we have not only promoted the 2004 reenactment—our capital city was, after all, the climax of the original excursion—but we have also celebrated the revitalization of our downtown riverfront. New housing, museums, and park space all reconnect our citizens and businesses to the river's potential in growing our city. Our efforts, and those of other cities along the Upper Mississippi, have resulted in billions of dollars in community renewal, as well as the Grand Excursion 2004 celebration itself.

Anniversaries indeed invite us to reconnect our past with our present. In concrete ways, Grand Excursion 2004 (www.grandexcursion.com) and Steven Keillor's book reconnect us to the trip itself. But they also reconnect us to how yesterday's events gradually shaped today's culture and will eventually shape tomorrow's world. In reading Keillor's account of the 1854 journey, we can understand more clearly how long-forgotten events of antebellum America affected the development of cities and towns along the original excursion's Upper Mississippi River route, and further affected the development of our nation. We can feel more keenly the anticipation of those nineteenth-century passengers and promoters as we anticipate the excursion's twenty-first-century reenactment. We can sense more fully the go-ahead, get-ahead spirit of the 1850s through our own excitement about the river's renaissance and our renewed commitment to our cities' limitless potential.

Ultimately, perhaps, we can see how the original journey continues to be our own, with many destinations realized and many more yet to be reached. Through lessons of the past and present, each generation determines its own path. The excursionists and entrepreneurs of today, for instance, are not just the descendants of that predominantly white male society of the 1850s, but also the descendants of the African Americans, Native Americans, Irish immigrants, and women who, in 1854, were considered second-class citizens. Ultimately, perhaps, we all can appreciate more deeply where we have come from and where we are going—and, in the words of T. S. Eliot, "arrive where we started and know the place for the first time."

Paul A. Verret
President Emeritus
The Saint Paul Foundation

VIEW ALONG THE MISSISSIPPI NEAR MAIDEN ROCK *by Edwin Whitefield, 1856–1859. The* Golden Era *carried poet Epes Sargent and his lady listeners past the famous Lake Pepin site of Maiden Rock on June 9, 1854, when Sargent supposedly retold the legend of Winona, a young woman who leaped from the cliff rather than marry a man she did not love. (Collection of the Muscatine Art Center, Muscatine, Iowa)*

PREFACE

I WROTE THIS BOOK with two purposes in mind: 1) to narrate the Grand Excursion of June 1854 for those who will celebrate its sesquicentennial in late June and early July of 2004; and 2) to paint a portrait of antebellum America for college students and others interested in an entertaining, focused, yet comprehensive account of that society. The two purposes are complementary. First, the variety, notable fame, and great influence of the excursionists make their excursion a usable model for such a portrait. The model did not sit still, of course, but was very much in motion and passed through a great many places that also become parts of this portrait of antebellum America. Second, serving as a model for such a portrait gives to the excursionists and to their excursion a dignity and a worth that is fitting, given the scale and scope of this thousand-person, three-thousand-mile trip. Contemporaries perceived it as more than a weeklong romp in the western woods, and so have I.

This portrait captures many of the features that other historians have noticed in antebellum America: sectionalism, the railroad-driven economy, reform movements, the literary renaissance, westward expansion, the second party system, the postmillennial optimism and pre-Darwinian religious fervor, the gradually changing notions of gender and class, and the romantic idealism of this period before realism. Yet these broad features are here personalized in the form of specific individuals—as it were, in concrete details, a Roman nose, a dimpled chin, ringlets of hair, a square head.

I do not claim that this is a definitive portrait. These travelers were not a representative sample of the entire class of antebellum Americans. This group contained far too many "notables & fashionables" to represent the society in any statistically accurate sense. And they tended to be older notables who had already gained the wealth or reputation that earned them an invitation; they represented the 1830s and 1840s, in many ways, and were not the cutting-edge, young leaders whose ideas looked to the future. The leaders on whom I focus—for example, Benjamin Silliman and George Bancroft—are also not a representative sample of all excursionists. I needed an individual's diary or letters mentioning the Grand Excursion to devote one of the "Excursus" chapters to that person. Several interesting notables—for example, the authors Caroline M. S. Kirkland and Elizabeth Oakes Smith—went on the excursion; however, I was unable to find their correspondence or journals referring to the event, and so I focused on Catharine Maria Sedgwick instead. Because the papers of ordinary Americans are not often preserved and collected at libraries, I was not able to focus on the many less notable excursionists, with the exception of John Munn.

Antebellum America often has to be content to have its portrait hang alongside another, more important one—its face merely a "before" view to contrast with the "after" view of the Civil War and Reconstruction. I have tried not to do that. There is no mention of the Civil War until the epilogue, and I use the term "antebellum" merely because it is the standard designation for that period in

American history. I hope you temporarily forget that the term means "before the war."

And yet the excursionists did not head to Chicago in the last week of May 1854 at a representative time in that antebellum period. That week was not a statistically average week. It was the week when President Franklin Pierce signed the Kansas-Nebraska Act into law. Most historians would agree that the act was a decisive turning point. Before it, North-South differences over the westward expansion of slavery appeared to be resolved to the satisfaction of most Americans. After it, these differences were reawakened and an action-reaction chain of events antagonized both North and South in ways that the political leaders of the time could not reverse or halt short of war. Accordingly, this narrative stresses that act, but so did the excursionists and their contemporaries, so that this emphasis is not anachronistic.

As the final editor of this narrative (which is based on the many shorter narratives written by newspaper editors and correspondents), I have occasionally emphasized details that point toward the coming tragedy of the Civil War because I believe that this theme of impending tragedy in the midst of celebration accurately reflects the ironic realities of human existence.

I have included many details that have no relation to that theme: for example, the incident of the potato hitting the nose of one member of the *Galena*'s crew (see chapter 7). Minute attention to such small events represents my own small protest against the "linguistic turn" in the historical profession over the past twenty years. The text has been increasingly privileged over the event—or the possibility of knowing past events has been denied and historical writing reduced to literary criticism of past texts. The Grand Excursion presents a great opportunity to stress the importance of the event—major events like the passage of the Kansas-Nebraska Act but smaller ones as well. About forty journalists went on the excursion, and almost all of them wrote detailed accounts for their newspapers; I obtained twenty-nine of these and tried to reconcile the few conflicting details in the eyewitness testimonies to arrive at a reasonably accurate, fairly complete narrative.

And yet these newspaper accounts are great texts, some of them with real literary quality. I am indebted to these journalists and, in some ways, am just an editor of this book. I have often quoted them, sometimes at length; the reader can often get a better feel for antebellum America by hearing its self-portrait in its own words. I also quote them to avoid the (often necessary) portrayal of the past only in terms of broad movements, large groups, abstract ideas, and wide geographic areas—all to the neglect of the specific, the particular, the individual. Letters and diary entries here demonstrate the very real way that past events had their impact on very real individuals.

A final caveat: this book does not try to prove the Baconian method was dominant in or representative of antebellum America. That method seemed to characterize several prominent intellectuals who are featured in the "Excursus" chapters, and so I chose it as the book's predominant intellectual theme. Other methods and ideas circulated in 1854, and these leaders gained their fame in—and thus partly represented—an earlier era. However, I did use that inductive method in researching and writing the book. In David Hackett Fischer's memorable phrase, I went "a-wandering in the dark forest of the past, gathering facts like nuts and berries." I did not begin with a hypothesis about the Baconian method; I was unaware of (or had forgotten about) Theodore Dwight Bozeman's *Protestants in an Age of Science,* an excellent treatment of "the Baconian ideal" in "antebellum American religious thought." I merely tried to find everything written about the Grand Excursion and to organize it in a coherent fashion. It helped to have a narrow topic, two weeks in early June 1854. It also helped to have people who assisted me in my wanderings.

My thanks go, first of all, to Patricia Johnston at Afton Historical Society Press for her confidence in this book's key concept from the beginning. Research for this book was funded in part by the Minnesota Humanities Commission in cooperation with the National Endowment for the Humanities and the Minnesota State Legislature. Some wonderfully hospitable folks hosted me on research trips to the East Coast and down the Mississippi: Don and Louise Campbell (La Crosse, Wis.); Phil and Ann-Britt Keillor (Madison, Wis.); Gerard and Jane Sundberg (St. Charles, Ill.); Dave Sikkink (Mishawaka, Ind.); Marc and Alison Kovac (Wooster, Ohio); David and Joanne Krehl (Buffalo, N.Y.); James and Alice Stewart (Scotia, N.Y.); Jim and Betty Warden (Ballston Lake, N.Y.); Pastor Wesley O'Neill (Schenectady, N.Y.); Pastor Steve Froehlich (Ithaca, N.Y.); Peter and Jill Stein (Harrisburg, Pa.); Harold and Pat Heie (Gloucester, Mass.); Steve and Gail Nyquist (Simsbury, Conn.); Rachel and John Diehl (Ambler, Pa.); Sam and Andrea Diehl and Bill and Carli Richard (both Washington, D.C.); James Milton (Laurel, Md.); Roger D. Schultz (Lynchburg, Va.); Eric Johnson (Louisville, Ky.); and Judy Locke (Greenville, S.C.). My thanks too to Grace Keillor of Brooklyn Park, Minn., for a mother's support and encouragement. My wife, Margaret, and my daughter, Amanda, cheerfully accepted weeks of a husband's and father's absence. My sons Jeremy and William will, I hope, cheerfully accept the idea of their father doing some literary criticism.

Many librarians have been of great help in locating information on the Grand Excursion. Special thanks go to Jeffrey M. Flannery at the Manuscripts Division, Library of Congress; Stephen E. Simon and Dawn Hutchins Bobryk of the Simsbury Historical Society, Conn.; Thomas Knoles of the American Antiquarian Society, Wooster, Mass.; Maida Goodwin of the Sophia Smith Collection, Smith College, Northampton, Mass.; Frank Orser of the Library of Florida History at the University of Florida; and Ann Southwell of Alderman Library, University of Virginia. Paul Clifford Larson of St. Paul, Minn., was instrumental in locating portraits and artwork.

Final responsibility for the edible or inedible quality of all these factual nuts and berries rests upon me alone, of course.

NIAGARA FALLS *by John Frederick Kensett, oil, 1851–1852. One of the Hudson River School of American painters famed for their wilderness landscapes, excursionist John F. Kensett focused on the sublime ruggedness of the falls' geology. Many excursionists visited Niagara before heading west. (Mead Art Museum, Amherst College)*

CHAPTER ONE

"Railroad Men from Near and Far"

TO SATURDAY, JUNE 3, 1854 (PART I)

THOSE WHO PARTICIPATED in it or read the many accounts of it knew that the Grand Excursion of June 1854 was a great phenomenon of antebellum America. The *New York Weekly Mirror* claimed that, for distance, a distinguished entourage, and "wildness, richness and beauty of the regions visited—it may safely be asserted that the world has never witnessed a more remarkable achievement." To the *New York Times,* the excursion was "perhaps the most magnificent ever projected"; to the *New York Tribune* it was "one of the grandest entertainments imagined." A more modest newspaper than the New York giants, the *Galena Daily Advertiser* ventured that it "was perhaps a little the grandest affair of the kind ever before got up in the United States." One thousand guests, by one estimate, were transported some thirty-six hundred miles at the expense of the Chicago & Rock Island Railroad and of Henry Farnam and Joseph Sheffield, the contractors who had recently constructed the C&RI, the first railroad to reach the Mississippi River from the East Coast. Originating at their widely scattered homes, the guests took free rail passage to Chicago, where they boarded C&RI cars for Rock Island, Illinois, from whence they traveled by steamboat to St. Paul, Minnesota, and thence back to Rock Island and Chicago—all

that in a week's time—and then back to their respective hometowns in another week.[1]

Such a band of travelers, enthused the *Mirror's* editor. Investors, stockholders, and bankers to be sure, but also "a liberal sprinkling of ladies by way of ornament; distinguished politicians, clergymen and scholars, by way of variety, and a miscellaneous crowd of no-bodies-in-particular to fill up the interstices and the state-rooms on board the boat." Such a collection of antebellum notables had never before been assembled, "from the Ex-head-of-the-nation, in the person of President Fillmore" to historian George Bancroft, the "dreamy" literary critic and author Henry Tuckerman, the "venerable Miss Sedgwick; the scientific Silliman; the learned Bartlett; the poetic Sargeant [sic]; the eloquent Bates; the benevolent Minturn; and a long catalogue of notables," not to mention forty-three newspaper editors and correspondents.[2]

These journalists did not spare the superlatives. The *New Haven Register* termed it "*the* excursion of *all* excursions—the largest, longest, and most respectable ever 'got up' since the days of Moses and the Children of Israel." The cautious ex-president, excursionist Millard Fillmore, who was not given to exaggerated language, asserted, "There will never be another such excursion, nor another such jubilee."[3]

Southerners were nearly absent. Only a few excursionists were listed from the slave states.[4] The C&RI tracks to the Mississippi represented a triumph for the growing East-West trade by rail, at the expense of the formerly dominant trade along the river between the South and what was then called the Northwest (the Pacific Coast was too distant to account for much in the nation's trade or nomenclature). The merchants of St. Louis and New Orleans were hurt by completion of the Rock Island Railroad. They saw no cause to celebrate their upstream customers and suppliers finally getting rail service to Chicago, Cleveland, Albany, and New York City.

Little of the Grand Excursion's luster derived from it being a "first." More than three months earlier, on George Washington's birthday, February 22, the first train to reach the Mississippi pulled into Rock Island before thousands of spectators to "the roar of artillery" and other symbols of festivity. The Grand Excursion was not the first such trip arranged by railroad promoters to celebrate the completion of a rail line. Nor was the steamboat trip upriver to St. Paul a first. The *Virginia* made that initial trip in the spring of 1823. For some thirty years, travelers with romantic notions of scenery and landscape had taken the "Fashionable Tour" past the majestic bluffs and wooded isles of the Father of Waters. Except for the west bank in Minnesota, the landscapes they admired so fervently were not wild, uninhabited frontier lands newly opened for white settlement. Illinois achieved statehood in 1818; Iowa, in

1846; Wisconsin, in 1848.[5]

The Grand Excursion owed its grandeur to its magnificent scale and scope and to its timing. It seemed to transport the East bodily to the West in one great tour of inspection on which the nation's past might analyze its future; its culture confront its bumptious expansiveness; and its politicians encounter a West whose slave-or-free status was proving their most insoluble problem—only days after passage of the Kansas-Nebraska Act ominously reopened a debate over slavery in the territories that had seemingly been settled. Western town boosters saw the excursion as grand because it brought the most distinguished crowd ever to visit St. Paul or Rock Island or Dubuque, Iowa. Its full meaning can be perceived only from a broader and longer eastern view, as the culmination of an eastern-financed effort to build local railroads, link them into regional networks, and thus link the Atlantic and Mississippi by rail. In the process, the American economy, politics, and society were forever altered. The Grand Excursion signaled a change not only for Rock Island and Dubuque but for the entire nation.

That change began on the East Coast, and so we must follow the excursionists from their starting points all the way to Chicago to understand the momentous transformations that led to the excursion. The C&RI's guests had to travel nearly a thousand miles between the Atlantic Coast and the south shore of Lake Michigan. For some, this trip would be their most extensive look at the East, as well as their first sight of the West. The excursion was an eastern event too: the travelers were mainly easterners; they passed through the East with free rail passes from their homes to Chicago (where the excursion officially began). As they passed through, they retraced the history of railroading that led to the completion of the Chicago & Rock Island Railroad.

The "venerable" author Catharine Maria Sedgwick began her free trip to Chicago, Rock Island, and beyond on Tuesday, May 29, by boarding the Western Railroad train at Pittsfield, Massachusetts, a county seat in the Berkshire Mountains less than a dozen miles from her home. Her party, which included her brother Charles, had to wait in Pittsfield over the noon hour due to "a change in the running of the cars," yet they enjoyed "an excellent dinner" and were on their way by 3:00 p.m. Boarding with them were Dr. Robert Campbell of Pittsfield, who was feeling unwell, and Miss Elizabeth Colt ("a very gentle ladylike girl," the novelist described), daughter of local attorney James Colt.[6] All had a tie to the Western Railroad. Catharine Sedgwick's brother Theodore had argued (in vain) that the Western lay its tracks instead through Lee, Massachusetts, which was closer to the Sedgwick home, but the chosen Pittsfield far outpaced its rival. A fifty-eight-year-old distinguished-looking, self-taught expert on most everything, Campbell served on the Western's board of directors and interested himself in all railroad matters, including which rock was most difficult to tunnel through and what statistics accurately reflected construction costs. On behalf of his "good friend" Charles

Chapin, the Western's president, James Colt was trying (in vain) to interest Boston investors in buying the New York Central.[7]

The Western was enormously important to Pittsfield but also to the United States. It was a pathbreaking railroad: the first to connect two different regions and the first U.S. corporation to organize itself into operating divisions, "the first modern, carefully defined, internal organizational structure used by an American business enterprise." And, using the Western's model, new railroad corporations of the early 1850s were set to revolutionize the entire structure of the U.S. economy.[8] There were good reasons that many Western investors from Pittsfield and Springfield, Massachusetts, went on the Grand Excursion. The Western not only supplied a prototype that railroads farther west could imitate, it also provided experienced managers and wealthy investors for those railroads, including the Chicago & Rock Island. Connected by way of other rail lines to the C&RI, the Western even provided freight and passengers for through trips from Boston to Rock Island. Although they had free tickets, the excursionists were harbingers of what would be a profitable link.

One excursionist, George Bliss, personified these chain links of railroad ideas and personnel. A former Western president, now president of the Michigan Southern Railroad, he sat on the C&RI board of directors. In his sixties, with a rather square face framed by long sideburns, Bliss was a Springfield lawyer who used the law to enter more profitable ventures. "There was something dry about him physically and mentally, and a curtness that made him sometimes pass for irritable; but this was his manner merely." Mental dryness was perhaps needed to focus on organizational charts, train timetables, stock stipulations—and Whig-Democratic politics (Bliss was a Whig and the Speaker of the Massachusetts House). Following spectacular train wrecks in the early 1840s near Pittsfield and Springfield, he helped to reorganize the Western into three separate divisions, with strict lines of accountability to prevent accidents. He helped to move the Western's management from jack-of-all-trades amateurs like Campbell (a director, not a manager) and himself to professional, career railroad men. He linked the Western to rail lines in New York, Michigan, and Illinois. He secured Grand Excursion tickets for Massachusetts leaders and investors.[9]

The Western did not yet have a bridge across the Hudson; indeed, this was the one missing link in the railroad chain between Boston and the Mississippi River. The Sedgwicks boarded a ferry to cross to Albany, New York, where they enjoyed "a nice tea at the Delavan" House, an Albany landmark.

Also stopping at the Delavan (albeit three days after the Sedgwicks) on his way west was one of the forty-three journalists, Charles Hale of the *Boston Daily Advertiser*. Only twenty-two years old but part of a prolific literary family, Hale had written two books on the South Sea Islands before graduating from Harvard in 1850, had edited the short-lived and aptly named literary journal *Today*, and now assisted his father, Nathan Hale, and his many siblings

in writing copy for the *Advertiser*. His father was famed patriot Nathan Hale's nephew. Few families were better connected to Boston's and New England's elite. The 1850s was not an age of specialization. The Hales were practical as well as literary people. Charles Hale's father was an early promoter of railroads in Massachusetts and a director and first president of the Boston & Worcester Railroad, which had a working relationship with the Western Railroad.[10] Newspaper editors naturally promoted railroads as new, noteworthy, progressive innovations sure to benefit the newspaper's town, its subscribers, and its advertisers. It was no accident that the C&RI invited so many editors on the Grand Excursion and that so many accepted the offer.

In mid-May, Charles Hale eagerly informed his brother Edward that "Father has cordially assented" to his going on "a select & discriminate railroad excursion" as the *Advertiser*'s correspondent (despite the elderly Nathan's need for Charles's services at the newspaper office). Charles hoped Edward or their sister Susan might go, but that was not to be. The one thing keeping Charles Hale from the trip was the legislative session, but it was "probable that Saturday [May 20] may witness the protracted, dying agonies of the legislature at which I must assist." By May's end, legislators and Hale could leave Boston— Hale, by the Boston & Worcester and Western railroads, taking lunch in Springfield and passing through Catharine Sedgwick's beloved Berkshires but ignoring them to concentrate on a fictional piece by William Thackerey in

Harper's. At the Delavan, Hale and his companions obtained "an excellent room at this first rate hotel and were soon 'cleaned up,' from the dustiness of the journey." They took tea and a walk, went to the theater, and prepared to leave for Niagara Falls the next day.[11]

The Sedgwicks also transferred to the New York Central at Albany and proceeded to Utica, New York, which they reached by 10:30 that night.[12] Very likely, none of these excursionists ever considered taking a boat on the Erie Canal that paralleled the Central line; railroads were making canals obsolete for passenger service. Although James Colt failed to arrange a Bostonian purchase of the New York Central, that line still funneled freight and passengers to the Western's terminal at Albany. The two lines were de facto allies, especially in competing against the New York & Erie Railroad that bypassed the canal route and Albany and went up the river valleys in southern New York to connect New York City with Lake Erie.[13]

At Utica, many excursionists boarded the New York Central—many on the same day the Sedgwicks came through—thanks to the numerous invitations extended by William Walcott, a Utica manufacturer and member of the C&RI board of directors.[14] Among them (though two days later) was John Munn, who typified the railroad investor of the early 1850s prospering from the rising value of railroad securities, the very tangible fruit of the Western's and other railroads' successful innovations. In fact, the forty-nine-year-old Munn lived off his railroad investments and his speculations in Chicago real estate (profitable due

to Chicago's excellent railroad connections). The son of a Connecticut veteran of the American Revolution, Munn was not born to wealth. He clerked in the Hartford store owned by author Lydia Sigourney's husband before heading south in the late 1820s to seek his fortune, which he found as store owner, bank cashier, and slave owner in Mississippi. There he married Mary Meek and fathered two children. Desiring a New England–style education for them, he moved his family to Utica, where he built a substantial three-story stone mansion with a four-story tower.[15]

John and Mary Munn only reluctantly parted from their children and their comfortable life in Utica to go on the Grand Excursion. In the 1850s, Americans undertook a lengthy journey with some trepidation. Before he left, John settled his affairs, "leaving memoranda of some things to be done if I do not return." No memoranda could ease the painful knowledge that "sad and heart rending scenes" could occur to the couple on their trip or to the children staying with Miss Harrington at home. As they walked to the New York Central depot around 7:00 a.m., the children came along as far as the street corner near their home, where Mary "parted from them," Munn noted in his diary, "& I returned a few steps with them, and with a gust of feeling I could not restrain & would not if I could, I embraced the sweet creatures, and taking a last look as they entered the house with the kind Miss Harrington I turned sadly toward the cars."[16]

John Munn also felt some trepidation about the vast mixed multitude going on the excursion. Railroad stocks and bonds were easily bought and sold on the New York and other stock exchanges; gone were the gate-keepers who restricted entry into the best businesses using old rules that admitted only dependable men from established families into partnerships. Nearly anyone could buy and sell a corporation's stock and be invited on a trip by its directors. "I fear a great crowd," Munn wrote, "& perhaps discomfort to those of the scrub aristocracy, who imagine all the world is intended for their comfort & all man & womankind should defer to their wants & pleasures." Hardly a representative of old money, Munn worked to acquire social polish and resented the parvenu all the more for being something of one himself. He also prided himself on his experience with Mississippi steamboats, with all their disconcerting discomforts, and so felt "certain this miserable class will have the wind taken out of them before they return. I truly hope so."[17] The ease of buying railroad stock could not prepare one to handle with aplomb the unease of being aboard a crowded western steamboat.

The Munns, the Sedgwicks, Hale, and other excursionists stopped at Niagara Falls on their way West.[18] Given a largely free vacation by the C&RI, these tourists used the eastern leg of their trip to retrace part of the Fashionable Tour so popular in the 1820s. Still scenic but now included in longer tours to the Mississippi that railroads made possible, the tour went from Albany to Niagara, then up Lake Ontario, down the St. Lawrence River, overland to Lake Champlain and Lake

George, then back to Albany. Antebellum Americans imitated their English cousins, who invented the tour in search of scenery and classified scenery into the beautiful, the picturesque, and the sublime. A beautiful landscape featured harmony, "simple and flowing forms," calm lakes, pastoral quietness, and an appeal to the rational, classical intellect. A scene suitable for a painting was picturesque; it had "striking, irregular, spirited forms" like a small waterfall or rapids, rough textures, some nonpastoral characters like gypsies or robbers, some "contrasts in light and shadow." In this Romantic Age, it appealed to the emotions—for example, admiring the Creator's power in fashioning variety and contrast. A sublime scene elicited awe or terror in the observer, either because it had "superlative degrees of beauty and picturesqueness" or because of some unusual "qualities of obscurity, power, privation (darkness and solitude, for example), vastness, infinity, magnitude or . . . magnificence." Moreover, an ability to distinguish these qualities in scenery helped to qualify one as truly genteel and not part of the "scrub aristocracy."[19]

The forty-three journalist-excursionists were familiar with these categories as they wrote letters for their newspapers describing the scenery from Albany to St. Anthony Falls north of St. Paul, Minnesota.

Niagara Falls was definitely sublime, and its immense sublimity satisfied Americans' nationalistic need to possess scenery equal or superior to England's and Europe's. From the 1780s to the 1850s, Americans and American writers sought "to establish a national identity";

viewing and describing the nation's unique scenery was one way to do so. Going on the Grand Excursion was one way of viewing and celebrating such scenery.[20] Samuel Bowles (a noted travel writer) of the *Springfield Daily Republican* took the same route as the Sedgwicks and, in spread-eagle fashion, described the falls: "Niagara Falls is a great Americanism. It would be inappropriate in any other country, and among any other people." To head west and not stop to see it was to be guilty "of a lack of patriotism, amounting almost to irreligion. America is written all over the Falls. . . . Its majestic sweep typifies the grand progress of America." Its sublime activity—"[t]he maddening, dashing, seething, bubbling, pitching, uneasy flood"—exemplified "the intensity of the American mind and the vitality of American action. Here is the fountain of true Young America."[21] For Whigs like Bowles, the expansionist, warmongering, bumptious Young America movement of Stephen A. Douglas's young Democrats was, almost by definition, false—an attempt to grab other people's territory instead of properly appreciating one's own.

Isaac Platt of the *Poughkeepsie Eagle* was not guilty of irreligion, but stopped and described Niagara, "the mighty Cataract looking, if possible, more grand, beautiful and sublime than ever, as the mad rapids dashed in their wild fury over the stubborn rocks, and the angry waters tumbled their vast volume over the crest of the great rock with a voice of thunder into the abyss below." He praised the moonlight view of the falls.[22] Niagara set high

standards for scenery. The excursionists' farthest stop was to be the Falls of St. Anthony, near the village that became Minneapolis, and those who saw Niagara on the way west could not help but compare the two. The falls of the Mississippi would have a hard time meeting their expectations.

Historian George Bancroft, "the scientific [Benjamin] Silliman," and many other excursionists did not take the Fashionable Tour route via the New York Central but took the Erie Railroad instead. Bancroft had ties to Springfield, Massachusetts: he married into its wealthy Dwight family, Western Railroad shareholders and business partners of George Bliss. Bancroft himself was "a large stockholder in [the] Western Railroad." But his first wife, Sarah Dwight Bancroft, had died; he now lived in New York City, and the Erie route was the shorter one from Gotham to Lake Erie.

Bancroft and William Bliss, his stepson, left home on Tuesday, May 30, and traveled with "the best of company" (including Silliman and a director of the "excellent" New York & Erie). The Sedgwicks had the flat New York Central tracks near the Erie Canal. Bancroft's trip through the upstate valleys across the Appalachians was more exciting, according to one New York editor: "This being whirled along at such a dizzy velocity upon a serpentine track, hung along the brows of rugged mountains, leaping across fearful chasms, and skirting the precipitous margin of rivers, requires either very strong nerves, or a comfortable degree of philosophical resignation." Bancroft seems to have had both—and perhaps a feeling that Providence would preserve him to complete the multivolume U.S. history he had half-finished. He and his stepson spent the night at Corning, two-thirds of the way to Lake Erie. On Wednesday, they continued through upstate New York to Buffalo. Thursday they spent at Niagara Falls. They "took the night train to Cleveland" and traveled to Toledo, Ohio, on Friday afternoon, June 2. Instead of stopping there, Bancroft wrote, "the evening was delightful, the moon bright, and we went on to Jonesville" on the Michigan Southern Railroad, "which we reached at eleven o'clock" on Friday night. He owned a section of land (640 acres) near Jonesville and no doubt hoped the Michigan Southern would raise its value appreciably.[23]

The next morning, the dawn's light awoke them just in time "to reach the train, which came whistling along, stirring the dust, heavy as it was with dew." Bancroft had no time to visit and inspect his Michigan land, if he had ever intended to on this trip. Like many excursionists, he had numerous western investments, not just this one, and he was on a pleasure trip after all. Yet he could not help observing generally the "rising villages in the midst of rich cleared lands" and perhaps calculating that the "civilisation . . . at work upon them" was also at work on their market values.[24]

The Michigan Southern was tied to the Western and C&RI railroads—by more than the person of George Bliss—and its value was rising too. It was one of several railroad corporations revolutionizing the U.S. economy in the 1850s. Like all revolutions, this one overthrew a previous regime—a regime of public service corporations specially chartered by state legislatures to accomplish public functions, such as canal and turnpike construction. These 1830s corporations were chartered much like municipalities, with public powers: they had perpetual life, but the legislature could revoke the charter; many had the right of eminent domain; they could tax (assess) shareholders to pay their debts; they had a monopoly within a certain territory and for a certain function (for example, a bridge). The state might appoint some directors (Campbell was a state-appointed director for the Western). These corporations were not for-profit private firms but had a definite public purpose from which they could not stray.[25]

In the 1840s, entrepreneurs stormed the Bastille (of state legislatures and constitutional conventions), demanding that individuals be given the right to secure charters without special legislative approval and the right to conduct these corporations for private profit but with the same public powers (such as perpetual life and eminent domain). Actually, the revolution took longer than a lobbyist does to dash up the Capitol steps, but railroad corporations were some of the first to secure quasi-private, for-profit status in the late 1840s and early 1850s, and they prospered during this period. Americans soon interpreted the railroads' success to mean the success of the new regime of private, for-profit corporations. The railroad's glory reflected on the private corporation.[26] The Grand Excursion celebrated the revolutionaries' success in building for-profit railroads that were linked together, from the Atlantic to the Mississippi.

Excursionist and ex-Michigan governor John S. Barry, who undoubtedly boarded the Michigan Southern train at his hometown of Constantine, personified the old, 1830s regime of public service corporations. Balding, a stern and forbidding personality in his early fifties, sparing his smiles as if they were hard money, Barry was a fiscally conservative Jacksonian Democrat. Reportedly, he "went so far as to sell the clippings from grass on the capitol lawn" and deposited the proceeds in the state's coffers. In the 1830s, Michiganders, and Barry, distrusted eastern capitalists and insisted the state build and own Michigan's railroads. Barry fought hard in the legislature for a southern railroad and against a bill to build only a central one. In 1837 the legislature authorized construction of the Michigan Central, Michigan Southern, and a third railroad. The financial panic of 1837 destroyed this state-owned effort, as it ruined public service corporations elsewhere, but Barry (governor from 1843 to 1845 and again from 1847 to 1851) was loath to admit that. He opposed proposals to sell the state's railroads to private parties; however, once he was out of office and the deed done he participated as an investor in the Michigan Southern and received his invitation to the Grand Excursion.[27]

In 1846, with a new governor, Michigan sold the Central to Boston investors headed by John Murray Forbes, and the Southern to upstate New York investors led by Elisha Litchfield. Both railroads would be most valuable as routes to Chicago. Litchfield's group was the first to grasp that fact and to secure needed rights-of-way through northern Indiana (George Bliss became president of the Northern Indiana Railroad too). That left the fourteen miles from the Indiana line to Chicago. Time was short. Realizing its error, the Central was making tracks for Chicago in 1851. Litchfield, Bliss, and John B. Jervis (the Southern's chief engineer) struck a deal with the fledgling C&RI: eastern capital would aid in financing construction of the Rock Island in exchange for the Southern's use of C&RI track into Chicago. Bliss, Litchfield, and Jervis joined the C&RI board of directors. Entering Chicago on February 20, 1852, the Southern won the race.[28]

The two railroads also competed by running rival steamboats on Lake Erie from Buffalo to their respective eastern termini at Detroit (Michigan Central) and Monroe (Michigan Southern). The Central formed a working relationship with Canada's Great Western Railroad, so that travelers who preferred to go west entirely by rail could take the Canadian cars from Niagara Falls (Canada) to Windsor, Ontario, and cross over to the Michigan Central station in Detroit.[29]

An Albany editor-excursionist found this last alternative decidedly unpleasant and dangerous. The Great Western tracks were "very rough," especially when combined with the "terrific" speed at which the engineer ran the train to make up for a late start. There was no bell rope allowing the conductor to communicate with the engineer up front. The crew locked the railcar doors "until the passengers raised a mutiny at *that*." Then, while the editor stood close to the conductor, who "was standing on the lower step of the passenger car, looking over the wheels" and axle that seemed to be heating up—and while the editor was "wondering at his carelessness," the conductor's head was "struck by a cattle-guard and he was thrown lifeless at some distance from the track." The engineer backed the train up to recover "his mutilated remains." Train travel in the 1850s was not for the faint of heart.[30]

Not surprisingly, the men whom the Chicago & Rock Island invited in May 1854 were from the Litchfield-Bliss-Jervis group, not from Forbes's Michigan Central–Great Western group. The C&RI directors did invite Forbes, but he declined.[31] (Even the anticapitalist Barry came as a friend of the Southern, not the Central.) Bliss invited his Massachusetts friends. Jervis (of Rome, New York) was now the C&RI president; many investors from Rome, Utica, Schenectady, and Albany went on the excursion. Millard Fillmore owned bonds of the Northern Indiana and the Michigan Southern railroads and was linked to this group.[32] But they also cultivated close ties with Democrats. Jervis was a Democrat; Michigan Southern director William Marcy of New York served as President Franklin Pierce's secretary of state and thus, they hoped, as the Michigan Southern's representative in the cabinet.[33]

Despite the seeming unity, once the pressing goal of reaching Chicago was achieved, the group began to split over the contentious issue of whether to run the railroad for its long-term reliability in generating passenger and freight revenues or to operate it for the short-term goal of raising the value of its stocks and bonds. Elisha and Edwin Litchfield thought Jervis's costly, high-quality standards for a railroad reduced their return on investment. They led "the anti-Jervis faction . . . who opposed Jervis's financially conservative policies." The rising value of railroad securities on the stock exchanges was tempting to investors. Jervis had his relatives and supporters too, and the celebratory excursion was hardly the appropriate time for bickering about strategies, but two cliques went west in June 1854.[34]

Bancroft arrived at the Michigan Southern–Rock Island depot at La Salle Street in Chicago at noon on Saturday, June 3. Two weeks earlier, Joseph Sheffield had assured him, "You have a *safe, regular* 10 percent invesment, with prospects of frequent 'Extras' [dividends]." The C&RI was already doing well; its link to the Michigan Southern brought it eastern freight and passengers (like him). Contractor Henry Farnam predicted that completing a railroad link between Chicago and the East would have a similar effect as "tapping into Lake Erie under a forty foot head." So it did. Although associated with a Democratic party traditionally skeptical of private, for-profit corporations, Bancroft must have been pleased, for he relied on investment income to support himself and family while he worked full-time writing his *History of the United States.* Driving around Chicago that afternoon, he noted the city was "full of the hope of boundless prosperity and increase." That could only help the C&RI. George Bliss was at his hotel, he reported, plus "half Connecticut; many from New York. . . . Miss Sedgwick, Silliman are of the number; railroad men from near and far."[35]

Catharine Sedgwick came on "John Forbes road," the rival Michigan Central. Its train did not reach Chicago until Saturday evening, but she was quite satisfied with its construction—"to my spirit[,] cushions underlaid the rails!" She remarked, "Oh the lots of rail-road Pres[iden]ts & directors! on the excursion." She was not thrilled at the thought of having dry-as-dust, profit-calculating railroad men accompany her on a scenic, romantic trip up the great Mississippi. "If William ever envies me," she wrote her niece Kate to remind Kate's husband, William Minot, "let him think of that."[36]

The May 1 letter sent with the tickets stated, "The object of this excursion is to afford the Stockholders and Bondholders an opportunity of visiting and inspecting their Road."[37] Sedgwick need not have wondered at the number of railroad men, which indicated the C&RI's capital needs, its alliances with lines like the Michigan Southern and the Western, and the rise of securities markets selling railroad stock and bonds. No longer were railroad promoters selling securities only to friends and relatives. For-profit railroad corporations were establishing the New York Stock Exchange as the nation's premier financial center. They were by far the major issuers of the stocks traded there.[38] Their profitability and reliability in the early 1850s, in turn, encouraged investors to view the stock exchange as reli-

able. It was no accident that the C&RI main office was in the Corn Exchange Bank Building on William Street, close to Wall Street.[39] Yet financial matters were still in transition in 1854. Some stock in the C&RI and related lines was still sold to friends and relatives.[40]

The C&RI Committee sponsored the excursion. It consisted of President Jervis; Sheffield and Farnam, the partner-contractors who built the railroad and controlled it until July 1; Thomas C. Durant, Farnam's partner in constructing the Mississippi & Missouri (M&M) Railroad that was to continue the C&RI line west of the Mississippi River; Ebenezer Cook, a Davenport, Iowa, banker who helped sell C&RI stocks and bonds; Isaac Cook, Chicago hotel owner, "chief lieutenant" of Illinois senator Stephen A. Douglas, and Chicago's postmaster; Azariah C. Flagg, a fiscally conservative Democrat, fiscal manager (controller) of New York City, and C&RI treasurer; William Walcott of Utica, who owned more than $7,000 of C&RI stock; and L. Andrews.[41] All helped to distribute tickets; Sheffield and Farnam were in charge, but Sheffield remained in New Haven and wrote Farnam, "As to the Excursion we all wish you to take the sole control & direction of it from Chicago."[42]

Evidence indicates that Sheffield, Farnam, and the C&RI directors originally planned for a relatively small group, what Charles Hale termed "a select & discriminate" group, more appropriate to the old era of personally selected business partners than to the new era of publicly traded shares.[43] As May advanced, these plans had to be gradually enlarged and Farnam's tasks in the C&RI's Chicago office grew dramatically. If Jervis invited his brother-in-law Henry Brayton, then he would have to invite other relatives. If Walcott invited only some Utica investors, then others might feel offended.

The committee had to be mindful of family and personal connections. Thomas Durant had family and friends in Albany, and his brother Clark was selling railroad stock to them in 1853. Thomas wrote to Clark, "Mr. A. Fish in the lumber trade in Albany has applied here through a friend for a ticket to the excursion." Thomas had heard that Fish held "14 bonds in this road," and, if true, Clark was to "give him a ticket for himself and Lady or Ladies." William Dey Ermand of New York wanted a ticket, claimed he knew Clark Durant, and was "a large stockholder in some of the western roads." Ever the manipulator, Thomas Durant asked, "Will he be of any service if asked?"[44]

Personal likes and dislikes still counted, even though shares changed hands indiscriminately. Sheffield explained to Farnam, "I could not ever extend an invitation" to two gentlemen, "but I shall not take the trouble here to make an apology—let it all go." Sheffield regretted that Hartford men were going on the excursion. De Forest "is an old commercial friend of mine, see to him a little. He is very rich, a good talker, and may do us a deal of good if he gets on well and is pleased. He is [a] Bachelor—put him with M. Gale." Sheffield was pleased that "Charles Thompson & Mr. Delano don't go (ahem!)" but that would

not detract from the excursion's glory. "I think in a while you will have the best collection of gentlemen & ladies ever congregated in one excursion or one party . . . public men and men of science and good manners." They invited foreign diplomats, artists, writers, and other luminaries. Sheffield was too unwell to go on the entire trip, but he would go out to the C&RI line. "I want to see the party, collectively, which I can do if I meet it on the line."[45]

Anxious about the safety of his western rail ventures, Sheffield felt that the Grand Excursion was "important to the whole western railroad interests." A pleasant and safe trip that impressed eastern investors with the promise of the West could do much to encourage them to buy more stocks and bonds. But it came at a crucial time, when any mishaps might have a damaging effect. In early May Sheffield complained to Farnam, "The excitement and misgivings in the money market continues in New York, and every thing is uncomfortable and as uninviting as possible." Railroad investments seemed to be "very much out of favor" in New England. Farnam's task of managing the excursion was a significant responsibility.[46]

Although the excursion's ostensible purpose was to have "Stockholders and Bondholders . . . visiting and inspecting their Road," it was clear from Sheffield's letter—and from other indications—that its real purposes went beyond hailing a fait accompli. In early 1854 when they sent invitations, committee members were selling bonds to build a bridge across the Mississippi at Rock Island and to finance construction of the Mississippi & Missouri line into Iowa.[47] If excursioning investors were pleased with the finished railroad, they would be more likely to invest in these new projects. Why else would Durant ask if one investor would "be of any service" if invited? Why else would Sheffield suggest another investor "may do us a deal of good" if he did not have a future project in mind? Why else would Durant play a more public role in the excursion than Sheffield? Sheffield had been Farnam's partner for the past completed project while Durant was his partner for the future one. Farnam and Durant were go-ahead promoters who hoped the excursion would interest eastern investors in a trans-Mississippi railroad that led to a transcontinental one.[48]

The Grand Excursion came just when railroad men were turning from lesser goals of reaching Albany or Chicago to the grand goal of reaching the Pacific Coast. The contrast between the older generation of Sheffield and Jervis and the younger one of Durant illustrated that transition.

Balding, white-bearded, the fifty-nine-year-old John B. Jervis was an engineer for whom a railroad was a technical apparatus that should be dependable and solidly constructed. "[H]e was never at ease among the promoters and manipulators who had emerged in railroading by the 1850s and who recognized the financial rewards that could come just from the sale of stock."[49] White-haired, clean-shaven, and sixty years old, Joseph Sheffield also represented the past. Born in Connecticut, he went south to engage in the tobacco and cotton trades in North Carolina and Alabama. He prospered as a cotton merchant in Mobile before returning to the Nutmeg State. Somewhat accidentally, he acquired Farmington Canal stock, met Henry Farnam (the canal engineer), and then shifted into railroads when the canal failed; but transportation had never been his career, and his early railroad projects were local ones in New England. He felt out of place in the 1850s political climate of hostile sectionalism, North against South.[50] Tired of risky investments, he wanted to end his rail-laying career at Rock Island. He dreaded another "enterprise involving liability and anxiety" and had no desire to reach toward the Pacific.[51]

Only thirty-four years old, Dr. Thomas Clark Durant was born in Lee, Massachusetts, the town the Western rejected, not far from the Sedgwick home. He was "tall and lean, somewhat stooped, with . . . long brown hair, drooping dark mustache and somewhat straggly goatee." Durant earned his medical degree at Albany Medical College but went into business at his uncle's grain exporting company in Albany, where he arranged the transport of goods to the West and developed cozy relationships with railroad men who did the transporting. That was how he met Henry Farnam. By 1853 they were partners in a railroad construction company. They "cast their gaze westward across Iowa" and formed the M&M Railroad.[52] It is unclear exactly when Durant began to think about building a transcontinental railroad, but the idea was in the air in 1854, having been agitated and promoted for a decade. For the previous two years, rival Pacific railroad legislative bills stirred interest and controversy in Congress as backers of a southern route fought against supporters of central and northern routes, St. Louis fought against Chicago, and New Orleans fought against both. In 1853–1854, Secretary of War Jefferson Davis dispatched four government survey parties to reconnoiter four possible routes. Which, if any, would be authorized by Congress and President Franklin Pierce was quite uncertain.[53]

Although he did not want his own dollars going west of the Mississippi, Sheffield wished the younger men well in their westward plans. The C&RI would soon be known "as the great leading line towards the south pass & california," he wrote in the summer of 1854. "This will help matters, the Land Bill *will* pass. That, too, will help you very much."[54] A "Land Bill" would grant government lands to a private firm (or firms) to finance construction of a transcontinental railroad.

One barrier to a central Pacific railroad from Iowa—the only route benefiting Farnam, Durant, and the C&RI—was that the area west of the Missouri River was unorganized. No civil government existed, so settlers were reluctant to move there, and railroad men were reluctant to lay track there. In 1853, "congressmen from Iowa, Missouri, and Illinois had introduced into the House a bill to organize" this area as Nebraska Territory. "[T]hey clearly stated that their purpose was to facilitate the building of a railroad westward through this region." Their bill passed the House; in the Senate, Illinois senator Stephen A. Douglas, chair of the Committee on

Territories, sponsored it. He too wanted governments in the region to make feasible a transcontinental line—if possible, one funneling western freight to Chicago, his home city. He was not aiding the M&M over its rivals. It was one contestant among several. And he preferred several Pacific railroads to none at all. In January 1854, he wrote to a Nebraska convention, "We must therefore have Rail Roads and Telegraphs from the Atlantic to the Pacific. . . . Not one line only, but many lines. . . . The removal of the Indian barrier and the extension . . . of Territorial governments are the first steps toward the accomplishment of each and all of these objects."[55]

There was one barrier to removing the barrier: southern senators demanded that Douglas amend his bill to eliminate the Missouri Compromise (1820) provision that barred slavery from this region. Douglas did not do that in February and March 1853, and the bill was tabled; however, he came under renewed pressure when Congress reconvened in December 1853. After trying to evade the issue, he gave in to their demands, and on Monday, January 23, 1854 (after the senators met with President Pierce on Sunday, January 22), Douglas reported on to the Senate floor a Kansas-Nebraska bill that repealed the Missouri Compromise line of 36°30' north latitude (which had excluded slavery north of that line in the Louisiana Purchase). In return for his concession, Douglas hoped to get the "Land Bill" passed in Congress. That did not happen. Douglas gave southern senators their *quid* (repeal of the Missouri Compromise line) without getting the *quo* (the Pacific railroad bill offering land grants to finance construction) that he wanted.[56]

To the older generation of Jervis, Sheffield, and Nathan Hale, this was madness. On January 27, 1854, Charles Hale wrote to his uncle, Edward Everett, U.S. senator from Massachusetts, to give his vacationing father's views on the Kansas-Nebraska bill: "a gross fraud"; "there is no good reason for disturbing the Missouri Compromise." As for the Pacific railroad that was one motivation behind the bill, "father is strongly opposed to any railroad at all."[57] None of the proposed Pacific railroad routes would benefit Boston. Yet Nathan Hale did not represent Douglas's boostering, boisterous Young America but the "old fogies" whom Young America opposed; Everett was soon to retire from the Senate; and Charles Hale had not yet found his own political voice. Douglas might represent the future, many northerners feared.

Railroads' westward progress had become entwined with the possible westward advance of slavery and with the sectional antagonisms aroused by that issue. Similarly, the Grand Excursion—indirectly and implicitly linked to hopes for a Pacific railroad—became entwined with the fateful Kansas-Nebraska bill. As they celebrated the nation's westward advance and the Upper Mississippi scenery that symbolized the nation's greatness, the excursionists could not avoid the unsightly advance of slavery westward and the nation's inability to resolve that issue. Other prospects

than Niagara Falls evoked awe and terror in their hearts and minds. While the "sublime" was merely a literary convention, events could have real and terrible future consequences. The committee sent out its invitations as Congress debated the bill. Bancroft and the Sedgwicks headed west just as the president signed it into law. It became Banquo's ghost that hovered around the joyous feast of the Grand Excursion.

Its sponsor, Senator Douglas, who seemed to personify the bill, became many excursionists' bête noire. He was small of stature, "dressed in a suit of black, with his frock coat buttoned to the chin, and his thick, dark hair swept negligently from his massive forehead," his piercing eyes protected by thick, dark eyebrows, his speeches full of profanities and insults (Harriet Beecher Stowe said they "resemble rather a bomb which hits nothing in particular, but bursts and sends red-hot nails in every direction") but full of remembered details and relentless logic too. One newspaper reporter referred to "impressions of the terror or senatorial might which he has at certain periods excited in certain portions of the country."[58] The senator, more persuasive than he had been even in 1850, a torrent of words and power, a mad rapids eroding away sensible caution about reawakening slavery agitation and attacking his foes with wild fury, a voice of thunder threatening to plunge the nation into the abyss—for some, he cast a terrifying shadow over the Grand Excursion.

Henry Farnam
1803-1883

Joseph E. Sheffield
1793-1882

John B. Jervis
1795-1885

Antoine Le Claire
1797-1861

Peter A. Dey
1825-1911

John A. Dix
1798-1879

Henry Farnam and Joseph Sheffield received significant organizational help in building the
Chicago & Rock Island Railroad, including that from excursionists John Jervis, Peter Dey,
and John Dix, as well as from Davenport, Iowa, founder Antoine Le Claire.
(Detail from collage, Minnesota Historical Society)

CHAPTER TWO

"New England Finds Her Onward Movement at a Stand"

TO SATURDAY, JUNE 3, 1854 (PART II)

THE OUTCRY AGAINST the Kansas-Nebraska Act was especially loud and angry in Joseph Sheffield and Henry Farnam's hometown of New Haven, Connecticut, the normally quiet seat of Yale College, pious center of New England Congregationalism, and home to more Grand Excursionists, per capita, than probably any other city. Sheffield and Farnam controlled the Chicago & Rock Island tracks until July 1, 1854, and were in charge of the Grand Excursion, to which they invited more investors and dignitaries than they had originally intended.[59] It was only natural that their city sent a greater percentage of its citizens than did any other. One who ventured west was forty-five-year-old James F. Babcock, editor of the *New Haven Palladium,* a "vigorous personality" and staunch Whig who wrote a detailed account of the excursion.[60] New Haveners considered their role vital for more important reasons than as Sheffield and Farnam's hometown: New Haven's (and the *Palladium*'s) Whig, evangelical views were the principles on which the nation's security rested. They must prevail in the West if America's future was to be secured. New Haveners could not travel to celebrate railroads' success in the West without worrying what liberty's fate would be there.

The Kansas-Nebraska Act threatened New Haven's and New England's future influence in the West. It organized Kansas and Nebraska territories with the legality of slavery left to settlers ("popular sovereignty"—or "squatter sovereignty," as its opponents derisively termed it), despite the 1820 Compromise. Throughout winter and spring, as it passed the Senate (early March) and languished in the House, northerners angrily attacked Senator Stephen Douglas's bill and flooded Congress with editorials and letters urging its rejection as a betrayal of the 1820 promise.

On Friday, February 24, the Reverend Dr. Leonard Bacon spoke on the bill in his Center Church in New Haven. His talk, Babcock approvingly noted, was "a faithful exposure of the monstrous injustice of the villainous scheme." A Yale student who attended Bacon's talk thought it "a very fine and eloquent sermon," but questioned the propriety of "bringing politics in the pulpit" unless there was "some great national crisis where the lives and liberties of the people hang on the issue." As the bill headed toward passage, however, more northerners came to believe this was the great crisis threatening liberty and justifying ministerial preaching on politics.[61]

On Wednesday, March 8, and Friday, March 10, two large meetings were held at

Brewster's Hall in New Haven to protest the bill. Babcock "made a short address" at the first meeting, in which he outlined the history of compromises with the South. Theologian Nathaniel William Taylor declared "the first thing which I have to say on this subject in *capitals:* THE NEBRASKA BILL IS A MEAN ATTEMPT TO VIOLATE A FAIR BARGAIN! (Applause.)" Taylor urged northerners to drop "all past differences of whig and democrat" to unite around a demand of no further expansion of slavery. Bacon spoke again to denounce the bill. The "scientific" Benjamin Silliman followed him, although Silliman claimed, "Never before this day have I addressed a public assembly upon a political question." He too called for a new political unity: "Let not the word whig, or democrat, be spoken—but let it be the party of liberty. (Cheers.)" On Friday night, excursionist Alexander C. Twining introduced the resolutions formally condemning the bill and stated that this issue of liberty was far greater than "commercial or agricultural or any mere financial considerations!" The resolutions were "enthusiastically received."[62]

These meetings were meant to influence the House debate on the bill. The final fifteen days of House debate were tense: "Amid scenes of wild excitement, weapons were drawn, and bloodshed seemed imminent." House passage did not come until May 22.[63] In protest, New Haveners held another mass meeting in Brewster's Hall on Friday evening, May 26. Babcock opened it with "a few brief remarks"; Silliman likewise spoke briefly after being chosen chair; and Twining again presented the resolutions, which pledged them all to "press on the repeal of this enactment to every justifiable extremity." After several speeches, at 10:30 p.m. the group passed the resolutions unanimously and departed the hall.[64]

Those who believed passage of the bill was an omen of troubles to come had a celestial omen to point to: a partial solar eclipse occurred that Friday afternoon before their protest meeting. Commencing at about 4:15 p.m. and continuing until 6:30 p.m., the moon passed in front of the sun and reduced its effects to a ring of sunlight that looked like a crescent-shaped new moon. During a "deep twilight," roosters crowed and strange phenomena happened.[65]

The following Tuesday, the day Babcock and many of the others left for the Grand Excursion, President Franklin Pierce signed the Kansas-Nebraska Act into law.[66] His signature did not end northerners' outrage or talk of new political alliances aimed at repeal of the hated measure. New Englanders were particularly outraged. Spreading slavery westward meant blocking New England's heritage of freedom from its own westward advance. That did not mean that Yankees were indifferent to commercial or financial considerations—and their interest in advancing west had a financial side too.

Farnam and Sheffield got their start in the transportation business here. The problem plaguing Boston and New England—being cut off from the western hinterland by New

York's superior river and canal connections—also plagued New Haven. The city had an excellent harbor on Long Island Sound, but rival Hartford had the Connecticut River, which provided access to the interior and entered the sound thirty miles east of New Haven. New Haven sought an artificial route to the interior that would bypass and outdo Hartford's natural route. An engineer, Farnam worked to construct a canal to Farmington, Connecticut, and beyond, to siphon interior trade away from Hartford. When that failed, Sheffield and Farnam led a project in the late 1840s to build a railroad near the Farmington Canal to accomplish a similar goal, an apprenticeship that prepared them for the more ambitious job of building the Chicago & Rock Island Railroad.[67]

Farnam, at least, had decidedly switched his ambitions to the West's more expansive, more lucrative opportunities. Yet the fifty-one-year-old Farnam mediated between the older generation of Sheffield (age sixty) and John B. Jervis (fifty-nine) and the younger generation of Thomas C. Durant (thirty-four). After his canal tribulations, Farnam badly wanted profits, but his trials taught him integrity so that he wanted honestly earned profits. James Woodward of the *New Haven Morning Journal & Courier* aptly described him: "There are but few that possess the extraordinary ability required to carry the Farmington Canal upon their back, with all its untold embarrassments and trials, for a dozen years or more," then go on to build the Farmington Railroad and the C&RI, "but Mr. Farnam has just that ability."

Years after his canal experience, Farnam would still have nightmares and awake with the words, "I have been spending the whole night repairing a break in the old canal."[68] After the purgatory of the Farmington River Valley, the excursion to the Mississippi River Valley was Farnam's well-earned heaven, and he wanted the New Haveners who witnessed his embarrassments to see his triumph too.

New Haveners he invited on the Grand Excursion had a chance to view the West first-hand, some of them for the first time.

Accompanying others, James Babcock experienced the tourists' frustrations. They left New Haven on Tuesday, May 30, and traveled to New York City—by train, no doubt on the New York & New Haven Railroad. Wednesday, they took "the 7 o'clock mail train from New York [City]" on the New York & Erie Railroad along the deep river valleys that cut through the mountains in the southern tier of counties in western New York State. One of Babcock's fellow passengers was Benjamin Silliman Sr., seventy-four years old but still tall, handsome, evangelical, and now professor emeritus of chemistry and natural philosophy at Yale. "Tall Mr. Silliman is attended by short Mrs. S[illiman]," observed historian George Bancroft. Silliman still lectured on geology, and his account of their trip through upstate New York focused on geological features ("the red sandstone region of New Jersey—then the granite ranges of Ramapo—then again a red sandstone region"). An author of travel books also—most recently *A Visit to Europe in 1851* (1854)—Silliman kept a detailed journal of the excursion, as if intending to turn it into a book. The perfectionist professor apologized in his journal for his poor handwriting and his uncertainty (due to "the rapid motion of the cars") whether the stones were red slate or red sandstone. The mail train stopped at all stations, so they missed their connection to the branch line to Buffalo. They had to continue on the New York & Erie's main line to Dunkirk, a small Lake Erie port that Silliman thought "a new place—not yet mature & not well arranged."[69]

Some of the group—including Silliman and Babcock's competitor, Woodward of the *Journal & Courier*—stayed in Dunkirk overnight, content to wait for the morning train to Cleveland. Impatient, Babcock went on ahead and experienced the unreliability of pre-railroad transportation. He believed "the lying assurance of an agent" for a lake steamer who told him the boat could travel to Cleveland overnight. The *Keystone State* got less than halfway to Cleveland, he complained, "and here I am in Erie [Pennsylvania], waiting for our friends to come along in the [rail] cars this morning." The train would beat the steamer to Cleveland by several hours, and Babcock had the humiliation of having to bow to a competitor's wiser choice and wait to rejoin him aboard the train.

While waiting, Babcock cast a critical eye on Erie, the Near West to a New Havener, and one with a dubious reputation. He granted that it was "a decidedly pretty place" with the advantage of being "laid out in squares like New Haven." Yet its citizens had recently engaged in a "rather infamous" episode of "rowdyism . . . tearing up rails and destroying bridges, and making themselves otherwise ridiculous." What was almost worse to a Whig was that the Democratic authorities did little to stop the rioting. What *was* worse to Silliman was that "even the women engaged in the savage work."

Babcock did not describe the riot's complicated origins. The rules for railroading were still being worked out when the excursionists headed west; American society and its economy were still adjusting to the new railway age. To stop New York railroads from using the narrow neck of Pennsylvania along Lake Erie to cross to Ohio without depositing any economic benefits in the Keystone State, Pennsylvania decreed that tracks west of Erie had to be of 6 feet or 4.71 feet gauge, and those east of Erie of 4.83 feet gauge. That forced travelers like Babcock and Silliman to change trains in Erie and spend money in the Commonwealth of Pennsylvania. The victory was temporary, for the "foreign railroads" got the law changed, by fair means or foul, and agreed on a common gauge through Erie. In December 1853, in response, the citizens rioted, tore up the tracks, and destroyed bridges. That created a seven-mile gap in civilized travel by rail and almost forced passengers to purchase transit and food in Erie.[70]

By late May, Silliman reported, an Ohio railroad had paid $500,000 to have the controversy "quieted" and the tracks linked—almost. "As a salvo for pride, however, we were obliged to change trains & walk over a platform to another car" to give "a pretense for stopping 20 minutes *to dine* at 10 1/2 or 11 AM!"—to drop some cash in Erie—"but few of the passengers left their seats today." This "puerile arrangement" would be abandoned for a complete connection "as soon as the popular irritation has died away." Presumably, neither Babcock nor Silliman dined nor disbursed funds but merely boarded the morning train for Cleveland along with fellow New Haveners.[71]

Another excursionist took the same dim view of Erie's people and their pretensions to rail equality. He saw street "urchins" with their parents' "true belligerent spirit." They "got up a small fight for our benefit, one of them raising a large stone in imitation of the fathers and mothers of the place, which he was about to hurl at his antagonist" until some in the excursion party stopped him. The riots were having a regrettable influence on the young. "The cars tarried long enough for dinner," but no one purchased dinner or anything else from "the boys who surrounded the cars with their baskets."[72]

Finally arrived in Cleveland, Babcock reported that the city had a reputation for beauty—"It has some resemblance to New Haven"—but needed the finishing work and final architectural touches that perfected "some of the older cities of New England, especially New Haven." The "exquisite finish" that made New Haven's architecture the best "I ever saw" could be brought to Cleveland by "[t]he two New Haven architects," if Ohioans had the good sense to hire them. The good

progress made to date was mainly due, he thought, to "the fact that the pioneers of this region were generally from Yankeedom."

In that Babcock was correct. As they rode the train from Erie to Cleveland, New Haveners passed through the last remnant of Connecticut's West, the so-called Western Reserve, a 120-mile-long tract of which Cleveland was the unofficial capital. Silliman noted that it was "formerly called New Connecticut." At the time of the American Revolution, the state of Connecticut claimed a swath of land between 41° and 42° north latitude (the exact latitudinal width of the state at its widest point) from the Pennsylvania border to the Mississippi River and all the way to the Pacific. Ironically, this claim included the sites of Chicago and Rock Island. New Haveners were hurtling toward their own patrimony, or what would have been theirs had their state not surrendered it, for purposes of national unity, to the new national government— except for Western Reserve lands that Connecticut retained and tried, somewhat unsuccessfully, to sell to earn revenues for its school system. In 1800, the nation took over the reserve and made it just another Ohio county, albeit one heavily settled by pioneers from the Land of Steady Habits.[73]

Reverend Dr. Leonard Bacon was the son of a Yankee couple, David and Alice Bacon, who toiled to found a model evangelical township in the Western Reserve. He looked back nostalgically on his parents' efforts to set "one conspicuous example of a well organized and well christianized township, with all the best arrangements and appliances of New England civilization." They hoped their model would encourage compact settlements and discourage that dispersal of population so injurious to "the best arrangements." His parents failed, and their son returned to New England, but he and other Yankee excursionists were going west partly to see if a market-driven, dispersed immigration had indeed produced the un-Yankee and un-evangelical results his parents feared.[74]

Silliman also encountered painful memories of failure when journeying west of Cleveland through territory also settled by Connecticut folk, including "my unfortunate [half-]brother Joseph Noyes . . . [who] purchased lands and toiled upon them many years like many other pioneers without success, buried his amiable wife and died at Pittsburgh." Yet Bacon, Silliman, and other New Haveners persevered in a passionate commitment to Christianize and civilize the West. A member of the American Board of Commissioners of Foreign Missions, Bacon participated fully in its work of sending missionaries to Native Americans in the West and in the American Home Missionary Society's work of Christianizing the pioneers. If New Haveners could not own a piece of the West outright, they could exert moral and spiritual influence on it.[75]

Departing from Cleveland on Friday morning, June 2, with three days to make it to the jumping-off point of Chicago, Babcock and the others entrained for Toledo. The editor did not bother his readers with any description of flat northern Ohio between Cleveland and Toledo, although he did detail the improvements in the latter city. "Much of the credit of the improved school system is due to our Yankee friend, Rev. Mr. Smyth, the superintendent," who formerly lived in New Haven.

(Possibly unbeknownst to Babcock, Woodward had gotten the jump on him and reached Cincinnati by Thursday evening, June 1, from whence he informed New Haven readers of the alcoholism and materialism— "The Money God"—prevalent in the West.)[76]

Ever the go-ahead traveler eager to steal a march on the slower excursionists, Babcock boarded the overnight train for Chicago "at 7 o'clock in the evening, just as a party of New Haven friends" arrived in Toledo. He had originally planned to spend Friday night in that city, but he changed his mind when he heard "that the hotels of Chicago were overrun with travelers." Reports of the greater-than-anticipated crowds of excursionists may have reached all the way east to Ohio. Better to be in Chicago seeking a hotel room on Saturday morning than to arrive there and try to find one at ten o'clock Saturday night. Babcock left his friends to fend for themselves and come along the next day. He boarded the Michigan Southern night train for Chicago.

He was surprised to find Connecticut company in the night cars. There sat Alexander Twining, a fifty-three-year-old civil engineer, surveyor of railroad routes, astronomer, and inventor of a new liquid-vapor refrigeration system. With him were

Colonel William Mather, president of the Farmington Valley Railroad that was Sheffield and Farnam's first rail project, and Jeffrey Orson Phelps, a self-taught lawyer, local judge, tavern keeper, postmaster, and amateur civil engineer who built a short section of Farnam's canal. Phelps handled legal cases for the FVRR. Mather and Phelps were residents of Simsbury, a town in the Farmington Valley with close ties to New Haven. The two-hundred-pound Phelps was a local notable and sometime legislator who was unafraid to express his views. He had worked with Sheffield and Farnam on the canal; he owned stock in several railroads, although possibly not the C&RI; still, it was time well spent for him to accompany his client Mather to the west on a free ticket. A Democrat and tavern owner, Phelps undoubtedly disagreed with Babcock and Twining on Connecticut's new prohibition law that was to go into effect on August 1—and may have told them so that night—but he probably shared their anti-slavery, anti-Nebraska views.[77]

Alexander Twining was a former student of Silliman's and now a New Havener. Although not a professor, he wrote articles for Silliman's *American Journal of Science and Arts* and had close ties to the Yale faculty. He had real estate and railroad investments in the West and a Chicago agent to look after them. He sometimes closed letters to the agent by referring to the Kansas-Nebraska Act ("I hope you forget not freedom & Nebraska"). A week before this conversation aboard the Michigan Southern, he wrote the resolutions opposing the act and attended New Haven's anti-

Nebraska meeting, chaired by Silliman.[78] He had written a lengthy article ("The Nebraska Bill and Its Results") just published in the May issue of *The New Englander,* New Haven's quarterly journal of religion, politics, and culture, edited by his friend Reverend Bacon and dedicated to advocating Congregational ideas to the region and nation.[79]

Babcock, Twining, Phelps, and Mather no doubt talked about the act while conversing on their all-night trip to Chicago—and Twining's comments likely paralleled those he made in his article.

Twining began his attack on Kansas-Nebraska with a metaphorical flourish on the barriers New England liberty encountered on its way west. Like Connecticut cut off from its western patrimony, like Boston merchants cut off from western customers by New York's superior rail and canal arteries, so liberty-loving New England found "her onward movement at a stand. Her leading and most prophetic minds are looking earnestly for some favoring defile around, or some passage across[,] impediments which appear more and more threatening"—namely, the Slave Power's aggressions in the West. The "pilgrim fathers'" idea of liberty had expanded "from the sea to the [Great] lakes and beyond the great western [Mississippi] river" due to "vast emigrations" of Yankees. Yet now it was blocked by slaveholders' unholy scheming.[80]

As might be expected of a writer from the long-settled East, Twining focused on history: "a grand inquest is demanded; at which history shall be made to take the witnesses' stand" by this attorney who would "summon the past with its persons and its papers" to testify. How could slavery annul the Missouri Compromise and triumph over liberty? Twining's case indicted the founding fathers as it exonerated the pilgrim fathers. Compromises at the 1787 Constitutional Convention encouraged a spirit of compromise that spawned further surrenders of liberty "till, at length, the Nebraska bill lifts its snaky form without a compromise" and strikes at liberty openly.

How could this process be halted and reversed? Only if that "multitude of minds" from "the religious, the learned, and the industrial occupations" could combine to create "newly formed agencies" that would defend liberty and defeat slavery. What those agencies might be or when they might be formed Twining did not say, but certainly the excursionists represented a multitude of religious, learned, and enterprising minds—New England's "leading and most prophetic minds." They would have opportunity to talk about Kansas-Nebraska as they were shut up together for a week in close quarters in railcars and on board steamboats.

If they discussed Twining's article that night, Babcock would have agreed wholeheartedly with his argument, even if the editor might not have used the geological and meteorological metaphors the scientist used to illustrate it. At the March 8 meeting, Babcock had also condemned the gradual reduction, by compromise, of freedom's share of the newly opened West.[81]

Unlike the steamer's agent, the railroad agent had not lied about Babcock's train reaching Chicago the next morning. Trains kept schedules better than boats. They immensely improved mid-nineteenth-century transportation but were accident-prone. A dozen miles from Chicago, the Michigan Southern train pulled on to a side track to make room for an outbound train, but it did so too vigorously and ran into a baggage car. The collision threw the locomotive off the tracks. The passengers had to wait for a substitute to come from the city and pull the cars the rest of the way into the La Salle Street station of the Michigan Southern and Chicago & Rock Island.[82]

As Babcock expected, "[w]e found the hotels all crowded, but luckily, were able to secure a room for four at the Mattison House." He couldn't help crowing a bit over getting the jump on his friends, who were to arrive that evening to the task of finding hotel rooms at a late hour. Fortunately, Reverend A. H. Eggleston had persuaded members of his "large congregation" to house those of "the New Haven representation" who failed to find a hotel with a vacancy.

Part of the representation had already arrived, "several with their families, booked at the hotels." Roger Sherman Baldwin and his wife, Emily Perkins Baldwin, were there. A native of New Haven, Yale graduate, descendant and namesake of Roger Sherman (signer of Declaration and Constitution), and a prominent Whig lawyer and politician, Roger Baldwin served as Connecticut's governor from 1844 to 1846 and as its U.S. senator from 1847 to 1851.[83] Like Phelps, but with a wider reputation, he handled legal cases for railroads. Like Phelps, he cemented his social and business ties to railroad executives by going on the excursion. Tall, bespectacled, with receding light (almost blond) hair, a light beard on jaw and chin but clean-shaven around the mouth and cheeks, the sixty-one-year-old Baldwin had a strong streak of Yankee independence that caused Connecticut legislators to refuse to reelect him to the Senate. His wife's "political zeal and acumen equaled those of any male in the Whig party." (Perhaps she was not as proud and independent and might have kept the Senate seat; she was as firmly opposed as he to slavery's expansion into the western territories.) In February 1854, Roger Baldwin called the Kansas-Nebraska bill "*base* and *fraudulent*."[84]

Baldwin personified New Haven's anti-slavery feelings. He inherited anti-slavery views from his father and grandfather, but these were strengthened by the famous *Amistad* case. He acted as chief defense counsel for Cinquè and fifty-two other slaves who killed the *Amistad's* captain and seized that slave-trading ship in August 1839. The ship ended up in Long Island Sound; the slaves, in the county jail in New Haven. "Each day, under guard," they walked to the green in front of Reverend Bacon's Center Church for exercise, "delighting crowds of spectators with their agility and gymnastic skill." The New Haven County jailor collected a fee from those who visited his charges and used the proceeds to improve their living conditions. Bacon and others gave "religious and educational instruction" to them; "Yale students and their professors . . . were able to teach them English."

It was abolitionist leaders in New York City who took the initiative in this case, but the *Amistad* brought the issue of slavery home to New Haven, and its residents rallied to the former slaves' cause. A Yale professor teased out the rudiments of the slaves' Mende (or Mendi) language so that Baldwin and his fellow attorneys could communicate with them. The prisoners were transported to their court hearing in Hartford along New Haveners' preferred route, the Farmington Canal; later, the slaves were moved to a house in Farmington, New Haven's inland ally. Primarily due to effective arguments made by former president John Quincy Adams, but also with the help of Baldwin, Bacon, and other New Haveners, the *Amistad* captives secured their freedom by March 1842, and their return to Africa, "accompanied by several Christian missionaries, who established a 'Mendi Mission,'" with Cinquè as interpreter.[85]

New Haven was not unreservedly, exclusively anti-slavery. Sheffield earned much of his fortune as a cotton merchant in Mobile, Alabama; even after he returned to Connecticut in 1835, he spent nine winters in Mobile "buying and shipping cotton." The 1830s witnessed a flurry of abolitionist activity that Sheffield strongly opposed, and "he never forgot to sympathize with the personal sufferings and hopes of his old acquaintances at the

South." New Haven was a center of carriage manufacturing. Although they may never have lived in the South, the city's carriage makers sold their product mainly to plantation owners and tended to favor compromise with the South. They supported the Great Compromiser, Henry Clay, the slaveholding Kentucky senator who had nearly personified the Whig party and who at his height had been as popular in New Haven as in Mobile. Baldwin's opposition to Clay's (and Douglas's) Compromise of 1850 had helped to end his political career in Connecticut in 1851. These Carriage Whigs resembled the pro-southern Cotton Whigs of Massachusetts.[86]

Although the Grand Excursion celebrated improved ties between East and West, and few southerners participated in it, strong commercial ties still bound East and South. These ties greatly complicated and fractured northern reaction to the Kansas-Nebraska Act and ensured that it was not totally denunciatory.

Another excursionist whom Babcock encountered in Chicago that Saturday morning—James Brewster—was New Haven's leading manufacturer of carriages. Balding, with graying hair over his ears and a large Roman nose, the sixty-six-year-old Brewster was New Haven's main civic leader, the epitome of a moral, enterprising, philanthropic Whig businessman. His carriage factory on Wooster Street was the largest of a dozen such plants in the city; it assembled "buggies, phaetons, victorias, and other forms of equipage for a large market, especially in the South." Brewster also found time for civic good deeds; he financed

an educational institute and lyceum in New Haven, "helped to found the community's pioneer savings bank," led in establishing a fire department and a city waterworks, and vigorously supported the new anti-liquor law.[87]

The *New Haven Register* called him "our enterprising fellow-citizen, who is always engaged in some good work." Brewster probably did not favor the compromise and certainly opposed the Kansas-Nebraska Act. He personified the spirit of civilization and progress that New Haveners looked for and hoped to see in the western cities they visited. They believed that slavery would dull that spirit if allowed into the western territories— as the hated act seemed to do.[88]

Babcock also met "many other Connecticut gentlemen" before walking to the C&RI office. "Mr. Farnam is busy at the railroad office," he reported, "receiving the names of the party who intend to push on to the Falls of St. Anthony." Farnam had time to reassure him that plans for the excursion were appropriate and adequate. "Friends and acquaintances will be kept together as much as possible," Farnam promised. Clean-shaven, his black hair starting to recede, with a dimpled chin, he had that straight-ahead, get-it-done look of the determined railroad engineer and promoter.[89]

Henry Farnam's optimism would be progressively shaken as throngs of excursionists poured into Chicago that evening and throughout Sunday. Babcock did not report on his friends' luck or misfortune in room-seeking on Saturday evening, but Isaac Platt of the *Poughkeepsie Eagle* described how "a cannon was firing near" as they approached Chicago that evening, "as if intended to give us a salute." Naive "green ones" concluded that this marked the prelude to "a grand or ceremonious reception" for them. Applying the metaphor for severe suffering on the 1849 gold rush to the relatively minor inconvenience of few hotel vacancies, Platt corrected that error: "on reaching" Chicago, "we were surprised to *see the elephant,* and to most decided advantage, tusks, tail, and all!" Stepping out of the train, they met alarmed cries, "'There is no room,' 'All the hotels are full, and running over.'" A few travelers "began to be alarmed and to repent of their temerity in visiting such a place."[90]

Catharine Sedgwick's published account of the Saturday evening arrival in Chicago emphasized joy, not alarm, and hilarity, not temerity. (Her brother Charles had telegraphed ahead to reserve rooms for their party at the Tremont.) Crowds "thronged the receiving-rooms, the drawing-rooms, and the passages of the Tremont Hotel." The Tremont was Chicago's premier hotel. A five-story brick building with a flag-flying cupola on its roof, it stood at the street corner, with its two-story-high portico, and took up one-fourth of a city block.[91] It was large and a difficult place to "throng," but the excursion was an even larger event. Still dressed in gray travel clothes and carrying "crumpled 'wide-awakes' in their hands" (a wide-awake was a soft felt hat with a wide brim and soft crown), they greeted each other joyously.

"Are you here?"
"How delighted I am to see you!"
"Two days only from New York, but not at all fatigued," says one.
"I," says another, "took the allowed six days for the journey, passed some hours at Albany, and half a day at Utica; spent a glorious day at Niagara; had a pleasant drive about Buffalo; saw all their princely residences; slept on the serene waters of Lake Erie; passed a delightful evening with my friends in Detroit; have glided to-day over the Michigan Central, and now am here as fresh as when I started!"[92]

Whether an observer perceived the hotels as sociably or alarmingly crowded depended, no doubt, on his or her chances for accommodations that evening. Or, perhaps, on the public or private nature of the writer's account. Writing privately to her niece in Massachusetts, Sedgwick sounded annoyed: they had reserved rooms at the Tremont "but the spacious entrance hall—the steps—all were a dense mass—& no one c[oul]d get to the" counter to register. Various friends and acquaintances and strangers then pushed offers of accommodations on her. She "accepted" one offer despite "dreading the horrors of social responsibility in a private house."[93]

An excursionist who arrived after 9:00 p.m. and failed to find a room reported the hotel hallway "filled like a merchant's exchange." He did reach the counter only to find the hotel clerk indifferent to his needs. The clerk did not invite him to sign the hotel register, but he signed anyway and asked, "Have you a room for me?"[94]

"Not a room in the house, sir."
"Well, give me a cot, then?"
"Not a cot in the house, sir."
"But I am ill, and can go no further.
You may give me a sofa,—anything."
"Not a sofa in the house, sir; nothing
in the house, sir."

The clerk "sa[id] the same thing to another applicant for hospitality,—and to another,—until he was so tired of refusing that he did it without pity, or even politeness."

Featured at the Tremont that evening was a panorama painted on canvas by a Monsieur Andrieu, showing "his views of a trip over the prairie by rail road, with scenes by the way, towns, cities, villages, etc., etc." While waiting for service and a room, excursionists could get an advance glimpse of what awaited them on Monday. Paintings of a single scene tried to reproduce the landscape a hiker saw; the panorama portrayed the much more extensive vistas seen from a speeding train.[95]

Crowded hotels were not solely a result of the excursion. "This state of things has existed here during most of the season," Babcock was told. "It is only made a little worse by the excursion party." Because he arrived in Chicago early and had to walk several blocks from the Michigan Southern depot to find a hotel, he had a good opportunity to examine the city. Chicago was in the midst of a tremendous growth spurt, triggered by rail-road construction—the building of the C&RI, but more important the Galena & Chicago Union that funneled western grain into the city, and the Michigan Southern (1852–1853) that connected it to the East and New York. The great moment came on February 20, 1852, when the Michigan Southern arrived and cut travel time to New York City from two weeks to less than two days. The 1850s were America's boom period for railroad building and for the railroad's multiplying ramifications. No city was more dramatically impacted than Chicago. "Forty-two trains of cars depart from the city daily," Babcock noted, "and as many more enter."[96]

"Four years ago it was a mere village," he marveled, "and now it is a city of about seventy thousand inhabitants, and having all the signs of a proportionate increase during the next ten years." This time he made no comparisons with New Haven. Chicago was sui generis. No Connecticut city exploded with such "rapid growth." To a New Englander, Chicago was nearly without a history. "The oldest native inhabitant of this place is a young lady twenty-two years of age!" he exclaimed in wonder. One of Chicago's few "relics of the past" was an "old block house used as a fortification against the hostile Indians," and it was only thirty-eight years old. Chicago was a village in 1838 when New Haven celebrated its bicentennial.[97]

Babcock's Connecticut regret over the loss of the past was considerably soothed by his Yankee delight at reports of the gain in real estate values. "In less than two years," the value of some low-lying marshlands "has risen from two dollars to one hundred dollars the front foot." He displayed an antiquarian's interest in inspecting the block house's dimensions and type of logs but admitted, after reporting land values, "I have got the Western fever well on me, as you have perceived." So much so, that he considered "going no farther than Rock Island" and then returning to Chicago, perhaps to buy a few properties himself. Some excursionists were land speculators who went west partly to spy out the land and pick choice parcels. One of Babcock's fellow editors climbed up in the Tremont's cupola to see "the magnificent prospect" of thousands of rapidly appreciating acres.[98]

Farnam persuaded him to continue, and Babcock's romantic view of the West prevailed over his pecuniary view. Farnam "informs me that the ladies of St. Anthony's Falls are preparing a *pic-nic* for the guests. . . . Think of that! Ladies at St. Anthony's Falls, where I had anticipated seeing only Indians, bears, catamounts, and other like citizens of a primeval forest." He turned the Northwest's speculative and rapid growth into a political statement against slavery. "This is a great country, especially the free portions of it" that were not "cursed with slavery." That conjured up the Kansas-Nebraska Act. "I have not found a man here that did not loath from his soul the perfidy of the South in basely swindling the North out of the free fruits of the Missouri Compromise. They are sworn to repeal at any hazard. The indignation is stronger here even than in New England."

That Saturday evening, Democratic federal officeholders organized a torchlight parade to support Douglas and his Kansas-Nebraska Act. The *Chicago Tribune* interpreted it as burlesque and dismissed paraders as habitués of North Side grog shops paid to march in the procession to the jeers of onlookers. "The head Marshal of the day was, of course, the Postmaster [Isaac Cook, member of the C&RI Committee hosting the excursion], aided by a Deputy" from the saloons, "the Port Collector, in his best clothes, looking very sheepish and ashamed of himself," and a Mr. Cameron, who patrolled "the rear and flanks of the procession . . . picking up the stragglers from the gutters." Fireworks sounded as the paraders neared the North Market. "The motley affair took up its zig zag, rail-fence march for the South Side," carrying a "white cotton banner" on which the words "Nebraska and Kansas Territory" were "daubed with charcoal." More jeers greeted them as they crossed Lake Street.[99]

The crowd made a left turn and headed east to Michigan Avenue. Here, "Dick Swift's artillery man, no doubt intending a practical joke, discharged his piece on the left flank of the procession" (firing blanks) in an enfilade blast whose "concussion, of course, extinguished three-fourths of the torches, and knocked over two or three of the most unsteady in the ranks." Survivors headed into Dearborn Park, where a Colonel Hamilton gave them a speech. "He said this was the most momentous occasion in the history of the country." And, "that Judge Douglas was the greatest man in the United States." That produced cheers from the marchers inside the park, "answered by three distinct and over-whelming groans from the outsiders." The *Chicago Journal,* also anti-Nebraska, was editorially embarrassed: "In view of the number of strangers in the city, we felt mortified at the ridiculous exhibition. . . . It was puerile in every point of view; in fact, *the* fizzle—such alone as Nebraska men could get up."[100]

Some excursionists were among the outside onlookers. Some attended the theater, including ex-president Millard Fillmore and his Buffalo ally, ex-postmaster general Nathan K. Hall. Famed actress Julia Dean was appearing in *Love Chase,* playing tearful Mrs. Haller and Constance. Tall and stately, twenty-four-year-old Dean had a "delicate, sensitive, refined, affectionate nature" and excelled at "delineating gentle phases of character and emotion and the milder aspects of human experience." She was a great hit with the audience that night, reported Hiram Fuller of the *New York Weekly Mirror.* "During the progress of the play, the sobs of Mrs. Haller were relieved by the reports of 113 guns, which the Federal office-holders were firing over the passage of the Nebraska Bill."

Babcock reported attending a social gathering on Saturday evening held at the *Chicago Journal* office for excursioning journalists, which no doubt featured some beverages that it would soon be illegal to sell in the Land of Steady Habits. "An hour was passed in a very agreeable manner, making new acquaintances, and inducing a happy feeling of unity among all present," reported the *Chicago Tribune.* Postmaster and C&RI leader

Isaac Cook also invited editors to his Young America Hotel, "where a basket of 'sparkling Micawber' [wine] was waiting" for them, but few of these mainly anti-Nebraska editors took Douglas's friend up on his offer. Like lawyers, editors formed a male fraternity given to occasional "frolics" of jesting and liquor—partly to form bonds that could survive the clashes of opinion that often divided them, as the Kansas-Nebraska Act now did.[101]

Dark-haired and black-bearded, Cook seems to have been the editors' bête noire like his friend Douglas, except they almost totally ignored his participation in the excursion, whereas some of them openly attacked Douglas. They could not very well critique one of their generous hosts. Perhaps in gratitude for the Micawber wine, Hugh Hastings of the *Albany Knickerbocker* did praise Cook as "one of the most untiring 'day and night' men that we ever met with," a very "attentive" host, and "the West personified—frank, hearty, generous and impulsive." (The marchers in Saturday night's parade may not have regarded him as generous; reportedly, they rioted on Monday evening after they went to the post office to receive their pay for marching and found Cook gone on the excursion.)[102]

Babcock said nothing about going to the theater that evening. He did inform his readers that Reverend Eggleston had told him that Dr. Eleazar T. Fitch, professor of divinity at Yale, would preach at Eggleston's church on Sunday morning "so you see that our delegation will be represented here in various ways."[103]

EXCURSUS
Catharine Sedgwick and Antebellum Gender Roles

AS THEY JOURNEYED to inspect the West and to discern the nation's future, prominent New Englanders were by no means united in their views of what New England had been, what the West ought to be, or what the nation should become. New Haven was not New England, nor did the *New Englander* actually represent some sort of Yankee consensus, despite the Reverend Dr. Leonard Bacon's dream that it do so. Even if New England's "onward movement" found a way westward around the Slave Power's obstacles, that movement was itself divided in ways bound to cause confusion among westerners as to what was the true Yankee heritage.

To non-Yankees, New Englanders seemed a quarrelsome lot. The English actor and playwright Dion Boucicault came west at the same time as the Grand Excursionists—he was in Chicago on Sunday, June 4—and some thought he would accompany them on their journey. Actually, Boucicault was accompanying his wife, actress Agnes Robertson (it is unclear if the two ever officially took marriage vows), who had enjoyed a stunningly suc-cessful U.S. debut at Moses Kimball's Boston Museum and was set to appear on a Chicago stage. Whether some Yankees questioned their relation-ship or some quarreled or some sounded self-righteous in their denunciation of the South, for whatever reason Boucicault later scathingly mocked:

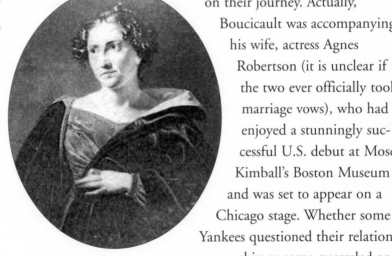

Novelist Catharine Sedgwick, ca. 1832.

> the New Englanders—who have preached
> [the southerners] out of meeting—why don't
> you put those hard gutted bluenosed canting
> sons of cod fishes outside the Union and

take their split with them—shut them up in a bag by themselves[,] shake them well together and they will reduce each other to fluff and claws. What a discontented, disputatious, ungenial, apostolic, dogmatic . . . race it is! bilious and biblical. None of them will ever get into Heaven, they will be sure to dispute at the door.[104]

Though not ungenial or bilious, Catharine Maria Sedgwick personified that segment of New England that emphatically did not identify itself with New Haven, although she would probably just as soon "preach the southerners out of meeting" as Bacon would. Raised in a prominent political family that was outspokenly anti-slavery, Sedgwick also hated the Kansas-Nebraska Act. On May 24, before she left for the Grand Excursion and before President Franklin Pierce signed the bill into law, she wrote to a friend, "I have just come from Washington, where I saw some of the fight about that horrid Nebraska bill whose infamous reputa[tio]n must have reached you." She fully shared abhorrence of the act with fellow excursionists Bacon, James Babcock, Benjamin Silliman, and Alexander Twining. "The majority [in the House] have put their damning seal upon it. But the end is not yet." Sedgwick could be counted on to give her moral support to that embryonic anti-Nebraska coalition forming as the excursion began. As a woman lacking a legal right to vote or society's approval to engage in partisan politics, she had to rely upon her brothers, Charles and Theodore

Sedgwick, to join other northern males to ensure that the act was not "the end," the South's conclusive triumph.[105]

Perhaps the act's unifying function in New England was one minor reason for the strength of Yankees' reaction to it. Why not stress what united most of them rather than dwell on disputes over the Calvinist Congregationalism that had shaped their ancestors and their region two centuries earlier but that now divided the descendants?

Sixty-four and unmarried, with streaks of gray winding through the otherwise black ringlets hanging over her ears, Catharine Maria Sedgwick traveled west as America's most famous female novelist. Edgar Allan Poe described her as "about the medium height," perhaps a bit shorter. "Her forehead is an unusually fine one; nose of a slightly Roman curve; eyes dark and piercing; mouth well formed and remarkably pleasant in its expression." She usually wore a cap. "Her manners are those of a high-bred woman, but her ordinary *manner* vacillates, in a singular way, between cordiality and a reserve amounting to *hauteur.*" As for her literary career, Poe commented, "Miss Sedgwick is not only one of our most celebrated and most meritorious writers, but attained reputation at a period when *American* reputation in letters was regarded as a phenomenon"—and he then named other literary pioneers like Washington Irving and James Fenimore Cooper, who, with Sedgwick, were partly esteemed out of American nationalistic pride as creators of an American literature.[106]

Sedgwick, at Stockbridge (or Lenox) in the Berkshires, was herself a monument or scenic site, often visited by European travelers to the United States who wanted to see two rarities at once: an American skilled at literature, and a woman at that. Alexis de Tocqueville, the Englishman Basil Hall, actress Fanny Kemble, English author Harriet Martineau, Swedish author Frederika Bremer—all included Sedgwick in their American tour. Bremer described her as beautiful, not picturesque or sublime: "Her figure is beautifully feminine, and her whole demeanor womanly, sincere, and frank. . . . I derived pleasure, also, from her highly sensible conversation and from her truly womanly human sympathies." The opinionated Martineau met her match in Sedgwick. As they walked along the Hoosac River arm in arm, Martineau suggested that southern slavery would lead to the breakup of the Union. "The dissolution of the Union!" Sedgwick cried, pulling her arm away from the Englishwoman. "The Union is sacred and must be preserved at all costs."[107]

By accepting the invitation and the free tickets on the crowded boats and trains, the "most celebrated" writer risked what Charles Sedgwick called "Lafayettism," the phenomenon experienced by the Marquis de Lafayette during his 1824–1825 trip to America: the unpleasant experience of being owned by onlookers and fellow travelers, who would gawk and question and even quarrel, while she would have to accept it all politely. During the heyday of Catharine Sedgwick's

fame, she hated "to fritter away in general courtesies [her] time and thought and feeling"; however, six years had passed since her latest book was published, and, in the spring of 1854, she may have sought to reawaken her creativity by means of new, spectacular sights and spectacular crowds.[108]

Characteristically, Sedgwick expressed no self-interested motive at all for going on the Grand Excursion—and wrote that "for my own sake" she would rather go visiting in Massachusetts—but justified the trip as a tonic for her ailing brother Charles. His wife and doctor favored the idea, and Charles rejoiced at "the news that the party was to be conveyed from Chicago to the Falls of St. Anthony and back free of all expense!" That itself was a tonic. "A bargain is the delight of a man's as well as a woman's heart," Catharine explained to Charles's son-in-law.[109] A woman who departed from antebellum norms by never marrying, she once stated, "The affection that others give to husbands and children I have given to my brothers. Few can understand the dependence and intensity of my love for them." She unstintingly gave that love to older brothers Theodore, Henry, and Robert—and they returned it in kind—but she suffered successive disappointments in love due to their marriages, to Henry's insanity, and to Robert and Henry's deaths. Only Theodore and Charles remained, and Charles's daughter Kate Sedgwick Minot, the beloved niece who would presumably outlive her father and give Catharine a love that would never disappoint or die before she did.[110]

Catharine Sedgwick's strong ties to her brothers facilitated her relative independence from men and yet also perpetuated a degree of dependence upon men. Like many antebellum women, she was freer of male dominance than her mother or grandmothers had been, freer to have a public life of her own and to work for public causes of social reform. Yet she was still reliant upon men to allow her freedom and sustain her in it. After New York City businessman Charles Butler invited her to go on the excursion, she delayed and finally wrote to him to accept and to explain, "I waited till I could see my brother on whose escort I depended." Charles Sedgwick had been "recently indisposed" but now felt well enough to go, and so she could go too.[111] Yet she was freer to go than were many women with children and homes to care for and manage. Her decision not to marry liberated her from a husband's legal control and motherhood's time-consuming obligations. She could focus on her writing. Her brothers' love compensated for the missing husband and children, while their influential role in New England's and New York's political and cultural life opened important doors for her as a writer. "They encouraged the initially reluctant author, applauded the novels and stories, and negotiated with the publishers."[112]

Women's relative emancipation, compared with social mores of the late-eighteenth century, was illustrated by the large number of women on the excursion. By one estimate, one-third of the participants were females, a proportion unthinkable in 1790 for a three-thousand-mile trip. Yet they went as a man's wife or daughter or sister. Antebellum proprieties prohibited female travel alone, without relatives or a chaperone—or brother Charles as an "escort." Catharine Sedgwick had a more egalitarian relationship to her brother than wives did to their husbands. Many men did not bring their wives. Remaining in New Haven with the children, Harriet Twining wrote in plaintive tones to her husband, Alexander, "I heard of your arrival at Chicago but have not had a letter from you." After giving some news, she added, "We all missed you very much and hope you will be able to take your seat at the table soon with us and your seat in the parlor where you may advise with your children and help along them that want help."[113]

Cornelia Martin agonized over whether to accompany her husband, E. T. Throop Martin, or "to watch over our large family in their father's absence." "[I]t was not without an effort that I determined to forego the pleasures" of the trip, but she decided "that I was in the way of my duty" to stay home. Perhaps rationalizing, she used society's perception of the fragile and vulnerable female constitution to justify her decision as a way to avoid "the *discomforts* of the excursion—a crowd of persons . . . fatigues of a long journey—The painful reaction of intense mental excitement etc. etc." Perhaps she could go the following year when "improvements on the route" would lessen the discomforts. She reconciled herself to the stay-at-home choice, only to receive a letter from her friend Francis P. Blair right after seeing her husband off at the train station—"and when I read in it that *you* were going to the Falls of St. Anthony, a thousand visions of enjoyment danced before me and for a moment gave me almost a feeling of regret that I had not made a greater effort to accompany my husband." Upon further thought, she told herself "that the same reasons" that were decisive before were just as compelling if Blair were going. To her letter to Blair, she added a patriotic explanation reminiscent of the Revolutionary era's ideal of "republican motherhood": Abigail Adams and Martha Washington stayed at home while their husbands traveled.[114]

Catharine Sedgwick did not face these agonies of conflicting duties and desires. Famous in her own right, she had received the invitation, after all, and she was free to go along with Butler and other friends, like historian George Bancroft, without neglecting any children. Yet she justified the trip as her duty to nurse Charles back to health. As a woman, she could not conceptualize herself as lacking *any* family responsibilities.

In all of this, she did not differ greatly from the New Haveners. Many New Haven wives went on the excursion. Nothing in New Haven's evangelicalism prohibited an evangelical female author such as Harriet Beecher Stowe from making the trip (she didn't). Nothing in New Haven evangelicalism excluded a woman like Stowe from becoming an author. Yet Sedgwick's career as a writer cannot be separated from her rejection of Calvinism, evangelicalism, and everything

New Haven and Yale represented.

Her first novel, *A New-England Tale* (1822), grew out of a religious tract on her move from Calvinist Congregationalism to Unitarianism, "follow[ing] her brothers' example." At brother Henry's urging, she wrote and rewrote until the tract became a novel. Raised in the Berkshires of western Massachusetts, in Stockbridge (where Jonathan Edwards closed out his ministerial career), the daughter of Theodore Sedgwick—a prominent Federalist politician, Speaker of the U.S. House of Representatives during Washington's administration, defender of New England's Congregationalism along with (but no more than) its other traditions—Catharine Sedgwick heard the Calvinist sermons of Reverend Stephen West and heartily disliked them and him, partly because she felt that both had harmed her older sisters. She joined the Unitarians in 1821 (after her father's death) and wrote her *Tale* satirizing Yankee Calvinists. In it, "Sedgwick's sympathies are barely disguised," for, although religious doctrine is not directly discussed, religious individuals are. "Her staunchest Calvinist is portrayed as a hypocrite" and that character's "behavior juxtaposed against the exemplary conduct of those who profess" what Sedgwick thought was "a more humane Christianity."[115]

She next turned her attention in *Redwood* (1824) to her accommodation with a rising Jacksonian democracy and her graceful retreat from her father's elitist federalism. Her brothers were making the same adjustment to the very different political realities of the 1820s and 1830s. She continued her literary success with *Hope Leslie* (1827), a story of warfare between colonists and Indians in seventeenth-century Massachusetts. *Clarence* (1830) satirized the get-rich-quick avarice of Jacksonian America. *The Linwoods* (1835) returned to her parents' era, the American Revolution, to reject their contemporaries' aristocratic and Calvinist values in favor of a more egalitarian and broadly humane view of life. Then she abandoned novel writing for two decades and wrote instructional books on manners and morals, short stories, a travel book, and children's books. She did some teaching at her sister-in-law (Charles's wife) Elizabeth's boarding school for girls at Lenox. Catharine Sedgwick's fame went into a long and gradual decline. The problems of Federalists' children adjusting to the Age of the Common Man did not interest 1850s readers. Newer issues of westward expansion and slavery preoccupied them, and she had little direct experience with the West or slavery. Perhaps she went on the excursion to remedy that in part.[116]

On the excursion, Sedgwick accompanied several noted Calvinist preachers: Reverend Dr. Gardiner Spring of Brick Presbyterian Church in New York City, a well-known man whose reputation she surely knew from her frequent stays in New York with brother Robert; Reverend Duncan Kennedy of North Dutch Reformed Church in Albany, likely known to her too from her visits to and occasional residence in that nearby city; and others perhaps unknown to her. Her excursion letters make no mention of them. However, in an autobiographical journal entry written less than three months after the excursion, she indicated a softening attitude toward Reverend West:

We had one clergyman in Stockbridge, of sound New England orthodoxy, a Hopkinsian Calvinist. Heaven forbid, dear Alice, that you should ever inquire into the splitting of these theological hairs.

Sixty years he preached to us . . . stern as an old Israelite in his faith, gentle and kindly in his life as my Uncle Toby. I dreaded him and certainly did not understand him in my youth. He was then only the dry sapless embodiment of polemical divinity. It was in my mature age and his old age that I discovered his Christian features, and found his unsophisticated nature as pure and gentle as a good little child's.[117]

Perhaps her perception of Stephen West had been partly changed by being refracted through her perception of Spring, Kennedy, and other clergymen on the sociable trip. Certainly, the reverse was true. Her initial view of them would have been influenced by her childhood and adolescent memories of Dr. West.[118]

On her way west to Chicago, before she encountered the clergymen, Sedgwick marveled at the sights and crowds. Writing to William Minot, Kate's husband, she regretted, "Oh if one of my beloved nieces were with me! But I have a very comfort[abl]e compan[io]n—in a Miss Colt of Pitts[fiel]d—

a very gentle ladylike girl." The rest of the crowd hurrying west to the excursion did not receive the compliment paid to Miss Elizabeth Colt. Sedgwick humorously called them "critters" ("what a multitude of creters!") In Albany they transferred to the New York Central and proceeded to Utica, and on to Niagara Falls, which they reached at 7:00 p.m., Tuesday, May 30. They spent the night and the following morning there.[119]

"Oh Kate," she exclaimed in a scribbled handwriting, "what a walk I had around Goat Island this M[ornin]g! alone—now think of that! alone!" (Goat Island is located in Niagara River just above the falls.) Ever setting self aside to relate to others, she immediately rejected that thought. "No, my darling, you were with me in your freshest youth—laughing—shouting, and many others who have shared this glorious scene with me, partak[in]g its loveliness now as I *felt*." Seemingly every feeling she shared with her niece. "Oh Niagara, what a place of delight but [the whole trip thus far] has been an unintermitted pleasure except this trial of a steel pen." The flow of ink was intermittent but the pleasure was not.

After a short journey from Niagara Falls to Buffalo, they spent part of an afternoon in Millard Fillmore's home city. "Y[ou]r father was rather tired," she confided to Kate, "but he took a nap while I was walking & after tea we had a nice drive." That night, they took a steamboat on "a delicious run over a glassy surface" of Lake Erie to Detroit. The voyage lasted until three o'clock the following

(Friday) afternoon. She was pleased with Charles's high spirits and improved health: "he was the charm of the boat—young men hang[in]g about him to hear his jokes."

But in Detroit on Friday night, she grew concerned again. Late-night guests cut into Charles's sleeping time. He did not appear well at breakfast the next morning. His sister fussed over him and over the western food: "You will understand my trials when I gently suggested that fried potatoes were not digestible—y[ou]r father w[oul]d do admirably if he merely encountered the necessary fatigues—but he will take care of every body & every thing & Hal instead of a help is a constant anxiety."

Saturday morning, June 3, they boarded the train to ride 280 miles to Chicago. At the depot they met more multitudes. "God be praised," Catharine Sedgwick exclaimed over the names of the few she knew (not over the multitudes). Here was Joseph Valerio from Sardinia, apparently the love interest of "Bessie"—for she wrote Bessie's name and drew a heart in a parenthesis following Valerio's name. The noted Italian educational expert Professor Vincenzo Botta was there too, "and oh a million creters." Despite the crowds, she found the train trip over "John Forbes road," the Michigan Central, fairly comfortable.

"Salutes were fired when we arrived here [Chicago]. We were taken in a packed Om[nibu]s . . . to the Tremont."

And the Tremont was packed, so they could not get to the rooms Charles had reserved. As a literary celebrity, Catharine

Sedgwick need not fear a roomless night. Businessman Charles Butler had secured rooms for her party; another friend told her he had done so; "a Mr. Ward a Washington acquain[tan]ce—offered me a room—but a little lady, a Broadway acquain[tan]ce of Kate pushed forward & said she had a room with a double bed & wo[ul]d move into a room with 5 others" to make a place for Sedgwick. She took this offer rather than risk the "social responsibility," the gawks and questions and obligations, that a celebrity would incur by accepting the favor of a night's lodging from one of the public. Her niece (not Kate) stayed in the donated hotel room with her; Charles and Hal "got a room at a hotel opposite" the Tremont.

To Kate, she complained the next day about Charles's masculine reticence. "He was tired last night but w[oul]d not express it." She wondered how he had fared in his lodging across the street. It was still early morning, "and I have not yet heard the report."

Like many antebellum males, Charles Sedgwick struggled to define himself and his masculinity in an age when women were assuming some roles previously held by men (teacher, social reformer) and regional types of masculinity competed against each other. "The rough-and-tumble style of southwestern frontier masculinity was much different from the self-control and sobriety" of middle-class manhood in the North. "The linking of manhood to fraternal love" in some circles competed with "notions of manhood embraced by other northern upper-class males who valued adventurous camaraderie more than sentimentality." An urban "sporting-male" culture of the Bowery Boys opposed the "emphases placed on personal restraint and sober chastity" by male temperance groups.[120]

For Charles, reticence may have been a device to help maintain his masculine distinctives. He had not achieved nearly as much as his Revolutionary-era father, Theodore Sedgwick Sr., a major in the Continental Army, Massachusetts political leader, congressman, U.S. senator, Speaker of the House, and associate justice on the Massachusetts Supreme Judicial Court. He achieved much less than did his older brother Theodore, a noted lawyer, author, and civic leader. The youngest brother, Charles "never thought himself as clever as his brothers, stayed in Lenox [the other brothers spent part of their lives in New York City] and was busy doing everything no one else had time for." But his "everything" was mainly family matters—writing letters that "expressed his overflowing family love"—matters society often assigned to females. The one business in his own family was his wife Elizabeth's boarding school for girls in Lenox. Between that and his sister Catharine, Charles was surrounded by women and feminine influence. The deaths of Henry and Robert were also devastating for him, in removing half of the males from the clan of Sedgwick siblings.[121]

One male visitor to the Sedgwick homes at Lenox came the day after George Bancroft's stepson, William Bliss, had departed. He reported to Mrs. Bancroft, "Men, as he [William] found, are at a great premium here. We chat & dance, & drive, & do nothing & the summer slips easily away."[122] The Sedgwick world was an overwhelmingly female one, and Charles had to adjust to that reality—and occasionally escape that world.

The Grand Excursion offered Charles an opportunity to perform on a more public, more masculine stage—to socialize with excursionists, a majority of whom were men; to engage in male bantering, albeit not of a coarse variety; to give speeches, chair meetings, and pass resolutions, all masculine duties in antebellum society; to debate politics, also a male sanctum; to play a broader, public role of an inspector of the West and predictor of the nation's future greatness. Despite her literary fame, Catharine Sedgwick was not called on to chair meetings or give speeches or discuss politics. Her response to scenery and events was expected to be a private one, expressed in private letters to family and friends. She did write an article on the excursion for *Putnam's Monthly Magazine,* but she cast her observations in the form of a private letter to her friend, Charles Butler.

*The hero of Young America and the bane of New England
clergy, Illinois senator Stephen A. Douglas, ca. 1840s.
He and the Kansas-Nebraska Act were hotly debated
on the excursion.*

CHAPTER THREE

"All Under a Full Head of Steam"

SUNDAY, JUNE 4, 1854

"SUNDAY IN CHICAGO," reported Isaac Platt of the *Poughkeepsie Eagle,* "I found much more quiet than I had anticipated after the confusion of Saturday night."[123] No official Grand Excursion events were planned; Henry Farnam had not dared to schedule the departure for a Sunday; many excursionists, many antebellum Americans, and perhaps Farnam himself held such strong views on observing the Sabbath that they would not have participated in such events or departed that day if he had planned it so. Many timed their arrival in Chicago for Saturday so that they could attend church on Sunday, June 4. A Saturday arrival was not required—the excursion trains would leave Chicago on Monday morning—but many preferred it to avoid travel on Sunday. For the same reason, Farnam scheduled the return to Chicago for the following Saturday, June 10, to allow for church attendance the next day.[124]

Although a quiet day, Sunday was not insignificant to the excursion. Antebellum America was a churchgoing nation. Several excursionists were prominent clergymen. This was their day to preach before distinguished audiences. Many of them were deeply involved in protests against the Kansas-Nebraska Act, and Senator Stephen Douglas had anathamatized them for using their

pulpits to deliver political sermons. In recent months, several had replied to Douglas in kind. That spring, politics in the pulpit was a major issue in American life. So, although the excursion's organizers had not planned anything for Sunday, neither had they planned on the Kansas-Nebraska Act or protesting pastors or senators whose egos had been bruised by Sunday sermons. So Sunday became a vital part of the excursion too.

Although a boomtown, Chicago generally respected the Sabbath rest. One visitor in the mid-1850s reported, "Sunday in Chicago, though not observed as it is in New England, is, I think, more respected than in any town of 20,000 inhabitants, or upwards, south of Philadelphia." New Haveners did not see the Sunday quiet of Connecticut, but that was not to be expected. "Some few stores are seen open, but not of a prominent class. The movement of the people is generally churchward, and the churches are well filled." Chicago's "streets are quiet." Although crime existed on all days of the week, "the Puritan element so far predominates in the population of the place, that wickedness is neither popular nor respectable." Speculation raised prices swiftly and tempted men to cut ethical corners, but they were willing to wait until Monday to harvest the weekend's rise in values.[125]

After a poor night's sleep "in cramped and dirty quarters," amid the noise of the pro-Nebraska rally and the commotion of hundreds of excursionists, Platt felt himself "in poor condition to enjoy the religious privileges of the day" but decided "to make an effort." He expressed displeasure with the results he obtained from his dutiful effort. He happened upon a high-church service (probably at St. James Episcopal Church) not to his liking. It lacked large Roman Catholic crosses but had "an abundance of small ones" and other ostentatious features. "The singing was done in the opera style, with many flourishes, trills, &c. by three persons, doubtless employed for the purpose"—like professional mourners and, presumably, no more sincere. The "minister preached in his surplice" with the mistaken notion, Platt implied, that fancy clothes make a man pious.[126]

George Bancroft likely attended the same church, for he noted that "the minister was high church," but that style "quite delighted Mrs. Oakley, whom I congratulated." It is unclear if Bancroft too liked that style or if he sided with her to win her favor. Mr. Oakley—officially, New York City Superior Court judge Thomas J. Oakley, a former Congressman and ex-attorney general of New York—disliked the service. Yet "she, triumphing over her husband, was won by my sympathy," he reported to his wife. (He seemed to delight in arousing his wife's jealousy with admiring comments about female excursionists.)[127]

Given the many religious disputes disturbing antebellum America, that Sunday in Chicago would have produced more such criticisms and divisions among the excursionists if they had all attended the same church. They didn't. And the excursion had no religious aspect that required a joint church service. Denominationalism and freedom of choice reigned in Chicago that morning, as they did throughout the nation, except in a few places like Mormon Utah or Catholic New Mexico, where one church dominated. Yet church attendance was high in Chicago and in the nation in the mid-1850s. By one estimate, nearly four million Americans were members in one of the nation's Protestant denominations; around eight million attended these churches but were not members; and there were nearly two million communicant Catholics (in 1850). That totaled fourteen million weekly churchgoers, or more than 50 percent of the population (higher than that, for many of the twenty-seven million Americans were children who could not be members).[128]

More than statistics made Sunday important to Americans. In a theological sense, the day symbolized eternity and proclaimed that there was more to human existence than the humdrum business of the regular six days. Human beings had an eternal soul and should lay down their weekday business to remind themselves of that fact. Since Americans disagreed greatly on the subject of eternity, however, Sunday was sure to reflect their divided state of mind.

Protestants too had their religious differences, as symbolized by the opposite tone of the texts that editor James Babcock of the *New Haven Palladium* heard expounded that day: in the morning at St. James Episcopal, "And they all forsook him and fled" (Mark 14:50); in the afternoon at First Presbyterian Church, "And the people heard him gladly" (Mark 12:37b). Other New Haveners attended First Presbyterian that afternoon: Roger and Emily Baldwin, Charles McCurdy and his daughter Evelyn, Professor Benjamin Silliman and his wife, Sarah, Dr. Eleazar T. Fitch, and Reverend Leonard Bacon.[129]

The Sedgwicks did not attend the same church as did these moderately Calvinist New Haveners. "We all went to the Unita[ria]n Church today," Catharine Sedgwick reported, "& heard a very pleas[in]g discourse from a lovely young clergy[ma]n." He led a "charming service," she informed her niece Kate, "and a communion, and your father staid." (Did Charles Sedgwick usually not stay for communion?) To another relative, she described the communion service as "an interval of sweet rest & religious elevation."[130]

If she had so described it to New Haveners like Bacon or Silliman, they would likely have asked her why Unitarians celebrated communion if they did not believe in the deity of Jesus Christ or in the substitutionary atonement to which the Lord's Supper pointed. Unitarians stressed ethical behavior. "As a good Unitarian, Miss Sedgwick believed that all men are inherently good"; the "major difference between social classes, she believed was manners; and the teaching of good manners became a central objective of her fiction." At the request of a Unitarian minister, she wrote *Home* (1835), a book teaching good manners

to "Farmers and Mechanics," and followed up with two more didactic tales that became her best-selling works. Not just to the lower classes did these books teach good manners, but also to westerners. "The Yankee boy," she wrote, "from the earliest period of forecast, dreams of seeking his fortune in the richer soil and kinder climate which his far-spread country provides for him"—in the West. Sedgwick's books taught him to bring New England manners with him and, thus, to civilize and "Yankee-ize" the West. Of course, her sister-in-law Elizabeth Sedgwick taught manners to Yankee girls who might be headed West and to some western young ladies.[131]

As the excursion took her west, Sedgwick curiously looked about her to see to what degree the region's people exhibited civilized manners.

Bacon, Fitch, and Silliman did not agree with Sedgwick on reducing religion to ethics, and ethics to manners. Bacon and Fitch represented New Haven Theology, a source of division in evangelical churches over the preceding thirty years. Yale Theological Seminary, where Fitch taught, housed this theology (the rival, Old School seminary for Connecticut was in rival Hartford). Begun in the 1820s, New Haven Theology refined or altered Calvinism to defeat the Unitarianism adopted by Catharine Sedgwick, her brothers, and other Yankees. Its chief theologian was Nathaniel William Taylor, professor at Yale Seminary. (One excursioning reporter, N. W. T. Root of the *New Haven Register*, was named after him.) To answer the Sedgwicks' (and others') objections to their father's Calvinism, it argued that

God's "moral government" of the universe must be perfect. "This governmental Calvinism meant a new understanding of all the old, defining doctrines—complete depravity, election, irresistable grace, limited atonement, and perseverance." That new understanding caused more dissension among the orthodox than conversions among the Unitarians.

Two months after the excursion, Sedgwick expressed her objections in a description of her childhood minister, Reverend Stephen West: "He stood up in the pulpit for sixty years and logically proved the whole moral creation of God . . . left by him to suffer eternally for Adam's transgression, except a handful elected to salvation." To answer that, New Haven Theology denied human beings were *necessarily* sinful through their descent from sinful Adam or were unjustly punished for Adam's sin—or that the elect were totally undeserving of salvation. Bacon and Fitch taught that each individual first sinned by choice, despite having the ability to avoid sin, and then had the power to turn away from sin and toward God but lacked the will to do so. Thus, revivalists acted correctly in urging sinners to repent since a sinner *could*. During the Second Great Awakening, New Haven theologians and ministers developed a view of human responsibility that fit their emphasis on revival. Defending revivalists became as important as refuting Unitarians.[132]

Reverend Bacon preached at Reverend A. H. Eggleston's Plymouth Congregational Church that Sunday evening. To evangelize the West and not hinder this goal by denominational rivalry, Presbyterians and Congregationalists had worked together since 1801 in the Plan of Union—and so it was not surprising that Bacon attended the Presbyterian Church in the afternoon. Yet in 1852 he led a Congregational move to repeal the Union on grounds that Presbyterians had used the Union to outpace their brethren in western church planting; so no doubt he was happy to preach that evening in one of the few thriving Congregational churches in the West. Eggleston had served as Bacon's substitute while he took a thirteen-month trip to Europe and the Middle East in 1850–1851, and Bacon was now returning the favor in a small way.[133]

Fifty-two years old, balding in front, with a full and rounded-out white beard encircling his determined mouth, Roman nose and bushy eyebrows projecting forward as if to unbalance him in the forward direction and hurl him into the very next controversy, Leonard Bacon stood at the height of his powers and his influence when he traveled west on the Grand Excursion. "Rather short and slight in stature," he did not have a "commanding physical presence" in the pulpit, whether at his own Center Church in New Haven or on the road. His head was his most prominent feature, and his intellectual powers the most impressive aspect of his sermons.

Called by some "the fighting parson," Bacon entered many ecclesiastical, theological, and political contests as pastor, denominational leader, Yale trustee, writer, and senior editor of *The Independent*, Congregationalism's national organ in New York. He served on many of the boards of the many societies that made up the Evangelical united front—societies for overseas and domestic missionary work, for founding colleges in the West, for encouraging temperance, for publishing and distributing religious tracts. (Many of these societies had just held their annual meetings in New York City in mid-May, including the American Congregational Union, thus freeing up its president, Leonard Bacon, and its secretary, Reverend T. Atkinson, to go on the excursion.) He wrote sermons, essays, and articles by the hundreds over a long career.[134]

Thus, Bacon could be forgiven for repeating "my Dudlean lecture" that evening and not composing a fresh sermon for Eggleston's congregation. He had preached a sermon on a text in the Gospel of John that morning at "the New England church" in Chicago, and had preached twice in Detroit the preceding Sunday. One Detroit sermon had been a warning, based on the text "on following a multitude to do evil"; presumably Bacon was not going on the excursion to do anything of the kind.[135]

Bacon "largely concurred with the central tenets" of the New Haven Theology but stressed cooperation among evangelicals and disliked doctrinal disputes. Still, when Old School Presbyterians had attacked Congregationalists' New School allies in the 1830s, Bacon defended both the New School and New Haven views. By the 1850s, Bacon and his Yale friends Silliman, Alexander Twining, and Fitch had distanced themselves from Taylor's suspicion of science and scholarship, especially German science and scholarship. "Taylor, for example, . . . rejected geologists' discovery of fossils and geological formations that challenged the Genesis story. Bacon, on the other hand, was a devoted proponent of scientific research." Geology, not yet biology, generated the most talk of a conflict between science and religion.[136]

Yale scholars like Silliman and their clerical supporters like Bacon denied any conflict existed. They had their own journals (*New Englander, Journal of the American Oriental Society,* and Silliman's *American Journal of Science and Arts),* in which they could publish articles that combined scientific, scholarly research and a Christian perspective or that merely assumed a Christian readership. They had their own scholarly methods. Silliman practiced the Baconian method of gathering facts, classifying them (red sandstone or red shale), and identifying God's purpose for various phenomena. No anti-Christian results were likely from this method. His Yale students and successors went further in scientific research, but they too tried to fashion "an intellectually complex middle way" between Taylor's Christian rejection of science and an atheistic science.[137] This middle way resembled Taylor's path between Old School Calvinism and Unitarianism, in its middleness and in its optimism that New Haven rationality could mark out an acceptable course between a conservative rejection of human reason and a liberal rejection of Scripture. "Scholarship gave the New Haven scholars the opportunity to rebuild religious belief on historically and scientifically credible bases."[138]

Many evangelical scholars traveled on the excursion: Silliman; Dartmouth chemistry professor Oliver P. Hubbard (married to Silliman's daughter, Faith); Edward Elbridge Salisbury, Yale professor of Arabic and Sanskrit; Alexander Twining, the former professor of mathematics and natural philosophy; and Fitch. Though not a Yale man, Edward Robinson, noted expert on Palestine's geography, typified this evangelical scholarly approach. An expert in Hebrew and Greek, in biblical philology and grammar, Robinson faced the heterodox danger, not of fossils but of German higher criticism that used textual criticism to cast doubt on the reliability and inspiration of the biblical texts. Partly educated at German universities, as well as at conservative Andover Seminary, Robinson solved his problem by using German critical methods on issues in Palestine's geography (hardly controversial), not on the biblical text, and by using the Baconian method of gathering facts by traveling. He "never took part in ecclesiastical agitations" and "stood aloof from doctrinal controversy." His wife, Therese Albertina Louise von Jakob (who published under her initials Talvj), was a well-known author, translator of Slavic literature, and essayist. For all of them, the excursion offered an expenses-paid pleasurable empiricism with friends and family along for the ride.[139]

For these evangelical scholars, traveling and gathering facts firsthand were the way to knowledge. They did not intend for this method to lead them astray from orthodox Christian faith and they did not expect it would, but they also did not want abstract doctrines—and doctrine could be the religious equivalent of theory—to keep them from their fact-gathering.[140]

Several excursionists represented the opposite, Old School view that shunned rational optimism, suspected science and German scholarship, and believed that humans were depraved by nature and unable to stop sinning, and that God's electing grace saved only some of them and not due to any merit on their part. They too believed in the Baconian method. They did not stand aloof from doctrinal battles. (The Old School's opposite was the New School; New Haven Theology departed further than did the New School from Old School Calvinism.) Most prominent among them was Reverend Dr. Gardiner Spring, pastor of Brick Presbyterian Church in New York City. He preached at Chicago's North Presbyterian Church that morning. Balding, bespectacled, with sideburns and curly white hair worn over his ears, the seventy-year-old Spring was perhaps the best-known northern advocate of Old School views and the author of several well-regarded books. In the 1820s, he crusaded against theatergoing and Sabbath-breaking in New York City—specifically against Sunday steamboat excursions on the Hudson. He undoubtedly agreed with Farnam's decision to spend the Sabbath quietly in Chicago and head west on Monday.[141]

Some of Taylor's "novel views" were first expressed in response to an 1829 book written by Spring, who summarized, "There was a boldness in the speculations of the New Haven Theology which has given rise to irreverence for the character of God." He believed the New Haven theologians departed from orthodoxy, and the New School accepted New Haven errors. In 1837–1838, Spring and other like-minded Presbyterians split off from the New School. Two separate Presbyterian denominations resulted. The following years only deepened the divide between them as the slavery issue exacerbated doctrinal differences.[142] The two were not unrelated. In worship, Presbyterians followed the regulative principle: anything not specifically commanded in Scripture should not be practiced in the church. In thinking about slavery, the Old School used a corollary that had a long tradition, especially in Scottish Presbyterianism: anything not condemned in the Bible should not be politically opposed by the church. No New Testament passage called for an end to slavery. Yet New School pastors called for just that—another indication of their departure from scriptural principles. Old School southerners argued thus, and some northerners agreed.[143]

Bacon was therefore much more involved in the crusade against slavery than was Spring, whose Old School group tended to favor compromise and to abhor anti-slavery agitation. Also, Spring's church was in New York City, a center of the cotton export trade with close commercial ties to the South. Beyond politics and economics, however, "Old School leaders were quick to point out" that there was a link "between New School theology and abolitionism. Both emphasized the rights of man and

his moral obligations. Both seemed to the orthodox to place rationalistic theories concerning man's nature above Biblical precedents." Old School Presbyterians in the North, by contrast, allowed the southern brethren to remain in the denomination and refused to allow the issue of slavery to be discussed at their General Assembly meetings.[144]

Spring's Old School stressed Protestantism's traditional concern with the individual's salvation; they regarded Calvinism as the biblical explanation of that phenomenon. In an age when death was an ever-present possibility for all ages, this emphasis was widely shared. The visitors feared cholera in Chicago that Sunday. Muddy streets and sidewalks, and unsanitary conditions, concerned them. "It would naturally be supposed that this must be a sickly place," remarked one correspondent, "but the citizens assert that it is very healthy." In fact, they "talk a great deal about the danger of cholera at their rival city, St. Louis; while the people of St. Louis (where I passed a few days) express serious apprehensions in regard to the health of Chicago." Another newspaper reporter found confirming evidence of Chicago's healthy condition that Sunday at church when "[a]n annual report was read." One item caught his attention: "No. of members 375—Deaths during the year, *two*. This ratio of mortality" was better than in eastern cities.[145]

Congregationalists, including New Haven ones, cared deeply about individual souls, and they would hardly have been true to their Puritan roots if they downplayed death's imminence. But they expected radically new behavior from new converts. They opposed slavery more openly than even New School Presbyterians did. The first two Congregational churches in Chicago were formed in 1851 and 1852 after members of two New School churches expressed "dissatisf[action] with the present condition of our General Assembly on the subject of disciplining those guilty of holding their fellow men in bondage." Eggleston's Plymouth Congregational Church, in which Bacon preached that evening, was the second of the two.[146]

Theological differences between Unitarians and New Haveners also carried over to the anti-slavery cause and the Kansas-Nebraska Act. Many Massachusetts Unitarians were cautious Cotton Whigs closely tied to textile-mill interests and reluctant to antagonize the South; thus, even though a few Boston intellectuals were anti-slavery Conscience Whigs, the Unitarians were deeply divided on the issue. Thus, New Haven anti-slavery activism could also serve as a sort of apologetic against Boston Unitarianism.[147]

There were few slaveholders on the Grand Excursion to complain about ministers' attacks on slavery, nor any German university professors to defend higher criticism from clerical critiques, but there were Democrats to complain about ministers meddling in politics with sermons against Kansas-Nebraska. This first Sunday in June came during a peak period in ministerial intervention in politics and in politicians' outcry against it. Bacon was one of three thousand New England ministers who signed a memorial against the act. Democrats

angrily charged that "anti-Nebraska clergy, by protesting as a class, sought to re-establish a theocracy." The main target, Senator Douglas, replied in kind. "A man of no deep religious convictions himself, he resented the interference of the pulpit in matters of government." Excursionists Reverends Eggleston and Harvey Curtiss were among twenty-five Chicago clergy who sent him a strongly worded protest against his attack in the Senate on their Yankee clerical colleagues as, basically, liars.[148]

Douglas seemed infuriated at this jab from his home city. In early April, he wrote a letter—one editor termed it "Stephen's Epistle to Chicago"—to the "reverend gentlemen" to deny their assertion that he had slandered clergy or had rejected clergymen's right to speak as citizens on public issues. In the Senate, Douglas had accused the Yankee clergy of "hav[ing] here come forward with an atrocious falsehood and an atrocious calumny against this Senate, desecrated the pulpit, and prostituted the sacred desk to the miserable and corrupting influence of party politics." This the Chicagoans objected to, but in his reply Douglas quoted other parts of his speech (and other senators' speeches) to prove he (and they) had not slandered the clergy. "I now call on you," he wrote them, "to withdraw this charge, and make an open and public confession of the injustice you have done me!"

What Douglas had done was to criticize ministers for making their protest "'in the name of Almighty God.'" After thinking about that wording, "I fear that it is your purpose to claim and exercise this prerogative of the Deity upon legislative and political questions." That was "asserting a divine power in the clergy of this country higher than the obligations of the Constitution." The twenty-five denied a "desire to interfere in questions of war and policy, or to mingle in the conflicts of political parties" but insisted on their "duty to recognise the moral bearing of such questions" and to preach upon that moral bearing. Douglas scoffed at any such political-prophetic office and recalled a failed Mormon prophecy that he would be defeated for Congress. Their "claims for the supremacy of this divinely-appointed institution [the ministry] are subversive of the fundamental principles upon which our whole republican system rests."[149]

There is no indication that Chicago's ministers replied, but Leonard Bacon did reply to Douglas's attack on the Chicago twenty-five. Free Soil congressman Joshua R. Giddings asked Bacon to "reply to Douglas with regard to the rights of ministers to have political opinions." (Bacon had aided abolitionist Edward Beecher in organizing the New England ministerial memorial.) Bacon wrote a lengthy article ("Morality of the Nebraska Bill") in the *New Englander* (May 1854). He countered Douglas's points: (1) ministers did not speak on the Almighty's behalf but as believers in an Almighty speaking to lay believers who could see immorality as clearly as clergy could; (2) ministers did not seek theocracy, for all men could see slavery's immorality—the clergy were egalitarian here; (3) Kansas-Nebraska was a moral, not a partisan, question because the act broke a solemn

promise, the Missouri Compromise. With Yankee pride, he ridiculed Douglas ("a Senator from Illinois") for demeaning "the intelligence of the clergy of New England." Bacon quoted Shakespeare: "Upon what meat doth this our Caesar feed, that he is grown so great?"[150]

"The ministers of the Gospel in this country," Bacon asserted, "never concern themselves in questions merely political." Disingenuously he insisted, "The memorial does not purport to come from ministers of the Gospel," although only ministers had signed it. Bacon did use his ministerial moral authority to oppose the Kansas-Nebraska Act. After an earlier Baconian thunderbolt on the issue, famed preacher Henry Ward Beecher wrote to Bacon, "It made me think of old-fashioned preaching in revivals, when a sinner was concerned, and the minister was poring down upon him the whole law of God, & he quite dissolving under it."[151]

Coming from a supporter of New Haven Theology, Bacon's most revealing argument was that all human beings knew that slavery was immoral and that "concerned" sinners *could* repent. "Just as Mr. Douglas knows it when he looks at it in the light of God's presence and of eternity; by the intuition of the moral sense." Indeed, the "whole force" of the Yankee clergy's remonstrance "depends on the assumption that those to whom it speaks are men with human capabilities," men "to whom the first principles of right and duty are self-evident." This confidence in human moral insight went beyond what the Old School acknowledged. It informed New Haveners' anti-slavery appeal. Seeing slavery's immorality required no "peculiar revelation." So Douglas, southerners, pro-southern Democrats, and Cotton or Carriage Whigs were without excuse.[152]

Drs. Bacon and Spring were not the only excursionists to preach at Chicago churches that Sunday. Reverend Timothy Pitkin of New Haven spoke at Trinity Episcopal Church in the evening, and Reverend E. H. Canfield of New York, in the morning; Reverend Dr. Duncan Kennedy of Albany preached at Second Presbyterian Church in the morning, and Dr. Ashbel G. Vermilye of New York spoke there in the evening. There is no evidence that any of these clergymen "desecrated the pulpit" or "prostituted the sacred desk" by haranguing against Douglas or his act.[153]

Reverend Sewell S. Cutting, who edited the Baptist *New York Recorder,* gave the sermon at First Baptist Church. A Vermonter who went on the excursion partly to gain knowledge of the West to more effectively "labor in the great cause of home evangelization," Cutting sent written reports back to the *Recorder.* At a colporteurs' convention in Chicago, "I could not refrain from weeping while I listened to the recitals of their labors" in distributing Bibles and religious tracts in the West. Such work was desperately needed, Cutting believed, because of "the vast immigration of foreigners, specially from Continental Europe," either Catholic or "nominally Protestant," who "bring little reverence for the Sabbath . . . and religious dogmas which do little to purify the heart or to adorn society." But he was far from being a nativist Know-

Nothing. Native-born Americans "have too many of them cast off religious authority, and respect for the Sabbath." Apparently referring to Isaac Cook's hotel and restaurant, he lamented, "It is impossible to look at a late hour of the night upon that lofty and elegant building known as 'Young America,' without feeling" the need for "a vast work for religion."[154]

One Old School Presbyterian editor and former minister did not speak at, or even attend, an English-language church. Edward D. G. Prime chose to attend Reverend Paul Andersen's Norwegian Lutheran church, Chicago's first, a modest frame structure on the North Side. Andersen had attended the school in Beloit, Wisconsin, run by the Congregationalists and the Presbyterians, and he started his church with the financial support of these denominations' American Home Missionary Society. That was probably how Prime heard of the church and why he went there. Andersen's Norwegian, he reported, was "a language far smoother and more musical than I had supposed, and although I could not understand a word, I listened to it with great pleasure." His text was Exodus 14:15, "Sig til Israels Børn at de skulle drage frem" ("Say to the Children of Israel that they should go forward"), appropriate for travelers about to take what was grandiloquently termed the greatest excursion "since the days of Moses."[155]

Many excursionists did not attend any church to assess the musicality of foreign tongues or the truth of Douglas's charge. Some attended only one service, not two or three. They prepared for the next day's com-

mencement or allowed their heightened anticipation to build to the bursting point. That
was Catharine Sedgwick's interpretation of the
prevailing mood in the hotels. "I wish I could
give you any notion of the scene here," she
informed Kate. "It is something new in the
world—the meeting at the time of the gift of
tongues was tame [compared] to it." A comparison to Pentecost might not have pleased
the clergy, had they known of it. "Many people of note" were there, "names long known
and honored—by *some*." Here she pointedly
began with Millard Fillmore, whom the anti-
slavery novelist did not honor, and included
Judge Thomas Oakley, Bancroft, dignitaries,
"most of them of some kind of note for something or other, a great many elderly people
(thank Heaven!)." Many callings were represented: politicians, writers, painters, travelers,
"rail road grandees, pres[iden]ts of banks."

Youth and beauty sometimes outshone
age and distinction: "pretty young women,
enterprising matrons, & all under a full head
of steam." The hotels were crowded, hallways
and rooms alike. Shouted greetings could be
heard from the room doors:

> *"You here!"*
> *"Bound for the excursion?"*
> *"Ho for the Falls of St. Anthony!"*

Everyone had "their 'steam up'—for the
Mississippi. Young belles dressed for conquest,
quiet interior matrons, young American lads,
men of all ages, and all on the alert, plumed."
Sedgwick herself was "now well fired up." As

for Charles, "his mercury has got to the very
top of the scale!"[156]

Human nature being variable, Catharine
Sedgwick's description was not true of all
excursionists, some of whom were weary from
their long journey to Chicago, their room-
seeking heroics of Saturday night, their insom-
nia perhaps, and their agitation at "the crowd
and din that were all around them."[157]

Some were beginning to worry about the
week ahead. After a busy day of churchgoing
and preaching, Bacon wrote to his wife, Catherine, "Many doubts are expressed here whether
the week will be long enough for the contemplated excursion, & whether it will be practi-
cable to get back" to Chicago before next Sunday. Devout Christians worried about the prospect of having to travel on Sunday, June 11.[158]

Those who had "their 'steam all up'"
probably did not worry about being back by
next Sabbath. Young belles, and the young
men who practiced the go-ahead, get-ahead
style of Young America, had absented themselves from Sunday evening services. So had
politicians and capitalists, who had other matters than Sabbath observance to worry them.
These men N. W. T. Root of the *New Haven
Register* called the "big bugs," but they were
not sticking their heads out of hotel rooms to
yell down hallways. "The drawing rooms of
the Tremont House were crowded on Sunday
evening by political, financial and editorial
celebrities from all parts of the country," he
reported. "Fillmore, fat, bland, and with his
hands behind him, seemed to be a center for a
system of highly respectable, and well-dressed

Senators, stock-brokers and gentlemen to revolve around." They were all fired up for a railroad building boom and the prosperity it would bring. The excursion celebrated the completion of one of its preliminary stages and implicitly heralded greater triumphs of investment and engineering to come.[159]

In his diary, John Munn of Utica failed to note any church service he attended. He did converse with friends, including a fellow Utican who had left on Friday and could thus report the Munn children all well as of then. He did note that the Tremont's "public room" was "a sort of Exchange" for conducting business. It was "crammed" on Sunday evening and "present[ed] an animating & astonishing scene to the many quiet denizens of the eastern states," who were newcomers to the West and its frenzied speculation.[160]

Typical in his speculative hopes and fears, but atypical in his occupation, was Reverend William Jarvis of Middletown, Connecticut. He apparently did not preach that day. Judging by his correspondence, his thoughts were very much on business. Jarvis served as a director of the Hartford & New Haven Railroad and invested heavily in others—the Cleveland & Toledo, the Lake Shore, the Cleveland & Erie—and in Ohio lands. He gloried in the railroad boom but worried about how events might have an impact on his investments. "The Erie troubles [the riots in Erie] will make bad work for the Lake Shore Road. . . . I should have sold out last summer." Yet on average, "My Rail Road stocks are paying me over 10 per cent on their

cost." They were better investments than were western lands. To cover subscriptions demanded of shareholders, Jarvis had to borrow funds occasionally. "The money market is very tight in New York," he fretted, "and it is almost impossible to get a loan at the Banks." Before leaving on the excursion, he had to pay an $1,100 installment on his Lake Shore stock; he requested his Ohio agent to borrow the money there. The need to shuffle funds around to meet such demands left him vulnerable to changing markets. Political storms like Kansas-Nebraska did not calm the money market.[161]

Jarvis and the "big bugs" were concerned. Financial conditions had worsened recently. "The excitement and misgivings in the money market continues in New York," Sheffield wrote Farnam a month earlier, "and every thing is uncomfortable and as uninviting as possible—the damage to Railroads throughout New England is immense, and sure to put investments in them very much out of favor."[162] The brouhaha over Kansas-Nebraska hurt investor confidence. Capitalists generally opposed agitation of the slavery issue, whether by New England or Chicago clergy, or by abolitionists. They had looked with favor on Fillmore's presidency, when he helped push the 1850 Compromise through Congress and then so stressed its "finality" as to take the wind out of anti-slavery activism. Small wonder senators, stockbrokers, and gentlemen "revolved around" the former president in the Tremont House's drawing room that night. Fillmore's political future and their railroad investments were bound together in symbiotic embrace.

EXCURSUS

Millard Fillmore and Antebellum Partisan Politics

FOR MANY OLD SCHOOL Presbyterians, conservatives, Cotton and Carriage Whigs, New York City merchants, railroad presidents east and west, and wealthy or moderate southerners, Millard Fillmore was the Union's palladium, the one statesman who could safeguard it from the perils of sectional strife. They approvingly associated his presidency with the Compromise of 1850, which quieted the stormy issue of slavery in the territories acquired from Mexico. In early July 1850, Texas seemed ready to send troops to settle its boundary dispute with New Mexico; Henry Clay's compromise seemed doomed by President Zachary Taylor's likely veto (if it even passed Congress); New York City merchants grew alarmed at canceled southern orders. Taylor succumbed to acute gastroenteritis after overeating at a July 4 celebration at the Washington Monument. The new president defused the Texas–New Mexico dispute, helped to rescue the compromise by promising his support for it and by using his patronage powers to secure its passage, and thus saved the Union. Supporters saw only these accomplishments.[163]

To his critics, Fillmore was a northern doughface who gave in to southern threats of secession and supported a Fugitive Slave Law that required northerners to help catch runaway slaves and return them to their masters. Writing for the Democratic *New Haven Register,* N. W. T. Root found this Whig politico fat and bland. Some thought Fillmore's dignified bearing pompous. Even his name sounded like a moniker thought up by a novelist seeking to suggest a mild, self-satisfied, dignified mediocrity. "Fillmore not only looked like a statue,

President Millard Fillmore, ca. 1850s.

he acted like one."[164] The Grand Excursion's wags and wits would have great fun with the ex-president who wanted to run for the office in 1856 but was forced by antebellum rules (presidential candidates must not campaign) to pretend he was sightseeing as a private citizen when he was actually traveling to make connections and to ascertain political opinions in the West. Fillmore was no fool. If scientists traveled to gather data, if historians traveled to acquire documents, if writers traveled to collect a cast of characters for later use in novels, then a politician could travel to take the pulse of public opinion and to meet acquaintances who might later prove helpful.

It was predictable that excursionists' humor would center on the most prominent politician on the trip. In the 1850s, one participant recalled, "politics was the very breath of life, every man was a politician." Men talked of politics morning, noon, and night. "The preacher was systematically scolded by one party because he preached politics and by the other party because he did not preach politics."[165] Party politics was man's occupation, his hobby, his recreation, his subject of thoughtful study, and his source of jokes and entertainment. He could no more ignore it than he could a traveling ex-president who looked the part and had played it.

The standard criticisms of Fillmore were a bit unfair in June 1854. Far from being mediocre, he had resolved a serious crisis in the summer of 1850, one brought on by the more colorful Rough-and-Ready's errors of judgment, and his policy of stressing the compromise's "finality" had worked for nearly four years. Anti-slavery agitation had been quieted and the agitators becalmed. Only the blundering of Democrats Franklin Pierce and Stephen A. Douglas now threatened to sink that policy. The Kansas-Nebraska Act was no fault of Fillmore's. The outcry that greeted the excursionists as they headed west resulted from abandoning his politics, not from following them.[166]

Nearly six feet tall, the fifty-four-year-old Fillmore had broad shoulders, a big chest, and a large head topped by a thatch of unruly silver hair, as well as blue eyes and a deep voice. He did not look meek and mild, but he was a jovial conversationalist who loved social gatherings (such as the excursion). A handsome man, he dressed impeccably and won the attention of many women while remaining faithful to his wife, Abigail. "It was proverbial in Buffalo that if women could vote Fillmore would win any election." He acted dignified to mask his lower-class origins. Both Millard and Abigail were raised in small towns in upstate New York and, once his legal practice enabled them to afford Buffalo's social life, they took to it with enthusiasm. "Formal dinners, chamber recitals, dances, visiting lectures, celebrities, plays—all crowded their lives."[167] Partly, Fillmore seemed to want to hold the Union together out of sheer sociability.

Like Catharine Sedgwick, the Fillmores became Unitarians, in Buffalo in 1831, even though Abigail's father was a Baptist minister (long since deceased). Unitarians prided themselves on their rationality; Fillmore "permitted reason, rather than emotion, to define the boundaries of his behavior." The Unitarians tended not to let doctrinal issues divide them, a trait appreciated by the sociable Fillmores. An optimist, or a man who sought optimism, Fillmore endorsed their rejection of Calvinists' doctrine of human depravity. By "embrac[ing] the idea of progress, they magnified the attraction of their church for Fillmore." He disliked the doctrinaire anti-slavery dogmas of a Leonard Bacon or a Henry Ward Beecher— which would divide a nation quicker than a debate over human depravity—as much as their religious views. No supporter of Stephen Douglas, Fillmore still would have been as offended as Douglas (had either of them read it) at Beecher's favorable comparison of Bacon's anti-Nebraska letter to "the minister . . . pouring down upon [the sinner] the whole law of God, & he quite dissolving under it." That was not how one spoke to people in the drawing room, at a formal dinner, or on the floor of the Senate.[168]

Abhorring and avoiding the drama of a sinner's sudden conviction and conversion or of clerical thunder hurled at southern slaveholders left Fillmore open to Root's charge of being "bland." Fillmore lacked Henry Clay's ability to make compromise exciting. Filllmore's Unitarian love of mild reasonableness may have contributed to his bland image. "There are many respects in which New England Unitarian thought of the classic era appears strangely pallid." Ralph Waldo Emerson criticized the "pale negations" of Boston's Unitarian thinkers.[169]

Root may also have found Fillmore bland because his oratory did not match that of the fiery preachers and anti-slavery agitators who passed through New Haven. "He spoke slowly, almost deliberately," in a low voice. "Usually he chose common household words to express himself, and these he arranged in short, direct sentences." That did not come up to the grandiloquent standards of antebellum political oratory. Fillmore did best "in private conversations and small groups," where he could be animated, well informed, and winsome.[170] One does not typically speak in a confrontational manner in small, face-to-face groups, where controversy seems out of place. Nor does one pour down "the whole law of God" or otherwise lecture people, as if from a pulpit, when in a small group.

In addition to reason, sociability, and soft words, Fillmore relied on commerce running along railroad tracks to unite the nation. If stockbrokers and other financial "big bugs" revolved around him to find political stability helpful to their investments, he also found their commerce helpful to his Union-saving politics. The relationship benefited sun and planets. Commerce distracted northerners from anti-slavery agitation and linked them closer to southern plantation owners. The cotton exports drove the antebellum economy and spread slavery's economic benefits liberally among northern merchants, cotton factors, and bankers. New York City's financial and wholesale predominance was built on its southern trade. That was mainly a coastal trade, but President Fillmore attended several celebrations of railroad projects completed: the New York & Erie Railroad (1850) and Boston's rail links to Canada and the West (1851).[171] He went on railroad excursions before June 1854. The railroad boom of the early 1850s helped to channel northerners' interests to profits and away from anti-slavery, and so he welcomed it.

In fact, there was some connection between Unitarianism and commerce, for "Unitarianism reshaped Christianity most fully to the market mentality" by linking rational effort to resulting success and denying that a predestining God's favor was needed for success.[172] All Americans could be united around the idea that hard work, prudence, and frugality would win out in a free-market economy. And what better united a commercial people than railroad tracks? If reason and commerce united a people in a common pursuit, if iron rails bound them, then why allow sectarian dogmas or doctrinaire anti-slavery passions to divide them? Fillmore's politics had a coherent logic: centripetal forces of commonsense reason, commerce, and technology could bind a people in harmony.

His politics sought to unify North and South, and his personality avoided confrontation and controversy too. His bitterest enemy—Thurlow Weed, political manipulator and editor of the *Albany Evening Journal*—accompanied him partway on the Grand Excursion, but there is no evidence that they tangled. While vice president before Taylor's death, Fillmore had sought peace with Weed while the editor was conniving against him.[173]

Fillmore began his political career, in 1828, in the Anti-Masonic Party with Weed; however, as he rose from Buffalo's congressman to comptroller of New York and vice president, his career path increasingly blocked the goals Weed set for his protégé, William Seward of New York. Now, Weed wanted the 1856 Whig presidential nomination for Senator Seward; Fillmore's own presidential ambitions stood in the way.

In the fall of 1853, seven months out of the White House, Fillmore hoped a Union party of compromise-accepting Whigs (excluding pro-Seward Whigs) and Democrats opposed to President Pierce might emerge to offer him a presidential nomination in 1856. Fillmore wrote "one of the more illuminating letters in American political history," a "brilliant analysis" of the political situation, couched in the laws of physics:

> [N]ational parties can only be formed by the action of the general government. Parties are broken up by local causes and that centrifugal force which throws individuals and masses beyond the attraction of the central power; but new parties of a national character can only be gathered from these fragmentary *nebula of dissolving systems by the magnetism of some great national and centripetal force at Washington. Will any question present such a magnet at the ensuing session of Congress? Is so, then we may hope to see a national Union party which will cast off the secessionists of the South and the abolition freesoilers of the North*

and rally around the Constitution and sus-tain it in its purity.[174]

The national Whig party had been formed by the vetoing actions of Andrew Jackson, by the national and centripetal force of anger at "King Andrew." This force gathered fragments such as the Anti-Masons and magnetized them into a cohesive Whig party. Now the party was breaking up due to Seward-versus-Fillmore factionalism, local bickering, antagonisms between northern and southern Whigs over the slavery issue, and the lack of a Whig president in Washington to bind the factions together. Fillmore hoped memories of his compromise presidency might become the magnet around which the nebula would revolve, then coalesce, and become a new party.

Fillmore's physics did not compare physical properties of the two national parties. Democrats were a localist and pluralist party, more willing to give local causes free play, and thus less broken up by centrifugal forces—which they celebrated. The Whigs stressed a central, entrepreneurial, quasi-evangelical vision for the nation; centrifugal localism seemed likely to break them up faster and farther.

Fillmore thought that the need to save the Union from extremists might become the new magnet creating a Union party. His friend and adviser, John Pendleton Kennedy of Maryland—novelist, former Whig Congressman, Fillmore's secretary of the navy—agreed. "To woo converts in the South" to this new party, he "urged Fillmore to accompany him on an ostensibly nonpolitical tour of the southern states in the spring of 1854, a trip the now nakedly ambitious Fillmore was eager to take."[175]

Neither could foresee that the dissolving *and* magnetizing question in the ensuing session of Congress would be Douglas's Kansas-Nebraska Act, which threatened to destroy their Whig party, rearrange political allegiances, and render both men's political networks obsolete. On February 9, writing to his friend, mental-health reformer Dorothea Dix, Fillmore worried, "I fear that this Nebraska bill is to open again the bitter fountains of slavery agitation, and if it does, little or nothing will be done for the good of the Country." Nine days later, he blamed renewed agitation on *"reckless demagogueism"* and hinted that Douglas and other demagogues renewed it for "mere bids for the Presidency" later and President Pierce's "favor, now." Angered at "knaves" foolishly tinkering with the Union's sole hope and his main accomplishment, Fillmore pulled back in the next sentence: "Prudence however, suggests that I should be more cautious." He trusted Dix to keep his comments confidential; women did not ordinarily intervene in party politics, especially a reformer like Dix, who needed support from both parties. And he said nothing publicly while the bill was before Congress. The slavery issue was such a bitter fountain that a potential Union-saving candidate risked alienating both sides if he dared come near it.[176]

The following month, Fillmore left on the two-month tour of the South (postponed a year due to his wife's death in March 1853). Although "ostensibly sightseeing," he planned to "visit the centers of 'National' Whig sentiment" to maintain ties among Union-loving Whigs during the Nebraska crisis. He seemed to try to unite the nation by his convivial, sociable presence. He carefully planned the trip. A book lover and friend of the literati, he invited Washington Irving to join him. Irving declined: "I have no inclination to travel with political notorieties, to be smothered by the clouds of party dust whirled up by their chariot wheels, and beset by the speechmakers and little great men and bores of every community." Fillmore did not mind if little great men gave speeches, for he went to listen and learn, to meet and greet. Their talk would lessen the chance that he would inadvertently comment on Kansas-Nebraska. The southern trip would be a trial run for the Grand Excursion (before he headed south, he was already planning on that) and would give him more knowledge of southern opinion than almost any other northerner possessed.[177]

He went with mixed feelings. He hated to leave his son and daughter—Millard Powers Fillmore, a twenty-six-year-old lawyer, and twenty-two-year-old Mary Abigail (Abby) Fillmore, an accomplished musician and his charming hostess now that his wife was gone. "[M]y children seem to be grieved at the thought of my leaving them," he informed Dix; he too regretted the separation, for "they are all that is left me of the dear, departed one," and, since his wife's death, "my affections are no longer divided, but concentrated on them alone." And yet marriage would take them from his home at some point, "[s]hould Heaven spare their precious lives," and their father's two-month absence might teach them "self-reliance" in preparation for that day.[178]

He worried about the cholera rumored to be widespread that year. One reason he decided to travel downstream on the Mississippi, then east to the Atlantic, and up the East Coast to New York (rather than taking the reverse course) was to minimize the risks: "We shall be more likely to escape the cholera should any exist on the [Mississippi] River; for that is more likely to be found among the emigrants who ascend, than among our own citizens who descend the River in less crowded boats." Furthermore, going downriver in March was better than returning upriver in May, for the cholera "will be less likely to exist early than late in the season."[179]

The Kansas-Nebraska Act worried his friends and advisers more than did cholera. Could he travel for three months through ten slave states and several free ones, give numerous short speeches, respond to many after-dinner toasts, and converse with secret foes or with friends who could not keep secrets, all without saying a word about the most discussed issue of the day? For company, he had Kennedy, who was a noted author of political satires and an experienced Whig politician who could advise him on avoiding controversy on the trip.[180]

The two gentlemen departed Cincinnati in a steamboat in early March. By March 18, they were visiting Henry Clay's home and tomb at Lexington, Kentucky. Then they were off to Louisville, where Fillmore referred to "gathering clouds" and an approaching "storm," but the reference was ambiguous. Northerners might infer that he meant Kansas-Nebraska, while southerners could infer that he referred to the agitation against that bill. Here, Kennedy and Fillmore boarded another steamboat to go down the Ohio River to the Mississippi, and then downriver to Memphis, Tennessee. They stopped at Vicksburg, Mississippi. In New Orleans, as April 1 ended, a band serenaded them at their hotel past midnight. They took a steamer for Mobile, Alabama, where Fillmore reported that, as president, he had determined no matter "what it might personally cost him, to do his duty fearlessly to the whole country." By April 15, they were in Montgomery, Alabama; by April 21, in Savannah, Georgia, where he reiterated that he had acted "with the sole view of restoring the harmony of the country which gave me birth." In Savannah, on Sunday, April 23, he diplomatically attended an Episcopalian church in the morning, a Presbyterian one in the afternoon, and a Unitarian service in the evening.

The highlight of the tour was Charleston, South Carolina, which Fillmore praised as "the New York City of the South." Flattery seemed the safest path through this hotbed of fire-eaters. He commended the late John C. Calhoun, who had opposed the 1850 Compromise. He admired the beautiful city and fine harbor. He toured the battery and Fort Moultrie, where cannon salutes were fired in his honor. The *Charleston Daily Courier* praised him for conducting his presidential duties "with a single eye to the country's good." He concurred and added that this singleness in 1850 had cost him some southern (especially South Carolinian and Texan) support.

From Charleston, they took the train for Augusta and Atlanta, Georgia, and then to Chattanooga and Nashville in eastern Tennessee, and back to South Carolina (Columbia). Here Kennedy heard that a family member was ill. They rushed back through North Carolina and through Norfolk, Virginia, to return Kennedy to Baltimore, which they reached on May 18.[181] "From everywhere he went—indeed, from southern cities he never got near—came stunning reports of extraordinary Whig enthusiasm for Fillmore, of certainty that he could carry the South as a presidential candidate in 1856."[182]

Finally back home in Baltimore, the exhausted Kennedy slept and rested for fifteen days (perhaps he exaggerated) and satirized the trip turned campaign:

Seventy-five days of constant propulsion by steam; one hundred and ten collations; thirty-four dinners; nineteen balls; one hundred and sixty-one committee-men, seven thousand bouquets; three thousand six hundred and forty volunteer infantry; twenty-six bands of music; twenty-three salutes of artillery in full complement of guns; with a vast number of attempts at the same performance on single instruments and several times on six-barrelled revolvers;—thirty-nine orations—in reply to set encounters by mayors and councils, and forty after-dinner effusions in response to toasts . . . twenty two excursions to see the peculiar wonders of peculiar neighborhoods; a limited quantity of miscellaneous kissing, with a decorous . . . struggle to prevent its extension;—one tremendous, overwhelming, unique and unrepeatable salutation by twenty-six steam-whistles . . . from twenty-six locomotives covered with flowers; and one thousand other assaults upon my nervous system."

He did not number the little great men and bores he encountered, but he was in no mood for a Grand Excursion to repeat the experience. Fillmore was; thousands of diners, dancers, committeemen, militiamen, musicians, orators, and kissers now felt a personal tie to him as a result of his trip. In a large nation, travel seemed necessary to politics.[183]

Antebellum politics were conducted in quasi-military fashion to mobilize the party faithful, convince independents of the party's strength, and entertain every onlooker in an age when other sources of entertainment were rare. Parades, dinners, balls, cannon, whistles, and speeches were common features during campaigns—even if Fillmore was technically not campaigning for office.

As they headed back, his friends urged him repeatedly not to stop in Washington on his way north. After congratulating him on having "succeeded in avoiding the discussion of dangerous topics," his law partner and

adviser, Nathan K. Hall, added, "You will of course avoid Washington." His other former partner, Congressman Solomon G. Haven, wrote to Hall that the Nebraska bill "will be up all next week. Wash[ingto]n will be in a blaze. He has done well & had better wind his way home & rest." The next day, Haven wrote Fillmore, "Nebraska will be up boiling hot all next week; don't come within the Steam of the Cauldron." Fillmore took this advice and kept his distance; he claimed he had never thought of visiting the nation's capital "when important political questions were under consideration." Kansas-Nebraska passed the House on May 22; he returned to Buffalo on May 25, as the bill awaited President Pierce's signature.[184]

Effective tactics in 1851, when Fillmore's compromise was lodged solidly in place and his opponents had to exert massive force to dislodge it, silence and a reliance on inertia were not so effective in early 1854, when Douglas's Nebraska bill had considerable momentum. Now Unionists like Fillmore would have to exert great force if they wanted to stop the moving object and restore the calm. But stopping an unbalanced bill in motion was harder than maintaining a balanced one at rest. Kansas-Nebraska was an anti-northern measure whose lurching, uneven flight demolished conservative, cautious opposition to it. Blocking it would be seen as pro-northern by many in the South. Doing nothing to stop it would be seen as pro-southern by many in the North. The course of events made these hypothetical dangers into realities. Free-Soilers—not conservatives as Fillmore hoped—led the early opposition to the bill; that caused southerners to perceive its foes as even more anti-southern; when southern Whigs therefore defended it, anti-slavery Seward Whigs pointed to that as proof that Fillmore's compromise failed to satisfy the ever-aggressive South. The bill unhinged his carefully constructed consensus.[185]

Once the House passed the bill, Fillmore could only avoid the issue, claim (as an excuse for his inaction) that an ex-president could not interfere, and then travel, look, listen, and wait to see what might turn up. He had no other choice. His allies in Congress could not ignore Kansas-Nebraska but had to cast a vote. Given their constituents' strong feelings, they had to oppose it, although that meant voting on the same side as the Sewardites.[186] But they did not have to run for reelection in the South. If he ran for president in 1856, Fillmore would have to—and so he had to keep silent now lest he alienate voters in one section or the other.

One day after returning home, on Friday, May 26, Fillmore reported to Dorothea Dix, "My journey was a most pleasant one, without accident of any kind, yet very fatiguing." He must start on another one on Monday. "Some six months since," he explained, "I promised to attend a celebration of the opening of the Chicago and Rock Island Rail Road, and since my return I have been notified that it will take place on the 5th of June." Daughter Abby would accompany him "and is so busy preparing for her journey that she desires me to excuse her [from reply-

ing to a letter from Dix] and remember her most affectionately to you."[187] A young woman with dark hair and eyes who had attended Elizabeth Sedgwick's boarding school, Abby could serve as social aide, introducing others to him, conversing with them when he tired of that, and shielding him from political talk (which she would not be expected to engage in) when he tired of that. Son Millard Powers also accompanied him.

So did a small group of Buffalonians linked to the ex-president. Born not far from Fillmore's home, Nathan K. Hall grew up in a similarly humble family and also tried to learn a trade (as had Millard) before clerking for Fillmore and becoming his law partner in Buffalo. "Tall, bony, dark-skinned," clean-shaven, with a dimple in his chin, Hall was six years younger than Fillmore and more serious, even more cautious, and more cerebral. The third partner, Solomon Haven, played the extrovert, the brilliant trial lawyer, full of oratorical tricks and an "impish tongue." That was not Hall's way. "Rather Hall was an ideal office lawyer and a safe counselor," who had a "clear analytical mind" that gave good advice in private, not emotional speeches in public. Fillmore mediated between Haven's exuberance and Hall's restrained caution, just as he attempted to mediate between North and South.[188]

After Fillmore became president, he named Hall as his postmaster-general; 1850s politics was oiled by patronage, and no department was a richer source of government jobs than the U.S. Post Office. As vice president,

Fillmore had been beaten and tricked by Weed at the patronage game. Now that he was in the White House, Fillmore desperately wanted a trusted supporter heading the post office. "Where Fillmore was mocked by even his supporters as passive, indecisive, and timid" in patronage battles, "Hall was renowned as a ruthless partisan who wanted all-out war against the Seward-Weed Whigs." While Taylor was still president, the Seward-Weed faction had deprived Hall of the post he wanted: governor of Minnesota Territory. Now he sought revenge. Loyal, without political ambitions of his own, committed to use postal patronage to further Fillmore's career, Nathan K. Hall was the ideal man for the job.[189]

Fillmore wanted Hall with him on the Grand Excursion to fulfill the role Kennedy had played on the southern tour. Now a judge in western New York, Hall was initially uncertain if he could go. His circuit court would hear cases in Canandaigua on Friday, June 16.[190] Hall decided he could return by that date and he joined Fillmore on the excursion; in fact, Hall handled the details of planning for both their families. He would get to see Minnesota Territory and the man who trounced him for the governor's post—Alexander Ramsey—after all.

Hall had added a bit of nativism to his resentment at Seward and Weed for depriving him of that job. Congratulating Fillmore on the southern tour, Hall noted that "the Seward People" had been silent about it, and they certainly "would be down upon you instantly if

you said any thing out of which they thought they could make Capital for Billy O'Seward." The Know-Nothing movement (that other "K-N" issue of 1854) experienced "dazzling growth" in early 1854. From January to July, Know-Nothing lodges multiplied across the nation. "Know Nothings tapped into and articulated a remarkably deep and widespread anxiety about, and antipathy toward, foreigners and Catholics"—anxiety that they were taking jobs from native-born Americans, were plotting to take over the country, and were manipulating the political system. During the 1852 presidential campaign, Seward and Weed had appealed to Irish and German Catholic voters. That aroused nativist ire and led to Hall's sneer at "Billy O'Seward."[191]

The Know-Nothings, however, were still not well known in late May 1854, as Fillmore and his party made plans for the excursion. Other Buffalo friends and supporters planned to accompany the ex-president. His good friend George R. Babcock, a former New York state legislator and congressman, had been Fillmore's floor manager at the 1852 Whig national convention. Forty-four-year-old Dr. Thomas M. Foote also accompanied him; he was from East Aurora, New York, Fillmore's home for his early legal career and the home of Fillmore's parents. Twenty years earlier, Fillmore arranged for Foote to take over the editor's chair at Buffalo's Whig newspaper, the *Commercial Advertiser.* Foote had served as a faithful ally and editorial promoter of Fillmore ever since. Like Hall, Foote was "a visceral foe of Weed," and he too had been denied a patronage job he sought—chargé d'affaires at Constantinople—by the Seward-Weed forces and had to settle for a lesser post.[192]

Hall, Babcock, and Foote were part of that conservative New York Whig faction called the Silver Grays, in the arcane vocabulary of antebellum politics. The name came from the flowing gray hair of Francis Granger of Canandaigua, who led an exodus of conservative Whigs from the 1850 Whig state convention at Utica. The men who followed Granger out the door took on his hair color too, so to speak. They favored the 1850 Compromise and walked out when the convention implicitly endorsed Seward's anti-compromise stance over Fillmore's pro-compromise position. Other Silver Grays went on the excursion: Francis's brother John A. Granger and Thomas M. Howell from Canandaigua, and others from upstate New York towns.[193]

Canandaigua was the geographical capital of Silver Gray–ness and Fillmore-dom. Settled by Yankees, at "the center of a rich agricultural region," it was the prosperous "seat of wealthy landlords" with "elegant, aristocratic homes, neat gardens, and broad tree-shaded streets." Here lived Old Fogy Whigs who vehemently opposed brash Young America Democrats like Stephen A. Douglas, who—in one of history's ironies—was educated at the Canandaigua Academy and socialized with the politically prominent Grangers. His stepfather was a Granger, a distant cousin of Francis and John Granger. He studied Greek and Latin classics at the academy but

his interest turned to politics early and he defended Andrew Jackson in that anti-Jackson town. He was only Canandaigua's stepson, and he soon headed west to Illinois and a brand of politics that Silver Grays hated. Now Canandaigua Whigs headed west to assess Douglas's rough western "Sovereigns."[194]

An article in that year turned to political taxonomy and tried to classify the great number of political species and subspecies: "What with whigs, democratic whigs, democrats, true democrats, barnburners, hunkers, silver grays, woolly heads, soft shells, hard shells, national reformers, fire-eaters, and filibusteros, it is not difficult to imagine how the exotic intellect should get perplexed." Even for those who were not foreigners but Americans, "the diversity of principle hidden under the diversity of names, is not palpable." And the dutiful young student of American political factions found it hard "to write their distinctive creeds in a horn-book."[195]

The Buffalo *Commercial Advertiser* (presumably, Editor Foote) tried to sort out, for its readers, which factions would be represented by whom on the Grand Excursion:

[1] "The barnburners [New York Democrats allied with Martin Van Buren and opposed to slavery] are going in great force. John A. Dix, Preston King, Mr. [Francis P.] Blair, formerly editor of the Washington Globe, S[amuel] J. Tilden . . . Van Dyke [sic] of the Albany Atlas, A. C. Flagg, ex-[New York City] mayor [William F.] Havemeyer, Judge [Amasa] Parker and

ex-Comptroller Wright will look after the interests of the Marcy portion of the party."

[2] "Among the hunkers [conservative New York Democrats favoring compromise with the South], en route for the Mississippi, are Mr. Bancroft, Mr. Polk's Minister to London, Judge [Thomas J.] Oakley of New York, Charles Van Benthuysen, Judge Hilton, and T[homas] W. Olcott of Albany, and Judge Paige of Schenectady."

[3] "The principal representatives of the conservative whigs [Silver Grays] are Mr. Fillmore, Dr. Foote and Judge [Nathan K.] Hall."

[4] "Thurlow Weed, Farmer [David H.] Abell, and Alderman Shultz of New York, will take care of the interests of Mr. Seward [and other anti-slavery Whigs] all the way to the Falls of St. Anthony."

Foote trusted that there would be "ladies enough to refine and harmonize the heterogeneous materials of which the party is to be composed."[196] No Fire-eaters or Filibusters went to make the materials too heterogeneous to be harmonized.

Actually, the materials of antebellum partisan politics were even more heterogeneous than Foote indicated. Softshells were Hunker Democrats who sought to go soft on (to reconcile with) Barnburners; Hardshells opposed this softness. Woolly Heads were anti-slavery; Fire-eaters sought secession to remove the South from anti-slavery agitation; Filibusters sought to annex Caribbean lands to the United States to add more slave districts to the nation.[197]

The heterogeneity of the Grand Excursion party and of antebellum politics could be clearly seen, for example, in the stark contrast between Fillmore and Francis Preston Blair, the prominent anti-slavery Democrat. The contrast extended beyond the obvious one between Whig and Democrat. Fillmore was large, tall, and handsome; Blair was thin, sickly looking, only average in height, and homely, even ugly. His head was a sphere (bald head and forehead) plunked atop a triangle (a sharp, angular jaw). Reporter Murat Halstead described him as "a little old gentleman, thin, slender, and feeble in appearance, yet moving about with considerable activity. . . . [H]e is given a top-heavy appearance by the fact that his head is too big for his body, and his hat too big for his head." His appearance caused people to assume he had tuberculosis and to predict his early death, yet, like a political party that loses but survives, Blair was now sixty-three and embarking on a three-thousand-mile trip.[198]

Fillmore was a self-made man whose son and daughter were not active in politics, whereas Blair was the patriarch of a politically prominent family. The Blairs acted as a unit in antebellum politics: F. P. (Frank) Blair Jr. was a St. Louis Democrat who served in the state legislature and had edited the *Missouri Democrat;* another son, Montgomery Blair, had been a judge in Missouri and active in its politics; "Blair's sons regarded their father as the noblest and wisest of all men, and deferred to his judgment in almost all matters." Daughter Elizabeth Blair Lee avidly followed politics and served "as her father's secretary and scribe for the long public letters, pamphlets, and ghosted speeches that kept him constantly busy." Living at the family farm at Silver Spring and at the Blair House across from the White House, the Maryland Blairs, at least, were the consummate Washington insiders—which Fillmore was decidedly not.[199]

Wife Eliza and daughter Elizabeth (Lizzie) were reluctant to allow the elderly, sickly patriarch to go on the excursion, to which fellow Democrat John A. Dix had invited him. "Father proposes to accept an invitation for a pleasure trip from the Railroad companies from New York to St. Anthony Falls," Lizzie wrote her husband. "Gen[era]l Dix and other press him to do so." Perhaps enviously, she observed that "all notable, & fashionables" were invited on "this railroad frolic." Her father pressed her to come along, but she did not "feel at liberty to go" and was "fearful to have him go in a Cholera region, so shall oppose the whole trip." Her mother opposed it for the same reason, but Preston promised Eliza that he would not go down to St. Louis, where the cholera reportedly raged. After he made his decision, Lizzie—like her brothers—"deferred to his judgment" and even rejoiced at it. "I am glad Father goes—because he is not well & a journey always has a good effect" on him.[200]

He eagerly desired to go, partly to see Frank out west and partly to exercise in person his still considerable political influence as the late Andrew Jackson's close adviser and official editorial spokesperson at the *Globe*. As Jackson's voice in life and the keeper of his "papers and reputation" (Jackson's words) in death, Preston Blair had the influence to bring many a Jacksonian Democrat into an anti-Nebraska coalition. Famous for feuds as well as friendships, Blair disliked the southern Democrats who aided President James Polk in ousting him as the party's official editor in 1845 because he opposed Polk's policy of annexing Texas as an added slave state. Anger aroused by these southerners' successful push for the Kansas-Nebraska Act gave Blair an excellent chance to help forge a coalition that could oppose slavery's extension but also bring him personal revenge on them. Frank wrote to his father in early May, "What a dog Pierce is, and what a pack of dogs he has about him." He agreed with this sentiment but cautioned his son, "Do not talk of him to others as you write of him to me."[201] Since he was not a potential candidate, Preston Blair could feud more openly than could Fillmore, but still there were limits. The act that threatened to undo Fillmore's plans promised possibly to fulfill Blair's.[202]

One thing Fillmore and Blair had in common was their role as brokers between the sections, a role that won political influence in this era of North-South strife. As a northerner opposed to abolitionists and free-soilers and willing to compromise with the South, Fillmore won acclaim on his southern tour in March and April. As a slave-owning southerner opposed to the expansion of slavery and sympathetic to free-soilers, Blair was popular with northerners who welcomed him as *their* kind of southerner. Apart from their shared appeal to women, that about exhausted their common features.

If Blair was Jackson's friend, Fillmore was his political opponent. Fillmore was a Unitarian who had rejected Calvinism; Blair's grandfather, John Blair, was a theology professor and vice president at Princeton College, and Preston never renounced his ancestor's Calvinism but seemed to transfer its sharp distinction between saint and sinner to politics, which became his religion. Total depravity characterized his political foes, whereas the Blairs and their many friends were counted among the elect. To friends, and to many women, Preston Blair demonstrated an irresistible graciousness that won him lifelong devotion. Fillmore won female hearts with his looks; Blair, with his "sensitive understanding" that was unusual for an early-nineteenth-century male and his gifts "of giving and inspiring personal affection." Cornelia Martin was one such friend. To his foes, however, he was a persevering foe. He was no quitter.[203]

Preston Blair needed his friends as he made his way west to Chicago for the Grand Excursion. He left home at 5:00 a.m., May 29, rather ill from overeating Maryland strawberries, and spent time in New York City talking politics before continuing west. "Father's ailment had come back on him at Buffalo," Lizzie reported, "but he stopped there a day & rested, Gen'l Dix nursing him almost after Mother's fashion—he was soon well enough to

start again." By Sunday, June 4, Blair was in Chicago, having a "very pleasant talk" at the Tremont Hotel with Cornelia's husband, who was also staying there. Blair shared a room with John Dix.[204]

Enos Thompson Throop Martin was the very opposite of a self-made man. Although the Age of Jackson had celebrated the man who rose strictly on his own merits without favors from anyone, and although corporate stock transfers did not exclude parvenus from ownership of crucial companies, antebellum America still valued family ties. Montgomery and Frank Blair rose partly on the strength of their father's connections and reputation. Martin epitomized the young man dependent on a patron, Uncle Enos Thompson Throop. His mother gave her son his name; the uncle became New York's governor, hired his nephew as his personal secretary, and gave the young man a legal, political, and social education, and then his upstate New York estate, Willow Brook. A Democrat, Martin was hardly the Jacksonian common man, and yet there is no indication that Blair, Dix, or their cronies looked down upon him.[205]

Martin wrote home to his wife to tell her the excursion news. William Walcott of Utica had secured him a room at the Tremont, "to be shared by me with John A. Granger," an unlikely pairing since the Canandaigua Whig's brother, Francis, ran against Martin's mentor, Throop, in the 1830 governor's race. Still, rooming with a Whig was a blessing compared to the roomless fate of many excursionists. Also at the Tremont were "your friend

Miss Sedgwick & *her train.*" Catharine Sedgwick "inquired with much interest & indeed affection about you. I told her you had not the courage to encounter such a crowd." Martin saw Dix, who "told me that your dear old friend F. P. Blair was here & rooming with him at this Hotel[,] & that he had talked a great deal about you on his way up." Fillmore was there, and former New York governor Washington Hunt "& indeed pretty much all the politicians, men of leisure, literary men, & capitalists together with a very considerable sprinkling of loafers of all kinds & sexes." Martin thought it "a most extraordinary assemblage of people"; Henry Farnam "told me he was constantly telegraphing for more steamboats as more guests arrived here." He promised to hurry home after the excursion ended; he forewarned Cornelia to get the house ready, for Preston Blair wanted to visit them on his way back east.[206]

So many officeholders went on the excursion that reporter N. W. T. Root joked, "There will be a chance for rising politicians, if any serious accident occurs."[207] For many on the trip, the serious accident had already occurred: the Kansas-Nebraska Act. That was Fillmore's worry, and Blair's complaint. The numerous species and subspecies that Foote listed might be what Fillmore called "fragmentary *nebula* of dissolving systems," which the act might magnetize and rearrange into a new system more conducive to Blair's revenge than to Fillmore's return to the White House. That might begin while these heterogeneous materials were together for the excursion. Preston Blair was sure to use his conversational charm. Did Fillmore have the resources to advance his very different cause? John P. Kennedy worried, "Have you a sufficient ammunition left from the late campaign to venture upon the expenditure of that?" But he mainly asked, "What is the real state of the Nebraska excitement in the North?" Was it "deep seated" or would it quickly prove "a worn out impulse"? Kennedy thought the act might "aid abolitionism" and so backfire on its originators. But the answers to all those questions lay in the future.[208]

ROCK ISLAND CITY *by Herrmann J. Meyer, engraving, 1853–1855. After arriving by train in Rock Island, more than 1,000 excursionists boarded steamboats bound for St. Paul, the territorial capital of Minnesota. (From* The United States Illustrated, *University of Minnesota Libraries)*

CHAPTER FOUR

"Off She Goes!"

MONDAY, JUNE 5, 1854

SOME TIME AFTER 5:00 A.M., excursionists in one Chicago hotel were awakened by a porter, "gifted with a strong pair of lungs," who strolled the hallways and yelled, "All aboard! All aboard! Omnibus ready for the Chicago and Rock Island cars!" Piles of carpetbags and trunks were "heaped up in the halls and passage ways." Porters hurried off with heavy loads of luggage. "Porters, waiters, guests, all are in quick motion," complained one guest, "and one or the other is pretty sure to knock you over." The hotel was "in a constant flux. The universe, in the Hegelian philosophy, is not more fluid" than this beehive on the morning when the Grand Excursion began.[209]

Although departure was set for 8:00 a.m., as early as 6:00 Monday morning, sidewalks outside Chicago's hotels bustled with activity: "all was hurry and confusion to be off; trunks, carpet bags, boxes, valises, and all kinds of baggage, began to descend like avalanches from the leading hotels, and load after load to start for the cars." The avalanches would have been greater, but some excursionists left their luggage in Chicago; they were uncertain whether they would continue past Rock Island, given the huge crowd and the likely dearth of steamboat berths. Still, "the scene for nearly two hours was most amusing," reported Isaac Platt of the *Poughkeepsie Eagle,* "well displaying our national peculiarity of being always in a hurry. . . . Before 7 [o'clock] omnibuses and hacks began to fill up and dash off with passengers, as if the place was on fire."[210]

Haste and confusion marked the construction of Chicago's streets and sidewalks, which consisted of planks laid on bare earth. "In the spring of the year, the ground asserts its original character of swamp," one traveler reported, and "planks actually float, and, as the heavy wagons pass along, ornamental jets of muddy water play on every side." Small wonder the road to every train depot in Chicago was called the "mud route." Sidewalks changed grade—from one to five feet—at nearly every block due to earlier decisions to change the street grade. Pedestrians had to ascend or descend steps or "short, steep, inclined planes of boards" as they went from one sidewalk level to the next. "It is one continual succession of ups and downs."[211]

The weather was cloudy and a bit cool, but this portent of a storm proved a false prophet in the city that day. The distinguished guests were not rained on; dozens of editors did not criticize Chicago's weather or call it the Windy City ("Garden City" was the term some used, with the hearty approval of the real estate dealers).[212]

Haste and confusion transferred to the La Salle Street Station of the Michigan Southern–Chicago & Rock Island Road, which the two allied railroads built in 1853 toward the southern end of downtown Chicago, on Van Buren Street, between La Salle and Sherman Streets.[213] Here Platt noted "scenes as amusing as those around the hotels." A huge crowd of well-wishers assembled at the depot, a wooden, whitewashed structure only sixty by twenty-five feet. C&RI contractor Henry Farnam had two trains ready, each locomotive festively decorated with flags and evergreens and flowers. Each train had nine large passenger cars. About twelve hundred excursionists filed into eighteen railcars, each new and "as clean as a parlor." Three baggage cars swallowed up carpetbags, valises, trunks, and boxes. By some watches, it was 8:30 a.m.; by others, "about nine o'clock"; others showed 8:15 a.m., when the moment of departure came.[214]

There was no standardized time in the United States; watches and "clocks were set according to the rules of astronomy: noon was the moment when the sun stood highest in the midday sky" and "every locale had a different noon." Excursionists came from dozens of localities, and even many newspaper correspondents had apparently not bothered to change their watches. Charles Hale of the *Boston Daily Advertiser* reported a fifty-minute difference between his watch and the Illinois clocks. Such imprecision was unacceptable to the new railroads. "Two trains running on the same tracks at the same moment but with clocks showing different times could well find themselves unexpectedly occupying the same space, with disastrous consequences." Railroads needed standard time, and Americans who adjusted to the more hurried schedules that railroads brought also wanted it. But they would not obtain standard time zones until 1883.[215]

At last the whistle shrieked; the "all aboard" came; someone shouted, "Off she goes!"; the first train pulled out "amid the roar of cannon, enlivening music and the cheers of the populace." They could almost have walked alongside. "The movements were slow at first, and the people, collected in groups, cheered us as we passed," Platt reported. "Soon the speed increased," but it never exceeded thirty miles an hour. C&RI contractor Joseph Sheffield was concerned lest a mishap occur to the large party of shareholders, bondholders, and notables. "Pray use *great care and prudence* with the trains," he wrote to superintendent John E. Henry that day, "so that no accident may mar . . . this beautiful and most important excursion—important to the whole western railroad interest." Investors' confidence in western railroads was shaky and might not survive a horrible accident to twelve hundred guests, with dozens of editors to chronicle the grisly details. "*Safety*—not speed, must be the motto."[216]

The Chicago & Rock Island had had some embarrassing difficulties with earlier celebratory events, so Sheffield's precautions were understandable. When their first train arrived in Joliet, there was no turnaround, so the engineer had to put the engine in reverse and back up the forty miles to Chicago. The night before their first train was to enter La Salle Station in triumph, Farnam and crew had to hurriedly lay the final mile-and-a-half of rails.[217] With the editors and notables on board, they could not risk a repeat of these fiascoes.

Farnam rode in the first train, no doubt with a careful eye on the engineer. John Henry supervised the second one and held it back a half hour to put a considerable safety margin between the two and minimize the chance of collision.[218]

Seemingly oblivious to any possibility of danger, the excursionists presented "a joyous and animated scene" inside the cars as the trains headed straight south past the first town, Blue Island, and onto prairie lands that were a new, exciting sight to many easterners. Someone picked "the wonderful prairie flowers" and brought them into a passenger car, where they were duly admired.[219]

The trains picked up new recruits as they stopped at the various Illinois towns. At Joliet, where the C&RI tracks crossed the Des Plaines River, Illinois governor Joel A. Matteson, wife Mary, and daughter Lydia boarded the first train around 10:00 a.m., amid "a parade of military and waving banners" and "the voice of a loud mouthed cannon." These rail towns had much more reason to celebrate the completion of a railroad than did the river towns they were headed for. "This was a Jubilee day for the people of this region," wrote Benjamin Silliman, "and we

were everywhere cheered by them; in the villages & towns, especially Joliet & Ottawa, the people assembled in great numbers—in their gala dresses & with banners flying and music and the firing of guns & cannon welcomed our arrival." One eastern editor reported that, on the Illinois prairie, with no hills to make sound reverberate, firing the cannon produced only "a single dead thump."[220]

A moderately anti-slavery Democrat, Matteson was a skilled businessman, now "independently well off," who dressed in a fashionable black suit and stovepipe hat. An excursion with eastern gentility would nicely emphasize how far this son of a New York farmer had come. He had grown rich from Joliet's early growth; from his woolen mill, store, and bank; and from his work as a contractor for the Illinois and Michigan Canal and the C&RI (he built the stretch between Joliet and Chicago). The rising tide of development in northern Illinois had lifted his boat considerably. After three terms in the state senate, his surprising nomination for governor in 1852 was perhaps due to the greater salience of railroad than slavery issues in that time of Millard Fillmore's "finality." Once elected, Matteson had the enviable dual role of influencing the legislature's chartering of railroad companies (as governor) and benefiting from those projects (as contractor). Farnam might claim that Matteson's contract work for the railroad earned him the invitation, but his political power didn't hurt. Free tickets to literary lights like Catharine Sedgwick might be innocent, but this extended free railroad and steamboat pass to a governor with direct power over the C&RI could not have been given without some thoughts, at least, of possible future benefits for the railroad company.[221]

A man on the make in his mid-forties, Matteson was being corrupted by the go-ahead, get-ahead exuberance of the 1850s. His tall, pretty, shy wife and his "quiet and reserved" and "most attractive" daughter likely did not demand the elegant lifestyle that he was cutting ethical corners to provide for them. He was not alone. The 1850s were remarkable for political corruption, some of Matteson's contemporaries noted with disgust. As the trains headed west, bills to give land grants to prospective railroads in Iowa, Minnesota, and Wisconsin—plus a bill to extend Samuel Colt's revolver patent—were sliding through Congress, well lubricated by bribes to congressmen and lobbyists' sizable fees.[222]

Others could still see only the railroad's benefits. William Bross, brother of excursionist John A. Bross of the *Chicago Daily Democratic Press,* wrote a panegyric hailing the soon-to-be-completed C&RI. It was printed as a booklet that year. William Bross saw another side of the railroad's moral effect:

It is astonishing how the opening of a railroad through a country arouses the energies and develops the faculties of the people. Contracted ideas take their departure with the 'slow coaches.' Great enterprises, sleepless activity and liberal views, follow in the wake of the Locomotive. . . . Men now begin to show of what stuff they are made. Individualities stand out in much bolder relief. . . . [T]he introduction of an important improvement . . . makes small men great and great men greater.[223]

The Joliet entrepreneur represented a small man made great, perhaps greater than his character could sustain.

Whatever politics was involved, Silliman admired the result: "This road has been constructed, as already remarked, by our New Haven gentlemen Mr. Joseph E. Sheffield & Mr. Henry Farnham. [sic] The work has been admirably done and a better road I have never seen at home or abroad." Ten years earlier, Silliman traveled by stagecoach from Peoria to Chicago, a heroic adventure as it turned out. It took "two days and the intermediate night" to go one hundred miles "over the wet & often miry prairie"; the coach wheels "often" sank so low in the ground that the stage was nearly stuck. Floodwaters rose above the coach floor as they crossed fords. Silliman gave his blanket to another passenger for the night and "suffered severely with the cold." The coach broke down, and passengers had to help repair it. In 1854 all was different. "Now we flew to the Mississippi with almost Eagle speed"—and that was "as an average speed of 22 to 23 miles an hour."[224]

The *New York Times* praised Sheffield and Farnam's speed: "Aladdin's Palace was built in a night, but that was in the days of magic. The Chicago and Rock Island Railroad was commenced on the 10th of April, 1852," and had reached the Illinois towns of Joliet by mid-October, Ottawa by mid-February of 1853, Geneseo by December, and Rock Island by February 22, 1854. "This is not exactly the magic of Aladdin's [P]alace, but it is very near it." If the two New Haven contractors "had done nothing else in their lives, this road would win them a lasting name."[225]

As they sped southwest through the state from Joliet to Morris, a well-meaning gentleman (possibly Reverend David Magie, fifty-nine-year-old Presbyterian minister, director of the American Tract Society, and author of religious tracts, or possibly Sewell Cutting of the *New York Recorder*) attempted to do his part to evangelize and Christianize the West, albeit with tactics that misfired. The trains passed "log huts and emigrant's shanties." Immigrant children, "well fed, happy, and independent imps of children, half naked, came tumbling out as we passed, to hail the wondrous cars." Perhaps thinking they were unschooled and unchurched, an "exemplary gentleman on board, who had brought with him a bundle of Religious Tracts," as the train passed "these huts and shanties, dropped good seed by the wayside, by throwing them out the car window." Alas, reported the *New York Times* correspondent, "[t]hey were taken by the wind, and by the draught caused by the rapid transit of the cars, and borne afar, sometimes over the roofs of the cabins. I saw 'The Path of Peace' lodge in the wires of the telegraph, and 'God's Judgment on Sinners,' I am afraid is being borne in the air across the prairies yet," he observed, not with any noticeable sorrow over the misfiring.[226]

At Morris, the jubilee continued. The local militia fired a brass cannon, "a hoarse one-pounder, rusty from lack of service. They could not get it to speak well," recalled the *Times* reporter, "for in about ten minutes they made it utter but four notes, and those were hesitating and uncertain,—perhaps from the hoarseness aforesaid." Yet excursionists cheered their effort, and the Morris folk cheered back. The trains stopped ten minutes to take on wood and water for the locomotives and a few new excursionists, then departed.[227]

They passed a few immigrant wagons camped not far from the tracks. Illinois's frontier period lay twenty or thirty years in the past, but a distinguished company of easterners had not been present then to observe it. This late and partial manifestation would have to suffice. "Some pioneers, as we might almost term them [the *Times* reporter seemed hesitant to use the term at this late date] . . . and a pleasant sight they were to see, bringing whispers to the heart, of hope and courage." The railroad's advance onto the prairie sparked added hope in settlers, who now could anticipate a ready supply of building materials on the treeless prairie, and a means to get their crops to market. Farther along, N. W. T. Root of the *New Haven Register* related, "[W]e passed a company of emigrants in their covered wagons, driving their herds before them—and at another sudden turn in the road we startled three red deer into a moment's wonder, and then into hasty flight."[228]

Not so easily startled were these tourists' "travelling companions": the Illinois River and the Illinois and Michigan Canal alongside it. "These serve to add to the interest of the changing views from the car windows," noted Charles Hale of the *Boston Daily Advertiser*. As in Connecticut's Farmington Valley, the earliest transportation artery (river) paralleled the first man-made one (canal) and the second (railroad). Antebellum America was slow to abandon waterborne transport. On board one train was William C. Redfield, a sixty-five-year-old jack-of-all-sciences who studied storms, steamboat explosions, and fossils but was invited on the excursion because he wrote an 1829 pamphlet that first suggested building a railroad to the Mississippi (near Rock Island, coincidentally). Otherwise, his pamphlet was wide of the mark: his railroad would link canal, river, and lake routes and let them do the heavy carrying; "[e]very true patriot and friend to his country's prosperity" would support it regardless of whether it ran through the patriot's hometown; knowledge of its civic benefits would bring it to pass without promoters like Matteson; the railroad would have fewer accidents than canals, and would not lower morals along the route as canals did, due to "the unhappy influence that boatmen often exercise upon each other."[229]

In 1829, Illinois was thinking canals. The river was navigable only to La Salle or Ottawa, depending on the season and year, and canal boats could haul freight to the Chicago River and Lake Michigan—or so Illinois promoters reasoned. The hugely successful

Erie Canal (1825) gave them a model; Congress gave the state a land grant in 1827 to help finance construction from Chicago to Ottawa. The state sold odd-numbered sections for five miles on either side of the canal, a system later used to aid railroad construction. The project fell behind schedule from start (1836) to finish (1848) but was completed. Farm crops were shipped up to Chicago and lumber down to rural prairie towns. Unlike the Farmington Canal, the Illinois and Michigan Canal was a profitable enterprise that was still useful for shipping bulkier products like lumber, even after the C&RI began to compete against it.[230]

As they traveled parallel to the canal, excursionist John Munn's mind was not on profitability or products but on an April 1849 trip "when Mary was so dangerously sick with Cholera upon the Canal Boat."[231]

At Ottawa, a growing town on canal, river, and railroad, the trains stopped and Millard Fillmore "came out and shook hands with several of our citizens," a local newspaper reported. "Ottawa was born as Chicago's twin," as the western end of the canal to match Chicago's eastern end, but the state government proved a much slower builder than private firms, and the eastern sibling far outpaced the western one. The canal that lay about one-tenth of a mile from the train station had arrived only six years before the trains, despite having a fourteen-year head start.[232]

Several prominent Ottawans boarded the trains to join the excursion (and perhaps shook Fillmore's hand): Judge John Dean

Caton, Illinois Supreme Court judge and "telegraph king of the West"; George H. Norris, a lawyer and early C&RI backer; Lorenzo Leland, a local leader and investor; Theophilus L. Dickey, a prominent lawyer; "glass merchant and farmer William Reddick," a former state senator and "the wealthiest man in town"; Mayor William Hickling, a wholesale grocer; and Burton Cook, a prominent anti-Nebraska Democrat. Caton, Norris, and Leland brought their wives; Mrs. Joseph Glover accompanied them. The delegation was mostly Democratic. In the 1850s, Ottawans "agreed to disagree on political issues while maintaining a united front in support of the town's economic interests." These men united to support improvements to the Illinois River channel and to encourage the C&RI to build through Ottawa. Hickling "pledged to subscribe $5,000 of his own money to the [C&RI] project." Senator Reddick introduced the bill to charter the C&RI corporation and used his "state-wide personal acquaintance among the members of the Legislature" to get it passed.[233]

Now was the time for the company to reward these early supporters with free tickets to St. Anthony Falls and back. The new railroad had needed their support. Contrary to what one might assume, Chicagoans "really had little to do with" initiating the new rail line but focused on aiding the Galena & Chicago Union Railroad. The C&RI resulted from the fervent desire of "venturesome promoters of Rock Island and Davenport" for connections to Chicago, not Chicagoans for

links to Rock Island. These promoters had to drum up interest among towns on the river-and-canal route to compensate for Chicago's lack of interest. They agreed to a provision whereby the railroad would reimburse the canal for lost freight revenue. Greatly helping them was their alliance with the Michigan Southern. In the race for the Mississippi, they left the Galena & Chicago in the dust, partly because they built along a water-transportation route with established towns, while the Galena road headed across open country.[234]

Ottawans also needed the Chicago & Rock Island. They had been jilted by the Illinois Central, the state's north-south railroad, which chose to cross the Illinois River at La Salle, not Ottawa. A town had the best chance to prosper if it became a railroad junction, and Ottawa had lost that chance.[235]

Many antebellum Americans were slow to perceive the railroad's revolutionary impact; even Redfield assumed the railroad would supplement existing water routes. Ottawa's growth in the late 1840s and early 1850s was due to the canal. "[T]heir total identification with and confidence in the canal" meant "that Ottawa's leaders did not initially view the new railroad technology as a threat to the canal's or the town's economic prosperity." They did not foresee the railroad taking freight away from the canal but "saw railroads as welcome adjuncts to the canal," as a way to connect canal towns "with others that lay beside distant lakes and rivers." Ottawa was a water junction where the canal, the Illinois, and the Fox River met, and slow to realize that the all-weather, ubiquitous iron rail was well on its way to making boats obsolete.

Despite town leaders' "united front," Ottawa was anything but united. Irish laborers came to construct the canal in the 1830s; many stayed to work on the canal boats or in the new shops and factories. Old Stock Protestants disliked Irish Catholics (but welcomed Irish Protestants like Reddick) and kept them from leadership roles. No Irish Catholics boarded Grand Excursion trains that Monday. Two days earlier, on Saturday, June 3, a serious fight broke out between Irishmen working on the "state scow" that repaired the canal and an Old Stock group on a canal boat, the *Flying Cloud*. Whig and Democratic papers (with Old Stock editors) agreed on details: Irishmen kicked a Captain Brown's dog into a canal lock, where it drowned; Brown returned to Ottawa; the Irish attacked him and his men, who fired several shots, seriously wounding Brady McGuire in the abdomen and hitting "another man in the hand." Monday, as the excursion rolled through town, Brown and a comrade appeared before a magistrate. "It appearing that [they] were fighting in self defense, they were acquitted."[236]

These ethnic and religious tensions fueled the explosive growth of the Know-Nothings in the spring of 1854, and they lay behind Nathan K. Hall's sneers about "Billy O' Seward."

The Ottawans who boarded the cars undoubtedly told of this episode after the trains puffed and whistled out of town. But easterners turned their attention to scenery

and Indian stories, not Irishmen. Soon, they passed close to Buffalo Rock on the north bank of the Illinois River, "down which it is said the Indians used to drive the buffaloes, killing them by the hundreds." Farther on, they saw Starved Rock on the south side—a 120-foot-high sandstone bluff looming above the river like a watchtower. Caton served as tour guide: he lived on a nearby bluff; he was an expert on the story of Starved Rock; and he told it to the *New York Times* reporter. "Two tribes of Indians, as the legend runs, had been very long in contention, and one tribe was nearly exterminated. The survivors retreated to this rock, and were hemmed in by their adversaries without the shedding of another drop of blood. The poor wretches were starved to death." This tale of the Illinois tribe's defeat by the Pottawatomies and Ottawas was told to Caton in the early 1830s by Méachelle, "the oldest Pottawatomie chief," who claimed to have witnessed the event in the late 1760s.[237]

Judge John Dean Caton was a jack-of-all-trades generalist, rather typical of the pioneer generation. Coming from the long-settled and specialized East, Silliman focused on his specialty, geology: "Limestone and sandstone are almost the only rocks in view. Near Ottawa about half way [to Rock Island], there are grand bluffs[,] vertical walls of sandstone which is also tunnelled for the rail road and deeply cut for the canal."[238]

They passed through Utica, Illinois, and then stopped at La Salle, Ottawa's successful rival for the rail junction. La Salle had experienced its own Erie-like insurrection when

Farnam tried to lay tracks through the Illinois River valley instead of on top of the bluff, where the Illinois Central tracks lay. The citizens organized themselves into a militia, drilled, and prepared to resist Farnam's army of tracklayers before delay and compromise defused the situation. However, no one seems to have informed the excursioning editors of this incident, and so La Salle escaped the editorial coals heaped upon Erie. Buffalo Rock, near La Salle, was the only place where Farnam's crew had to cut a path through rock.[239] At La Salle, they picked up Ninian W. Edwards, Abraham Lincoln's brother-in-law, and Edward Bates, a Whig lawyer and ex-congressman from St. Louis. Edwards, his wife, Elizabeth (Mary Lincoln's sister), and daughter Julia came from Springfield via the Illinois Central. Bates came without his family; he probably also took the Illinois Central.[240]

Bates, a sixty-one-year-old moderate Whig, was just the sort of man Fillmore wanted to see. "His massive forehead, large Roman nose, and firm mouth and chin presented a facial solemnity" that matched his depressed mood, caused by the Kansas-Nebraska Act, which Bates saw as the result of "monumental errors of judgment." He was inclined to favor the pro-compromise Union coalition that Fillmore sought. They had been allies before. President Fillmore had tried to persuade him to accept a cabinet post; Daniel Webster praised him as "a *North Western*" man, "well known, not only to the people of Missouri, but also to those of Illinois, Wisconsin, & Iowa & I believe highly respected by the Whigs of those States"; Bates led in early balloting for vice president at the Whig convention in 1852 as a broker, a border-state man acceptable to northerners. He declined Fillmore's offer and lost the Whig nomination. Kansas-Nebraska aroused his ire. Coming on the excursion signaled his reentry into politics.[241]

Hiram Fuller of the *New York Weekly Mirror* hailed him as "a valuable addition to our company" and hinted at a future Bates presidential bid: "He is one of the few modest, affable, agreeable great men of the right sort, whose head is sufficiently well set upon his shoulders as not to be 'turned' by all the exhilarating honors heaped upon the 'head of the nation.'"[242] (Fuller implied that Fillmore's head was turned by the attention he received.)

Ninian W. Edwards was not modest, nor was his the sort of head to remain fixed despite honors. His had been nearly rotated by merely being the son of a former Illinois governor. He was an aristocratic snob, a big fish in the small pond of Springfield. Elizabeth and he hosted fancy soirees at their mansion, where Lincoln met Elizabeth's sister, Mary Todd. What better to confirm their high social standing than to go excursioning with eastern notables, whose bright light could be reflected in Ninian and Elizabeth's party talk once they returned, and thus further polish their own luster? The Grand Excursion was a bigger pond for them to swim in for a time, to return as bigger fish themselves.[243]

The sixteen miles from La Salle to Bureau passed quickly. At Bureau the allied

Peoria & Bureau Valley Railroad headed south to a coal mine, and the Illinois River ran southwest, away from the C&RI tracks. At Bureau, nearly two hundred people gathered to greet them as they took on wood and water. While the crews were loading these supplies, a local resident "remarked quite audibly":

"Nebraska couldn't come it!"

"We'll see," replied New York City businessman and land speculator Charles Butler, "let us take a vote.—All you citizens of Illinois who are in favor of the Nebraska bill please hold up your hands."

No one raised a hand for Douglas and Kansas-Nebraska.

"Now," he resumed, "those of you opposed to the Nebraska bill please raise your hands."

The crowd responded with upraised hands "accompanied by a waving of hats and hearty cheers."

"Such is the unanimous voice of Bureau county," an old settler commented, "Douglas is politically dead and only wants to be pitched into the demagogue's grave!"

The crowd gave resounding applause to the local man, and Josiah Harris of the *Cleveland Herald* reported, "[T]he extempore incident quite enlivened a party of pleasure seekers that was getting rather dull." Someone asked Fillmore to give his aye or nay on Kansas-Nebraska, but he was quoted (perhaps inaccurately and maliciously by an opponent) as evasively saying he "couldn't possibly discuss a subject which had already been decided." Of course, he couldn't discuss it in February and March when it was being decided, either.[244]

It was about 1:00 p.m. The excursionists had been confined in the cars for five hours, without a meal since they breakfasted at 6:30 in the hotels. Fortunately, beyond Bureau the trains entered a beautiful prairie. Easterners "were now lost in general admiration." A New Yorker told a Springfield editor, "You have never given us a true picture of the west; you have never told us half its extent, its richness and beauty." Hurrying to the car's rear platform, a newspaperman exulted in a "magnificent rolling prairie, which, in its way, was as grand as the White Mountains or Niagara Falls." Easterners tried to fit this prairie scenery into the familiar categories they had applied to the Grand Tour to Niagara and the White Mountains. "Eye glasses were in constant requisition as wave after wave of the great land ocean broke into view." Scenery set metaphors and similes flowing from editors' pens, and most compared it to the sea: "like the swell of a mighty ocean"; "[o]ccasionally a house could be seen looming up in the far distance, like a sail in mid ocean"; "hundreds and thousands of acres lie in one body as smooth and level as a house floor"; "vast Prairies resemble Lake Huron, the occasional ridges and groves answering for its Islands"; "the monotony of the prairie was broken by graceful swells, looking like fixed waves in the midst of a great ocean."[245]

Fuller of New York invented his own figures: "a rich, smooth, luxuriant and highly cultivated English meadow expanded beyond the line of vision," so huge that it seemed "a sort of Titanic culture—as if the gods themselves had rolled out these infinite lawns whereon the children of the assembled universe might have ample room to run and play."[246]

Flatness and monotony suggested that this landscape was merely beautiful; however, its oceanic vastness made it almost sublime. It possessed "vastness, infinity, magnitude." Fuller domesticated the prairie but on such a gigantic scale as to suggest the sublime.[247]

Practical jokers also broke the monotony eight miles beyond Bureau, at Tiskilwa, Illinois. A small crowd came to greet the trains and Fillmore, who (unbeknownst to Tiskilwans) was on the second train. At every stop, spectators wanted their first glimpse of a president. A few "wags" in the first train "played quite a joke on the crowd by representing one of their number to be Mr. Fillmore, and this gentleman made quite a speech. But at last [the crowd] got on the right scent, and, after some cheering, Mr. F. came out of his car and spoke with some of the 'oldest inhabitants.'"[248]

Around two o'clock, the first train halted at the village of Sheffield (named after the New Haven contractor). While waiting here for the second train, they were treated to the drama of a prairie thunderstorm that "had for some time been rising from the horizon" and then "came with full force upon us. It was a grand spectacle." The rain drummed on the car roofs harder and faster than back East. "It shut out all view of the prairie, all view of anything within a hundred yards of the car

windows. The thunder crashed heavily, and the lightning was most vivid." The "violent squall" hit the second train and caused the cautious John Henry to slow down "for fear of running into the first train." A reporter in Henry's train estimated less visibility, no more than one hundred feet. That called for more caution "and after much singing [of brakes] and whistling," the second one "at last came to a dead stop until it cleared up enough for us to proceed." Finally, the rain left; clouds lingered; Henry's train caught up to Farnam's; and they both stopped for a welcome lunch break.[249]

Lunch consisted of cold turkey meat and bread-and-bacon sandwiches, passed from car to car. After their seven-hour fast, the "[New] York girls went into the turkeys with a good relish," reported an amused western editor, "reminding us that the substance of beauty is no more nor less than what grows in cornfields, and struts about in turkeyish regalia." Yet the eastern young women knew best. They would need nourishment to look their finest for a Rock Island audience of critical westerners, and their eastern male companions eyed them curiously to see if they could endure the strain of travel. Approvingly, if condescendingly, Fuller found them "as lively as blackbirds and as fresh as morning glories" and predicted that, if they endured, males' talk of the weaker sex might end.[250]

In a spirit of boisterous fraternity, a group of men—"the noisy ones," including "a large preponderance of editors"—gathered in a car right behind the engine, to imbibe liquor and enjoy freedom from wives, advertisers, and deadlines.[251]

Others were not free from the worry of investments. Only a half-mile from the railroad lay the Coal Creek mine, in which Farnam, Sheffield, C&RI chief engineer William Jervis, poet Epes Sargent, and other excursionists had invested. Their company dug "about one hundred yards into the bluff, on the west side of Coal Creek" to reach a four-and-a-half-foot-thick vein of coal. Mining operations had begun less than a year before, and the results were still quite uncertain. There was no time to exit the cars and inspect the mine, but there was time to worry about possible difficulties or failures.[252]

The trains resumed their slow progress across the fifty-mile-long prairie. Then they crossed the Rock River on a covered bridge, over twelve hundred feet long, and came into "a finely wooded land" that took them to Moline, Illinois. Here, they approached the Mississippi; "every eye is straining to catch through the trees a glimpse of the magnificent River." Some cheered; some broke open liquor bottles and celebrated; some merely uttered "the thrilling words 'the Mississippi'" to mark their first sight of the great river.

The Mississippi had a mythic power that awed some first-time observers. E. T. Throop Martin felt a "tumultuous rush of thoughts & sensations" when he first saw it.[253] It was the continent's longest river, the goal of several generations' worth of American westward migration, the commercial unifier of the trans-Appalachian West. "And when I took

into consideration the thousands of miles of its length, the great tributaries that poured their waters into its swelling flood," Martin reported to his wife, "when I reflected that its source was in a region of almost eternal snow, while its terminus was in a land of never ending summer, I assure you I was almost overcome with the grandeur of the great stream & the great associations connected with it." Suggesting the inaccurate myth of its origins in a land of eternal snow, Leonard Bacon traced its "majestic sovereignty" that reached "from its icy springs to its palmy delta," and, thus, seemingly encompassed all possible climates in between.[254]

Other observers, like Charles Hale, were impressed ("splendid—broad, very broad even here") but not overawed.[255]

At four o'clock, right on schedule, the trains pulled into Rock Island. Moored there, "with their bows run upon the shore," were six steamboats: the *War Eagle, Lady Franklin, Galena, G. W. Sparhawk,* the *Golden Era,* and the *Jenny Lind. New Haven Palladium* editor James Babcock noted, "A Mississippi steamboat is a queer looking affair to a green Yankee. The hull is little less than a sharp pointed scow, while the upper works, two or three stories high, look in some respects like an Indian pagoda." On each steamboat's upper deck, a band played welcoming airs, but each band did not always play the same airs at the same time as the others, which sometimes produced a cacophony.[256]

The thousand westerners awaiting the excursionists at Rock Island's depot saw the river and its steamboats frequently enough. They came to "see the lions," the eastern celebrities. Cannon roared, bands played, and "loud and enthusiastic cheering" came from the crowd. The trains' whistles blew. On the depot hung a large banner: "The Mississippi and the Atlantic shake hands." Few easterners seemed interested in shaking hands with the crowd. Light rain fell. Guests were painfully aware that there were fewer accommodations onboard the steamboats than seats onboard the trains.

Saturday's Chicago hotel scenes were repeated. "There was a frantic rush after choice tickets to the different steamboats," and an equally frantic effort to secure berths on the same steamboat as family or friends. As in Chicago, some succeeded. John and Mary Munn were booked on the *Lady Franklin* in Stateroom C, which John knew from his riverboat experience to be a good location. Martin shared a room with William Davenport of Philadelphia, a retired Army colonel. Charles Hale reported, "I have half of a nice stateroom, an upper one, opening both into the saloon and on the guards, of the G. W. Sparhawk steamer." Babcock had to bunk with his competitor, James Woodward of the *New Haven Morning Journal & Courier,* but that was better than the fate of many temporary "bachelors," like Judge Jeffrey Orson Phelps of Simsbury, who had to sleep on the floor, "my Carpet bag for Pillow & no covering but my clothing." On the train, cards showing assigned boat and stateroom were given to some excursionists but not to all.

Some steamboat tickets had been left in Chicago by mistake. Others were lost. Confusion reigned; "complaints long and loud resounded on every side; President, Directors, Managers, &c. were all at fault." Others blamed the guests. Woodward expressed disgust at "the conduct of others, principally from New York, who brought their male and female friends uninvited."

John Munn was "greatly provoked by the conduct of [Thomas R.] Walker & family on coming on board" the *Lady Franklin*. He clearly regarded them as part of the "scrub aristocracy." The law partner of Roscoe Conkling and a former mayor of Utica, Walker was a respected local leader (except for the story that "the firing of a cannon in one of the college halls" kept him from receiving a Hamilton College diploma). Perhaps it was Walker's wife, Sarah, or one of their two daughters who complained, despite having "good rooms provided for them," in Munn's opinion; "their pretensions were too great & they rebelled" at the room assignment. "The scene was amusing and yet annoying," Munn felt. "There was this family of 4 persons, with really no right to be the guests of the occasion, complaining of want of accommodations equal to most others, making themselves conspicuous, abusing their friend & neighbor Mr. [William] Walcott, one of the managers of the excursion, insisting upon returning home etc." That move, Munn asserted, "would be a great relief to all of us & which they threaten to do on reaching Galena tomorrow."[257]

The Walkers were by no means the only

complainers. To such disgruntled guests, railroad officials replied that this affair "was altogether too big for them" and "they coolly said we will try to-morrow to do something." They had already added a sixth steamboat, the *Jenny Lind.*

That did not calm matters. "Not only were most of the gentlemen obliged to look forward to a prospect of beds on the floor of the cabin, but most of the parties and families on the excursion were separated—one member being on one boat, and another on another." Married couples had been assigned to different boats; "several young fellows were obliged to part from the fair ladies about whom they had revolved with the most laudable devotions," lamented Charles A. Dana of the *New York Tribune.* Another newspaperman complained they were not told the trip schedule: "In fact, we are all 'Know-Nothings.'" Some "guests" were gate-crashers. "A. B. Elliott & Lady" expressed a wish to go on the *War Eagle*, but the clerk wrote *"Imposter"* over their preferred accommodation. The officers were "*rather* busy" trying to arrange things right then.

What finally, but only partly, solved their dilemma was the decision of many guests to give it up as a bad business and make other travel plans—some for St. Louis, some for a stay in Rock Island or Davenport across the river, and others for a return to Chicago. Eager to take the Upper Mississippi cruise, yet appalled at the overbooking, many "changed their minds . . . some of them as often as a dozen times"

before finally giving the excursion up.[258]

One who dropped out at Rock Island was Thurlow Weed, famed editor of the *Albany Evening Journal,* legendary Whig politico, archenemy of Fillmore, and oily manipulator. "Tall and dark-complexioned, with a large, long head and stooped shoulders," Weed acted in a "secretive manner: He always spoke in low tones, almost in a whisper, as if he feared being overheard." Even his frequent opponent Horace Greeley stated that Weed "can call more men by name, than any other living American." C&RI director John B. Stryker of Rome, New York, had sent several excursion tickets to Weed, who had tried to persuade some of his friends and allies to accompany him on the trip—with mixed results. With Weed's reputation as a wheeler-dealer, his distribution of free tickets took on the character of rewards to friends and allies. He had planned to go at least as far as Galena, Illinois, but his traveling companions, or the applause for Fillmore, or the danger of being overheard on crowded boats, or "trouble in your leg" changed his plans. He took a boat for St. Louis instead.[259] Fillmore's supporters charged that Weed dropped out because of "the obnoxious presence of Mr. Fillmore; it was too much for the sensitive nerves of the editor . . . to witness Mr. F.'s warm receptions."[260]

Prior arrangements of George A. Mix, the organizer of the steamboat flotilla, and Farnam came to the rescue, with excellent timing: "an elegant dinner" after five o'clock at tables in each boat's cabin (or saloon), a long, elegant, chandelier-lit room (really, a wide hallway) extending down the center of the second deck. Before the eight hundred excursionists who remained sat down for dinner on their steamboats, sad faces were everywhere, "pouting lips on pretty faces met one at every turn, and eyes unused to weep were very much disposed to do that little thing," noted travel writer Samuel Bowles. "However, an abundant dinner upon the boats" and a good "appetite sharpened by long fasting . . . partially restored good humor" when added to the band music and "the novelty and excitement of the whole scene presented at and upon the river."[261]

A politician's after-dinner speech was not a novelty to the diners, but it occurred even if it did not excite. When they learned a president was on the *Golden Era,* a thousand local folks "gathered on the landing, and by repeated cheering and calls for 'Fillmore,' the ex-President made his appearance," reported editor William Schouler of Cincinnati. A Davenport editor liked Fillmore's appearance: "a fine looking, portly man with gray hair, bowing repeatedly to them," with his hat in his hand. Schouler sounded a Whig's cynical note (he was from Massachusetts originally) on western commoners: "as soon as he was recognized, the 'Sovereigns' on the landing raised 'their most sweet voices,' in loud acclamations." Fillmore tossed out some flattery: what a grand reception his "fellow citizens" were giving him in the Great West; what a grand railroad, soon to be part of a transcontinental track to the Pacific. That led to the safe old Whig issue of government aid for such "internal improvements." Then the steam whistle blew, and he used that as an excuse to end his brief talk before dangerous topics like the Kansas-Nebraska Act could arise. "When he concluded, he was again cheered, shortly after which he retired to the Cabin."[262]

The steamboats' bands, "by some strange coincidence" and not by any advance coordination, all began playing "Jordan Am a Hard Road to Travel." An anti-Nebraska editor from Chicago observed, "We fear Mr. F. will find his road to the Second Term, a hard one indeed to travel."[263]

At seven o'clock, the steamboats headed across the river for Davenport, so Iowans could greet the party and the guests could better view that night's fireworks. These side-wheel packet boats with wood hulls usually carried both freight and passengers. Mix arranged that only the *War Eagle* carry freight for this trip, and that discretely so passengers would not see it. Fearing they might have cholera, he also excluded "all emigrants & deck passengers." At 296 tons, the *Galena* and *War Eagle* were the largest; the *Lady Franklin* (206 tons), the smallest. The captains were well known and experienced:

Galena—Captain D. B. Morehouse
Golden Era—Captain Hiram Bersie
G. W. Sparhawk—a Captain Green
Lady Franklin—Captain Legrand
    Morehouse
War Eagle—Captain Daniel Smith
    Harris

Legrand Morehouse had captained vessels for a dozen years; Bersie, for sixteen; and Harris, for twenty-two. No racing would be allowed, but the captains competed to offer the best food, drinks, and music. The bow of each boat was decorated with wreaths of evergreens and prairie flowers.[264]

After an overcast afternoon, the sun came out as the boats departed the Illinois shore for Iowa. The sun's rays threw "a flood of golden and mellow light over the water and the land."[265] Crossing the river, the boats passed the western tip of Rock Island, a three-mile-long island "covered with a very dense growth of young timber—oak, hickory, ash, birch, etc." This was second-growth forest, for soldiers had cut down much of the original timber for fuel and lumber, and fire had destroyed the rest. Easterners might imagine this was the frontier West, but Fort Armstrong had guarded the lower end of Rock Island Rapids for thirty-eight years. Built in 1816 of red cedar logs, with three blockhouses at three corners, the fort stood near the island's western tip atop a twenty-five-foot limestone bank that added to its military strength. After the Black Hawk War (1832), it lost its military role. No soldiers had been stationed there since 1836. Even a fairly new country could have a historical relic.[266]

In view of the travelers, on the western bank of the island not far from Fort Armstrong, stood the Davenport house, a two-story frame house in the Greek Revival style, with a columned front portico. It too had historical associations, a Chicago editor noted, as "the house rendered famous as being the scene of the dreadful and mysterious assassination of Col. [George] Davenport" in 1845. Davenport served as the sutler at Fort Armstrong and expanded into the fur trade before becoming a key early leader of Rock Island and Davenport (named for him, of course). (He was murdered in one of the upstairs bedrooms of this house, but the *Davenport Gazette* improbably listed him as an excursionist. The paper meant Colonel William Davenport of Philadelphia and later printed a correction.)[267]

The steamboats "now swept out into the stream, and rounded to at the bank opposite, up whose ascending heights of magnificent green" lay Davenport, a city of six to seven thousand people. The boats anchored off the shore, near the foot of Iowa Street. When Iowans heard the *Golden Era* had arrived, "a crowd again assembled," and Fillmore did not disappoint them. He spoke "at some length" and touched on the safe Whig topic. "He believed, he said, that the General [National] Government, the States and individual capitalists should unite to extend these internal improvements wherever they might be wanted." He won local approval when he proclaimed "the duty of the General Government to remove all obstructions from the navigation of the Mississippi river." The Davenport editor was impressed that Fillmore's voice carried four blocks: "His voice is very loud and remarkably distinct." Also four blocks away were the Mississippi & Missouri Railroad tracks on Fifth Street. Farnam had his sights set on Council Bluffs, and he wouldn't mind if the "General Government" aided his internal improvement there.[268]

The setting sun dimmed prospects for political speeches and made possible more romantic entertainments. Bonfires lit up the river shores. Well-lighted steamboats cast brightness into the gathering dark. Preparations for setting off fireworks at the old fort neared an end. For nearly two hours, "there was an almost constant display of fireworks, including many splendid pieces." The sky was lit "by fires on the shore, and the bands on the boats enlivened the scene with delightful music." As the final rockets burst in the air, the moon "shone clearly, and made visible the outlines of the scenery," and "its beams danced gaily" on the water. Lightning flashed "from a dark cloud in the south-east." The crowded excursionists on board the boats, the ex-excursionists who decided to stay in Davenport that night and not continue, and the crowds of locals in both cities all watched the magnificent display of many lights— moon, rockets, bonfires, lightning, and boat lights—illuminating the darkness. [269]

Around ten o'clock, the hour of departure, sounds took center stage. Amid pealing bells, "the booming of cannon, the shouts of the multitudes on the shores, the music of the bands and the puffs of the engines (the respiration as it were of a strong man at work,) we glided off," recalled Schouler, "and were soon hid from sight by the windings of the river." The bands played "Old Dan Tucker," "Sweet Home," and "Push Along, Keep Moving" as

the boats headed north. Being hid from sight did not lessen the night's romance. The moon shone as they pushed upriver, single file, the *Sparhawk* in the lead. A few young women and "their gallants" stayed on the decks. A few editors headed inside, to the *Golden Era* cabin, where "you could see a half dozen editorial pens in full swing, enlightening" six different parts of the nation "in regard to the excursion." On the *Galena,* Edward Prime of the *New York Observer* sat down to write his article "in the midst of passengers hurrying to and fro in the eagerness of starting upon such an expedition." So great was the confusion, he reported, "[I] scarcely know what I have put down."[270]

Night brought reality: the problem of where to sleep. One fellow "lost his trunk" with his fine clothes. "Another gentleman finds that his wife has a berth in a state-room and he has none." Cheerily, someone congratulated the married men for their good fortune. The disconsolate husband replied, "[I]t is better to have no wife at all than to have one and be thus torn from her." Bachelors "had to sleep on the cabin floor, piled side by side, like so many saw-logs."[271]

Apparently—on the *Galena,* at least— having a wife was a better way to secure a stateroom than having wealth. Several rich men were on board: New York merchant Robert Bowne Minturn, Mississippi & Missouri partner Thomas C. Durant, Shepard Knapp. "Other millionaires are plenty," noted Harris of the *Cleveland Herald,* "and just now the floor of the long [cabin] of the *Galena* resembles an encampment of them. . . . [T]hey snore as lustily as the man who earns his bread by the sweat of his brow." These "venerable 'silver greys'" were just as useful to the nation as workingmen, Harris affirmed. "Honor to the American merchants and capitalists." They were more useful than politicians. "May they all live to enjoy a Railroad excursion to the Pacific!"[272]

For other editors, like Schouler, the attractions of a night voyage and the discomforts of the accommodations encouraged a postponement of sleep. "I stayed on deck till the first short hour of the morning, and then camped on the cabin floor, amid a gorge of cots and mattresses."[273] He may have been the last excursionist on deck, as the flotilla steamed north between the Iowa and Illinois banks.

EXCURSUS

Antebellum America and the Mississippi Steamboat

TO INFORM NEW HAVEN readers unfamiliar with the western steamboat, James Babcock of the *New Haven Palladium* described it: "[A]s there are no wharves on the river, the boats are constructed expressly to lie up on the edge of the banks." Their bows extended far on to the shore. "Their hulls, if hulls they can be called, are shallow and much resemble an elongated tea saucer. Of course, the bottoms are flat and draw but little water," so hulls could be shallow. "The furnace, boiler and engines are all within this shallow enclosure. Above all this, are the saloons [cabins] and state rooms, running the entire length of the boat," and fancifully furnished. "The saloons are therefore very splendid; but I cannot say as much for the State rooms, which are too contracted.—They have each two berths, one above the other. In these state rooms there is no room for a writing table or even a wash stand, and hardly room for dressing. The state room doors open outside upon a narrow promenade, and inside into the saloons." Saloons and staterooms were on the main deck, on whose outer ring was a railed gallery ("the guards") where passengers could stroll or sit to view the passing scenery. For a better view, they could go up to "the promenade [hurricane] deck," or, with permission, "still above that [to] the wheel-house and pilot's room, all enclosed in glass. So these boats are really three stories high, and these stories all rest upon mere planks, or a saucer, called the hull." This would hardly do for Long Island Sound or anywhere "the winds are fierce and the seas rolling." But it made "a very showy appearance" where waves and winds were slight.[274]

"A 'world in miniature'" was how "literary travelers were wont to describe the western steamboat, and such in truth it was. Here all the essential processes of living went on. . . . Here all ranks and classes were represented. . . . Here was a society with a distinctive life and folkways of its own."[275] Here was antebellum America in miniature. Protection from wind and wave allowed three-story Indian pagodas on small hulls, just as America's protection from European wars (partly due to the British navy) allowed elaborate federal systems of

The cabin (or "saloon") of the Grand Excursion's War Eagle, *with the sign on the chandelier apparently the one that excluded gentlemen unaccompanied by a lady from the ladies' curtained end of the cabin. (Murphy Library, University of Wisconsin–La Crosse)*

local-state-national governments to rest on a small military base. However, snags and sharp rocks lurked beneath the seemingly safe waters. A steamboat boom of the 1850s paralleled the nation's prosperity and led to fierce competition and "steamboat gothic" architecture to attract customers. The flimsy luxury of cabins, the main architectural attractions, so ornate with their "heavy gilt, gingerbread, brilliant illumination, and red plush," and yet sunlight and a few years' time revealed this as "sham splendor all around"—a Melville or a Hawthorne might make a telling comparison to antebellum American culture. The centrality of this public space—all staterooms opened on to the cabin—mirrored a republican emphasis on the public good that was fading but was still preached. A ladies' cabin divided public space into separate spheres for men and women just as antebellum society did; class division into deck passengers and cabin passengers reflected 1850s America.[276]

So many distinguished Americans traveled on the Grand Excursion that antebellum society here boarded its own world in miniature.

That was not exactly true. The lower ranks and classes (except for the crew) were excluded. The organizer of the steamboat flotilla, George A. Mix, wrote to Henry Farnam, "I deem it very proper that all emigrants and deck passengers be excluded to preserve health."[277] Fear of cholera would not permit them to take lower-class passengers, whom experience showed to be more susceptible to that disease due to terrible sanitation, poor food, close confinement, and other causes.[278] Yet the railroad company's desire to impress the eastern elite would have ruled out the lower classes even without the health consideration.

With the lower classes excluded and their boats making a showy appearance, excursionists could congratulate themselves that theirs indeed was a classless society in which all were equal, but they were more equal than others. In the steamboat's cabin all could mingle freely. The inside door of each stateroom opened onto the cabin, a room (more like a wide hallway) nearly two hundred feet by twenty feet, the miniature steamboat republic's public space where

meetings were held, letters written, politics debated, and dances celebrated. Steamboat owners outdid themselves to decorate this public space with candelabra, fancy woodwork on the walls and ceiling, chandeliers, carpets, mahogany furniture, and velvet upholstered chairs. Toward the stern was the ladies' cabin, carpeted and adorned with sofas, piano, and rocking chairs. Here were separate spheres for men and women; no door or wall separated gentlemen's and ladies' cabins; however, men could enter the latter only by invitation or by marriage, while it was not deemed proper for women to be in the former except at meals (the gentlemen's end became the dining room).[279]

"The ladies cabin" of the new *War Eagle* was "decorated, among other embellishments, with several beautiful paintings: . . . views of Galena, Pike's Bluff opposite Prairie du Chien, Lake Pepin, Fort Snelling, St. Paul, Falls of St. Anthony, Little [Minnehaha] Falls, &c," reported a Galena newspaper. Female excursionists viewed an artistic representation of each scenic sight before they glimpsed its reality. The *War Eagle* had forty-six staterooms, with sleeping berths for 120 passengers. "The cabins are finished with just enough of the gilt work to give them a cheerful appearance," reported the *Cincinnati Times,* "and barber shops, wash rooms, &c., are on a liberal scale." The carpets were velvet. The new boat cost an estimated $33,000.[280]

The many staterooms almost encircled the cabin. Their doors opened inward into the cabin and outward onto the gallery, or "guards." Catharine Sedgwick complained about her stateroom door opening onto the gallery, "with men of all aspects & conditions traversing between me & the guards." The classes were not separated enough for her taste. The Baptist editor, Sewell Cutting, shared a stateroom toward the rear, or ladies', end of the ship, "far away from the noise of the engine, and with a door opening directly out upon the deck." Most of the time, he appreciated the outer door, for it gave "us always a view of the river, excepting when 'Maria' [evidently a washerwoman] hangs her table linen to dry directly in our faces. This is the fashion of the river, however, and we do not complain."[281]

At the far end of the gentlemen's cabin were the clerk's office and bar, so the men were not far from the boat's dollars-and-cents management or from its liquid refreshments, and ladies were mostly separated from both. Of the westerners on board the boats, Catharine Sedgwick observed, "The drinking of these people is inconceivable." Yet Charles Sedgwick had "not seen a drunken person."[282] Very likely, the excursion's managers took measures to control drinking during the trip.

"At the bow-end of the cabin, on one side, is the clerk's office, on the other is the bar," Catharine Sedgwick noted. The *Sparhawk*'s barkeeper was "a personification of Dickens's 'fat boy.' He claimed acquaintance with me on my first appearance; showed me his daguerreotypes of his wife and two pretty children; said my writings

lay on his table with these treasures, and how fond his 'ma' was of them." Here was the Lafayettism that Sedgwick dreaded. "He begs me to go and see her at St. Louis; gives me 'Muscatine Journals' and 'Iowa Gazettes' to read, and as often as I pass his bar, begs me to stop and partake his ever-flowing hospitalities."[283]

The clerk's job was partly to impress passengers more than this bartender did Sedgwick and to assuage their hurt feelings. His main duty was to handle business details of freight and passenger service: taking travelers' money for tickets, securing cargo, negotiating freight rates, doing the boat's payroll, keeping its books, buying needed supplies, and filling out waybills and other forms. A second ("mud") clerk assisted him.[284] The *War Eagle*'s clerk was William Faucette, a New Orleans Cajun and newcomer to Upper Mississippi steamboats. Faucette impressed high-class passengers. "Polite in address, a fine dancer, a good story-teller and conversationalist, his personality went far toward attracting the public who travelled for pleasure—and that was the best-paying traffic, for which every first-class packet was bidding."[285] Not all clerks were so smooth and personable. The *Lady Franklin*'s clerk was rather ill-mannered; when passengers saw "Roast Pig" on the menu, one wag suggested that perhaps the clerk had been butchered and cooked.[286]

Not all the accommodations were appreciated, either. Near the clerk's office was the men's washroom (the ladies' was at their end of the cabin). It received frequent use, and some excursionists complained about its towels.

One gentleman asked, "Can't you give me a clean towel, Captain?"

"'No,' said the Captain, 'more than fifty persons have used that towel there, and you are the first one that's said a word against it.'"[287]

It was also the clerk's job to arrange for the purchase of firewood at the various "wooding-up" places along the river. A Mississippi steamboat consumed around forty-five cords a day; the price varied from $2.25 to $3.50 per cord. The woodmen stacked the wood in an eight-foot-high "rank" that was eighty-four feet long and contained about twenty cords. The clerk or his assistant negotiated a price and measured the ranks to make sure he was not being cheated. The captain oversaw the process, and much else on the boat.[288]

The clerk's office was above the boilers and engine and beneath the pilothouse (which rested on a texas deck that sat on the hurricane deck, the cabin's roof). The men were at the business end of this high-pressure engine on a raft; the ladies' cabin was some distance back from the boilers. Engineers' wages were not as high as pilots' wages, but tending a high-pressure steam engine and boiler on river steamboats with reputations for explosiveness was a high-responsibility job. The experienced Robert Scribe Harris served as engineer on the *War Eagle;* he was an innovator, brother to Captain Daniel Smith Harris, the upper river's most famous

captain, and a part-owner and sometime captain himself. Robert Scribe Harris had higher status than most engineers. Strong currents and rapids required a river steamboat to have "a wad of steam," a burst of power to push upstream or to maneuver in fast waters. Its engine ran at more than one hundred pounds of pressure to the square inch; a factory steam engine ran at "but a few pounds' pressure." A shallow hull and high-pressure engine produced "the excessive vibration of western steamboats when in full motion." Benjamin Silliman ("Chirography bad on account of the jarring of the machinery of the boat"), Catharine Sedgwick, and George Bancroft all complained about how hard it was to write legibly due to the vibration.[289]

Visible at the wheel high up in the pilot-house, his brain stocked with memorized details of every twist and turn in the ever-changing river, the pilot commanded public respect and a wage sometimes as high as the captain's. The pilot had to know the outline of every range of

bluffs and hills, as well as every isolated knob or even tree-top . . . the man at the wheel must know these outlines absolutely, under the constantly changing point of view of the moving steamer; so that he might confidently point his steamer at a solid wall of blackness, and guided only by the shapes of distant hills, and by the mental picture which he had of them, know the exact moment at which to put his wheel over and sheer his boat away from an impending bank.

Thirty seconds' inattention could lead to disaster on this always-winding, often-changing course. The *Sparhawk* had two pilots, Harlow and Gregg, for the excursion, as was typical.[290]

Several hazards lurked menacingly in the Mississippi's waters. Security from high winds and waves did not mean safety for the steamboat. "Leaning trees, snags, islands, sandbars, and rapids delayed or blocked navigation" on a river that remained largely unchanged since Father Louis Hennepin traveled these waters in 1680. Leaners could knock freight or people off the boat. Partially or completely hidden in the water, snags could tear a hole in a steamboat. Pilots named different kinds of snags: "sawyers swayed back and forth with the current, preachers bowed in and out of the water, planters lodged themselves in the river bottom, and sleepers hid beneath the water's surface." Islands divided the river and posed navigational conundrums for the pilot, whose boat might enter a cul-de-sac and have to back out if he steered to the right of the island when the main current went left. Especially during low water periods of late summer and early fall, the many sandbars greatly hindered navigation: boats went aground or their hulls were damaged when a captain forced his boat across a sandbar or valuable time was lost poling a boat off a sandbar. Sharp rocks at Rock Island Rapids threatened to ground steamboats or tear holes in their hulls.[291] The excursion occurred during a high-water period, so the river's per-

ils were largely hidden from the excursionists, who may not have realized how challenging was the pilot's job.

Ranking above the pilot was the captain, who had a large cabin cum office on the hurricane deck below the pilothouse. He had to know the essentials of the pilot's and clerk's jobs, have "sufficient polish to commend himself to his passengers," know the business of freight and passenger service, handle labor relations with an often fractious deck crew, and give correct commands in emergencies. Each boat had a crew of about thirty, who were treated "very shabbily," one editor complained. The captain often was part or sole owner of his steamboat, with a strong financial interest in beating his competition to passengers and freight.[292] The captains of the five Grand Excursion boats (the *Jenny Lind* returned from Dubuque after Tuesday) cooperated for that trip but could not forget they would be competing again in a week's time.

By most accounts, Captain Daniel Smith Harris was the most competitive of the lot. Forty-five years old with hawkish nose, thin lips, and full beard (clean-shaven around the mouth), looking oddly like a bird of prey, Harris had piloted, owned, and commanded boats on the Ohio and Mississippi Rivers for thirty-one years. He earned much of his capital from his West Diggings lead mine near Galena, which aided him during price wars or slow times on the river. He displayed his competitive daring by battling river ice to be the first boat to arrive in spring and the last to depart in the late fall; by steaming up "hitherto unnavigated" streams; by introducing innovations in steamboat construction; and, of course, by racing. Winning steamboat races brought a double reward: reaching the next landing first to secure freight and passengers and gaining the admiration of travelers, who then bought tickets on his boats to share in his glory. He, in turn, would allow them to taunt the rival boat as they passed it. "To Smith Harris, the sine qua non in any steamboat was speed." His boats held records and won races. On top of his latest racehorse, *War Eagle,* he mounted his "chicken cock," a bird carved from oak. Profane, impatient, hot-tempered, combative, he found himself carrying "the piety of the party" to St. Paul. His fast pace kept the *War Eagle* from being lashed to the other boats for dancing, which some of his passengers may have appreciated. But they may have preferred that the devout Sabbatarian Orrin Smith be their captain.[293]

Smith accompanied the excursion as president of the Galena and Minnesota Packet Company but did not captain a vessel. For three years in the early 1850s, Harris fought a bitter battle against the Minnesota Packet Company, a price war that drove the cost of a Galena–St. Paul ticket down to fifty cents. Westerners with nothing better to do shuttled between the two towns just to enjoy the river's "cooling breezes." The two combatants eventually saw this was a losing proposition, and the company invited Harris to be on its board of directors. They joined together, but "Captain Harris continued to manifest his pronounced individuality."[294] They cooperated for the

excursion as well, but Harris would prove difficult to tie down to any common endeavor.

The *War Eagle* and the *Galena* (both 225 feet long and 31 feet wide and both owned by the Galena and Minnesota Company) were new boats, finished in Cincinnati that spring. The *Golden Era* and *Jenny Lind* were only two years old; *G. W. Sparhawk,* three years old; *Lady Franklin,* four years old. A steamboat lasted only about five years on average, and the 1850s were the peak decade in the construction of new ones. Competition was fierce. New, fast boats had the edge. More speed came with longer and narrower boats; the *War Eagle* and *Galena* had a length-breadth ratio of 7.26, very high for steamboats of their tonnage class. Daniel Harris had his new racehorse.[295]

George Mix hired these five boats (plus the *Jenny Lind,* later) to carry the excursionists. From Rock Island, he wrote to Farnam that he hoped they would "meet your fullest expectations." On June 1, he assured Farnam, "I hear of no sickness on the river and *I believe* that the present high stage of water will render the Valley *perfectly healthy.*" By Friday, June 2, Harris had the *War Eagle* at Rock Island, the first to arrive there. "Capt. Harris came down [from Galena] to clean up and prepare," but other captains got the jump on him in buying food and supplies at Galena, so "I send his steward by this morning's train to Chicago to procure some supplies." Mix planned to send freight with Harris's boat, out of sight of passengers, "for 100 Tons will neither retard his speed nor be observed on board." He estimated the five boats would house seven hundred travelers, and that should be adequate; it was certainly as many berths as Farnam could expect Mix to come up with on short notice.[296]

With racing forbidden by Farnam and Joseph Sheffield, the captains' competitive spirit turned to food, and Mix seemed to sense that already by Saturday, June 3. "The expenses will be largely increased from rivalry in entertainment on the Boats." Not only was there rivalry between five captains, but the five boats represented two rival companies: the Galena and St. Louis, and the Galena and Minnesota. Great rewards beckoned for the company and boat that favorably impressed influential guests, including editors whose articles would reach thousands of potential customers. It is highly likely that Sheffield and Farnam and the C&RI paid the food bill, so a company could advertise itself at someone else's expense. After the fact, Mix reported to Farnam how much expenses had been increased: the *War Eagle*'s expenses came to $5,000 (Harris won here too); the *Galena*'s, $4,750; the *Golden Era*'s, $3,783.73; the *Sparhawk*'s, $3,726.69; "and *Lady Franklin* yet to be determined." (These figures may also include the costs of hiring the vessels and their staterooms; one source puts the total cost of the "Excursion in June" at $22,000.)[297]

The result was fine dining on the *Golden Era,* as Babcock reported:

[O]urs has been a succession of luxuries from the first meal to the last. We have had oysters and lobsters daily, though two thousand miles from the sea. . . . Hens, turkeys and ducks have given their last squeak every morning. Two cows, on the lower deck, furnish us with fresh milk twice a day. Meats are cooked in every variety of style, and the dessert consists of all kinds of fruits, nuts, cakes, confection, ices, [etc.]. . . . Then there are meats for supper, with tea and coffee— with toast dry and wet, cold bread, warm bread, Indian bread, biscuit, rolls, &c., &c.

As a reward for this munificence, Captain Hiram Bersie of the *Golden Era* had his reputation as "a prince of a man" established with thousands of Connecticut readers. The *New York Times* hailed George Mix as "a splendid fellow," who was "the general favorite of all" the excursionists.[298] The *Chicago Democratic Press* printed a menu, probably from the *Galena.*[299]

No expense was spared to satisfy guests. Pineapples from the West Indies ("only four days and a half from Havana!") arrived in New York on Sunday morning, came by express train to Rock Island, and were loaded on the steamboats Monday evening.[300]

One fly in this editorial ointment was the placement of passengers on various boats. Friends and family members were separated. Yet travelers on the individual boats developed camaraderie and a sense of pride. Isaac Platt of the *Poughkeepsie Eagle* at first complained when "myself and one friend [found] ourselves placed on the *War Eagle,* while our associates were on the *Golden Era.*" However, he soon saw the *War Eagle* was "a first rate craft, new and splendidly fitted up" and, though Millard Fillmore was on the *Golden Era*, the *War Eagle* "was the flag ship of the fleet, capable of distancing any of her associates in speed, and having first rate officers."[301] Parties on other boats discovered their identity and rejoiced in their good fate.

A young woman from Utica generalized about the passengers on the various steamboats: "The *Golden Era* has the official dignity"— Fillmore, Nathan K. Hall, and other politicians; "the *Lady Franklin* the fashion"—there "one finds the accomplished ladies from the city of New York"; "the *Sparhawk* the Massachusetts men and women; and the *War Eagle* the piety of the party."[302]

Considered by its guests as the flagship because it had the "official dignity" (dignitaries on other boats had not made it to the presidency), the *Golden Era* carried President Fillmore; his son, Millard Powers; his daughter, Abby, and her friend, Matelda Stuart of Buffalo; his political allies Hall and George Babcock; and Silver Gray John A. Granger and his wife, Harriet. Eight editors accompanied them, perhaps to be near the main newsmaker. Poet and former editor Epes Sargent, best known for "Life on the Ocean Wave," and his wife, Elizabeth, were there. "In stature he is short—not more than five feet five—but well proportioned," Edgar Allan Poe noted. Long, scraggly black hair framed his round face. "His demeanor is very gentlemanly"; his prose, "not quite so meritorious"—punchy and unoriginal, like an editor's quick *"hits."*[303]

MENU

SOUP
Green Turtle
Salmon
Oyster
Pickerel

FISH
Lambeau Eels Baked
Baked Pike
Clam White Fish Baked
Mackinaw Trout

BOILED
Ham Corned Beef
Chicken   Egg Sauce
Veal Ducks
Turkey

ROAST
Beef Pork Pig
Tongue Mutton
Turkey, Oyster Sauce
Lamb Mutton

GAME
Prairie Chicken
Snipe
Buffalo Stock
Quails
Boiled Chickens

ENTREES
Oyster Pie
Chicken Pie
Brazed Fillet of
Mutton
Truffle of Fowl,
Wine Sauce
Broiled Brook Trout

PIES
Cranberry   Rhubarb
Currant   Cocoa Nut
Lemon   Plumb

DESSERT
Raisins and Kisses Figs

PUDDINGS
Prunes   Colinet
Pecan Nuts
Spice   Lemon
Pineapples

ALMONDS
Pound
Filberts
Oranges
Currant

JELLIES, & C.
Calf.
Lemon
Madairi

ICE CREAM
Blanche Mange
Sherry   Orange
Chorlds Rasb

Also on board were E. T. Throop Martin; John R. Bartlett, an author, book dealer, and Whig who served on the commission to draw the U.S.-Mexico boundary but was dismissed by Democrats for siding with Mexico's claims—he was recovering from two deaths in his family; Vincenzo Botta, the Italian educational expert; noted landscape painter John F. Kensett; investor cum clergyman William Jarvis and his daughters Hetty Hart and Mary, whose sister Elizabeth later purchased a Kensett painting; Amelia Tyng, Jarvis's relative and wife of a Havana sea captain; Alexander Twining and other New Haveners, including Eleazar Fitch, Babcock, and Henry Farnam, his wife, and two sons.[304]

The *Sparhawk* carried Massachusetts railroad investors invited by George Bliss, the C&RI director from Springfield. Fourteen Bay Staters were onboard, including Moses Kimball, an anti-slavery Whig who dabbled in politics and who presented respectable plays and exhibits without liquor for proper, self-improving Bostonians at his Boston Museum; Samuel Bowles of the *Springfield Daily Republican;* George Dwight, George B. Morris, and R. D. Morris of that city; and William Schouler, now of Cincinnati, but earlier a well-connected Whig editor in Boston and Lowell. Leonard Bacon's friend, Reverend A. H. Eggleston, was there, along with Professor Henry Boynton Smith of New York's Union Theological Seminary, a church historian vacationing with his wife, Elizabeth, after a taxing academic year of teaching and writing. Roger and Emily Baldwin traveled on the

Sparhawk, as did others from Connecticut. The Imperial Austrian consul general in New York, Charles Frederick de Loosey, accompanied them. But the Massachusetts men—most, without wives—set the tone.[305]

The witty young lady from Utica could not characterize the *Galena*'s entourage, perhaps because it included so many undistinguished westerners from Illinois (including Governor Joel Matteson, Judge John Dean Caton, Ninian W. Edwards, and others from Ottawa, Galena, Joliet, and Chicago) and some easterners who were not yet distinguished (railroad man Thomas C. Durant, railroad construction engineer Peter A. Dey, and American Express founder John Butterfield and his wife, Malinda). Durant brought his extended family, who invested in his railroads and who all traveled on the same boat: E. A. Durant and his wife, Charles W. Durant (a brother), Thomas H. Durant, and William C. Durant. Some notables took this boat: former New York mayor William Havemeyer, an anti-Nebraska Democrat and prominent banker; New York philanthropist and merchant Robert Bowne Minturn; John A. Dix, former U.S. senator (Democrat) from New York, a railroad investor, lawyer, and director and president of the Mississippi & Missouri Railroad; Francis Preston Blair, the sire of the political Blairs; Edward Prime of the noted Presbyterian Prime family; and Reverend Leonard Bacon.[306]

Lady Franklin accommodated more than "accomplished ladies" from New York.

Catharine and Charles Sedgwick boarded her, as did reporter N. W. T. Root of New Haven; John and Mary Munn and their friend John L. Boswell (editor of the *Hartford Courant*) and his wife; Francis P. (Frank) Blair Jr., a scion of the Blair family who moved west to try his political fortunes; editor Sewell S. Cutting, the Baptist; E. Church Blackburn of St. Louis; Stephen A. Goodwin of Auburn, New York; and Sarah and Thomas Walker.[307]

The Harris brothers speedily transported several pious persons, who held evening prayers on the *War Eagle:* Silliman; Reverend Gardiner Spring and one of his lay leaders, Shepard Knapp; and Captain Orrin Smith. George Bancroft, New York Democrat Samuel J. Tilden, and Alexander Hamilton's son John C. Hamilton, a New York City lawyer, also enjoyed the prestige of traveling on Daniel Harris's new racehorse.[308]

It is not clear who waited to board the *Jenny Lind,* which was "already loaded with freight for a downward voyage" that Monday evening, when Mix and Farnam realized they would need her and "hired [her] to discharge [freight] and follow" the other boats "up the river the next day." Bringing up the rear, hours behind the other boats, her passengers could not imagine she was the flagship. Best-laid plans of excursion organizers—like those of a nation's political leaders—could go awry

and force less than ideal adjustments.

The Kansas-Nebraska Act was similar, an expedient tossed to southerners who felt they had not benefited equally from the main program, the Compromise of 1850. The act was a last-minute boat, a concession to the South hastily approved by President Franklin Pierce at a hastily called Sunday meeting in the White House that threatened to swamp antebellum America. A complicated three-story structure of executive, legislative, and judicial branches—of federal, state, and local governments, with all the checks and balances between Senate and House, Senate and president, Supreme Court and Congress, states and the national government, and with the several compromises over slavery built in to its three-fifths rule and fugitive slave clause—all this carefully crafted political gingerbread rested on a flimsy "tea saucer" that could survive light winds and no waves. This fragile hull that the Framers had not designed was a two-party system of Whigs and Democrats competing as *national* parties in all regions and thus compromising all regions' demands. Now, in anger at the act, some northerners—some excursionists prominently among them—planned to create a sectional party. Did this top-heavy structure contain a built-in check to balance the boat against such a move?

GALENA, ON THE FEVER RIVER IN ILLINOIS *by Henry Lewis, lithograph from painting, ca. 1850s.*
Like "a drove of sheep going down to water," Galena's houses descend to the Fever River.
Excursionists took the road (center) to the Marsden Mine.
(From The Mississippi Valley Illustrated, *Minnesota Historical Society)*

CHAPTER FIVE

"Rain and Speaking, Words and Water"

TUESDAY, JUNE 6, 1854

AROUND 4:30 A.M., the men who slept on "cots and beds" on the cabin floor were awakened "by the novel method of the waiter coming along and pulling each sleeper by his big toe." Waiters must set tables for breakfast, and sleepers were decidedly in the way. The novelty of it partly compensated for the "unpleasantness" of it.[309] Some easterners privileged with a stateroom complained about that. Catharine Sedgwick wrote home, "What think you William of a state room about twice the size of Katie's Linen Closet with 4 berths[?] I confess I didn't pass a refreshing night!"[310] Secure in his stateroom, Charles Hale of Boston dismissed the complaints: "*Home* is the only place where one can truly 'make himself at home.' If he chooses to go abroad, he must expect an occasional disappointment." A good breakfast on well-set tables helped restore the spirits of insomniacs and claustrophobes.[311]

The six Grand Excursion steamboats had pushed upriver all night, with the *War Eagle* in the lead, followed by *Lady Franklin, Sparhawk,* and the three laggards.[312] One hundred miles separated Rock Island from Galena, and many miles were now behind them. Water was high; it was still spring; the boats had no trouble with rapids or sandbars. The morning dawned overcast but pleasant; the

previous day's rain and thunderstorm were behind them.[313]

In the old era, of which this excursion signaled the end, travel on the Mississippi was "relatively unobstructed, rapid travel" compared with taking wagons or stagecoaches along frontier roads. A traveler seemed "immune from all the delays and hindrances of travel off the main road" and seemed to acquire an almost transcontinental reach compared with the rough roads that promised him only the next county—and did not always deliver on that.[314] Yet these excursionists had just come halfway across the continent by rail at fast speeds; the great river could not seem to them the most modern route they had taken. They were primarily interested in its romance and its scenery. As a commercial highway, it led ultimately to the slave-owning South. That aspect they would not glorify.

Men and women wandered on deck and in the cabins of the various boats "eager for every varying scene and object that breaks upon the vision." For many, this was their first extended look at the Mississippi River, and they sought to characterize it—as beautiful, picturesque, or sublime—and to compare it with other sights and other rivers. Early in the morning, an editor named Moore of Springfield (Illinois) already seemed tired of the comparisons of Upper Mississippi bluffs to castles on the Rhine (or tired of his own youthful dreams, or of the talk of those youths promenading the deck): the river's scenery was "exceedingly handsome and stirs up all the nonsense of earlier days; till we have built our glittering castle upon the verge of every charming cliff and dream of poetry and bliss in their nestling shadows." Moore was not interested in romances about scenery and idylls on the Mississippi but in obtaining a realistic "aboriginal view" of the river before its role as "this great channel of commerce" forever altered it.[315]

His boat, the *Jenny Lind,* was "a full half hour behind the rest"; he had ample opportunity to take note of the scenery. The bluffs sometimes towered near the stream, which was from one-half to one mile wide here, then "the deep interval of over-flowed swamps" separated the two so that he could not glimpse the bluffs:

> But we move on, on—more deep set swamps; more antlered elms and branching sycamores; more wavy willows, shooting up from watery islands; more circling vines; more dead, uprooted trees on the shore, ready to embark with first coming freshet; more bluffs; more castle grands; more voluptuous swells; more hanging steeps; more bends; more islands, and so on, I expect, till night, and then a new bright page in the morning.

Tomorrow's "aboriginal view" farther upriver could be described for tomorrow's new edition of his daily paper.

The more distant future would not be aboriginal. Already, "[c]ivilization shows its advance here and there": "a small village spreads out under the brow of a cliff, and a few stores and commission houses [stand] along the water's edge." The channel of commerce carried more and more goods. "Wood piles crowd down upon the water." They fueled commerce's advance as they went. Late, and not wanting to stop on shore, the *Jenny Lind* picked up wood from an "old scow" that "hitched alongside" for the transfer. A small boat carrying "rough looking sovereigns"—whites hunting or fishing—"darts from its swampy moorings." Popular sovereignty certainly applied to the citizens' right to take game or fish. "Big rafts of logs" floated by "now and then. A few minutes ago we passed a load of German emigrants, making for Minnesota." The great river was already a busy highway in June 1854. Moore's hopes for an "aboriginal view" this late were romantic and unrealistic.

Not sharing Moore's opinions, R. L. (Charles) Wilson of the *Chicago Journal* anthropomorphized and romanticized the scenery. His bluffs were "towering stern and solemn, like temples built without hands"; his small tributaries were "brawling" and hiding brook trout; his Mississippi was "a noble river." Hiram Fuller of the *New York Weekly Mirror* outdid everyone in ascribing human (or superhuman) behavior to nature: "the bold bluffs which we gazed at but a moment since, have leaped over to the other side of the river. . . .

Kensett, the artist, is trying to sketch the outlines of these rugged hills; but it seems hardly possible for the prominent features to *hold still* long enough to be caught." A prominent artist of the Hudson River School (tourists compared the Upper Mississippi with that river too), John F. Kensett painted mainly landscapes—of the White Mountains and other scenery that had become, or were soon to become, tourist destinations. He did not sketch Moore's log rafts, commission houses, scows, or rough sovereigns. Moore's realism was probably a minority opinion.

A correspondent for an Albany paper reported, "[T]he scenery much resembles, I was told by a gentleman on board, that of the Rhine, wanting the old castles and ruins."[316]

Tourism and landscape painting enjoyed a symbiotic relationship. While studying art in Europe in the 1840s, Kensett sold paintings of scenery to travelers making the Grand Tour and desiring souvenirs. Back in America, he drew "dozens of landscape vignettes to illustrate *Lotus Eating,* a travel book about the major tourist sites of the northeastern United States." Tourists needed to know which scenes were worth seeing, and his drawings told them. In fact, guidebook authors called a worthy scene "a Kensett." Guidebooks encouraged the traveler to select a good vantage point, to view the surroundings, and then to "appreciat[e] natural scenery by mentally composing it into pictures resembling well-known works" by noted artists. Painters enabled tourists to appreciate certain landscapes, and the tourists then aided the painters by purchasing their

pictures of those sites.[317]

Around eight o'clock, the three leading boats halted, "moored side by side," and waited for the stragglers. Passengers on the *War Eagle, Lady Franklin,* and *Sparhawk* exchanged social visits—like genteel Americans did on New Year's Day, following the example of New York City's elite. Gentlemen were the active visitors going from boat to boat while the ladies stayed on their "home" vessel and acted as the visited. They exchanged "notes upon the magnificence of the river, the beauty of the weather, the adventures of the night, &c"—perhaps on whether the scenery resembled the Hudson or the Rhine, perhaps on whether it was picturesque or sublime. Ever the active observer, and proud of his status as a Mississippi steamboat veteran, John Munn went to other boats and talked with their passengers. He was pleased to hear that *Lady Franklin* was less crowded than the others and to see that "the delights of the morning"—the scenery—had even begun "to operate powerfully upon our disaffected 'Snobs,'" Thomas and Sarah Walker.[318]

They halted partly because their destination, Galena, lay not on the Mississippi but five miles up a tributary, the Fever River (Galena boosters were renaming it the Galena River). The excursion's organizers wanted the boats to enter the city together as an impressive flotilla rather than straggle in one by one. Once the *Galena, Golden Era,* and *Jenny Lind* caught up, "the line of boats began its progress up the Fever River." The river was narrow, only three times as wide as one steamboat; the visitors were surprised that a Mississippi steamboat could navigate it, for it twisted and turned between "high bluffs"; but for all its faults it was deep, and the boats could come up single file if not six abreast. They "formed a line, put up all steam, and bore down upon the city in fine style. The whistles screamed a shrill 'how d'ye' to the inhabitants." The steamboat bands played their music, "a variety of patriotic airs and colored melodies" (African-American spirituals). Banners streamed from the boats. Excursionists crowded the decks to catch their first sight of Galena. Between 9:00 a.m. and 10:00 a.m. (editors' watches varied) the six boats landed at the wharf.[319]

Galena wanted to impress them. (The day before, one local newspaper urged "citizens to give them a reception worthy the occasion.") A cannon stationed on a small bluff fired at intervals. Hundreds of male westerners crowded the lower streets and cheered the guests, while women and girls stood on housetops and waved handkerchiefs from house windows. Men occupied public spaces and women private ones in this gender-conscious age. "[T]he people were out by crowds . . . to see the great menagerie of human beings from the far-off East." Built on levels ascending from the riverbank uphill, Galena seemed to one editor to be "a three story place, being located at the foot, on the side, and on the top of a high and steep hill." (One earlier observer compared the descending houses to "a drove of sheep going down to water.") This amphitheater amplified the "tumultuous applause," as the welcoming crowd was stacked up like the audience in an opera house, from first floor to mezzanine to balcony.[320]

On levee and wharf, "great quantities of ingots of lead of 62 lbs. weight each lie in piles," noted Benjamin Silliman, "and indicate one principal business of the place." Each bar (or "pig") had the owner's name stamped upon it.[321] Galena owed its existence to lead mining. That day the *Galena Daily Advertiser* printed a history of the industry (begun by white settlers in 1819, it said) and its statistics: in 1853 more than $1.6 million of lead were shipped. Lead mining had recruited a population of wild-living, free-spending males in the early years, of which neither Sedgwick nor Silliman would have approved.[322] In the 1840s Galena became a major wholesaling center for the Upper Mississippi region and the home port for steamboats transporting dry goods and groceries to the new settlements upriver. Several Grand Excursion steamboat captains had their homes there: D. B. Morehouse, Daniel Smith Harris, and Hezekiah H. Gear. As a port, Galena had more family life, a more balanced gender ratio, and sounder business methods, with wholesalers and clerks who kept closer watch over their expenditures.[323]

To easterners, Galena lay on the frontier. Sedgwick saw "more people on the street than I supposed there were north of St. Louis!" (The 1850 census showed 6,000 in Galena; 1854 estimates ranged from 7,000 to 10,000.) Excursionists "were much surprised to see so many people in an apparent wilderness" and so many prosperous-looking brick buildings on Main Street.[324] Yet lead mining was thirty years old there, and Galena's wholesale trade depended on steamboats when the railroad was the up-and-coming transportation technology. Several excursion steamboats belonged to the Galena and Minnesota Packet Company that was owned by Galena interests.[325] Yet this was a railroad excursion, after all, even if it was now joy-larking upriver and allowing boat captains to show off their hometown. Galena still had a greater wholesale trade than Chicago, but the town's steamboat-oriented leaders had been outmaneuvered by Dubuque and Chicago in the railroad location wars and were in danger of being left in progress's wake. The *Chicago Journal* writer treated Galena as yesterday's news: he doubted they would get a chance to visit the mines and said nothing about the place except that its temperature had dipped to "thirty degrees below zero!" the previous winter. "Pretty cold that."[326]

Chicago's U.S. senator, Stephen A. Douglas, the "Little Giant," had aided and abetted Dubuque's maneuver. Therefore, the welcome song ("Come on the Steamboat") Galena offered the visitors included a dig at "Little Doug," which they would interpret as a reference to the Kansas-Nebraska Act:

> *You may have heard that in the West,*
> *Great giants have been born?*
> *We had a* very little one,
> *But now his head is shorn.*

The next lines went on to replace political notables with railroad builders as the heroes for a new age:

> *The only giants now you'll meet,*
> *Are those whose minds and hands*
> *Are binding up the East and West,*
> *With railway-iron bands!*

That stanza was sure to please Henry Farnam and the Chicago & Rock Island Railroad directors.[327]

Rain was falling that forenoon. Galena's streets had turned to mud. The *New York Times* reporter called it "one of the muddiest places I ever beheld"; another journalist described it as "a dirty looking place" with mud "ankle-deep" and dubbed it the "City of Mud." Mud and rain prevented Galena leaders from holding the intended official ceremonies on the city's streets—and caused some ladies to stay on the boats.[328]

As soon as the six steamboats landed, citizens of Galena came onboard to have a good look at the eastern dignitaries. Boarding the *War Eagle,* one man kept asking for Millard Fillmore. He ran across Silliman talking with Reverend Thomas C. Pitkin of New Haven. After Silliman walked off, the man strode up to Pitkin "and inquired if that gentleman was President Fillmore?"

The minister answered, "No—that was Prof. Silliman."

With both hands, the westerner excitedly pulled his hat down nearly over his eyes. "Prof. Silliman, did you say?—Prof. Silliman. Why, where is he? where did he go? Good gracious I must see Professor Silliman, anyhow."

He ran off, having seemingly forgotten which eastern celebrity he had originally boarded the boat to find.[329]

Galena's city fathers had arranged for more than forty wagons, which could carry around three hundred persons, to transport the guests to the Marsden lead mine four miles south of town. Discovered that March, when its landowner dug in the ground to enlarge a spring, the Marsden Mine gave promoters a convenient chance to show visitors that lead mining was not an old, played-out story around Galena. The wagon train lined up on the east side of the river, but there weren't seats enough for all. Many ladies and not a few gentlemen decided against the rough wagon ride over muddy roads. The adventurous engaged in "a grand scramble" for seats, and those too shy to scramble had to stay behind.[330]

Charles Sedgwick regretted his adventurousness: "I went with the cavalcade to the Lead Mines riding in a lumber wagon 8 or 10 miles [round trip] over the wheels on a board which was too short & came tumbling off."[331] Mining consultant Silliman did not regret it. His son-in-law Oliver Payson Hubbard, Gardiner Spring, Shepard Knapp, a Mr. Comans (also a New Yorker), and the tall professor climbed into a "rough wagon" for the half-hour ride. Headed by Galena's mayor seated on horseback, the "long and picturesque procession" about a half-mile long wound its way from the Fever River, up a creek valley, and across farming country, dotted with hills in the distance.[332]

James Woodward of the *New Haven Morning Journal & Courier* boarded a wagon driven by "a venerable Dutchman" who had migrated to Galena in 1827. He unloosed his life story on his passengers: hard times, the Black Hawk War, present prosperity. He confided that he "'had four boys, 3 *big* ones, and *all* teetotalers'; he also had 'four daughters, three big ones and one little one, had a fine farm and was offered for it $10,000 last year.'" The reporter from soon-to-be-dry Connecticut was happy to hear about the teetotalers, and "some young men in the wagon" were interested to hear about the farm and the daughters.[333]

At their destination, they disembarked at a grove of trees on a small hill and were welcomed by Captain Hezekiah H. Gear, a native of Connecticut who had owned and operated mines near Galena for a quarter-century.[334] At the wharf, no formal ceremonies had greeted the excursionists, who now discovered the formalities were at the mine site.

Silliman spoke "with a calm, scientific enthusiasm" on the mineral riches of the mines. A Galena editor noted: "[A]ge hangs lightly upon him and when speaking, his voice was clear and strong, and he looked quite young. He is a tall, fine looking man." His comments probably paralleled his travel notes, in which he praised the progress made on the three-month-old mine and described it in geological terms: "The head is contained in a yellowish limestone, the old transition l[ime]stone, and, as far as I saw, the ore is without a vein stone or gangue. The ore is broad, foliated galena—very rich and brilliant—often distinctly crystallized in cubes and breaking in that form."[335]

Gear gave "a speech in the true western style, expressing the high gratification he felt to meet so many friends from the east, and giving them a cordial welcome." James Babcock of the *New Haven Palladium* reported that Gear "was in an ecstasy of delight with the visit of the strangers" to the mines. Some may not have been strangers to Gear, unbeknownst to Babcock. Certainly, the admiration bestowed by visiting dignitaries like Silliman, from his own home state, upon his own western mining industry, would have meant far more to Gear than mere words from "strangers." For the first generation of pioneering Yankees, excursionists' praises represented almost a parental approval and blessing, coming as it did from the land of their parents. It was because the visitors stood for something near and dear, and not strange, that Gear was in ecstasies of delight.[336]

For Yankee and non-Yankee Galenans, who had painstakingly been constructing a respectable society out of what had been a parcel of wild bachelor miners, this visit from eastern ladies and gentlemen consecrated and finalized their efforts. An exclusive set of easterners condescended to pay them a visit; that confirmed their genteel standing in national society.[337]

Many guests descended into the mine by a "rough stairway" to have a look for themselves. The shaft was dug horizontally into the hillside, to follow the horizontal vein of lead ore. A twenty-foot vertical shaft provided ventilation and an opening through which to hoist lead to the surface. Guests stepped down the stairway a few feet to reach the horizontal shaft, and then exited by a similar stairway at the other end. "We went in as far as it had been worked," reported Charles Dana of the *New York Tribune*, "the metal lay in masses and in great purity; a richer show no miner could desire." They grabbed samples of lead ore to take home as souvenirs. The ore was 90 percent pure lead, and so loose "that large chunks can be pulled out by the hand." Babcock was busily "knocking off some specimens" to take home when he "found someone who had approached from the opposite side engaged in the same business." That was ex-governor and ex-senator Roger S. Baldwin. "A queer spot in which to meet a fellow citizen"— and such a distinguished one! The horizontal shaft did indeed have a leveling effect, and there was no genteel way to knock off ore chunks that Baldwin could use to keep himself elevated above his fellow citizens.[338]

Back on the earth's surface, Galenans offered visitors a genteel "collation" complete with champagne, Catawba wine, crackers and cheese, and claret. It was around noon. Dana apologized—as if to his teetotaling editor, Horace Greeley—"I am sorry to say that total abstinence is not the rule of the Mississippi Valley."[339]

Then came the after-dinner speeches. Fillmore had already seated himself in a carriage for the ride back to town, but the miners "loudly" prevailed upon him to return to the picnic site and make a few remarks, as if to bestow the nation's blessing on their endeavors. Speaking for the excursionists, Judge Amasa Junius Parker of the New York Supreme Court then performed the main and necessary oratorical task of eloquently thanking their Galena hosts for the feast and the C&RI company for making the entire trip possible. A native of Connecticut, the forty-seven-year-old Parker was a Democrat; he may have been asked to speak after the Whig Fillmore to keep easterners' praise a bipartisan consensus. Then they all headed for the carriages and wagons that would take them back to Galena.[340]

Rain, muddy roads, and a mine shaft combined to make the returning excursionists look less than genteel, due to "the bespattered state of their garments" and other factors. George Bancroft "was as gaily spotted as a South Sea Islander, yet his enthusiasm carried him far beyond all considerations of dress."[341] A reporter "noticed several returning guests, each having the neck of a champagne bottle protruding from his pocket." One had a bottle in each pocket, like a pair of six-shooters, "and when I said something about it he assured me that he wished them 'only as chemical tests.'" (That was perhaps a witty sally at the teetotaling chemistry professor, Silliman.) Woodward did not find these Galena donations of liquor to be humorous but regrettable.[342]

Awaiting were the less adventurous ones, who had been writing letters home or walking Galena's streets and hills. John Munn was adventurous but somehow had the impression that the mine tour and carriages were only for "the Lions," the notables. He had climbed the steps to Galena's highest point and had writ-

ten a letter to Miss Harrington, who was minding his children. Edward Prime of the *New York Observer* went to the "rooms" of Alexander Hesler, a daguerrotypist whose pictures he had seen at the New York Crystal Palace exhibition the previous year. Hesler had just returned from the Falls of St. Anthony, and Prime looked at daguerrotypes of scenes he would soon view in person.[343] Those who had taken sick or who were dissatisfied with the accommodations on the steamboats had also been discussing their options. Galena might be the last place to turn back.

On the levee was a crowd "impatient to hear from their distinguished visitors" and perhaps fearful that they had missed the oratorical action. Naturally, they demanded a speech from Fillmore first.[344] A Democratic newspaperman was amused at the predicament of the nonpoliticking Whig politician: "'He could not talk of politics, he could not talk of religion, in Heaven's name what could he talk about?'"[345] He could talk about Galena and its bright prospects, a subject sure to please a bipartisan local audience even during contentious times.

Several men addressed the crowd "from the decks of the steamboats . . . in response to calls from the crowd that gathered on the river banks": Edward Bates, Reverend Leonard Bacon, Charles Hudson of the *Boston Atlas,* Dana of the *Tribune,* former state senator James E. Cooley of New York, and Judge Parker. "The concentrated essence of what was said," Samuel Bowles noted sarcastically, "was that ours was a very great country, and just this particular place was the greatest and smartest part of it."[346]

These speeches could easily be dismissed as meaningless blather, but with so many influential editors, writers, and leaders present, this was a chance to make one's reputation—or polish it, if already made. Men eyed Bates as potential presidential timber; he was, in effect, auditioning for the role before critical eastern editors. Dana noted that Bates's speech "was listened to with particular interest by those of us who had not before enjoyed the opportunity of seeing this distinguished man." The Missourian's talk "was simple, and without effort, spoken in a very quiet and straightforward manner, but with one or two fine touches that betrayed the orator." Bates had declined Fillmore's offers of cabinet posts and lost the Whig vice-presidential nomination in 1852. After hearing him, Dana "regretted that Mr. Bates has never taken that leading part in our public affairs which he might have filled so honorably and advantageously to himself and the country."[347]

After the speeches—"all on one key, namely, in praise of the West"—an Irish miner hurried to board the *Golden Era*. He approached John A. Granger and addressed him (as best the newspaperman could recall), "Misthur President, Surr: I mek bould to presint to yer honor this illigant specimint." He gave Granger a "fine stalactite" from the mines. Granger informed the man that he was not Fillmore but pointed out to him the ex-president. The miner went to Fillmore and "repeated his concise speech and presented the specimen with a grace that many committees of receptions are not possessed of." Fillmore graciously took it. The miner then departed—perhaps assuming that all these genteel people must be Whigs—with the comment "that he was a good whig" and not a "dimmecrat."[348]

Now that the ex-president had a souvenir of Galena, the full agenda seemed to be accomplished. The day was far advanced; Galena had taken some of the visiting time her rival Dubuque wanted. In mid-afternoon, the six steamboats departed amid great fanfare: "the boats, banks and buildings upon shore were crowded by enthusiastic and happy people; guns were fired; the bands played from the decks of the steamers, cheers echoed and re-echoed, handkerchiefs waved."[349] Compliments from distinguished men had validated Galena's progress to date, and its citizens had cause to celebrate. Hubbard left a note for the Whig editor, assuring him that the guests "are greatly delighted with what they see" and, by implication, that the town's extensive preparations for the visit had paid off.[350] Whether this would help a river town in a railroad age remained to be seen.

The flotilla steamed down the narrow, twisting Fever River in "something of a wild goose course, heading close upon each other," with the *Golden Era* in the lead, apparently out of respect for Fillmore's exalted status. As they headed toward the Mississippi, the competitive Captain Harris acted quickly to regain the lead for his *War Eagle*. Some three miles south of Galena, the Fever River split into a main channel that entered the Mississippi three miles farther south, and a secondary channel that in low water was a slough but in June's high water was separated from the Mississippi by only a hundred yards of fast-flowing water—and a sandbar. Taking the secondary channel saved six miles. "The 'Golden Era' took the long one round," reported Henry Tobey of the *Kingston (N.Y.) Journal,* "while the Captain of our boat [Harris] just ran his bow full speed upon a sand [bar]. . . . We were to go through this channel and head the 'Era.' That was clearly the game." The *War Eagle*'s bow hit the sandbar "and she laid for a moment broadside to the stream, but the next instant the waters carried her off." Harris would not quit after one try. "Then she rounded to, and there was a great clattering of bells and machinery; soon she headed again for the passage, and this time, by running her bow some fifteen feet in the sand, it held fast while her stern swung round; but then the reaction threw her bow on the opposite shore, and we left the impression of every bucket in one [paddle] wheel, at least four feet in the dry sand bank." Harris made it, and the *Eagle* "beat the 'Era' some distance into Dubuque."[351]

Steamboats had several ways of getting over sandbars; this was a particularly dangerous and potentially destructive one.[352]

Heading back onto the Mississippi, the steamboats encountered three ominous-sounding landmarks. Smallpox Creek flowed into the main channel of the Fever River, the one taken by the *Golden Era* and its followers. On the west (Iowa) bank of the Mississippi, a small stream with the unusual name of Tête des

Morts flowed into the great river. Death's Head cliff rose some 150 feet above the creek of that name, which they both inherited from a grisly episode—likely in the eighteenth century—when a band of Dakota warriors was slaughtered by their Sac and Fox enemies at the top of the cliff. The names of the two streams struck a solemn note on this joyous occasion. But at least there was no Cholera Creek.[353]

On the Mississippi again, the advance steamboats halted to allow the slower ones to catch up. They ran up on the bank beneath a tall rock, which some compared to a feudal castle, near a log cabin and a woman engaged in the unromantic task of hoeing her potato patch. Despite the unannounced visit and despite being "the focus of six or eight hundred pairs of eyes from the steamers," she kept on with her work as the impromptu party landed at her place. Excursionists went from boat to boat. The rain having let up, "the shore was alive with the curious among our travelers, some gathering wild flowers, others cutting walking sticks, and others hunting and finding turtle's eggs." Others noticed that the woman was wearing homemade wooden shoes, and so they went boldly to the log cabin to examine her handiwork. "They had been dug out of blocks of bass wood, and resembled much the old India rubber shoe as originally imported, but were more clumsy." The woman had customers, wanted or unwanted but certainly unexpected, and she sold "[s]everal new pairs of different sizes" to a few passengers. Apparently after viewing this scene, one of the western women on the trip remarked that frontier life "is very well for men and dogs, but hard for women and oxen."[354]

Steamboat bells rang and they re-embarked for Dubuque, a few miles farther upriver.[355] The organizers placed the fast-paced *War Eagle* in the rear, probably to prevent their impressive parade of boats from again being separated and diminished by distance as it steamed into Dubuque. Captain Harris projected his impatience onto his vessel, which was "behaving very uneasy," according to him, for, "being unaccustomed to such slow progress, it was exceedingly difficult to hold her back."[356]

Two miles south of Dubuque, excursionists saw the mouth of Catfish Creek and, on its north side, a tall bluff upon whose summit lay the grave of the area's pioneer white settler, Julien Dubuque. "Passing the romantic grave of Dubuque, and the castled crag near it," one reporter noted that these sights "were beautifully sketched by Mr. Kensett, the distinguished artist of New York," onboard the *Golden Era.* Perpetually comparing American to European scenery and finding the former deficient in ancient historical associations, New York writers and painters sought associations to remedy the primitive and unfinished character of American landscapes. Catfish Creek did not connote European-style grandeur; however, the grave of the eighteenth-century French-Canadian fur trader, lead miner, and local grandee dignified the site with a historic aura that made it worthy of a noted landscape artist's sketch pencil. George Catlin had painted bluff and grave; the region's folklore had already made the spot of

"great notoriety" so that Kensett could make use of an existing perception of its antiquity.[357]

The tall bluff represented a geological feature that Kensett could paint with scientific exactness. Many landscape painters (including Kensett) studied geology and chose natural scenes rich in geological interest: bluffs, waterfalls, rocky mountain peaks, gorges, natural bridges, etcetera. No hard and fast line separated antebellum science and art; Silliman wrote a guidebook for tourists, and Kensett painted rocks with such detail that Silliman might learn their makeup from his paintings. The growing interest in and knowledge of geology aided artists' and tourists' appreciation of scenery. Painters and travelers understood that rock strata imparted a history to the site, a geological history that rendered the site ancient even if it lacked ruins of human civilization. America "had the equivalent of a cultural past in its natural phenomena." If there were a historic relic like Dubuque's grave next to a geological bluff, so much the better. That imparted aesthetic, historical-associational, and geological-scientific interest to Kensett's sketch of the scene.[358]

Around five o'clock, the flotilla neared Dubuque. A "violent rain-storm" had started, and Silliman noted some hail, a most unwelcome turn of events for Dubuque's boosters, who had 130 carriages lined up on the levee, ready to take excursionists on a sightseeing trip around the town and its hilly environs.[359] A week before, the *Dubuque Miners' Express* urged "our citizens to spend a little time and money" on hosting their guests. "Such attentions . . . may and probably will lay the foundation for important additions to our population and valuable contributions to our capital and business." The day before, the *Express* reemphasized, "It is the most magnificent excursion of the age. Hundreds of men will be present, who make their mark wherever they go." Making a good impression on them "may be of invaluable benefit to us and our city." Good preparations were all the more vital because Dubuque leaders suspected Galena captains would time their journey so as to stop in their rival city at the most inopportune time.[360]

More than three hours of daylight remained, but the rain made the Dubuque stop most inopportune. The city gave a "canonical" salute and sustained applause, but few excursionists went ashore. Carriages sat there while the Mississippi's current flowed past. Prominent easterners looked out on "a motley sea of 'upturned umbrellas'" as Dubuque's citizens gathered at the levee. If not picturesque or sublime, this umbrella scenery seemed "novel" to Edward Prime of New York: "the immense array of umbrellas of all colors and hues, even to the red, . . . which, as we looked down from our elevation, entirely hid their persons from view." One excursionist "facetiously" remarked "that if any gentlemen had lost an umbrella within the last year, he might step ashore and claim it, as the lost umbrellas must all certainly have collected there." The umbrellas sent a delegation headed by Iowa governor Stephen Hempstead to board the *Golden Era* and greet the visitors formally. Under the circumstances, the dele-

gates not only represented the crowds that would have liked to greet them but also substituted for the rich feast that had been prepared (in vain) at the main hotel. When presented to Fillmore and even as he began speaking, Hempstead "forgot to take off his hat until one of his friends touched the rim over his shoulder, when he doffed it with electrical haste." Woodward of New Haven thought Governor Hempstead "quite *unfinished*" and his speech a sure sign "that he had risen in the world a little too fast." Whig editors and "big bugs" on the steamboat were sure to note these bad manners coming from an old-fashioned Jacksonian Democrat who defended the Kansas-Nebraska Act.[361]

Fillmore stepped out on the hurricane deck and spoke to the crowd on shore, which sent one Democratic reporter into a paroxysm of partisan scorn: "President Fillmore here again laid his hand on the spot where his heart is supposed to be, and with a most profound bow, assured the multitude that he was not on a political tour." But "this was the *twenty-seventh* time he had said the same thing since leaving Chicago. The fact is, he has made an ass of himself by running out upon the deck every time a dozen boys could be got to cry, 'Fillmore, Fillmore.'" The reporter thought Fillmore's friends should see this was hurting his cause and should ask him to stop.[362]

The crowd on the levee then "vociferously called for" John A. Dix, a fifty-five-year-old former U.S. senator from New York, a Democrat (popular in Democratic Dubuque), and president of the Mississippi & Missouri

Railroad, the planned westward extension of the C&RI through Iowa from Davenport to Council Bluffs. Of medium height, with a dignified bearing and a determined look, used to dealing with presidents and financiers, Dix gave "a neat little railroad speech." A strong advocate of a transcontinental railroad, he intended that the C&RI–M&M group build it and seemed the well-connected man to get it done. He wanted a railroad built west from Dubuque to join his road at Council Bluffs and partake in the transcontinental bonanza. That was what Dubuque wanted to hear.[363]

The Iowans had outmaneuvered Galena in railroad planning. Dubuque had an open hinterland stretching west across a prairie; laying railroad track here would be easy. Galena's hinterland was a steamboat-supplied Upper Mississippi frontier whose frontier status and traditional mode of transport seemed about to end. Dubuque's leaders got Congress to make their city, not Galena, the northern terminus of the Illinois Central. In 1853, they formed the Dubuque & Pacific Railroad Company (whose far-reaching pretensions a Galena editor ridiculed by suggesting it be named the "Dubuque, Pacific, Japan and Shanghai Railroad"); in early 1854, they decided this railroad should head west via the Catfish Creek route. Obtaining Dix's support for their plans would help them to interest railroad investors (many potential ones were unfortunately kept by the rain onboard the steamboats) in their project. However, their hopes were a bit unrealistic. "The plan was to run the line to the next county where enthusiasm would push it on to the next county and so on to the Pacific." That was not the way railroads pushed west. It required interlocking directorates of successive railroad companies—the Michigan Southern, C&RI, then the M&M—not successive counties' boards.[364]

James A. Cooley, Judge Parker, Judge James R. Lawrence (also from New York State), and E. Church Blackburn gave brief talks to the crowd. Then attorney, Democrat, and candidate for state representative Benjamin Samuels "replied in behalf of the people of Dubuque . . . thanking the men of the East for their capital and confidence." The gist of his remarks were: "You at the East, have the capital; we at the West, are anxious to supply the labor. Send us money then, and we will build railroads, and send your money back to you in car-loads of the produce of our fertile soil." Perhaps surprised to find eloquence on what they considered a frontier, the eastern editors' verdict was favorable: "a regular Western oration"; "We heard no better speech than this one of Mr. Samuel [sic] on the entire route"; "an animating address."[365] He spoke for "we" westerners, but the western towns competed against each other for eastern capital and confidence; Dubuque's choice of the eloquent Samuels and his careful preparations were competitive acts designed to make Dubuque look better than its rivals.

To put down Dubuque's one-upmanship, Galena editor Dr. Charles H. Ray parodied the orators, "all of whom adopted the line usual on such occasions. 'Great and glorious country,' 'the mighty west,' 'the iron horse,' 'links of iron and hooks of steel,' 'wonderful people,' were the staples" of their oratory. No doubt, those words were spoken at Galena also, but the rivalry between the two cities freed (or forced) Ray to critique speeches on the river's west bank. He exaggerated too: "No one went ashore, and, except for the committee of reception, no one came aboard." In fact, some excursionists did go ashore, and more than the committee came onboard the steamboats to greet the visitors. But Ray was having too much fun at Dubuque's discomfiture to stop at the facts. "Our entertainment was speaking and rain, rain and speaking—words and water. A bill of fare well adapted to the town."[366]

Incensed, the editor of the *Dubuque Miners' Express* rebutted Ray's account. What Ray called a "bank" on which the boats docked was "a stone Levee which Galena might brag on if it had it"; some visitors went ashore; the weather was to blame for any deficiencies in Dubuque's welcome, plus the fact that "no official notification of the intended visit" had been given to the city. Indeed, experience led the Iowans to suspect "that where Galena Steamboats had anything to do with a party of the kind, the programme would be so arranged, as to land here about night, which was the case." (Indeed, some passengers were told the Galena visit was to last only three hours, but it took more like six, and there was little time left for Dubuque—perhaps intentionally.) The one "serious blunder" Dubuque's citizens committed was "in extending their hospitality to" Ray and other Galenans.[367]

This was not a tempest in a teapot, but part of a serious competition for the eastern capital Samuels invited. As they traveled, eastern editors and investors eyed towns carefully and analyzed each one's prospects. Babcock of New Haven sized up Galena: "The town will always be one of importance, though it can hardly make the show of Davenport, because away from the main river and shut in somewhat by the high lands about it." Moore noted one defect in Dubuque: the tendency of the Mississippi's current to run nearer the eastern bank and to leave "a sloughy channel" near the city.[368] Like debutantes at a ball, western towns expected to be closely inspected by outside investors and tried to highlight their advantages and distract observers from seeing their disadvantages.

Westerners, including their editors, eyed towns' shifting fortunes, including their own. Many were loosely committed to their own towns. In June 1854, Ray was discouraged about Galena, his low circulation, his unappreciative readers, and the change in the Illinois Central's plans. He was looking for a more promising city for a newspaper—just as he was discouraged with his Democratic party, his paper's Democratic name (*Jeffersonian*), and the Democratic Douglas's Kansas-Nebraska Act, and was looking for an anti-Nebraska coalition that he might join.[369]

Although he commented on Dubuque's favorable location and evident prosperity, Reverend Leonard Bacon was more concerned about the religious than the economic competition. "A huge Roman Catholic cathedral, in a most pretending if not imposing style of architecture, is a very conspicuous object, as we begin to ascend the river, leaving the city behind us." Bacon interpreted the cathedral's presence, size, and imposing style to mean "that the great power of the Papacy . . . is aboring to establish itself everywhere in our country"—even in the West—but he did not recommend an end to religious liberty. "Let them build their cathedrals and their convents, but let us build school-houses, colleges," and churches and, thus, "in the exercise of our liberty, resist them with the legitimate and peaceful weapons of 'light and love.'"[370]

Around 6:30 p.m., the steamboats pushed off from the handsome stone levee and headed north. Hearing that there were "several invalids" and some who did not want to proceed farther, the organizers sent them back on the *Jenny Lind,* whose slowness had forced the faster boats to stop and wait for her. They also told the captains that each boat was free "to take her own course" on the understanding that all would meet "some twelve miles below" St. Paul and steam with style into the next sizable town. (Racing was still forbidden supposedly, although what Harris did at the Fever River was really racing.) This was welcome news to Captain Harris; "the War Eagle left her companions out of sight in her rear in a very short time, and dashed ahead in the best style."[371]

Dubuque's poor luck was further proven as the evening progressed: "the sky cleared up and we had as gorgeous a sunset scene as fancy ever painted," Moore noted. "The bluffs grew more bold, the banks less marshy, the islands more spicy, and the scenery more enchanting." The Upper Mississippi won over this realist's heart. Even "panorama painting" could not do it justice. "All must see with their own eyes, and from seeing, will come believing." Excursionists who had traveled to Europe assured Moore this scenery was "unmatched either in Europe or America." National and western pride encouraged him to accept their word: "It looks as if it must be so."[372]

John Munn appeared more interested in what kind of scenery the flotilla of steamboats presented to onlookers on shore as they steamed upriver "& to us as they float upon the water they have a very picturesque appearance." A steamboat veteran from his southern sojourn, he prided himself on his ability to make friends of the boat's officers, and he clearly had struck up an acquaintanceship with Commodore George Mix, "an intelligent gentleman . . . exceedingly affable and courteous in his manners and untiring" in replying to Munn's questions. Even so, he doubted that Mix's "equanimity of temper" would survive this stressful, overcrowded excursion and the complaints of the "scrub aristocracy." The Walkers, however, had not left the party at Galena, as they threatened. Mix was happy to hear that the excursionists were delighted with Tuesday's river scenery, but added that "the scenery is tame compared with what is beyond."[373]

At dusk, tea was served. Then, as night fell, the *Golden Era, Galena,* and *Lady Franklin* were lashed together (while continuing to steam north) and planks were placed from deck to deck so that excursionists could walk from one to the other, socialize, and dance with their neighbors. Dignitaries on the *Golden Era* could join fashionable New York City ladies on the *Lady Franklin,* and both could visit Illinois governor Joel Matteson and the snobbish Ninian W. Edwardses on the *Galena.* (The *War Eagle* steamed ahead as if to avoid the dancing altogether.) The three cabins were "handsomely decorated," the chairs and tables removed to make "three grand ball rooms," and, in the center of each, a band played dance music. Soon, "ladies' feet fairly twinkled in their graceful evolutions," many heads "unconsciously nodding time to the measure." On the *Golden Era,* "eight or ten editors, or their correspondents," sat at a table at the far end of the cabin, tried to ignore the hubbub, and recorded "this day's observations." Near them, two players sat "completely abstracted in a game of chess," while cries of "ladies change" and "first four forward" rang out from the dance floor. Eventually, the editors were cajoled into joining the party that lasted "till long after midnight."[374]

Outside, the rain had resumed, but the action had shifted indoors; no one seems to have complained about the weather.[375] Moore found the human scenery picturesque: "Here were poets, artists, travelers, authors, editors, lawyers, ministers, judges, senators, and all sorts of great men; besides a full complement of amiable matrons, and their bright eyed, rosy-hued daughters. It was a scene fit for Byron to have gone mad over. I can only let our Journal readers *guess* at the poetry."[376]

Lashing boats together ran counter to Joseph Sheffield's fatherly, cautious advice to Henry Farnam: "I would not lash Boats together—the noise of their steam & etc. will give the appearance of crowd and confusion—but sailing separately, and in sight of each other, will be pleasing, and add to the variety."[377] For entertainment, excursionists seemed to desire crowd and confusion at night. They ignored Sheffield's aesthetic, and Farnam ignored his advice. Sheffield wasn't there.

Massachusetts railroad men were on the *Sparhawk;* most had not brought their wives; and their boat was not lashed to the others. Therefore, they held a railroad meeting in their cabin in honor of their C&RI hosts. Alderman Nathan C. Ely of New York City served as chair. Some investors expected the C&RI directors to issue a financial report during the excursion, which resembled a traveling shareholders' meeting. When asked for a financial report, C&RI president John B. Jervis replied, "None to be obtained here, but they are plenty in New York." That was disappointing to shareholders, who were "here," not in New York. Yet they held this night session to thank their hosts, not to complain, which would have been seen as inappropriate at a social event. Several men gave humorous speeches, and the evening was devoted to male bonhomie.[378]

One group began to regret the late-night sociability: the young bachelors, men without wives, and other unfortunates who had to sleep on the cabin floors. "We poor 'cotters' couldn't get to bed very early," complained one, and they had to anticipate an early awakening from waiters pulling big toes.[379]

EXCURSUS

Benjamin Silliman and Antebellum American Science

BENJAMIN SILLIMAN, evangelical scientist and Yale professor, was a worthy representative of that New England piety that sought to extend its sway to the western states. An indefatigable note-taker and an author of travel books, Silliman carefully recorded the Grand Excursion scene on the evening of June 5, but he began with a characteristic attention to history. "The island proper is in the river and a fort of the United States still remains there. It was used in the Black Hawk's war in 1832-3." He marveled at historical change since then: "Only twenty years have passed since this region was transferred to our dominion and now it is full of the stir of high civilization." The excursion caused quite a stir for this new-born region. "From the fort on Rock Island splendid fireworks were displayed in the evening and until after 10 o'clock when our

Yale professor Benjamin Silliman.

Steam Boats began their night voyage." After the long day's journey, the elderly Silliman was not tempted to remain on deck, but turned in and enjoyed "quiet and refreshing slumber" until morning.[380]

So impressive were the West's "high civilization" and grand scenery that New Englanders might think "how insignificant geographically is their small territory," he later summarized. Yet size and grandeur did not count for everything. Such persons "would find compensation in the prevailing influence of New England intelligence and energy and moral and intellectual power which infuses an active element into the new States and the love of liberty and free institutions is not the least important." He echoed his friend Alexander Twining's concern that Yankee morality and liberty continue to advance westward. Silliman wrote impersonally of "all" easterners feeling overshadowed, but he was clearly—albeit temporarily—tempted to see his native region as "insignificant." Yet he was intellectually strong enough to resist inferiority: "although the prairie is beautiful poetry I prefer the sober prose of New England."[381]

Westerners would see few better examples of "New England intelligence and energy and moral and intellectual power" than Benjamin Silliman Sr. His father, Gold Selleck Silliman, served as a general commanding Connecticut troops during the American Revolution; "four generations" of Sillimans "had been prominent in Connecticut"; Benjamin's first wife was the daughter of Jonathan Trumbull, Connecticut's governor during the Revolution. Benjamin was born in August 1779, in the midst of dark days for American patriots, when his father was imprisoned by the British in New York. When his mother, Mary Silliman, wrote to her husband to ask what to name the child, Selleck replied, "I am perfectly at a Loss what to call the Dear little Stranger, name him as You please."[382]

The dear little stranger entered a family enduring great and patriotic sacrifices for the nation's liberty and free institutions. At Benjamin's birth, his father mused over Jeremiah's *Lamentations,* comparing New York's fall to Jerusalem's, and his own captivity to Israel's. After Selleck's release, the family's fortunes plummeted just as the infant nation's rose. As a youth, Benjamin "was disturbed by the disjunction and tried many times to reconcile the history of the Sillimans with that of

the rising Republic."[383] When he wrote of Rock Island "transferred to our dominion," he well knew it was a dominion his father had suffered to help create. Rock Island was located within the lands Connecticut claimed but had given to the new nation. His father's state's patrimony, in a sense, was sacrificed along with his father's personal estate. As a young man, Silliman studied his father's war letters and battle plans intensively, to make sense of the past.[384]

His study of history did not yield an original answer, only the old Puritan one that Providence was to be trusted and praised ("But let me not complain: the hand of God has done it," he wrote in his diary regarding his father's death).[385] He did not choose to devote his life to composing that answer in the minister's study and proclaiming it in the pulpit. Yet he retained a passionate interest in the history and fate of the Republic. At New Haven's March 1854 meeting against the Kansas-Nebraska Act, he spoke in "chiefly historical" terms: "It has happened to me by the favor of God, to be born amid the scenes of the revolution" when his hometown "was burnt by the British troops" and "[m]y father served in our armies." "I remember every capital event—every event of prominence which has occurred to us since our history as a nation began." Excursioning westward, the seventy-four-year-old Silliman was a living embodiment of the nation's relatively brief history.[386]

Science became his way to retrieve his family's fortunes by patriotically contributing to the rising republic and defeating that rising infidelity that partly resulted from France's different ideas of republicanism and science. In July 1801, Yale president Timothy Dwight met him under the campus elm trees and asked him to become Yale's first professor of chemistry and natural history. A friend of Silliman's father, Dwight presented a challenge sure to appeal to him:

> [T]here will be no rival here. The field will be all your own. . . . Our country, as regards the physical sciences, is rich in unexplored treasures, and by aiding in their development you will perform an important public service, and connect your name with the rising reputation of our native land.

Having graduated from Yale in 1796, Silliman was then studying law, but he gave that up to accept Dwight's challenge. The established reputation of European science made it advisable for him to travel there for two years of study (1805–1806).[387]

Dwight's offer was a godsend. Here was a new, fertile field for a Connecticut young man to cultivate (unlike played-out farming or overcrowded lawyering), with opportunity but without having to leave his elderly mother and to move west to New Connecticut as his step-brother Joseph Noyes had done in 1800 with disastrous consequences. Moreover, scientific fact-finding could justify trips westward to examine "unexplored treasures."[388]

Chemistry, geology, and mineralogy became Silliman's frontiers, and he became the pioneer advancing into new realms and bringing New England's religious faith with him into realms that would otherwise be seized by French infidelity. In doing so, he carried on the life work of Timothy Dwight, the father figure who gave him a patrimony (a "field" of "unexplored treasures") that his own father had been unable to leave for him. Dwight gained a defender of orthodoxy (unlike the suspect Jeffersonian Republican, Josiah Meigs) as Yale's pioneering scientist. Silliman was "already well insulated by Dwight's personal instruction against the infidelity that seemed irresistably to flood the domain of science."[389]

With Yale's financial help and Dwight's encouragement, Silliman succeeded: "he did more than any other man in the first half of the nineteenth century to establish science in America as a profession." He brought to Yale a fine mineral collection; he wrote widely admired articles about the Weston meteor of 1807; he edited for twenty years the nation's premier scientific journal, the *American Journal of Science and the Arts,* often called "Silliman's *Journal*"; he trained many of antebellum America's major scientists, including his future sons-in-law Oliver P. Hubbard and James Dwight Dana, as well as Charles Upham Shepard, Edward Hitchcock, and Denison Olmsted; he trained his son, Benjamin Jr., and gave him a patrimony, the professorship in chemistry, which "Young Ben" held after his father retired; he founded America's first real graduate school in science, Yale's Sheffield Scientific School (whose main benefactor was Joseph E. Sheffield); he traveled widely (starting at New Haven with James Brewster's course for mechanics), popularizing science as an entertaining and energetic lecturer; and he explored the nation's mineral treasures as a mining consultant.[390]

Shepard described Silliman's famous chemistry lectures:

During the lecture hour there was no lull or intermission; all was rapid movement, a constant appeal to the delighted senses. Here were broad irradiations of emerald phosphorescence, there the vivid spangles of burning iron, or the blinding effulgence of the compound blow-pipe. . . . Strange sounds saluted the ear, from the singing hydrogen tube, the crackling decrepitation up to the loud explosions of mingled gases and detonating fulminates. As forms of matter once regarded simple were torn into their elements, or these again compounded in manifold ways, a very kaleidoscope of changes came into view, of which the greatest was the transformation of the whole seeming fantasy into science, through the lucid rationale of the gifted lecturer. [391]

Here was a dramatic show that greatly appealed to audiences and established Silliman as a popular attraction in lecture halls.

He went on the Grand Excursion as professor emeritus, although on May 28, two days before departing, he finished a course of twenty-five lectures on geology. "The duty has been arduous but my health and mental power (God be praised) remain unimpaired," he noted.[392] His fame was secure by then. He could take a month off to travel past sites he had visited as a mining consultant, now in the company of celebrities who had attended his public lectures and of several students now become well-known scientists—his sons-in-law Shepard and Hubbard. He could bask in fellow excursionists' praise of him as the pathfinder of American science.

By 1854, his pioneering work was accomplished; American science had entered an age of increasing specialization, in which few men would tackle three sciences (chemistry, geology, and mineralogy) as he had; Silliman's students were making major contributions. Young Ben was analyzing the crude liquid accidently oozing out of Oil Creek in Pennsylvania. His 1855 "Rock Oil Report" laid the scientific groundwork for Pennsylvania's oil industry.[393] Mainly a mineralogist, Shepard taught at Amherst and in South Carolina. He epitomized antebellum science's collecting mania. Silliman described his former student's mineral collection ("cabinet") as being "very rich especially in gems and meteorites including meteoric iron. In this department it has no equal except in the Imperial Cabinet of Vienna."[394] Hubbard had a less spectacular, more general career as a professor of chemistry and pharmacy, mineralogy, and geology at Dartmouth College.

All had family ties to Silliman. Shepard married Silliman's adopted daughter; Hubbard, one of his biological daughters. Another of his daughters married James

Dwight Dana, America's premier antebellum geologist. Both Shepard and Hubbard went on the excursion alone, without their wives.[395] Benjamin Silliman could almost be called the father-in-law of antebellum American science.

One other scientist accompanied them on the excursion: William C. Redfield of New York City, although he went mainly as the author of the pamphlet (1829) that first suggested the route of a railroad to the Mississippi River. Redfield had also published an article on meteorology in which he successfully argued that "the circular movement of wind around a storm center" was the cause of storms and hurricanes.[396]

Americans did not yet surpass Europeans in any science. In chemistry, their contribution was "mostly practical . . . or else descriptive and analytical." In botany, zoology, and other life sciences, they were busy collecting and identifying new species. In the earth sciences, they had a varied geology to work with, and they had begun to make contributions to theory. In mathematics, they had achieved little. American astronomers were more successful and had proven the Europeans wrong on Neptune's orbit. "In astronomy as in other fields of science, Americans were strongest in observation, description, cataloguing, and technique." American study of physics had hardly commenced.[397]

The trip itself served as a metaphor for the peripatetic, hurried, fact-gathering, non-speculative character of antebellum American science. No need to speculate on origins or to theorize until all data were in—and, with the ever-receding western frontier offering still unexplored treasures, all data would not be in for decades. Writing in Silliman's *Journal,* one observer stated that "in a country so unexplored as ours . . . for a time, general and abstract researches will, and legitimately may, give place to the labors of the literal historiographer of nature." Coming from Switzerland to America in 1846, Louis Agassiz was so struck by new objects "and brought into such a state of excitement that I at last was taken sick." American entomologists traveled "like so many scientific Robinson Crusoes" looking for new species. When someone inquired what his field of specialty was, a naturalist replied, "I am studying Wisconsin." The West prolonged the Baconian task of fact-gathering and delayed theory-making.[398]

The method advocated by Sir Francis Bacon was to eschew speculative hypotheses and to gather facts like nuts and berries in the woods, until the facts themselves almost shouted out a general law.[399] That suited Silliman (and antebellum American science) exactly. In his lectures at Yale, he began by stating "that geology is erected upon facts, and not upon mere speculation." Speculation had its uses, but "positive" geology was "incomparably more important than speculative, and it proceeds, like the other natural sciences, upon a careful examination of particulars. From particulars, it ascends to generals, and upon these builds legitimate conclusions." Positive geology reasoned inductively from a set of facts. Silliman did not condemn hypothesizing but preferred to gather facts before making a hypothesis. He distinguished inferior hypotheses, which built upon few known facts or even analogies, from superior ones, "which, being built upon analogous facts, approximate to legitimate theory." By theory, he meant a scientific law that explained natural phenomena.[400]

Even "positive geology," even as early as the antebellum years, seemed to many Americans to conflict with a literal reading of Genesis. A strong evangelical and a follower of Timothy Dwight, Silliman confronted this public perception in his efforts to popularize science. In a speech given not long after the excursion, with a metaphorical anecdote clearly based on his experience on the trip, George Bancroft compared historians' task of analyzing recent ages to geologists' analysis of "remotest antiquity":

The student of the chronology of the earth may sit on the bluffs that overhang the Mississippi, and muse on the myriads of years during which the powers of nature have been depositing the materials of its delta. He may then, by the aid of induction, draw nearer to the beginnings of time, as he meditates on the succession of ages that assisted to construct the cliffs which raise their bastions over the stream; or to bury in compact layers the fern-like forests that have stored the bosom of the great valley with coal; or to crystallize the ancient limestone into marble; or, at a still earlier epoch, to compress liquid masses of the globe into seams of granite.

The geologist-on-the-bluff sought to discover "the revolutions through which our planet was fashioned into a residence for man." Viewing geological strata exposed on the Upper Mississippi's bluffs, he gathered "particulars" from which "generals" (generalizations) could be induced.[401]

Similarities linked geology and history. Like the convenient four-year periods of presidential administrations, geological strata classified natural history into periods for analysis. However, rocks and strata were residue resulting from past events, not witnesses who could testify exactly about them. Presumably, a skilled scientist could tease some testimony out of them, but it would be limited by the scientist's tools, concepts, and knowledge. History relied on eyewitness testimony about unique, nonrepeatable past events, and Bancroft did not need to deduce "generals" in any real scientific sense. The historian did not usually rely on inference in interpreting that testimony to the same degree as did the scientist. The "student of the chronology of the earth" relied on observing the results of past physical events, from which general laws could be inferred. He "could draw nearer to the beginnings of time" but could he actually get at the beginning, which by definition was a unique, nonrepeatable event?

English geologist Sir Charles Lyell's *Principles of Geology* "had compellingly presented the uniformitarian thesis in geology, holding that the operation of currently observable processes explained all geological change since Day Three [of the Genesis account]."[402]

That aided "the induction" done by the geologist sitting on the Upper Mississippi bluff; he need not wonder if processes themselves changed over time, as well as the rocks. A historian, however, suspected that time changed most everything, even the processes of change themselves. So how could one examine the results of change and reliably calculate how long it had taken to produce those results?

It was easy enough for Bancroft to use a geological figure of speech in a talk to a historical society. He was merely a historian, and one certainly not charged with instructing youth at an evangelical college. Three sentences later, without offering any evidence, he could transition to "the higher subject of man. It is but a few centuries since he came into life." For the scientific Silliman, those "myriads of years," a succession of ages, and that "still earlier epoch" posed problems for the prevalent view that Genesis taught a six-thousand-year-old Earth and a six-thousand-year-old human race. (And yet Silliman would have appreciated the comparison of geology to that historical study he had practiced as a young man; he "was prepared to treat natural history as an extension" of his youthful "'retrospective viewings'" of his father's letters.)[403]

Throughout his long career, Silliman confronted clergymen and theologians, such as Moses Stuart of Andover Seminary (Edward Robinson's teacher), who contended that "either the doctrine of the entire infallibility of the Bible must be surrendered, or geology be rejected." Stuart preferred the latter course. In March 1830, Silliman wrote to his former student Edward Hitchcock, "I only glanced at Mr. Stuart's geological remarks. My previous correspondence with him showed me how poor a judge he is of such matters, and I must include nearly all our theological gentlemen here, who discover no disposition to listen to reason and evidence on the subject."[404] Silliman often sounded as annoyed over clerical forays into geology as Stephen Douglas was over preachers meddling in politics. Silliman's standard rejoinder was that clergy did not understand the facts of geology and that he always tried to reconcile geology and Genesis. True to Yale's "middle way" between a reason-only infidel science and a faith-only conservative theology, he also encountered fierce opposition from the unbeliever Dr. Thomas Cooper of Columbia (South Carolina) College, who objected to Silliman the scientist referring to a Creator.[405]

Silliman could not have been surprised when, aboard the *War Eagle,* he met a clergyman questioning geology. Gardiner Spring and he held a "protracted interview" on the steamboat. Spring believed that geologists could dig up and examine only a veneer of the Earth's surface, an insufficient basis for generalizing about the Earth's age. The Old Stock clergyman condemned geologists' "speculations" that conflicted with Genesis. Somewhat defensive over the implication that he had not fulfilled Dwight's charge to defend orthodoxy through science, and convinced that geologists possessed an adequate collection of facts (and clergymen, very little), Silliman argued that geology was "not a dream" of visionaries and did not contradict, but rather vindicated, Genesis. In Silliman's stock phrase, "there is a perfect harmony between the works and the word of God." He probably explained his view that a "day" in Genesis could mean an indefinite period of time, long enough for geologic changes to occur and geologic strata to be deposited and eroded.[406]

He had talked to many ministers about geology: "Some of them are candid and forbearing; others find no insuperable difficulties [between geology and Genesis]; others are silent because they feel that they do not understand the matter; but a few are loud, confident, and uncharitable, while it is obvious that they know not whereof they affirm."[407] Reverend Dr. Spring was not loud or uncharitable. He expressed his views "with Christian fidelity and gentlemanly courtesy," Silliman admitted to him. It was Silliman who made concluding "abrupt" remarks that could be interpreted as signs "of arrogance and presumption" (they were not, he assured Spring).[408]

He referred Spring to his "Outline of the Course of Geological Lectures," where he reconciled the *"philosophy of geology"* with the book of Genesis. "It is true, that the Bible is not a book of physical science" and, when speaking of "physical subjects" Scripture "adapted to common apprehensions" of those subjects. Yet it was not a book about moral matters only, for the creation and flood were physical events. "Why should any one refuse to attend to a history of these two stupendous events, merely because that history professes to

have proceeded from the same author as the work itself[?]" When pushed far enough back to "the beginnings of time," geology became history, reliant on the testimony of the Divine Author, the only eyewitness present. The one point, Silliman acknowledged, where his view "differs from the common understanding of the Mosaic account of the creation [not from the account itself, he carefully stated] is, not in the order of the events, but in the amount of time, which they are supposed to have occupied before the creation of man." Implied here was his day/age view of Genesis 1.[409]

He may have sounded impatient and irritated when speaking to Spring because he knew his scientific judgment was no longer immediately accepted, as it had been twenty or thirty years earlier. When Silliman lectured in Boston in 1835–1836, most Americans were uninformed about science; they eagerly listened to the tall, handsome professor with the melodious voice. His five-foot-square drawings appealed; his mineral samples aroused curiosity; his chemical experiments flashed, bubbled, and burned on cue; so his *"philosophy of geology"* reconciling "works and words" was accepted without question. He recalled, "The Orthodox and Unitarian influence was united in my favor. . . . These deductions of natural theology were out of the bounds of politics, and were equally acceptable to the wise and good of all religious denominations."[410] When he spoke at Yale in August 1850, a young colleague (James Hadley, professor of Greek) critiqued his speech as "the usual lurry about 'words and works' with the usual shadiness about the reconciling exegesis."[411] A better-informed generation was harder to satisfy.

Even in middle-way Yale, Silliman encountered sarcasm. By 1850, New Haven Theology was divided on science. Nathaniel W. Taylor rejected it as a threat to faith. Yale's tradition of natural theology, of Dwight's science as apologetics, demanded ongoing engagement with it. The day after Silliman spoke, Leonard Bacon sermonized for science and against Taylor, to impress the American Association for the Advancement of Science that was meeting in New Haven—or so Hadley implied. Hadley did not accept Bacon's view "that, though the Sacred Scriptures are infallible, our interpretation is fallible and must be modified to answer the demands of science." Not so, Hadley commented (to his diary), only the science of critical exegesis could modify our interpretation of Scripture, not "astronomy, geology, physiology, etc. . . . Every tub on its own bottom. If Moses calls a thing black, the fact of its being white does not prove that he meant white when he said black." Linguist Hadley focused on ascertaining what Moses actually called it. Analyze the Hebrew word for "day"—not the age of rocks—to ascertain its meaning in Genesis.[412]

Bacon, Silliman, and their fellow New Haven believers in the perfect compatibility of science and religion were a bit naive. Bacon may have been bluffing when he offered to change his scriptural interpretation "to answer the demands of science." He probably believed future science would not be too demanding. Yet even American scientists would, at some point, finish collecting and begin speculating, especially as they narrowed their focus and specialized. And theories hostile to the Genesis account could come from Europe. Geological evidence of a "succession of ages" could always be reconciled to Genesis through the day/age theory. The study of rocks was never going to disprove the Mosaic account of humanity's origins, but there was more to science than geology. Uniformitarianism could be applied to biology. In 1844, the *Vestiges of the Natural History of Creation* (anonymous, but written by Robert Chambers of Edinburgh) argued for the inheritance of acquired characteristics and a gradual development of species. Critics, including James Dwight Dana in Silliman's *Journal,* pointed to its many factual errors, but a better-informed advocate of the idea might come along.[413] A day/age theory would have more difficulty answering a theory that claimed an alternate explanation for the origins of the human species.

BLUFFS AT TREMPEALEAU, WISCONSIN *by Edwin Whitefield, lithograph from watercolor, 1859. Adventurous excursionists climbed the bluff at Monteville, Wisconsin, later named Trempealeau. (Minnesota Historical Society)*

CHAPTER SIX

"Bluffs like Gigantic Sentinels"

WEDNESDAY, JUNE 7, 1854

SNOW FELL DURING the night. When the big toes awoke or were pulled awake early Wednesday morning, their owners found a cold and rainy day. A strong wind greeted them from the north. "On Wednesday it was awfully cold, windy and wet." In words hardly welcome to river town boosters who hoped eastern newspaper readers would hurry west after the Grand Excursion, one correspondent noted the abrupt change in weather since Monday: "I am informed that these sudden changes are peculiar to the Mississippi in this latitude until about the 15th June."[414]

Peculiar western weather was hardly welcome to eastern bachelors, unaccustomed to sleeping with their clothes on, with a mattress or carpetbag for a bed, and in damp, cold air to boot. Combined with Mississippi drinking water, to which their digestive systems were unaccustomed, these conditions "produced much sickness on board." Two sick bachelors on the *War Eagle* "receive the sympathy of the ladies," for there was "no doctor on board who owns a diploma," although there were some "fifty self-made physicians" ready with free advice. Pitying the sick men, "the kind ladies prepare them beds upon the sofas in the cabin," which moved a *New York Times* reporter to "wish I had been sick myself, that I might have shared the attention which they got."[415] (Female attention must not have been peculiar to sick bachelors only.)

Yet this amazing scenery was also peculiar to the Upper Mississippi, or so the eager sightseers believed, and despite the raw fact that "the cold pierced to our bones," travelers hungry for scenery hastened to "the wheelhouse, the hurricane deck, and the cabin promenade" to take a look.[416]

The old fur trade town of Prairie du Chien was the first sight with notable associations—historic more than picturesque ones, for the Wisconsin town was situated, not near the bluff, but on a mile-wide prairie north of the mouth of the Wisconsin River. "It is one of the oldest places on the river," one editor was pleased to report, "having been settled as long ago as 1820." For excursionists who had taken the Grand Tour in Europe that was not so long ago, but it was as ancient a Euro-American history as they were going to find here. "The little houses with their steep roofs and fantastic architecture, give unmistakeable evidence of their French origin, and it is really quite refreshing to see some of them growing old and toppling into decay, for not often in the west does one see a house that appears to have been finished more than a week ago." Prairie du Chien offered more recent history: the late President Zachary Taylor, then a colonel, commanded Fort Crawford. Jefferson Davis, now President Franklin Pierce's secretary of war but then a lieutenant under Taylor's command, served there. He met and fell in love with Taylor's daughter Sarah, much against Taylor's wishes. So the fort had romantic associations too.[417]

Only twenty-five years old, Fort Crawford was a simple rectangle of connected white limestone buildings (some two-story, some one-story) with a parade ground in the center. It was located close to a good landing.[418] The sight of the fort's white buildings overlooking such a "quiet scene [so] peacefully" led the editor to pronounce a benediction on the fort: "May their deep throated cannon in the black port holes never belch their sullen roar to a more hostile flotilla than the one which now swims so gracefully past."[419]

The order of the boats as this flotilla steamed upriver was as follows: *Galena, Lady Franklin, Golden Era, Sparhawk,* and the *War Eagle* last in line, not due to the editor's denigration of war, but (in vain) to prevent the speediest vessel from pushing so far ahead of her companions.[420]

Their next noteworthy sight was a battlefield, that of Bad Axe, at the mouth of Bad Axe River. John Munn was in the pilothouse on the top deck of the *Lady Franklin* when the "gentlemanly and communicative" pilot pointed out Bad Axe Bluff. Here, on August 5, 1832, soldiers on the steamboat *Warrior* and on land, General Henry Atkinson commanding, battled Black Hawk and his Sac warriors. The battle turned into a massacre in which

Sac women and children were shot on the river islands, on the east bank, and in the river itself as they attempted to swim across to the west bank. A Dakota band then killed many Sac survivors. Colonel Taylor led U.S. regular army soldiers onboard the *Warrior* during this, the last battle of the Black Hawk War. In his report, written from Fort Crawford four days later, Atkinson noted, "A great advantage was derived from the presence of the steamboat, on this occasion, as it retarded the enemy in crossing the river."[421]

Around nine o'clock, the peaceful flotilla passed a camp of about two dozen Indians, the first the excursionists saw on their trip upriver. The Indians (no one seemed to know which tribe they represented) watched the steamboats pass. Their camp was on a low-lying level spot near the river. "They had their bark wig-wams, a few dogs, guns, and dug-out canoes," reported Moore of Springfield. "They were all standing outside in the wet grass, with their blankets thrown above their heads, and falling near the ground." Apart from the blankets, they appeared to have no clothing. A few shelters consisted of animal skins held up by four sticks. There were a few canvas tents. But the strange sight of five crowded steamboats had drawn them out of all shelters. "The rain was coming down in torrents" and the northeast wind blew strong and cold.[422]

The Indians' exposure to the harsh elements aroused pity and compassion in the excursionists, protected by roofs and warm greatcoats. Isaac Platt of the *Poughkeepsie Eagle* thought they "look[ed] the very picture of melancholy and desolation," and "seemed to feel the weight of despair upon them," for "they had nothing to do but await their impending fate" while the excursionists "could rejoice and boast of our progress." Moved (temporarily) to repent of westward expansion, William Schouler of Cincinnati remarked, "[T]here they stood by the banks of their own great river, expatriated, forlorn, miserable; aliens in their own country, and the victims of an inexorable cupidity, which we are pleased to call by the softer name of destiny." Moved even to tears, the *New York Post's* Andrew Aiken told one of his fellow passengers "that they must suffer beyond comparison," only to hear the response, "Oh, they are as well satisfied with their lot as you with yours." Aiken did not think so.

Yet, in the end, tears and pity seemed mainly to supply a romantic association to the passing scenery. Henry Farnam told several passengers on the *Golden Era* that they would see more Indians and that he hoped "to take on board a few of them for a sail up and down the river." As the boats passed, the Indians stared at them silently. The excursionists "gave them three cheers as we passed, which was answered by a wave of the hand, and deafening peals of—silence." Moore described the Indians "look[ing] on as unmoved as statues" after the whites' "loud cheer." Whichever Indian nation they represented, and whatever their legal status vis-à-vis the white government and white settlers, they did not choose to join in celebrating the rail union of the Atlantic and the Mississippi.

The tourists returned to their various activities, which the sudden, unexpected meeting with Native Americans had interrupted. Some played whist; some individuals read books. Young singles flirted. "The girls, notwithstanding the scowling elements outside, were happy and delicious within, and the boys were as busy as bees among the flowers." Having long ago taken care of their matrimonial needs, older men discussed the churches' needs and controversies, or those of the nation. James Woodward of the *New Haven Morning Journal & Courier* assured his readers that "among such a party . . . political questions have been somewhat discussed," especially the Kansas-Nebraska Act, on which he found "a unanimous sentiment of opposition." So there was talk of "Bill Nebraska" and Stephen A. Douglas, not in flattering terms. "Not one word could we hear for Douglas," observed the Whig Moore (hardly an unbiased observer). "If he had set himself ahead on the Pacific railway project, in room of his Nebraska business," he would have won favor among this railroad-investing crowd. However, excursionists were divided, Woodward reported, over "whether old party associations should be given up, and a new organization effected" or whether the Whig party was still a useful vehicle for anti-Nebraska men. The cold weather drew them all close together but not into a new party, not all of them at least.[423]

On the *War Eagle,* Benjamin Silliman noted "a temperature so low that a fire in the stove was highly acceptable and drew our party into more intimate communication around the focus of heat." Indoor activities better acquainted them with each other; fellow passengers became the scenery for a time.[424]

On the *Lady Franklin,* Charles Sedgwick stayed indoors, warmly dressed in a "flannel waistcoat & my overcoat & am sitting now by the stove." Grousing over the "heavy nasty" bed coverings in the staterooms, he also complained of the fickle weather: "unfortunately the weather which was hot yesterday has changed and there is a cold north easter & rain all night & all day so far which threatens to last. That cuts us off from the sight of a great deal of beauty & from occupied landing[s] on interesting points of the River," he wrote to the folks back home; "nevertheless we have enjoyed a great deal & the beauty of the scenery far surpasses anything I had anticipated."[425]

On the *Sparhawk,* a male frolic erupted, a satirical dance, "a quadrille, dancing wholly by gentlemen in which the *ladies* are distinguished by having cigars in their mouths."[426]

On the *Galena,* Illinois governor Joel Matteson and two Ottawans conversed with editor Josiah Harris of Cleveland. They spoke admiringly of their role in promoting the Chicago & Rock Island Railroad, Matteson claiming to have overcome Chicago opposition to starting the new railroad by promising to build the first forty miles himself in ten months, a feat he said he accomplished. He would take only C&RI stock in payment, he boasted, to show his confidence in the venture. A Whig, Harris was delighted to find a Democratic politician who supported internal

improvements and entrepreneurial progress. "Though not a speech maker," Harris admitted, Matteson "has won and retains great popularity with the people of all parties" (the source for this information must have been Matteson or the two Ottawa Democrats). The governor, "estimable lady [Mary] and daughter [Lydia] have been the life of the social circle and participants in the merry dances on the *Galena.*"[427]

On all the boats, some tourists stayed out on the deck to watch the scenery despite the discomforts of wind, cold, and rain. Editor Daniel Wager of Rome anthropomorphized "the envious bluffs" that tried to hide other scenery and even "approach closely" at some points "and frown savagely at each other across the still water." He noticed a shy duck floating near the boat "until alarmed by the sonorous clank of our engine," when "he hurriedly dashes from the water, and stretching out his long neck sails gracefully away." At another spot, a "tall crane, stalking about in the long grass of the shallows, eyes us languidly as we pass." The crane too did not seem to appreciate the significance of this rail-made union of Atlantic and Mississippi: he did not comprehend "the fact that if he was shot and bagged, his slender legs and delicate body could be transported to the Atlantic Ocean in forty-eight hours, and . . . served up hot at Delmonico's before his mate had noticed his absence."[428]

Around one o'clock, they stopped at La Crosse.[429] Like Prairie du Chien, it was situated "on an extensive prairie" of some thirteen square miles and was still often called Prairie la Crosse. High on a five-hundred-foot bluff some two-and-a-half miles east of the river stood "a large wooden cross." Yet that was not the origin of the town's name, which derived from the Indian game of lacrosse: the prairie here made an ideal site for playing this game. Founded in 1841 as a fur trading post, the town's main economic hopes in 1854 were lumber milling and waiting for a railroad. (The prairie site, forty feet above the river and rarely flooded, was good for buildings and steamboat landings, but Galena dominated the steamboat business and would resist any La Crosse competition.) Entering the Mississippi a mile north of town, the Black River drained an extensive hinterland of excellent pine timber. Logs were floated down to La Crosse, sawed into lumber, loaded on flatboats, and transported to the St. Louis market. Logging, retailing, farming, and other economic activities supported a population of 745, and that was before the railroad from Milwaukee neared the town. La Crosse hoped to supplant Galena as the main supplier to the Minnesota frontier once the railroad came. Boosterism ran high. A jest laughed off Chicago's progress: "Getting to be considerable of a village, but it has one drawback,—it is almost too far away from La Crosse."[430]

A crowd awaited them at the landing, near Front Street, "a wagon road running parallel with the river, the banks of which were high and irregular," but two narrow landing spots existed "at the foot of State Street and Pearl Street," and storekeeper John Levy's dock stood at the foot of Pearl Street. One dock was made of small willow trees, each a dozen feet long, with a hundred tied together in each one-foot-thick bundle. The bundles "are so ingeniously arranged and woven together, that it is impossible for the sand to work out or the water in." They were placed on "an inclined plane, so that steamboats can land at high or low water." The willows would "sprout and grow," reportedly, to make a living dock.[431]

Between river's edge and road, a disembarking passenger had to climb twenty-five feet to Front Street, up a steep rise and across hillocks of drifting sand. "Street" was a somewhat honorific title: platted on maps, these paths "were made of sand, and sand burrs thrived in goodly manner." La Crosse was building and booming: steamboats disembarking immigrants; "teams carting freight, lumber and stone in every direction"; "stores, dwellings and mills in process of erection on every street, with the everlasting pounding and noise of the carpenter's tools fencing yards and lots." The ferryboat *Wild Kate* hauled settlers across the river to Minnesota Territory. On Wednesday, June 7, however, with rain and Grand Excursion excitement, *Wild Kate* was probably not competing with the flotilla for attention, and carpenters were likely at the landing, in a crowd standing on the twenty-five-foot rise, with horse-drawn teams temporarily parked nearby.[432]

Excursionists onboard and westerners on shore eyed each other, and the La Crosse crowd called for Millard Fillmore. One "denizen" of the place "call[ed] out at the top of his voice that if the elephant did not make his appearance at the command of the Sovereigns, *he* would never vote for the 'old feller' again." That brought loud laughter. Then "the ex President appeared on the guards of the Golden Era, and returned his usual address of thanks," which with "his winning smile . . . drew down upon him the cheers of the crowd."[433]

Some travelers, however, were in no mood to cheer a speech they had heard a dozen times already. They were pleased when Stephen Goodwin followed up with "a most capital speech" that satirized "all the 'big bugs' on the other boats, who only talked about 'the last link,' 'the iron bands,' 'Atlantic and Mississippi,' 'the Pacific Railroad,' &c, &c."[434]

Charles A. Dana reported that a dozen excursionists decided to climb the bluffs here (an "optical illusion" led visitors to think these were half a mile from the river when they were two-and-a-half miles away). A "tedious and tiresome ascent it was," he reported. The bluff looked "like a cleft sugar-loaf, with its flat side toward the river," and the summit "was not more than fifteen feet wide . . . covered with grass." From the summit, "the eye swept to the horizon on both sides of the river over a panorama that only superlatives could describe."[435]

(Dana's, and Horace Greeley's, *New York Tribune* had forty subscribers in La Crosse in 1854. While they may have been pleased by Dana's panoramic superlatives, they were outraged by his description of their town as "a wooding place" with only "two or three frame houses." They fired off two angry letters to the editor assuring Greeley that La Crosse was not a wooding place, had far more than three houses, and had been visited by the excursion—but its bluffs decidedly had not been. Printing the letters constituted Greeley and Dana's apology for what was evidently the editor's mistake. It is unclear where Dana's party ascended the fifteen-foot-wide bluff.)[436]

Two La Crosse leaders boarded the boats: Cyrus K. Lord, a Democratic lawyer from Maine and register of the U.S. Land Office by the grace of President Pierce; and John S. Simonton, a co-owner of the town's first sawmill. Lord and his partner, the land office receiver, were buying out the *La Crosse Democrat* and starting the more ambitiously named *National Democrat.* His land office post benefited Lord's law business; land dealers' and lawyers' advertisements were sure to benefit the register and receiver's new paper; and a trip with forty editors was sure to benefit the neophyte publisher.[437]

Headed back upriver, the flotilla threaded its way through the islands north of La Crosse and into a broad, two-mile-wide stretch. As they progressed northward, throughout the day they "met several immense rafts [of logs], some guided by five or six men each," who ate and slept "for weeks" on the rafts. "They cheered our boats, swung their hats, and one of them, for the want of a piece of artillery, fired his rifle several times in the way of a salute."[438] These rafts were coming down from the Black and Chippewa Rivers.

Some of the many rafts they encountered on the river were larger ones, of sawed lumber, not logs. One editor described these rafts as "no small affair." A crew of twenty was needed for "the largest class, which often contain 200,000 feet of lumber. One that we examined was made up of inch boards, laid one upon the other, with great regularity," in eighteen layers, "and these layers lashed together over a surface of about 30 by 200 feet." The lumber on this raft "was worth $30,000," or so he was told. It was bound for a market in the South.[439]

Onboard the *Sparhawk,* the men held a mock trial.[440] Cincinnati editor William Schouler stood accused of assault and battery for falling through the slats of his berth in "state room No. 4" onto Dr. Robert Campbell, who occupied the bunk beneath him. The Pittsfield medical doctor, railroad director, and jack-of-all-trades had appeared that morning "with a scar upon his face." The Sparhawkians declined to indulge in vigilante justice. They arrested Schouler and drew up an indictment in the name of "Sparhawk county, in the State of Upper Mississippi River."[441] It charged Schouler with "beating, bruising and maiming him (the said complainant) in a manner to endanger his life, and all against the peace and dignity of the steamer Sparhawk." Antebellum lawyers, especially on the western circuits, held mock trials to spoof their profession, vent their frustrations with judges' rulings, and bond with each other in the male legal fraternity. In this trial, journalists and non-lawyers took the lead in what was also an eastern spoof on the rough and

ready West. William C. Prime (Edward's brother) of the *New York Journal of Commerce* served as prosecutor; Moses Kimball represented the defendant. Author and journalist William H. Bogart presided as judge.

The tradition in mock trials was to break all the normal rules in trying a ridiculous indictment, to make satirical speeches, and to allow the jury to sentence the defendant to an equally absurd penalty.

A crier opened the proceedings. Bogart attempted to call jurors. The first man he called was not present. That led to convoluted citing of cases and precedents, as Prime maintained that the accused had no right to confront the jury—and therefore the juror's absence was no problem. Bogart sustained Prime "and cited and read various authorities . . . to show that" when an impaneled juror was "absent from the court, he should nevertheless be deemed to be present, and an empty chair should represent him." That problem resolved, Bogart then instructed the five jurors (present or absent) that, in carrying out the court's duty, they should use "no other weapons but those of Mercy and Justice." While he gave this charge, he lay "upon the table before him an enormous pair of duelling pistols, and a bowie knife eighteen inches long." Thereupon, it turned out that both Kimball and Prime were similarly armed. They surrendered their weapons, "a double-barrelled rifle and a bowie-knife of portentous dimensions."

From time to time, the "Sheriff" replenished the court's supply of bottles filled with some liquid refreshment.

The "legal" reference works consulted during the trial included Senator Thomas Hart Benton's *Thirty Years,* a memoir of his lengthy career in Washington, and "Grace Greenwood's Works and the Dodd Family Abroad."

Prime gave "an able opening speech which made the hair of the auditors stand on end with horror" at the atrocity. Schouler "was visibly affected and covering his face with his hands appeared to weep as a bad boy at school."

The "witnesses" to the "felonious assault" then testified "with infinite humor." Campbell testified first, with a brown piece of paper covering his wound. Others confirmed his account. Attorney Kimball cross-examined each witness, but his client kept interrupting with "innocent corrections of witnesses" that effectively undercut Kimball's otherwise successful efforts to trip up prosecution witnesses. Schouler "thereby restor[ed] the force of their testimony against him, excited continual quarrels between himself and his counsel, who threatened to desert him" if he continued.

By this point, two hours had passed and the jurors cried for an end, "and some of the ladies thought the weather was beginning to clear up and were anxious to go on deck."

Still, Kimball gave a forty-five-minute closing speech, which was deemed "a very fine and eloquent burlesque." He ended by suddenly turning to Schouler in the defendant's box and announcing, "But if, my poor young friend, you are to be hung, and I confess I think this Court and jury intend to hang you, and I don't know but you deserve it, I beg you to console yourself on the gallows, with the reflection that it won't hurt you at all the next day, and that's the only consolation I can imagine that is fitted to a man like you."

Both Prime and Kimball bribed the jury. Then the court adjourned until the following day, when the jury was to issue its verdict.

While the trial dragged on, passengers on the other boats also amused away a rainy afternoon. On the *Lady Franklin* after dinner, tablecloths were taken off, Charles Sedgwick was elected chair, and "toasts and speech making" commenced. Sedgwick gave the opening one in praise of the Mississippi's beauty "and the increasing growth and prosperity of the illimitable West." He "proposed" that the excursionists "make an inscription legible from the River suitable to [their] sentiments & fit for one of the eternal monuments of Rock that crown the summits" of the bluffs. It should read: "Glory to God in the Highest on Earth Peace & good will to men."[442]

Various men were asked to reply to various toasts: Stephen Goodwin, to a toast to the Empire State; E. Church Blackburn of St. Louis, to a toast complimenting the "'Great West'"; Frank Blair, to a toast to the press.[443]

Blair objected "that there must be some mistake in calling upon him"; his father had edited a newspaper; he did not belong to the editorial "fraternity." They must have confused his name with his father's, Blair Sr., who was traveling on the *Galena* with Mississippi & Missouri Railroad owner John A. Dix. Preston Blair had sold his interest in the *Congressional Globe* nearly ten years earlier, after President

James Polk made it clear he wanted a supporter of his expansionist policies to edit the Democrats' chief organ in the capital. Part of Andrew Jackson's kitchen cabinet, Preston Blair turned against the pro-slavery expansionism of Jackson's successors, who had unseated him from the *Globe*. Frank Blair had briefly co-owned and helped edit the *Barnburner,* a St. Louis free-soil newspaper, in 1848; in 1854 he was part owner of the *Missouri Democrat.* His disclaimer of any journalistic experience was somewhat disingenuous.[444]

"Never mind, no excuses, go on, go on," Sedgwick interrupted, "you have read your father's paper and are therefore well qualified to make a speech, so go ahead."

"If," said Mr. Blair, "I must speak, I will speak as a western man, of western things; and as a chief ornament of our state, the West and the nation, I will refer for a minute to the Great Missourian—'Old Bullion'—known to you as Thomas H. Benton."

A Hard-Shell Democrat from New York State who sat "near the head of the table" then called for three cheers for Benton, which were given enthusiastically.

Frank Blair cast his lot with the West by moving to St. Louis from the family homes in Maryland and on Pennsylvania Avenue. Ex-senator Benton (called Old Bullion for his fervent support for hard currency) was Blair's political mentor and was then engaged in a bitter election battle against pro-slavery Know-Nothings angered at his opposition to the Kansas-Nebraska Act.[445] Frank Blair could not stay away from the topic of the day.

Father and son spent "most of their time" on the excursion talking politics, specifically, trying to convince anti-slavery Democrats to join the anti-Nebraska coalition that was rapidly forming. For the Blairs, who had supported Pierce in 1852, the act was the last straw, the final error by doughface or pro-slavery Democrats, the final indication that "Pierce would use Blair's talents in any way possible, but had never intended to accept his advice on anything" (Blair Sr. had advised the president not to support Douglas's act).[446]

Picking up on Goodwin's comment on the Northwest Ordinance of 1787, which prohibited slavery in lands north of the Ohio River and east of the Mississippi, Frank Blair stated that, although he was raised in slave-owning Maryland and lived in the slave state of Missouri, "yet he regretted from the bottom of his heart, that the great territory which stretched far to the westward" of the river they were following "could not in consequence of the Nebraska bill, come into the Union as free from the taint of slavery as was intended" by the founders who wrote the great Ordinance.[447]

Catharine Sedgwick reacted enthusiastically, "by clapping of her hands, waving of her handkerchief, and other signs of approval." She was also pleased that her ailing brother presided so winsomely over the meeting.[448] She had spent a lifetime reconciling herself to the Jacksonian democracy her Federalist father would have abhorred; the main barrier to full reconciliation was the slavery issue; to hear the son of Jackson's close friend attack slavery was to see the removal of that last barrier. It was also a good omen indicating that a strong anti-Nebraska coalition was a real possibility, and anti-slavery Whigs on the *Lady Franklin* likely noted it.

The Baptist editor, Sewell Cutting, reported that Frank Blair's praise of Benton and attack on Kansas-Nebraska was greeted by such "warm applause" that "it was difficult to restrain the cheers within the limits of decorum." On this rainy day or at another time, Cutting met Blair, talked with him, and was impressed by him. He found "in him a man who, though born in the midst of slavery and himself a slaveholder, holds unflinchingly the sentiments on the subject of slavery which distinguished Washington and Jefferson."[449] That is, the sentiment that slavery should not expand but should be allowed to die out slowly in the southern states where it existed.

By this time, the slower boats were approaching the Black River, whose delta deposited peninsulas and islands in the Mississippi and narrowed its channel. Past the delta, four boats (apparently not the *War Eagle*) stopped to wood up at Monteville (Trempealeau), Wisconsin. Cords of firewood cut for use in the fireboxes were stacked along the shore. The crews loaded it on the vessels while passengers disembarked to look around. The "rain had abated" and they took advantage of the break in the weather to escape their onboard confinement.[450]

Nearby stood a two-room log building. James Babcock of the *New Haven Palladium* described it: "Over the door is written, on a log, the words 'Post Office.' Two girls stand on the steps, and a woman, with a true Yankee face, sits at the window. She was from New Hampshire," he discovered, and (naturally, being from New England) was "quite intelligent and communicative." The postmaster was her husband, "a Massachusetts man," who "invited us to ascend the mountain, back of his house, and see the extensive prairie beyond."[451]

Some half-dozen excursionists—including Babcock, Charles B. Lines of New Haven, and Charles Hale—took him up on his offer. John Munn noted that "our adventurous passengers ascended"; he was surprised and almost apologetic that he was not among them: "[I] lost my enthusiasm." The postmaster led the way. The ascent was fairly steep, but the hillside "was thickly strewed with pretty wild flowers" blooming in early June. After much effort, they were at the top of a bluff they estimated as five hundred feet above the river.[452]

A "glorious view" greeted them, Hale discovered, with "the whole country for miles around laid out at your feet like a map. You can trace the broad current of the Mississippi above and below, as it winds along"—and can distinguish the byways and side channels from the main one. Looking east, they saw "a rolling prairie ten miles across, with a few enclosures of cultivated land, looking like garden plots, and one road track stretching across on which a few pigmy men and horses were traveling." Across the prairie was the wooded lowland of the Black River delta, and the wooded bluffs that towered over it. "The steam-boats beneath us appeared like toys and the brawny crew like ants as they busily loaded them with wood."[453]

Babcock looked down at their fellow excursionists, many of whom had seen and heard the climbers shout at them from the summit and were following their example. "Passengers are scattered about the shore, and winding their way up the mountain. Some are hunting wild flowers." Miss Williams, daughter of whaling-ship owner, banker, and railroad promoter Charles P. Williams of Stonington, Connecticut, rode a pony "back and forth to the amusement of the company" below. Far above, looking at "her red shawl, with uncovered head," Babcock could almost "imagine her to be some fair Indian maiden" riding horseback with abandon.[454]

Babcock and others offered to pay the farmer-postmaster "for his trouble in piloting us up the mountain." He adamantly declined any compensation, "saying he would willingly pay fifty dollars if every man and woman in the boats would come up and see what a country was lying around him."[455]

As if they heard his invitation, "Hundreds" of excursionists (perhaps an exaggeration) now trekked up the steep slope, as the few pioneer climbers descended. The newcomers included a young lady and Edward Prime, who "overtook" her "near the summit." Observers noted "the rich bloom which the exertion brought to her cheek," but Hale obeyed "that well founded decorum which leads journals conducted with good taste not to put ladies' names into print." He simply

called her "Countess Montoville." Prime did not obey any such rule, but stated that Margaret Bogart's ["Miss Maggie B."] "courage and perseverance, and enthusiastic love of nature, as tested by this exploit, deserve a memorial"—in this case, mention in the *New York Observer*.[456]

From the summit, Prime could see the Mississippi Valley, dotted with islands and castlelike bluffs, and also the ten-mile-wide prairie that Hale reported. It was "covered with the most beautiful verdure, unbroken by a single tree. . . . As we stood gazing down upon it from our elevation, we saw in the distance crossing the prairie an ox-team preceded by three men, but all looking like the merest pigmies."[457]

Suddenly, Prime heard "the tolling of the bells of our several steamers, and the scream of the whistles [that] made it necessary for us to descend with some rapidity." The later climbers had to cut short their look at the glorious view and return for imminent departure. Many brought down wildflowers with which to decorate their staterooms. Someone gave a few flowers to Catharine Sedgwick, who had not been so ambitious as to climb the bluff.[458]

The two-hundred-pound Judge Jeffrey Orson Phelps of Simsbury had found a less strenuous way to use the postmaster's services. At 2:00 p.m., he wrote a letter to his wife describing the trip so far: "we move slow—as there is speeches made at every village—the villages some times consist of two log houses & are 10 or 15 miles a part . . . this forenoon has rained very hard & is very cold . . . every moment from Rising till 12 at night is like 4th of July—Cotillions were danced Last evening composed of one person only from a State." As for the "Table, the Astor House don't sett as Good." As for the politics, "Mr. Fillmore is speaking while I am writing," and here he had to end "In good health & great Haste" (the boat must have been about to leave). Phelps paid the postmaster three cents postage.[459]

But a delaying incident occurred at river's edge.[460] Three Dakota men and one woman came out of the woods to see the excursionists and apparently to request alcohol. The men "were dressed in blue coats with brass buttons, carried rifles" on their shoulders, and each had a gray blanket wrapped around him. Their faces were daubed with war paint. Whites believed them to be Dakota spies sent to Winnebago territory. Governor Matteson invited them to come onboard, which they did. "They were led to Mr. Fillmore, and through an interpreter, had a talk with the Ex-Father."

Eastern excursionists and western Indians were unsure of each other and uncertain of what constituted good manners. One Dakota man had a pipe of some kind in his belt, which he took out and lit, "and very complacently began puffing his smoke into the faces of the ladies." Moore was surprised that the men seemed unimpressed by the well-dressed ladies and by "the glisten and glare of our costly trappings." The Dakota men were given "cake, candy, cigars . . . and liquor."

The Dakota woman also went onboard,

into the ladies' cabin. "The crowd of passengers press close around her," Babcock reported, "and she grows timid. She drops to her knees and creeps along among the gentlemen until she gets to the plank" that stretched between deck and shore. She hurries ashore, "where, rolled in her blanket, she stretches herself at length."

Meanwhile, the Dakota men were also leaving the boats. As one walked across the plank to the shore, he dropped "his whiskey flask in the drink." Feeling sorry for him (he "looked disconsolate") some excursionists threw dimes, quarters, and sugarplums to him. He gingerly gathered them up as the woman and the other Dakota men looked on. Some travelers regretted that others threw these "contributions," which would undoubtedly encourage him to buy more whiskey and so complete the process of corruption that white liquor dealers had already begun.

On the *War Eagle,* which had surged far ahead of the other boats and which did not stop at Trempealeau, an afternoon meeting was held, and speeches were made by Samuel J. Tilden, Reverend Gardiner Spring, George Bancroft, Silliman, and others. The focus was not on current politics but on a resolution of thanks to the C&RI Railroad and to the *War Eagle* crew "for their marked kindness and courtesy . . . and for their thoughtful attention to our wants and comforts"—not for their superior speed.[461]

Silliman chaired the meeting and also lectured for a half hour "on the geology of the Mississippi mountains."[462] This was spontaneous at his fellow travelers' request as they "pass[ed] through scenery of great grandeur and beauty." He had to do without his usual exhibits and experiments. Passing scenery substituted for his lecture pictures. "I took occasion to explain upon geological principles the peculiarities of the features of the country," he noted. "On both sides of the river there were frequent cliffs of limestone and sandstone arranged horizontally & made conspicuous as regards their arrangement by the denudation of their fronts." Silliman estimated their height to be from "several hundred feet" to "800 in some instances." Cliffs "were separated by valleys of denudation, which often wound away into the country & were united to other valleys." He deduced, "The strata in the different hills were evidently once united & in the view of the whole scene it appeared highly probable that they were originally united across the valley which is now the bed of the Mississippi at a period anterior to the formation of its channel." He did not assign a date to this period or say if it was "anterior to" dates commonly cited for the Genesis account. "I explained the geological powers by which these effects were produced and added an outline sketch . . . and I received warm thanks for the effort."[463]

(Silliman's "interview" with Spring may have occurred after this lecture, as a result of Spring's objections to the implications of Silliman's remarks.)

Far behind the *War Eagle,* the *Galena* stopped on the Minnesota shore, at a small embryonic settlement called Mount Vernon,

to pick up more firewood and to drop off a mailbag.[464] Here Stephen M. Burns operated a store, a post office, and a sizable business employing "a large number of men cutting steamboat wood on government lands." The large number of men were not present but the wood was, and one Minnesotan—probably Burns himself—stood on the woodpile to greet them. The man agreed to sell the wood for $2.25 per cord and the loading of wood began.

Reverend Duncan Kennedy decided to have a little fun with this westerner and with politicians. In appreciation of this one-man welcoming committee, he climbed up on the wheelhouse to speak to the Minnesotan. "Friends and fellow citizens, this demonstration was wholly unexpected to me. . . . It quite overwhelms me with gratitude."

"Gentlemen, I trust you will believe me, when I tell you, that I came here as a private individual, without reference to the distinguished post which I have occupied in the Government of my country, and that I did not expect to be called upon to address you." Nevertheless, he was grateful for this "enthusiastic reception," the first ever given him in Minnesota Territory, and he could not put his gratitude into adequate words. Minnesota "is a great country. This is a mighty river, and the bluffs like gigantic sentinels keep watch and ward upon its shores." No other part of the Union, "of the universal Yankee nation," nowhere that "the great American eagle flew," could at all compare to this place.

The lone man "stood with open mouth

gazing on the crowd in perfect wonder."

Kennedy announced his campaign for the presidency and commenced to angle for votes. "I intend, gentlemen, to remove all the snags from the Mississippi, to construct railroads from city to city, from town to town, from village to village, throughout the Union, and to insure to every man the greatest reward for the least labor." Those who supported his campaign would indeed get the least labor and greatest reward: a government job. "Give me all your votes, and in return I will bestow upon you, fellow citizens, all the offices."

That promise brought a shout from the excursionists. And that seemed to awaken the Minnesotan "from the stupor into which he had been thrown by the harangue of the Doctor."

"Gentlemen, as a private citizen, I bid you farewell."

The passengers roared with laughter and applauded loudly.

"The boat slowly moved from the shore as the Minnesotian extended his arm towards the speaker, and exclaimed in very decided tones, 'Hold on, old feller, come up here next year and I'll show you more nor one house in this 'ere place.'"

On the *Lady Franklin,* John Munn won the friendship of Catharine and Charles Sedgwick with his proper appreciation of the grand scenery. Catharine Sedgwick informed him that these bluffs looked like castles or forts that she had seen in Europe. "Miss S. thinks me quite enthusiastic," Munn noted in his diary, "and has become as well as her

brother very social with me, enjoying with me the glorious scenes we have passed this day." Properly enjoying scenery was a mark of genteel status, which the Sedgwicks bestowed on the former Hartford store clerk that day. Munn showed himself not to be one of the vulgar people they had feared might ruin the trip.[465]

A few miles past Mount Vernon and the nearby village of Winona, Munn (and probably the Sedgwicks) looked up to the summit of a bluff on the Minnesota side and saw "the modest home of some new settler, with a love for the picturesque and beautiful beyond others. His Dwelling, Barn & other buildings were there to the eye." The group "looked upon it with pleasure as it seemed the only spot where art had stepped in to improve the scene." As the *Lady Franklin* moved upstream and cut the distance between them and the bluff-top farm, "we exclaimed with surprise our self deception." What had seemed to be man-made buildings "were massive rocks detached & occupying a position to render the illusion complete."[466]

The scenery's grandeur had only partially had what should have been its morally uplifting effect on the Walkers. Munn duly admitted, "The selfishness of our Utica clique has somewhat thawed under the influence of the scenery witnessed this day." Yet the improvement could not erase the memory of their "contemptible" behavior, and only the parents had "thawed." The daughters were still ruining their reputations with "flirtations & other modern modes of passing time among would be fashionables," in Munn's opinion. They had followers, now, a "train [of] several upstarts" who were exhibiting their moral deficiencies by ignoring the scenery ("natures grandest work"). They flirted, paraded, and showed off instead. They drew attention to themselves instead of paying attention to works of nature much greater than themselves.[467]

As the afternoon wore on, the weather cleared. Shortly after four o'clock, "the sun came out in all his glory." The *War Eagle* was first to snake through the narrow channel—created by the Chippewa River, which deposited silt and sand and formed its own delta—and into Lake Pepin, which it reached "just before sunset." Lake Pepin was a reservoir of sorts, about thirty miles long and four miles wide, created by the partial damming effect of the Chippewa delta.[468]

The tourists were delighted with Lake Pepin, for there were no islands to block the view and they could "view the Father of Waters from bluff to bluff, and behold him in his natural and unshorn glory." Near here, Captain Daniel Smith Harris had named three adjacent bluffs the "Three War Eagles" in honor of his first boat of that name.[469]

Harris took the *War Eagle* a few miles up the lake, until dark, and then landed on the Wisconsin shore below a high bluff to give the other boats, now three hours behind, a chance to catch up. His passengers went on shore under a full moon; many went looking for agates, other stones, and carnelians, a type of reddish quartz with a waxlike luster that could

be used for seals. They found few, "but from the trees on [Pepin's] banks we had the notes of the whip-poor-will, and the breeze . . . laden with the aroma of millions of prairie flowers." They stacked up fallen trees and lit a bonfire, which "blazed up as high as the chimneys of the steamboat, cast a lurid glare upon the dancing waters of the lake, and lit up the rearward forest and the distant bluffs." It burned "for several hours" as the passengers sat on the *War Eagle*'s deck till past midnight, "warming ourselves in its genial rays, and listening to the voices of the forest."[470]

Some returned to the boat and "brought their stones" to Silliman (who acted as a sort of scientific Adam) "to be named and there was much amusement at the marble table" where the specimens were identified.[471]

The *Sparhawk* did not near Lake Pepin until eleven o'clock that night. The moon was out, "and the scene was, if possible, more bold and romantic than ever." So thought C. Cather Flint of the *Chicago Tribune*. He went to the upper deck "to drink in the loveliness of the scene, and remained there, in silent but deep admiration until the shades of night shut out every beauty from our view." (Clouds may have passed between lake and moon.) He "wished for the pencil of a Hogarth to paint that landscape" but recognized the inadequacy of his words.[472]

The captains blew the signal whistle to call the boats to rendezvous. Four boats "near[ed] each other to enter the lake, like chariot horses all abreast. We are now all in a platoon," Babcock reported. "The vessels are made fast amid the cheers of seven or eight hundred passengers." Lashed together, side by side, the *Sparhawk, Golden Era, Lady Franklin,* and *Galena* made one "magnificent floating palace" sailing up the lake. "The remaining part of the night was spent by the companies in visits from one boat to the other, dancing, music, flirtations," reading books, and writing letters—including those obligatory reports from the editors. "Several of the ladies who are promenading past the tables of the editors," Babcock noted, "tell us not to be sparing of *adjectives,* in describing the things of this afternoon and evening. If we follow them, we shall write only 'beautiful'—'wonderful'—'charming,' from the beginning to the end of the letter."[473]

The ladies onboard the *War Eagle* were perhaps not so pleased with the night's voyage, for they could not promenade from one boat to another. When they passed Wisconsin's Maiden Rock, where the maiden Winona had leaped to her death to avoid

a marriage with a man who was not her true love (or so the legend went), these "ladies run from their state-rooms to behold it, and the unmarried [ones] show a moisture beneath their eyelids" (or so a *New York Times* reporter wrote). But perhaps the tears partly resulted from their exclusion from the magnificent floating party going on until the wee hours of the morning so near to them—but without them.[474]

At midnight, on the *Golden Era,* Babcock finished his letter and was ready to turn in. Aboard the *Lady Franklin,* Munn went out on the deck to enjoy the moonlit night while Mary went to bed. Then those still awake were "called to the Cabin" for an evening prayer by Reverend Samuel Osgood, "a venerable old man," a Congregational minister, abolitionist, and keeper of an Underground Railroad station (his house) in Springfield, Massachusetts. Munn pronounced this "a most fitting close of a day of enjoyment granted us by Heaven."[475]

EXCURSUS

George Bancroft and Antebellum American Historians

LITTLE MORE THAN A WEEK after finishing the sixth volume of his *History of the United States from the Discovery of the American Continent* (on May 13, 1854) George Bancroft received a letter from Joseph Sheffield, who reported recent Chicago & Rock Island Railroad earnings and assured him, "You have a *safe, regular* 10 percent investment, with prospects of frequent 'Extras' [dividends]"; and updated him on plans for the Grand Excursion. Bancroft was invited. Sheffield initially hesitated but ultimately included Bancroft's stepson, William Bliss, who was "a considerable holder of our Bonds" and had shown an "early . . . confidence" in the railroad—although not all bondholders were invited.[476]

A major reason that Bancroft could devote nearly full time from 1849 to 1854 to

Historian George Bancroft, ca. 1890.

working toward completion of the first major scholarly history of the United States—and then embark on a one-month trip—was that he had a good eye for safe, regular investments, particularly western ones. He had married into the wealthy Dwight family of Springfield, Massachusetts. In the 1830s, Jonathan Dwight often sent Bancroft, his son-in-law, to inspect the family's Bank of Michigan (Detroit) and potential family investments in Cleveland and Cincinnati. His first wife, Sarah Dwight Bancroft, died in June 1837, but he maintained his keen eye for a western city's prospects, even as he headed west with the older son of his second wife, Elizabeth Davis Bliss Bancroft.[477]

George Bancroft was a shrewd analyst of western railroads too. After seeing a description in "the Railroad Journal" of a Wisconsin line that Charles Butler was promoting and that Bancroft had invested in, he wrote to Butler:

[I]t alarmed me. The route from Chicago to Janesville is manifestly a good one; that from thence to Fond du Lac, I am ready to believe a good one; at least a time out [in the future]; but that through the wilderness to Lake Superior I cannot persuade myself can be worth the expense of running it. The climate, the wilderness must render the return inconsiderable or nothing; land there will not bring the prices estimated; the necessity of raising large sums of money will lower the credit of the whole concern, & as it seems to me change it from a safe to a speculative one.

Bancroft did not like risky, speculative investments.[478] In his early fifties, the historian was at the height of his powers. With short hair, a well-trimmed beard, tightly pursed lips, and sharp nose, he looked every bit the judicious, penetrating observer, sure of his analytic skills and of the accuracy of his observations.[479]

Bancroft and "Billy" Bliss left their home in New York City on Tuesday, May 30, and traveled with "the best of company"— Professor Benjamin Silliman, Shepard Knapp, Miss Van Schaick, and others. Knapp was a director of the "excellent" New York & Erie Railroad, which brought them to Corning, New York, where they spent the night. They proceeded to Buffalo on Wednesday and spent

a day (Thursday) at Niagara Falls before taking "the night train to Cleveland." On Friday, June 2, they traveled to Toledo ("I have no doubt the town must be both prosperous and agreeable," Bancroft predicted). They continued on: "the evening was delightful, the moon bright, and we went on to Jonesville" on the Michigan Southern Railroad, "which we reached at eleven o'clock," he wrote to his wife. "The country inn was somewhat picturesque; we turned in upon feather beds; I soon fell asleep, & I know not what genii rested in my eyes & lips & ears, but all who I had ever known in my youth came about me, and I seemed to expire amidst the sweetest offices of friendship & love."[480]

Not exempt from life's trials, Bancroft had known "the sweetest offices of friendship & love" in his fifty-four years. He was born in 1800 to Lucretia and Aaron Bancroft, a Congregational minister in Worcester, Massachusetts. Taking an anti-Calvinist position, Aaron Bancroft endured a church split over his views and served as an early president of the American Unitarian Association. By 1813, when he sent George to Harvard College, that ancient bastion of Puritanism was solidly Unitarian. Rebelling against his father's theological liberalism to a degree (as Catharine Sedgwick rebelled against her father's pastor's Calvinism), George avidly read Jonathan Edwards, wrote a conservative essay on "The Use and Necessity of Revelation" that rejected the Enlightenment's religion of reason, and sought some thematic, reconciling Union between Calvinism and

Unitarianism.[481] Donors at Harvard funded two years of his graduate education at the University of Göttingen in Germany, from which he received his doctorate in 1820; several months at the University of Berlin; and a year's Grand Tour of Europe, during which he met Goethe, Lord Byron, Lafayette, and other European geniuses.[482]

Returning in the summer of 1823 full of the zeitgeist of European Romanticism, George Bancroft arrived in staid Boston dressed "in velveteen trousers, with a silken beard, lisping Italian phrases." After he kissed his Harvard mentor on both cheeks, the man did not speak to him for six years.[483] Romantic genii—and not Jonathan Edwards—had certainly been playing about his eyes, lips, and ears.

Researching and writing American history, using scholarly German methods he learned at Göttingen and Berlin, enabled Bancroft to reconcile his Continental, Romantic education with his American nationality and New England upbringing. In 1834, Little, Brown published the first volume of his *History of the United States*. Reviewers praised it highly; Massachusetts senator Edward Everett called it "a work which will last while the memory of America lasts, and which will take its place instantly among the classics of our language"; previous efforts had not displayed such extensive research, balanced interpretation, literary style, and inspiring theme. The spine was adorned with a seal showing an eagle astride the globe and a quote from Bishop George Berkeley, "Westward the star of Empire takes its way." Aided by Dwight wealth and his own western investments, Bancroft planned to work full-time to complete the history.

A patronage job as collector of customs at Boston (1838–1840), a cabinet post as James Polk's secretary of the navy (1845–1846), and the post of U.S. minister to London (1846–1849)—plums given to reward his loyalty to the Democratic Party—delayed his work. So did the campaigning he was expected to do to earn such jobs. When Bancroft was collector of customs, one journalist recalled, "I do not think that he much cared to deliver stump speeches; but he had no choice." Democratic jobholders were expected to do so, except Nathaniel Hawthorne. "Mr. Hawthorne, who could no more speak than jump over a wide river, was of course excused." Bancroft was not. "Mr. Bancroft brought the rhetoric of his History to the platform. . . . he seldom deigned to descend from his stilts." He would begin his speeches "with an expression of astonishment at the audience, and exclaim, with the gesture of Hamlet at the first sight of the ghost, 'This vast assemblage might well appall me!'" Campaigning, collecting tariff duties, helping Polk write a message to Congress, making the social rounds of London—and his meticulous thoroughness—resulted in only six volumes in twenty years.[484]

In his *Democracy in America,* published not long after Bancroft's first volume, Alexis de Tocqueville critiqued the historians of democratic societies. Unlike historians of aristocratic nations whose books reflected a Great Man theory of history, democratic historians minimized individuals' influence on events and looked to "general causes" instead. This "exaggerated system of general causes," he argued sarcastically, served as a crutch for "second-rate historians." It gave them "a few mighty reasons to extricate them from the most difficult part of their work [identifying causes], and it indulges the indolence or incapacity of their minds, whilst it confers upon them the honors of deep thinking." It perniciously encouraged determinism, the belief "that societies unconsciously obey some superior force ruling over them." In a democracy, no one individual seemed powerful enough to avoid being shaped by a general cause, so people concluded "that mankind cannot resist it." Historians who succumb to determinism "subject [the people] to an inflexible Providence or to some blind necessity. . . . They take a nation arrived at a certain stage of its history, and they affirm that it could not but follow the track which brought it thither." Such thinking reduced people to helpless pawns; in such books "the author often appears great, but humanity is always diminutive."[485]

It is highly doubtful if de Tocqueville had Bancroft in mind, and the latter was certainly not lazy or second-rate. The overseas post and his government income aided Bancroft in collecting primary sources from English, French, Dutch, German, and Spanish archives.[486] He felt committed to basing his historical narrative on the best primary sources

available, to analyzing these critically, and to writing in an elevated, literary style. Like those of antebellum American scientists, his achievements consisted largely in collecting new evidence and in categorizing it, rather than in theorizing. He collected primary source documents indefatigably and at considerable expense: employing two copyists in London's State Paper Office, writing letters to government archives overseas, purchasing Samuel Adams's papers, engaging friends and colleagues to collect documents, and purchasing books. Unlike those of American scientists, perhaps his most important collections were specimens from European archives previously closed to or unused by American historians.[487]

Bancroft considered the study of history to be a science, as his German professors taught him. However, the German words *eine Wissenschaft,* sometimes translated as "a science," more accurately meant "a scholarly discipline"—whether or not that discipline used methods of the natural sciences. History was an "organized body of information" and, thus, a "science" in this German sense. Like American antebellum physical sciences, it used a Baconian inductive method of gathering data, classifying them, and then generalizing about possible "laws" of historical progress. Hypotheses were avoided.[488]

In his preface to Volume VI, written in mid-May 1854, Bancroft described his method. After a seven-page account of his data-gathering efforts, he concluded that, if his *History* failed to provide "a lucid narrative . . . , it is not for want of diligence in studying the materials, which I have brought together, or of laborious care in arranging them." For him, chronology was the main criterion for classifying data: "The strictest attention has been paid to chronological sequence, which can best exhibit the simultaneous action of general causes." Accuracy was more highly valued than theory. "The abundance of my collections has enabled me, in some measure, to reproduce the very language of the principle actors . . . and to represent their conduct from their own point of view." That did not mean he had to accept their point of view, but his own judgments had to be fair and objective, "neither exaggerating vices of character, nor reviving national animosities, but rendering a just tribute to virtue wherever found."[489]

Yet these Baconian methods did not prevent Bancroft from writing with literary style, or narrating events with a sense of drama, or discovering "laws" of human progress. The "law" of advancing liberty need not be proved in the same way as the law of gravity; reproducing the actors' own words might enhance the drama; chronological sequence was essential to a dramatic plot; virtue's just tribute could be stated in elegant style. The historian could even discern Providence's hand; belief in God and belief in science were not seen as contradictory. The scientist, whether it be Silliman or Bancroft, could discern the hand of God in the phenomena of nature or the events of human history.

In all this, Bancroft was a leader among antebellum American historians, although by no means the only one to use scholarly methods, literary style, or extensive fact-finding. Indeed, he returned from London in 1849 to find a rival, a Harvard graduate and Bostonian who promised "plain facts in plain English," in open contrast to Bancroft's dramatic language, many adjectives, and providential theme. Richard Hildreth saw no inexorable march of Progress: "If in certain parts of the American Union, the experiment of Democracy be steadily and quietly pursued . . . in certain other parts of the country it is quite overshadowed." However, Hildreth's "hard, dry prose, failed to strike forth the spark that [Bancroft's] volumes lighted." Bancroft's *History* far outsold Hildreth's.[490]

Other historians of the 1850s did not attempt to compete directly against Bancroft's *History*. They used similar methods, in some cases just as skillfully, but on more exotic and romantic subjects: Francis Parkman's *The California and Oregon Trail* (1849) and T*he Conspiracy of Pontiac* (1851), which began his epic account of the seventeenth- and eighteenth-century battle between France and England for control of North America; William Prescott's *History of the Reign of Ferdinand and Isabella* and other works on the Spanish Empire; John Lothrop Motley's *The Rise of the Dutch Republic*. Readers appreciated the narrative style of these historians, but Bancroft's dramatic narrative, providential theme, theistic piety, and patriotic fervor made him the most popular historian of antebellum America. "Bancroft's books filled shelves in thousands of American homes"; many Americans "knew American history only as he wrote of it"; the name Bancroft was "very nearly synonymous with American history."[491]

The mid-1850s idea of history as a discipline did not require the historian to achieve "authorial invisibility" and such scientific detachment as to eliminate his personality.[492] Writing about the colonies in the seventeenth and early eighteenth centuries, this son of the anti-Calvinist Aaron Bancroft optimistically reconciled his father's views with those of his Puritan ancestors and Jonathan Edwards. God sovereignly directed American history, but he predestined America to greatness, not individuals to salvation, and he did so to bring about a vague Progress, not to vindicate narrow religious dogmas. Indeed, "it is hard to be sure that at all times the theism of the *History* is actually Christian." The Romantic Bancroft conveniently enlisted Edwards and Puritans in his war against Enlightenment rationalists and French atheists, but their views were altered in the process. The enemies, Enlightenment and atheism, were soundly whipped in Bancroft's *History*, as the American people's closeness to nature enabled them to maintain their faith in God.[493]

In his confidence in Providence's guiding hand, Bancroft seemed to flirt with the determinism that de Tocqueville critiqued. However, his Common Man intuited Providence's goals and was no helpless democratic pygmy, as the Frenchman feared. And Bancroft included Great Men like George Washington and Daniel Boone, who exerted decisive influence over events. They were just not aristocrats but men taught in western forests to discern Providence's goals. Since those goals were Progress and greater liberty for ordinary people, the people had no desire to resist the providential scheme anyway. The nation had to have followed that track, but that was not the European rut that de Tocqueville feared. It led onward and upward.

On May 26, 1854, Bancroft received a letter from Charles C. Little and James Brown expressing surprise at the length of his *History;* Bancroft had reached only the contractions that predicted the birth of the Republic, and these did not seem to be getting any more frequent. His first three volumes covered colonization and early development, to 1748. Little and Brown understood their contract to call for the next three volumes to cover the American Revolution; however, Volumes 4, 5, and 6 dealt with its causes and ended well before a shot was fired at Lexington or Concord. They expected a complete account of the Revolution "& shall insist upon a performance on your part" of the contract. (His English publisher was even more annoyed.)[494]

Bancroft shot off a letter to Little and Brown. He wanted the proof sheets back. He thought the contract called for six volumes on the causes and events of the Revolution. "I am on the point of leaving New York for an excursion to the west; and shall hope to find your answer awaiting me on my return." He hoped their answer would help to clarify matters, so "that we may go through without any further misunderstanding."[495]

He seems to have given the matter no further thought as he and his stepson traveled through upstate New York, northern Ohio, and southern Michigan to Chicago. In his mid-twenties, bachelor William Bliss admired the young ladies—he was "struck dumb" by Miss Cornelia and later was "dividing his heart between Miss Walker & Miss Charlotte"—while Bancroft admired the scenery of the West—"rising villages in the midst of rich cleared land." They "passed several prairies; but civilization had been at work upon them; and all the difference between prairie farms & cleared lands is that the one have not a stump to mar the smoothness of their surface; & the others are thick-set with girdled trees & ruins of old forests." They spent Saturday afternoon, June 3, "driving through the streets" of Chicago, "this wonderful prairie city" whose "oldest native inhabitant is but twenty two years old." Bancroft thought the only European city with a commerce equal to Chicago's might be Le Havre. The city was "full of the hope of boundless prosperity & increase," he informed Elizabeth.[496]

His *History* was a vote for the West in six volumes that did credit to Bishop Berkeley's motto. In it, perhaps the least comprehensible British act leading up to the Revolution was the Proclamation of 1763 prohibiting American settlement west of the Appalachians. There was a reason, Bancroft noted: British officials' feared that settlers in "the Valley of the Mississippi . . . would establish manufactures for themselves; and in the very heart of America, found a power, which distance must emancipate." A paper barrier to westward advance was useless. "But the prohibition only set apart the Great Valley as the sanctuary of the unhappy, the adventurous, and the free. . . . The boundless West became the poor man's City of Refuge, where the wilderness guarded his cabin" from British authorities. It was not possible to stop the westward, stump-clearing, cabin-building surge. "Nothing could restrain the Americans from peopling the wilderness. To be a freeholder was the ruling passion of the New England man." By the late eighteenth century, Yankees could fulfill that passion only in the West, not in long-settled Connecticut.[497]

Although Aaron Burr had conspired to start an independent nation in the Mississippi Valley, Bancroft did not fear that westward expansion—resulting from a love of landowning liberty and producing still greater liberty—would lead to disunion. Providence acted in American history to guarantee that centrifugal forces of liberty would never destroy the Union, for a love of union also existed and exerted a balancing, centripetal force. Providence provided Common Men, the "Sovereigns" that excursioning Whig editors and "big bugs" were quick to sneer at, with an intuitive reason that caused them to reject anarchic freedom and despotic, centralizing union, and to achieve freedom-in-union.[498] Union protected each man's freedom, and each free man would willingly fight to protect the union. (Conceivably, a part of the whole might decide that its sectional unity better guaranteed its freedom.)

Bancroft pointed to the West as the natural home of liberty-loving men. In the early 1770s, he noted, the inhabitants of Illinois requested the British authorities to grant them "some part in the election of their rulers"—which the British refused. The Illinois men protested against "a Government so evidently tyrannical," which the British were planning for them. Bancroft rejoiced, "The chord of liberty vibrated on the Illinois, and the sympathy of the western villages with freedom was an assurance that they too would join the great American family of Republics."[499]

Statesman Alexis de Tocqueville, ca. 1865.

Faith in the West and the Common Man enabled the scholar Bancroft to unite with ordinary folk in the Democratic Party, and to distance himself from Boston's genteel, Unitarian elite who, he felt, had never accepted the son of Worcester.[500] He had

supported Andrew Jackson, and Preston Blair even hoped that Bancroft would write the biography of Jackson that Blair had intended to write.[501] The Boston elite hated Jackson. They looked with condescension and distaste on the westerner, the Squatter Sovereign. Bancroft had full faith in him, and in the popular sovereignty doctrine of Stephen A. Douglas that placed the West's and the Union's future in his hands. He had just as much confidence in the men of 1850s Kansas-Nebraska as he had in the men of 1770s Illinois to decide their own fate. With Douglas, Bancroft believed westward expansion would cement the Union (Northeast and Southeast quarreled, not Northwest and Southwest); westerners were the best guarantors of freedom and union.[502]

The westerner Andrew Jackson had prevented South Carolina from tearing the Union apart with her claim to a right to nullify federal laws. In his fifth volume, in a Democratic-Jacksonian gesture of reconciliation, Bancroft devoted a chapter ("South

164

Carolina Founds the American Union") to celebrating that state's unifying role in 1765, when its legislature approved a call for a Congress to coordinate colonial opposition to the Stamp Act.[503] In a further gesture, Bancroft was careful to blame the British, not southerners, for the existence of slavery in the colonies.[504]

Bancroft's faith in the West and the Common Man rested, ultimately, on his faith in human Progress.[505] History went from East to West, from aristocracy to democracy; if western democracy was inferior to eastern aristocracy, then Progress was doubtful. But Bancroft was no agnostic on Progress:

> The course of civilization flows on like a mighty river through a boundless valley, calling to the streams from every side to swell its current, which is always growing wider, and deeper, and clearer, as it rolls along. Let us trust ourselves upon its bosom without fear. . . . Since the progress of the race appears to be the great purpose of Providence, it becomes us all to venerate the future.[506]

The future must be better than the past, as surely as the Mississippi River was wider at New Orleans than at La Crosse.

That did not mean, of course, that he denigrated the study of the past. Progress could be expected forward but could only be understood backward, by examining how Providence worked in past ages. "It is because God is visible in History that its

office is the noblest except that of the poet," Bancroft argued, and because History studied "the last work of creation," mankind. "The mineralogist takes special delight in contemplating the process of crystallization, as though he had caught nature at her work as a geometrician. . . . But history . . . sees the mind of humanity itself engaged in formative efforts, constructing sciences, promulgating laws, organizing commonwealths," and "history, therefore, stands first" above the natural sciences that studied only matter.[507]

That did not mean that historians experienced a radical separation from other scholars or scientists. Antebellum intellectual life still knew considerable unity among the disciplines. Historians used the same Baconian method as geologists. In his 1854 address to the New-York Historical Society (quoted above), Bancroft praised the data-gathering advances made by anatomists, zoologists, biologists, chemists, meteorologists, astronomers, and geologists. Sitting on the Mississippi's bluffs (and reading other geologists' books), the geologist "has been able to ascertain, in some degree, the chronology of our planet." But gathering data did not encourage atheism; God remained the Author of whatever data were discovered. Intellectual progress itself was due to humanity's glory as "the last work of creation." Bancroft denied that the human being bore any "marks of having risen to his present degree of perfection by successive transmutations from inferior forms"; no, he was "created separate and distinct from all other classes of animal life."[508] All humans were so created at one time. He did not accept Louis Agassiz's theory of polygenism, of separate origins for separate races.[509]

For Bancroft, the unity of the human race was the spring of Progress and its ultimate goal. "The reciprocal relation between God and humanity constitutes the UNITY of the race." Providence was binding the peoples closer together, was using Christianity and America to accomplish that unity. "To have asserted clearly the unity of mankind was the distinctive glory of the Christian religion," Bancroft maintained. And America's westward expansion was forging a geographic link of liberty between Old Europe and Old Asia. East of the Rocky Mountains, "the Western nations of Europe [find] a theatre for the renewal of their youth," while west of the Rockies, "the hoary civilization of the farthest antiquity leans forward from Asia to receive the glad tidings of the messenger of freedom." America "stands, therefore, more than any other, as the realisation of the unity of the race."[510]

Unity would not come at the price of liberty; "the organization of society must more and more conform to the principle of FREEDOM" even as it tended "towards unity and universality." Unity would develop out of Common Men's wisdom, not be forced on them by their superiors, "and still less by the reckless violence of men whose desparate audacity would employ terror as a means to ride on the whirlwind of civil war."

Concluding his address, Bancroft summarized Progress: "Every thing is in movement, and for the better . . . [man's] last system of philosophy is the best, for it includes every one that went before. The last political state of the world, likewise, is ever more excellent than the old, for it presents in activity the entire inheritance of truth."[511]

With this optimistic certainty about the future, Bancroft was, understandably, not alarmed or worried as he traveled west on the Grand Excursion. Progress since his earlier trips west was everywhere evident. People were more numerous, towns larger, roads better, railroads present where none had been before. Because of these improvements, land prices were higher and bound to rise even more. The "universal Yankee nation" was spreading liberty and union to new territories. Common folk were settling the West and contributing to the ultimate unity of humanity. They could be safely trusted with the governance of the West, the anti-Nebraska agitation notwithstanding. They were worthy successors to Revolutionary patriots who defied British prohibitions against westward expansion, to Jacksonian Democrats who defied Biddle's Bank. (Nicholas Biddle was the president of the Bank of the United States that Jacksonian Democrats opposed.) One could hardly lose by betting on even greater Progress in the future. Bancroft had calculated history's trajectory, and it was upward.

Accordingly, Bancroft sounded quite positive about the Grand Excursion and the sights he saw after leaving Chicago. "I am converted into one of [the prairie's] most enthusiastic admirers," he wrote home to his wife. Galena was not mud-ridden but the site of an interesting lead-mining process and of a beautiful "rolling prairie." "The rest of Tuesday and all Wednesday, we ascended the Mississippi, which we found more beautiful than was expected or can be told. The magnificent stream, the countless islands, the bluff, the villages, the hollows, the prairies all combined to give delight." Some excursionists said it "surpassed" the Hudson River Valley. "I make no comparisons but say the scenery along the Mississippi is surpassingly beautiful as well as peculiar & unique."[512] He summarized his impressions: "The beauty of the Mississippi Valley far exceeds any account you can have read of it; and as to its resources, they are scarcely begun to be developed."[513] So had liberty and union scarcely begun to be developed in the valley and in the West. Such a beautiful region would surely find itself matched with a fitting politics and government.

ST. ANTHONY FALLS *by Herrmann J. Meyer, engraving, ca. 1853. Excursionists expected to see wild, sublime falls akin to Niagara's when they reached Minnesota. Instead, they found sawmills and a fledging city that became Minneapolis. (Winona County Historical Society)*

CHAPTER SEVEN

"The Greatest Epoch that has Ever Dawned"

THURSDAY, JUNE 8, 1854

THURSDAY DAWNED CLEAR, sunny, but rather cool for early June, thought some eastern passengers aboard the Grand Excursion. That was not an impression Minnesota boosters wanted them to publicize, but several editors wrote back home that they felt they were now in "these upper regions" characterized by "this high northern atmosphere." A *New York Times* correspondent reported, "A bright day, but chilly. It is never very warm in this region." There was talk that there had been frost the previous night.[514]

Led by the *War Eagle,* but close together to make an impressive landing at St. Paul, the steamboats pushed north against the early-morning current. On the west bank, the travelers saw Little Crow's village at Kaposia, or the remains of it, and a nearby burial ground where poles supported frames on which the dead were placed. The Mdewakanton band of Dakota had begun to leave the village in September 1853 (and may have taken their dead with them) for their new reservation along the Minnesota River. After a long delay in preparing fields and constructing buildings for the Indian agent in their new home and after much wrangling over implementation of the Treaty of Mendota (1851) that called for their removal, the move was now largely accomplished. Little Crow had just returned from a steamboat-and-rail trip to Washington, D.C., to finalize the details. Surveyors had already platted lots at Kaposia. Yet it is possible that a few Mdewakanton remained near the Mississippi's banks in the spring of 1854; a *New York Times* correspondent reported seeing signs of a recent Indian camp at or near Kaposia: "the poles of the wigwams are yet standing, and the ashes of their fires are visible upon the sand."[515]

On an eastern bluff, farther north, excursionists saw "vast myriads of birds resembling swallows." These cliff swallows flocked to "a high perpendicular bluff of soft limestone, which they had pecked full of holes" that they used for nests. "They have completely honey-combed the face of the bluff," Cincinnati editor William Schouler observed, "and there they were, as happy as security could make them, chattering and fussing away in the expectation of soon bringing forth their numerous progeny, to the particular delight of 'their anxious mothers.'"[516]

About eight o'clock, before Benjamin Silliman and party "had hardly time to finish our breakfast," Sewell Cutting was standing at the front of the *Lady Franklin's* cabin, "looking ahead for new scenes as they came," when he saw "that we were approaching a sudden bend in the river—and through the trees I discovered St. Paul! I shouted for companions to gaze on the scene." Astonished, they saw the frontier city. "The dome of the capitol glistened in the rising sun, and towers and spires of churches rose amid clusters of buildings, of brick, and stone, and wood, and some of them of large and stately proportions." They were amazed that such substantial buildings had been raised in "scarcely half a dozen years."[517]

The flotilla began to swing around the river bend that brought the excursionists in sight of St. Paul and its startled citizens—and St. Paul in sight of them. It was hard to say who was more surprised. Minnesotans did not expect the excursion to arrive in St. Paul until late Thursday or early Friday, and the visitors did not expect to find such a solid, attractive, prosperous, stone-laid and brick-built city on the nation's northwestern frontier. Minnesotans had been told of Henry Farnam and Joseph Sheffield's original plan for the boats to travel only in the day but not of the revised plan to return to Chicago by Saturday, "that the rest and order of the Sabbath should not be broken." That plan required travel by night, departure from St. Paul by midnight Thursday, and, hence, arrival in St. Paul on Thursday morning. No telegraph lines reached St. Paul to communicate this change of plans to the welcoming committee.[518]

Before the boats rounded the bend, Captain Daniel Smith Harris's cannon on the *War Eagle* fired a warning shot to notify the Territory of Minnesota that the Grand Excursion had arrived. The steamboats blew their whistles.[519]

"Coming! Boat's coming!" shouted St. Paulites on shore. Crowds hurried down to the Lower Landing to see the spectacle. Others hastened to make quick adjustments to the capital's appearance. Someone raised the Stars and Stripes in front of a major hotel, the Central House. A few horse-drawn vehicles were driven down to the landing. Most surprised Minnesotans just stood and watched the five steamboats approach.[520]

Excursionists stood on deck and gazed. "As we rounded the bend and the city appeared in sight," wrote one editor, "every one was astonished at the rise, solidity, and beauty of the four-year-old." (Platted in 1847, St. Paul was seven years old, or perhaps only a three-month-old infant, for it was incorporated on March 4, 1854.) Another reporter heard the cannon and went up on deck "just in time to see . . . the Capitol, with its glittering dome, the six church steeples, and the freshly painted frame houses. Truly, a commanding site for a city." The site was a "bluff rising perpendicularly from the water, then forming a broad *plateau,* and then again gradually rising" to hills farther back. "At two places the bluff recedes from the shore, forming the upper and the lower landings," where warehouses and a levee served river traffic. Others were more impressed with how many structures were not wooden frame ones: "it is quite certain that no town in the country of the same age, has more large stone and brick buildings than St. Paul." Author William Bogart—and others he talked with—expected to see a makeshift frontier camp of "the canvass and shanty order" but found "a city set on a hill," shining in the sun, with "its handsome buildings—its churches—its warehouses—its streets crowded with citizens. . . . It was the diamond where we expected to find a pebble."

So civilized did it appear, one editor noted, that "it seems as if all the world and the rest of mankind were mere outsiders—away from them, and not they from the world."[521]

Rather than pull up to the landing immediately, the *War Eagle* halted in midstream and waited for the other four. The *Galena, Sparhawk, Golden Era,* and *Lady Franklin* came up to form a line, "in as much order as [if] they were an armed squadron in a line of battle." The band onboard the *Galena* "struck up lively airs" and the boats glided in formation to their landing spots "amid the clash of instruments, the roar of escaping steam, [and] the huzzas of the great gathering"—excursionists on the decks and Minnesotans on shore and on the docked *Admiral.* Church bells rang up above the bluff, in the streets of St. Paul.[522]

As the boats were moored close together, an African-American crew member on the *Galena* stood on deck, seemingly taunting the *War Eagle's* crew by the manner in which he ate "some second-hand ice cream." "He would take a spoon-full, stretch out his arm, make a grand sweep through the air over his head, and deliberately settle the delicacy" in his mouth. He did this a few times, and had the spoon close to his mouth for another delivery when "a huge potato" thrown from the *War Eagle* "carried away his spoon" and hit him

square in the nose. "It almost knocked the fellow down, but for all that he took it in good part, and after a moment joined in the general laugh, as if it were common sport on the Mississippi to get one's nose knocked off with a raw potato."[523] It was not hard to see why fights often broke out among the crews.

"It was not a matter of regret," felt editor Charles H. Ray of Galena, "that the intended speeches, no doubt eloquent and apropos, were omitted." The crowd on shore did not call for Millard Fillmore. Taken by surprise, local dignitaries were wholly unprepared to address such distinguished visitors on such short notice. Minnesota territorial governor Willis A. Gorman (Democrat) and former governor Alexander Ramsey (Whig) made it down to the landing to greet the tourists but gave no speeches.[524]

Excursionists' first priority was securing transportation to St. Anthony Falls, the northwestern-most, ultimate goal of the excursion. Some were under the mistaken impression that they had to leave St. Paul as early as three o'clock that afternoon.[525] Westerners' first priorities were to apologize for their unpreparedness, to explain it, and to secure the needed transportation as soon as possible.

Apologies arrived before wagons and carriages, and they all came spontaneously, from all directions, without a committee's organizing control. A German-American resident of St. Paul told Bogart that they had picked out a corn-fattened ox and a bear to be Friday's dinner for the visitors but "you did come one day too soon; I hope you do not cherish any *animosity* because we were not ready." Bogart assured him that they did not resent the unpreparedness, "and the Bavarian seemed in heart, delighted that we thought kindly of St. Paul." Other residents talked of plans to exhibit a group of Indians and a buffalo, plans spoiled by the early arrival. A committee had announced a ball at the Capitol. The day before, the City Council passed two "Whereas" and four "Resolved" clauses complimenting the visiting "wise men of the East," hailing the rail-made "union between the East and the West, of this Great Confederacy," flattering the Chicago & Rock Island Railroad "so far in advance of all its rivals," hinting broadly that its advance should proceed through Minnesota to the Pacific, and calling on St. Paul's citizens to entertain the guests and so "to do something toward establishing the good name of our infant city, for warm-hearted, generous hospitality." Unfortunately, there was no time to set these words in type before the wise men arrived the following morning.[526]

"For the Falls," excursionists shouted, not halting long to hear apologies, "for St. Anthony's." A few managed to hire and board carriages at the lower landing, yet those accommodated only a few, and hundreds demanded to see the falls. "Ladies stood in anxious groups about the boats and the wharves. While gentlemen, eager and perspiring," climbed stairs and streets to downtown and "rushed about the city seeking horses." No one stood on ceremony. "Countrymen coming in with loads of produce were seized, their loads pitched off and themselves and

wagons rapt unceremoniously to the wharf." Men paid $10 for a horse; others offered to buy horse and carriage for the morning and then "sell them at a liberal discount in the afternoon." About one hundred conveyances of one sort or another took on passengers for the falls. "Every sort of a team, from old line stages down to carts and wheel-barrows, were quickly chartered." Pine boards were laid across wagons to make temporary seats for New York City's finest. When one wagon was loaded with ten or a dozen occupants, so that not a spare inch remained, it set off for the falls, and the next one stopped at the landing for its load.[527]

The *Palladium*'s James Babcock described New Haveners' efforts to hitch a ride.[528] "There sit Gov. Baldwin and Mrs. B. in high back chairs in a long lumber wagon, in company with a dozen more on similar seats." Charles J. McCurdy, the former minister to Austria, sat with his daughter Evelyn in a lumber wagon. Judge Jeffrey Orson Phelps of Simsbury, attorney Charles B. Lines, and James Woodward of the *New Haven Morning Journal & Courier* did not wait for a welcoming committee to provide for them but hastened to a livery stable and hired "a very handsome one horse buggy." Carriage-maker James Brewster knew what to look for; his wife and he rode in a "similar carriage." "There is Rev. Dr. Bacon, Rev. Mr. Eggleston, Rev. Dr. Fitch and others, in a lumber wagon." Babcock now needed a seat.

"Have you room on top of that coach?" he asked.

"No," said A. P. Cummings of the *New York Observer,* "this coach is engaged." Cummings seemed "to have monopolized two or three coaches, and to have turned out of one of them the wife and daughter of Mr. [Azariah C.] Flagg," the C&RI treasurer and "one of the principal originators of the excursion."

Contradicting Cummings, a St. Paul man insisted "that no one had *engaged* the coach, except the committee, and they had provided it for *any* of the party."

"Here is room," Alexander Twining offered, "come up here."

Babcock climbed up on the stagecoach and sat between Twining and former governor John Barry of Michigan. Also on top were George Bancroft, Billy Bliss, the driver—"and back of all was stretched out one of the editors of the *New York Times*. The inside of the coach was chiefly filled with ladies."

Several excursionists commanded a respect commensurate with their station in life. (There were too few completed arrangements and too many high-status individuals to provide that to all.) Charles Dana of the *Tribune* was taken in tow by William G. Le Duc, a member of the Committee of Arrangements, who in 1853 brought a Minnesota exhibit, including a buffalo, by steamboat and train to New York's Crystal Palace World's Fair. A correspondent for the *Tribune,* a guide worthy of the distinguished Dana, Le Duc and his wife, Mary Elizabeth ("our *cicerone*"), drove Dana and his companions to see the sights: Minnehaha Falls, Fort Snelling, Lake Calhoun, and St. Anthony Falls.[529] Former governor Ramsey gave the *New York Post* correspondent "a seat in one of his carriages."[530] Colonel Matthew Simpson, the army's road-construction supervisor in Minnesota, guided editor Josiah Harris of Cleveland and told him of plans for a government road to Lake Superior.[531] Others found Minnesotans who had emigrated from their area, and these acquaintances provided them with a ride to the falls.[532]

Hiram Fuller of New York had to be content "to meet a couple of my fair name-relatives," Jane Gay Fuller and her sister Abby, his cousins who had been six weeks in St. Paul, "long enough to be considered 'old inhabitants.'" Jane Fuller was an aspiring poet and writer; one of her letters from Minnesota had appeared in Fuller's *Mirror* five days earlier. They drove him and his party around in a two-horse carriage and, with infectious enthusiasm, described the sights of their newfound land.[533]

Not finding anyone—distinguished, acquainted, related, or otherwise—to transport and guide him, one eastern newspaperman hired a "water-barrel" and "straddled" it into St. Anthony "much to the amusement of the lookers-on . . . he cut a ludicrous figure—his legs and coat dangling in the air, while his white hat" reminded one St. Paul editor "of the notable Greeley sauntering up Broadway." Three New York editors rode a "one-horse water cart" toward St. Anthony.[534]

It took nearly two hours to find conveyances to carry all the visitors who wanted to go. The road to St. Anthony was "lined with loads of passengers, many crowded and piled up to a very unusual extent."[535] Ray of Galena thought the "motley cavalcade" highly amusing:

> *Here was a Governor bestride a sorry Rosinante of which even the great Don would have been ashamed; here a U.S. Senator, acting the part of footman, stood bolt upright in the baggage boot of a coach, holding on by the iron rail surrounding the top; here the historian of which the country is justly proud, squatted on his haunches on top of a crazy van, unmindful of everything but himself, his book, hat and spectacles; . . . here a corpulent madam, whose idea of a ride is bounded by luxuriant cushions, shining hammercloths, spirited horses and obsequious flunkies, was seated in a hard bottom chair, in an open one-horse market wagon, first cousin to her husband's vegetable dray or perhaps his pedler's cart.*[536]

Moving by land, without the ordering and beautifying luxury of a steamboat, the excursion's "freight of wealth and dignity" could seem absurdly mismatched to its means of transportation.

Nevertheless, the mood was cheerful and celebratory, John Munn of Utica felt: "[A]s we passed others, they gave us cheer upon cheer. Such an animating, novel & amusing ride will never again be ours." That was easy for him to say, for the Munns and Boswells had hired "a comfortable Barouche." They passed a miserable party in a wagon "drawn by a small French pony" wholly unequal to the task of transporting a dozen persons. At each uphill climb, the passengers had to get off and walk.[537]

Some self-conscious dignitaries undoubtedly noticed the incongruities, but most excursionists looked at the scenery, not at themselves. They admired rolling prairies, prosperous-looking farmhouses, wheat fields greening up, corn fields whose stalks had not yet overshadowed the rich black soil, oak openings, the many small lakes and trout streams, both presumably full of fish.[538] Those who entertained notions of investing in this real estate, and editors whose readers entertained such notions, paid careful attention to Minnesota's agricultural potential. Some were suspicious; Minnesota had a reputation for being overpromoted with less than accurate facts.[539] Yet this farmland looked more aesthetically pleasing than Illinois's flat prairies, even if it might not produce quite as many bushels per acre.[540]

Listening to the Le Ducs' descriptions and looking at the pleasant June landscape, Dana still sounded cautious: "[I]t was whispered in my ear that the winters, when the prairies are covered with snow, are bitter and merciless, and that the wind goes over them with fatal asperity. Distrust the land speculators at St. Paul, said this malignant whisper." Though his Minnesota guides told him it was not so, he passed this warning on to the *Tribune*'s many readers, along with his hosts' reassuring denials.[541]

Some in Schouler's party asked their driver if prairies were healthy places. "Yes, he said, people never really die on them, they keep living until they kind a gradually dry up, and *then they blow away*. Sometimes when they want to die as they do East, they move out of town and go down the river."[542]

Intense interest was shown in technical details too. Benjamin P. Johnson, corresponding secretary and editor for the New York State Agricultural Society, rode in one coach and served as its agricultural tour guide, pointing out purebred cattle and soil types. His party stopped to examine a sod-breaking plow pulled by four yoke of oxen, driven by two men. The plow, about a dozen feet long with two side wheels, was "of peculiar construction—very large and strong." Once set in the ground, no one had to hold it to keep it down in the soil. "Two or three large knives preceded the share, cutting a way through the tangled and thickly interlaced roots of the prairie grass." Then the share turned the sod over "and up comes the black rich earth." It made a four-inch furrow. The two-man team charged the farmer $3.50 per acre to break sod. A farmer could harvest a crop from that soil the same year it was broken, reported one editor (he may have been mistaken). "Really this is a fast age and we are a fast people."[543]

Johnson's group passed a poorer farm, "where a tender female of perhaps thirty, and the mother of a half a dozen hopeful Minnesotians, was out in the garden hoeing among the tops of the potato. She wore a fashionable short sleeve gown (and short at both ends besides), a calico sun-bonnet, and *no* stockings, or shoes." They thought they saw "the rich, black loam, ooze up between her tender toes" as she gardened.[544]

Editor Moore of Springfield was pleased to discover that land speculators controlled lands only a mile or two from St. Paul. Five or six miles out, actual settlers had acted to keep lands out of speculators' hands. "Squatter sovereignty" ruled, but not Stephen Douglas's or Democrats' "kind of squatter sovereignty, that allows the white man to make *cattle* of his brother black man"—as in the Kansas-Nebraska Act—but the real kind, "free and equal to all, holds here supreme."[545]

The motley cavalcade came to hills, from which they could see the Mississippi ahead (it was also behind them; its S-curve around Fort Snelling and St. Paul put it to their east and west). Here Babcock's fully loaded stagecoach suffered an accident. Across the prairie, George Bancroft had at first paid close attention to the sights. "Gradually the novelty of the thing wore off, and he drew from his pocket a copy of Dante's *Inferno*. In that he buried himself, seemingly unconscious of the beauty of the scene around him." That was not so hazardous on level prairie, but on hilly terrain he lost his balance—perhaps when "the forward wheels dropped into a rut," although Bancroft blamed his act of reaching into his coat pocket—"and away went our historian, topsy turvy, heels over head, to the ground." His fellow passengers feared he had been run over by the wheels. Billy Bliss went to rescue him, but Bancroft was unharmed. "Gathering up his hat, spectacles and *Inferno,* he clambered back to his place, unhurt, and thoroughly cured of the fit of untimely studiousness that had caused his fall."[546]

A mile or less from the falls, they passed a ninety-foot-tall wooden observation platform, Cheever's Tower, built by the eccentric St. Anthony hotel owner William A. Cheever. Some stopped to see it. The bottom was as wide as a house, some forty feet square, but higher up it partly lost in length and width what it gained in height, until it was only six feet by six feet at the top, where the Stars and Stripes waved. There was a fee of a dime to climb the stairs. Cheever placed mottoes on his hotel doors and windows, and here he had painted in black letters, "Pay your Dime and Climb." From the top one could enjoy the "view of the country for forty miles around, embracing Fort Snelling, the Falls, the river, and a number of bright and sparkling lakes." Babcock did not stop to ascertain whether this western claim to forty-mile scenery (perhaps with the aid of a telescope) was accurate or not.[547]

Now they were at the falls, and they climbed down from their awkward and crowded perches to have a look around. Those who visited Niagara on the way west, or those who made that comparison mentally, were disappointed.[548] St. Anthony Falls were about one-tenth the height of Niagara Falls and had no major historical or romantic associations, beyond the visit of Father Louis Hennepin in 1680 (Hennepin had also been one of the

first whites to see Niagara Falls).[549] Lumber milling, logging, and other economic activities had tarnished the sight from an aesthetic perspective: "Its real beauty is much diminished by an immense quantity of saw logs and drift wood, which is piled up above and below the fall in most gigantic masses." St. Anthony Falls appeared to some to be not sublime, not picturesque, and not beautiful—but only industrious.[550]

There was no discernable organization to this visit en masse to the falls. Finally arrived at their farthest destination, excursionists scattered along the riverbank to sightsee, collect souvenirs, rest, and converse for two or three hours. New Haveners shook hands, congratulated each other on reaching this far-off site, searched for souvenirs—"some cutting canes to carry home as mementos, others searching for agate stones which are occasionally found here, and others knocking off pieces of the limestone rock, in which are embedded fossil shells." Some of Schouler's party gathered agates and carnelians, "which they are going to have set in rings, pins and other Eastern notions" back home. Some walked the streets of St. Anthony, where Yankees were pleased at their Maine cousins' progress and impressed at the New England order evidenced when a schoolroom of pupils kept studying despite the colorful throngs walking past their window.[551]

Some adventurous tourists crossed the Mississippi, divided into two channels here by Nicollet and Hennepin Islands. Above the falls, a rope ferry operated to take carriages from one island to the west bank; Hiram, Jane, and Abby Fuller took their carriage (accompanied by a second one) on this "tit-tlish little ferry," which Hiram found "immi-nently perilous" given the rapid current, jammed-up logs, and the fact that "the lives of the passengers all hung upon a single rope."[552] They made it and drove down the west bank to Fort Snelling. They need not have risked the ferry; Silliman noted that the river was "fordable by horses and carriages, and some people in our party came over in that way."[553]

Others crossed over to the island on a plank footbridge above the falls or on a similar one below the falls. One was "the width of only a single plank, with a slight hand rail at the side." The one Silliman crossed did not have a handrail. Many were nervous about trusting their weight to such slender supports. Bachelor reporter N. W. T. Root crossed the plank bridge "with a dizzy young lady," which he probably did not mind.[554] Silliman did mind. He "regretted" he did not know about the upstream ford,

as it would have saved us a perilous passage on foot over a miserable row of planks of no great strength imperfectly secured at the ends to cross forms set in the water among the stones. There was no hand rail, except that for a short distance there was [a] dangerous substitute in a few narrow slips of boards imperfectly secured by nails. The rush of the torrent beneath the planks is, in some places terrific, and might cause some who have not strong nerves to fall; I led

Sarah with a firm grasp of a strong hand & was rejoiced when she was safe over; she became faint and dizzy in transit.

Nervously guiding his wife did not prevent Silliman from making a careful scientific observation of the falls: "The ledges are fossiliferous limestone arranged in strata as distinct as a pile of books and the torrent has shoved off some large layers which have slid over each other with beautiful distinctness."

Water erosion had undermined some limestone cliffs and caused them to tumble down. Silliman noted the logs jammed up in piles.[555]

Not all excursionists made it across without getting wet:

"There goes the editor of the New York Times. He has stepped upon a log—it rolls, and he has gone down. He rises, and holds on to the log—a friendly hand is reached out and he is drawn up, somewhat scared and a good deal wet."[556]

The point in crossing to the island was to see the main part of the falls, which stretched from the island to the west bank. A number of excursionists, from the *Sparhawk* especially, crossed to Nicollet Island and held an organized ceremony to mark their farthest point reached. Hamilton Morton of New York City had judged a yacht race off Sandy Hook on June 1 (at 2:00 p.m.) and had brought with him a bottle of Atlantic saltwater, to be mixed with the Mississippi's waters, exactly a week later, on June 8 (at 2:00 p.m.). Benjamin Johnson, the agricultural expert, took charge of this ritual occasion, which one editor termed "the marriage of old Atlantic to Mrs. Sippi." Present on the west side of the island just below the falls to witness this event were Catharine Sedgwick, Bogart, Morton, several Albany men, and several other ladies. They chose the sixty-year-old Johnson to give the main speech and do the honors, apparently because he was present at the Erie Canal groundbreaking in 1817.[557]

Before emptying the bottle, Johnson invited witnesses to taste its contents to verify that it was the real Atlantic vintage. Some did; the others were amused, for "their faces gave incontestible evidence that this was simon pure saline from the ocean." Johnson broke the bottle on a log and tossed the saltwater into the newly fallen torrent. He gave a speech expressing delight at reaching his long-sought goal at his advanced age, thanking Sheffield and Farnam for the excursion, praising a nation with such improved transportation that Atlantic saltwater could be mixed with Mississippi freshwater in one week's time, prophesying the Atlantic and Pacific would also be joined soon, and hoping this act symbolized national unity. "Let our prayer be, that the complete union which is now secured between these waters, shall be secured throughout our entire country, never to be severed while time shall endure," Johnson concluded.[558]

Finished viewing the falls, the excursionists broke into dozens of small groups with different sightseeing agendas and different means of transport. Those who crossed to the west bank drove south to see the "Little Falls" (by comparison to St. Anthony Falls) or southwest to Lakes Calhoun and Harriet. Others returned to St. Paul to inspect the capital in more detail (the rush for wagons had kept them from paying it much attention earlier). Others went elsewhere. They were on their own until a scheduled ball at the Capitol that night.

Observers were more delighted with "Little Falls" than with St. Anthony Falls; perhaps their expectations for the latter were too high, whereas the former came as a surprise. Samuel Bowles called it "the most charming little water-fall imaginable," hidden in the trees—"and you might pass within ten feet of it without noticing it but for its merry music." There, a small creek "pours itself in one gush over a straight ledge of rock into a softly beautiful pool sixty feet below." Underneath the ledge was a narrower ledge some twenty feet wide, where one could stand behind the waterfall and look through it. "Nothing could be more bewitching in its way, than this fall of Minni-Haha, which is Indian for laughing waters," he enthused. Another editor expanded on the simile of waters laughing: you discover a creek with "its face clothed with the calmest gravity, when, all at once, it suddenly smiles, and then giggles, and at last bounds down in a hearty roar of inextinguishable mirth." The "Little Falls" was picturesque even if it too lacked the sublime character of Niagara.[559]

Some westerners were annoyed at a sophisticated, overdressed, diamond-bedecked, perfumed eastern dandy who was sightseeing at both falls with the aid of an opera glass he carried "in a patent leather box hung over his shoulder by a strap." When he saw a picturesque scene, "out would come the opera glass, and after a momentary squint, . . . his note of admiration—'Demnition foine!— Exquisite, 'pon me honor!'"[560]

Some excursionists who had crossed the river continued by wagon or carriage from Minnehaha Falls to Fort Snelling; however, the steamboats were to take the party from St. Paul to the fort in the late afternoon, and most of them waited for that trip to see the fort. Many returned to St. Paul immediately after viewing St. Anthony Falls.

That might necessitate rental of a return conveyance, to the surprise of the renter, who thought the original fee was a round-trip charge. A party of five excursionists who had hired a driver and his horse-drawn wagon for five dollars asked him if he didn't think it was time to return to St. Paul. "He replied he was ready to do it, if they paid him" another five dollars.[561]

A New York lawyer asked him, "[D]id you not agree to take us to the falls for $5?"

"And by jabbers," said he, "have I not done it? And if you wish to go back I will take you for the same price."

The "greatly fatigued" group had no choice—either pay twice for the trip or walk the nine miles back to St. Paul. Once there, they asked him to drive them to Fort Snelling.

"Sure your honor would not expect me to carry you there for less than $3!"

So they ended up paying a grand total of $13, which the Albany correspondent thought quite excessive. (Perhaps the driver charged for the entertainment of the motley cavalcade.)

Excursionists started arriving back in St. Paul at 2:00 p.m. They had three hours to tour the city or to rest onboard before the steamboats took them to Fort Snelling.

Some New Englanders onboard the *Lady Franklin,* including Catharine Sedgwick and Sewell Cutting, were happy to invite Harriet Bishop, pioneer missionary schoolteacher of St. Paul, to visit them onboard.[562] The delight was no doubt mutual. For them, Bishop personified that civilizing and Christianizing Yankee influence they hoped would shape the West. For Bishop, they represented her home region and pronounced its blessings on her self-sacrificing labors.

Born in 1818 in Vermont, close to Lake Champlain, Bishop attended schools in Vermont and upstate New York. When Catharine Beecher and former Vermont governor William Slade set up the National Board of Popular Education in 1847 to train and dispatch New England young women to teach school in the West, Bishop was in Beecher's first class at Albany. (Beecher asked Sedgwick to aid her western education project, and the author may have been minimally involved.) When missionary Thomas Williamson wrote to Slade to urge him to send a schoolteacher to the steamboat landing in Minnesota— which "has been baptized by the Roman

Catholics by the name of St. Paul" and whose dirty children were untaught and virtually unchurched—she volunteered. Williamson warned, "A teacher for this place should love the Savior, and for his sake should be willing to forego, not only many of the religious privileges and elegances of New England towns, but some of the neatness also." Bishop was willing. She represented the best New England had to offer the West. Baptized in Champlain at thirteen, "the youngest member of her Baptist church," educated by a Beecher, she reportedly missed a boat disaster on Lake Erie because she refused to travel on Sunday. In the seven years since arriving, she had succeeded in getting St. Paul's young children taught, washed, and married off. She fought for Yankee-style temperance and for a female, purifying influence on the frontier town.[563]

"The ladies on board were deeply interested in narratives which their inquiries drew from her," Cutting reported.[564] Catharine Sedgwick especially rejoiced at this story of Yankee pluck and piety. Despite being told (only miles from its very real location) that St. Paul did not exist, this "New England missionary girl had faith in her instructions, . . . opened her school, had, to begin, eight white children, and now came on board to tell us of her flourishing boarding-school, amid five thousand inhabitants!" Sedgwick concluded that Bishop's story "urges promptness, constancy, and heroism in the cause of Western education." Unimpressed by tales of profitable land speculations and prosperous farms in the West, she wished instead "that each emigrant

from our instructed Puritan country might realize that he had more precious seed to sow than the finest of the wheat." Only the schoolhouse could ensure "the safety and progress of a democratic republic."[565]

Less charged with New England's missionary zeal, editor Isaac Platt and his Dutchess County friends reconnected with their guide, Augustus Morgan, a St. Paul citizen from Poughkeepsie. Morgan showed them the Capitol, a substantial two-story brick building, 117 feet long and 63 feet wide, set partway up the hill in back of town to increase its visibility. In front its 42-foot-wide portico was supported by four columns, and its dome rested on a hexagonal brick base. Territorial secretary Joseph Travis Rosser, "although busily engaged in his office" when the Dutchess delegation called, "most obligingly conducted us through the building," Platt noted, "and to the dome, from which" they had "a splendid view" of St. Paul and environs. They counted six churches, three hotels completed, two more under construction, a courthouse finer than "a majority of those in New York," and "a market that equals the best found anywhere. Besides these, spacious, neat and comfortable dwellings . . . some of them elegant, built of brick and stone"—and all this little more than a dozen years since the first building of any kind appeared. St. Paul seemed to Platt "in some degree like the famed palace of Aladdin."[566]

C. Cather Flint of the *Chicago Tribune* chose a different vantage point. He climbed the hill in back of the Capitol. From here, he could see perhaps twenty miles in all directions, he estimated. "The country is spotted all over, at distances of one to three miles, with bright and cool little lakes, that abound in excellent fish." He could see "bluish hills" off to the southwest, up the Minnesota River Valley.[567]

Flint walked downtown to inquire of the merchants about exact statistics of St. Paul's commerce but could not obtain any. He noticed that most merchants specialized and there were fewer general stores than he expected in a frontier city. "Thus we saw exclusive hardware, queenware, dry goods, hat and cap, boot and shoe stores, &c." (Queen's ware was creamy-colored containers, dishes, knives, and forks made of baked clay.) St. Paul had twenty-five lawyers, ten doctors, and four daily newspapers.[568]

Four dailies had sprouted within a fortnight of each other: *Daily Minnesota Pioneer* (May 1), *St. Paul Daily Democrat* (May 1), *Daily Minnesotian* (May 11), and *St. Paul Daily Times* (May 15). The *Pioneer* was Democratic, the organ of Henry H. Sibley, former fur-trade leader and delegate to Congress; the *Democrat* was allied with current delegate Henry M. Rice; the *Times* and *Minnesotian* were Whig, with ties to former governor Alexander Ramsey. The former two supported Douglas's popular sovereignty; the latter two opposed it and the Kansas-Nebraska Act.[569]

Conversing with a "very large number of individuals" and consulting his Whig preconceptions, Flint found "the great majority" in St. Paul were "strongly anti-Nebraska." They all "laugh[ed]" at the "'Popular Sovereignty'

humbug" and were "sincerely opposed to the repeal of the Missouri Compromise."[570]

Another Whig correspondent passed on an unflattering story about Democratic governor William Gorman (possibly told by his predecessor, the Whig Ramsey): "I am told that Governor Gorman argues by the hour with an Irishman who keeps a horse grocery [a saloon] opposite the American [House]. It is needless to add that the Irishman holds his own with uninterrupted success. . . . Governors teach Irishmen out west the rules of oratory and get used up at their own business."[571]

Four dailies (and two political parties) meant fierce competition, and that included coverage of a major event like the Grand Excursion. Earle S. Goodrich, editor of the *Pioneer*, tried to get the jump on his rivals by traveling with the party upriver from La Crosse and by giving his readers a synopsis of the excursion to date; however, John P. Owens of the *Minnesotian* also made it to La Crosse and reported Wednesday's events from "the Grand Flotilla." Goodrich made another try by printing Friday's paper on Thursday afternoon—which enabled him to give a copy to visiting editors, who might reprint a paragraph in their home papers. He wrote one article as excursionists boarded wagons for the falls.[572] Yet David Olmsted, the *Democrat's* editor and St. Paul's mayor, matched him ("while we write, the levee is occupied by steamers' gaily decked with bunting"), also published on Thursday with excursion news, pleased St. Paul pride by saying nothing of the visit to St.

Anthony, and bustled about so much gathering news that he missed the eastern editors who called at his office.[573] Owens and the *Times's* Thomas N. Newson mingled with the guests and waited until Friday to tell the story.[574]

Visiting editors commented on the difficulties of one embryo city sustaining four dailies.[575] The *St. Anthony Express* poked fun at its rival city's dilemma. The editors of the four St. Paul dailies tried all sorts of stratagems to attract subscribers. "One editor will . . . make a statement in regard to some topic, as for example, that 'the price of putty has riz.'" His rivals then attack him and "accuse him of being a 'truckling,' 'vacillating,' 'time-serving' poltroon, 'prostituting the vast power and influence' of the press for the most dishonorable purposes." Finally the putty issue "is exhausted, and ends by the belligerents shaking hands . . . and stepping into Ranch's and ordering 'ice cream and mint julep—strong—for two.'"[576] All St. Paul dailies were careful not to report any negative news of the excursionists' visit (apart from the surprise at their early arrival)—no accidents, complaints about exorbitant charges, or unflattering comments about the falls—and not to give noticeable publicity to St. Anthony.

In fact, there was an accident on the return trip from St. Anthony to St. Paul. Some mishap, either frightened horses or a broken harness, caused a carriage to lose control, careen down a hill, and smash into one in front of it. They were both destroyed, the rear one "shivered into fragments, almost every spoke being broken from three of the wheels,

and the body completely demolished." Benjamin Silliman reported that "providentially" no one was seriously injured. Edward Bates, the auditioning Missouri politician, and Azariah Flagg were in the runaway carriage, "and also two ladies, who are highly praised for the self control and presence of mind which they exhibited under the circumstances." Miss Walton of Utica was one of the two, and she suffered a "slight injury," Silliman reported.[577]

As the excursionists returned, group by group, to their steamboats for the scheduled trip upriver to Fort Snelling, they received cards inviting them to a ball to be held at the Capitol that evening.[578] Banners flying and bands playing, the boats left the upper landing at 5:00 p.m. for the fort.[579] The four-mile trip did not take them long. Having traveled down the west bank to the fort that afternoon, some excursionists were already there and watched the steamboats' arrival from the ramparts, "and as they rounded to the shore and took position, side by side, one after the other, the flag of our country was saluted with cheers long and loud." Major Thomas W. Sherman seems to have been caught by surprise by the arrival, however, for no cannon saluted the flag or Millard Fillmore.[580]

When the guests landed on the flats below the fort, they found a lone white tent and a lone sentry whose mission was "to keep guard, and see that we committed no depradations," or so Isaac Platt interpreted it. "I felt sorry for the poor fellow as he walked back and forth among the tall grass, shouldering his musket, apparently as much at a loss to decide what he was there for as we were."[581]

A "long procession of guests" trudged up a steep road to the fort "in groups" dressed wildly different, in "the pretty colors of dress and shawl and costume," and making "a most irregular army" that took the peaceful fort by surprise. "The soldiers were scattered round, in no other order than as they came together to gaze at this curious invasion," William Bogart remarked. Secretary of War Jefferson Davis's army seemed unready for action. Peace had lulled this far-off frontier fortress into complacency. The visitors were unsure who was in charge: Major Sherman or Colonel Francis Lee. A group of soldiers led artillery horses down a road. Some watered horses. The Stars and Stripes flew over the round tower. Guards paraded back and forth by the gate. Portions, at least, of the Fourth Artillery and the Sixth Infantry Regiment's Company K, and remnants of the Third Dragoon's Company E were stationed here (most dragoons were off to New Mexico).[582]

Reactions to the fort's exterior were mixed. One editor called it "a sombre pile of stone in our dear Uncle Sam's own peculiar style of architecture."[583] To another, a "gray stone" wall "encloses a lozenge shaped area of considerable size, around which are the officer's quarters, barracks, offices, etc." At one acute angle was the magazine; at the other end, the commandant's house, located "nearest the angle of the" bluff, below which point the Minnesota and Mississippi Rivers met. "A picturesque octagonal tower is situated at the end of the south wall, from which there is a most splendid view over the surrounding country."[584] The view disclosed a higher point from which a few cannon could render the fort indefensible. Swallows built nests in the sandstone bluff below, the sandstone "crumbling easily between the fingers and making an exceedingly fine sand." Cannon balls might have a similar effect upon it, one editor thought.[585]

Officers showed their guests around: officers' quarters, barracks, the magazine, the chapel. The visitors "poked their curious heads into all the guard-rooms—accoutrement-rooms—gun-rooms—magazine-rooms . . . picked the flowers which hung like Macbeth's banner from the outer wall," and discussed the fort's merits and demerits. Opinions were mixed. To C. Cather Flint, the barracks seemed "ample, commodious, well ventilated," and the officer's quarters, "which occupy two sides of the grand enclosure which forms the parade ground, are very elegantly furnished." Most officers had their families with them. As a Whig, Flint was most "pleased to see . . . a large and well filled reading room," where the men could improve their minds and profitably occupy their time.[586] Bogart felt "the Fort was not in good order. There were old hats in the windows and other appearances of neglect." Green grass on the parade grounds he took as "an emblem of the peaceful condition of our affairs"—a condition not conducive to well-kept fortresses. It seemed odd the cannon were not fired in a salute to Illinois governor Joel A. Matteson or to former president Fillmore.[587]

Having been informed about the fort in advance by his onboard roommate, retired Colonel William Davenport (who had commanded at Fort Snelling), E. T. Throop Martin had few grand expectations and felt no disappointments.[588]

They were also shown the battery that Captain Braxton Bragg used to good effect at the battle of Buena Vista (February 23, 1847) in the Mexican War. Major Sherman was present at that battle; he was ready for another, but the cannon were not ready to be fired in salute. Excursionists had to imagine the sound of these famous artillery pieces.[589]

Colonel Lee served cake and wine to his guests, including Fillmore and Catharine Sedgwick, in his parlor. Edward Prime was pleased to see a copy of his family's newspaper, the *New York Observer,* on Lee's table. They could also go out his back door, as Sewell Cutting did, "to view the valley from the rear of his quarters, on the brow of the bluff," where the two rivers meet "at your feet."[590]

Silliman was also pleased with the fine view from the platform behind the commandant's house: "The two rivers flow at your feet. The walls repose upon a sandstone so soft and disintegrated that it is fast becoming sand and the swallows make their nests in the bank." He found Lee and his officers to be "very polite" but their fort "of little or no use."[591]

After an hour's visit, the steamboat whistles loudly blew the command to board and depart. Walking down the steep road to the landing, they could look up the Minnesota River and reflect on the historic, romantic, and picturesque associations of this site.[592] Across the Minnesota, at Mendota, stood the American Fur Company's "old buildings . . . ancient and deserted," reminders of a bygone era and "the whoop of the Indians, or the gasconade of the French trapper." Even a new country had ancient ruins. Now, "the quiet pursuits of agriculture" made the fur post as obsolete as the fort was made by the prevailing peace.[593] One visitor wondered what Fort Snelling had ever protected and why it had ever been built.[594]

They crossed Pike's Island and boarded the steamboats for the return trip to St. Paul, which they reached about 7:00 p.m.[595]

Trying to outdo the other boats once more, Captain Harris took the *War Eagle* up the Minnesota River "a short distance" before heading to St. Paul. Harris told his own tall tales to his passengers: the Minnesota River seldom flooded; it was navigable for "some 300 miles," and Harris had steamed up it that far; he "proudly boasted that his wife was the first white person to land so far up upon its shores"; he claimed that the Dakota were "quite as well satisfied" with their Minnesota River reservation lands as they had been with their old homes along the Mississippi.[596]

It was only an hour until the grand ball was to begin, but that was enough time for William Schouler, Moses Kimball, and company to entertain the crowd at the St. Paul levee.[597] Several wags proclaimed Schouler to be the mayor of St. Paul, and he proceeded to give a speech welcoming excursionists and parodying the spread-eagle, whisky-soaked rhetoric of Douglas's Democratic Young America enthusiasts, with their support of fili-bustering expeditions to seize Cuba and of Republican revolutionaries trying to over-throw European monarchs.

"We welcome you, gentlemen, to the 'horse-pie-talities' of St. Paul," the "mayor" opened. "You came up here expecting to find us a half-civilized, half-fed race of beings; but now you may go home and tell that we are jest as good looking and well dressed as any of you Yankees." He then launched into his own Young America rhetoric:

Feller Citizuns[.] I am glad to see you here in the Great Northwest—in this part of a great kendtry which is bounded on the East by the Atlantic, on the West by the Pacific, and is split in two by the Big Ditch of the Mississippi. I have said that this is a great kendtry, but feller citizuns, it's getten' to be more than a great kendtry—it's getten' tremend-i-o-u-s! We stand with one foot on Cuba and the other on the Sandwich Islands, and our arms stretched out over all creation, and I'd like to know where you can scare up a bigger figur than that is? *Feneul Hall was the cradle where our kendtry was rocked in infancy, but, feller citizuns,* whar *will you find wood enuff to make its coffin?*

Schouler urged easterners to come to Minnesota to raise wheat "to feed the poor, miserable people that are crushed down the other side of the Big Pond by the iron heel of the Dees-pot." He warned of price-gouging speculators at St. Anthony, "whar' they sell lots for $10,000 an acre. Dont go thar, I beg of you. We can, in this flourishing place, sell you lots, at a very great sacrifice, for half that sum." He closed on a wet note. "Feller Citizuns, I reckon you're mighty dry by this time; I am; and if you'll come over to the gro-cery across the square, we will all take a drink to our better acquaintance."[598]

Bogart of upstate New York and W. E. P. Haskell of Boston replied to the welcome, as had been the custom at prior stops along the river. But the main rhetorical effort came from Kimball, who was suffering from a bad cold that amusingly distorted his voice but did not dampen his presidential ambitions.

"Mr. Mare," Kimball replied. With no regard to the mayor's exact remarks or the spe-cific occasion, he threw his hat in the ring while imitating Fillmore's "manner, gestures, &c." "He defined his past and present posi-tion at length; he was in favor of all the great principles of all parties; was in favor of the next war; in favor of the largest liberty for everybody to do as they pleased; was in favor of dividing the whole property of the country equally *twice* a week; was in favor of all the women having the right to vote, and should, if elected, as he expected to be, appoint none but women to any public office."

The crowd cheered each and every promise.

One fellow came to announce that Fillmore was going to speak at the Capitol, and the mock candidate down at the landing used that real announcement also to poke fun at the candidate up on the hill.

By now it was time to head for the uptown festivities. Hacks, carriages, and coaches stood by to transport ladies and some gentlemen to the Capitol. The rest had to walk.[599]

Brightly lit with candles in its windows, the Capitol could be seen from quite a distance. Placards had been posted around town to announce the ball. A large crowd of Minnesotans stood outside the brick building, while St. Paul's finest waited inside.[600] Guests entered through the columned portico and front door into a large vestibule, on one side of which was the governor's office. They climbed the stairs to the second-floor Council chambers, the evening's reception room. On the speaker's platform were Sibley, Gorman, Fillmore, and Bancroft, facing "a large company of ladies and gentlemen."[601]

Sibley opened the proceedings by introducing the governor—a fellow Democrat, not as popular as his predecessor, Ramsey the Whig. A Mexican War veteran, a rough and profane man, Gorman recognized that this high-class affair was mainly Whig in numbers, in polite expectations, and in the presence of the last Whig president.[602] To him, Gorman spoke first, praising Fillmore's help to the Minnesota Territory and, in the 1850 Compromise, to the nation. While an Indiana Congressman, Gorman was privileged to vote for the compromise that "had hushed the war of factions and given peace to opposing sections of the country." Aware of protocol and

of Whig scorn for rough-hewn Democrats who violated it, Gorman thanked the excursion's organizers; welcomed men of various professions, the arts, the sciences, "and those who had occupied high positions in the nation"; and praised editors, whose publicity was sure to benefit the territory. He boosted Minnesota in words they could copy for wider circulation: "But six short years ago, on the spot where I now see so much of the talent and beauty of the country assembled around me, there stood an Indian wigwam, a sugar camp." Now Minnesota had more than 30,000 inhabitants with room for more: "the oppressed emigrant from Europe," "the enterprising New-Englanders and the hardy Westerner." The excursion was a bigger boost for emigration than anything Minnesotans could devise. So these visitors were heartily welcome. "And especially do we welcome the ladies, whose bright eyes to-night lend a charm to these legislative halls."[603]

Fillmore replied with a longer speech than any he had delivered so far on the excursion. He came as a private citizen and expressed his surprise at this public reception. He complimented Henry Farnam, whose spirit of enterprise had helped to link East to West and to organize an excursion to celebrate that. The crowd applauded that compliment loudly. Fillmore responded to Gorman's unexpected praise, in terms the *Tribune*'s Dana paraphrased: "[N]ext to the approbation of his own conscience he valued that of his fellow citizens." The 1850 Compromise "which had been so kindly singled out for comment was a trying one." In supporting it "he was aware that he ran counter to the feelings of many whose esteem he could not but desire and value, but he trusted that all would now do him the justice to believe that that act was done honestly and fearlessly."[604] Fillmore noted that St. Paul was located on one potential route of a transcontinental railroad, so needed to bind Pacific Coast, Mississippi Valley, and East Coast "in one Confederacy." He advocated its construction—by a route through St. Paul, the city's boosters could infer.[605]

(Two days earlier, Sibley had written a letter to Isaac I. Stevens, governor of Washington Territory and a leader in the 1853 government survey of a northern transcontinental route from Minnesota to Washington. Sibley assured Stevens "that hereafter the great overland travel will be via St. Paul to Puget's Sound" and urged him to lobby for the northern route "if you have half the affection for Washington Territory that I feel for Minnesota." Fillmore's comment may have been the result of Sibley's lobbying him that Thursday.)[606]

Fillmore likened the Mississippi "to a great tree, loaded with fruit, whose roots were in the Gulf of Mexico," near which New Orleans was positioned to gather the fruit as it dropped down. And yet the "rich fruit . . . might be snatched from the proud city" by "enterprize and railroads . . . and only by these two powerful engines could the fruits of the West be directed Eastward." The excursion evidenced that the fruits were headed East. "Messrs. Sheffield and Farnam in building the Chicago and Rock Island Railroad have set up a great ladder, with its base at New York, to bear the fruit safely and securely to another commercial point."[607] Fillmore did not criticize this fruit-snatching. Nor did he discuss its impact on the Union his Compromise was meant to strengthen. Did the C&RI and a northern transcontinental railroad marginalize the South or nudge it out of the "one Confederacy"?

Fillmore also sounded his appreciation for the beauty of St. Paul, of Minnesota, and of the ladies assembled there.[608]

All that now stood between the gentlemen and a dance with a beautiful lady was the final speech, George Bancroft's. The audience knew his reputation as a skillful historical writer, but few had heard him speak, and many were unsure of his ability to give an impromptu address, with his only source his wit and his own observations. Bancroft may have doubted his ability to speak well when "tired & banged up & dusty."[609] He had no current political ambitions; he spoke for the railroad and its investors; he did not speak on historian's stilts. He began by mentioning "the kindly relations" now inaugurated between the C&RI and Minnesotans, whom it had linked to eastern markets and who would gratefully respond by patronizing it (via steamboat to Rock Island). He praised the "unprecedented" excursion, with "so large a number of persons . . . conveyed in so agreeable a way, as the guests of the Railroad Company." Unlike Fillmore, he included the South in a Union to be "dovetail[ed]" by railroads. Progress would bring Minnesota into that rail-bound Union. Picking up on Gorman's regret that the winter freeze cut Minnesota off from the East for five months, Bancroft gallantly and democratically reversed the usual geographical hierarchy: "Do not talk of being locked up for five months in the year. It is us who are shut out from you."[610]

While Bancroft spoke, Gorman led Fillmore outside the Capitol and introduced him to the crowd of people who lacked the status or came too late to secure a place at the proceedings inside. (A *New York Times* man called them "the *plebs* of St. Paul's.") Here Fillmore repeated his speech.[611]

His voice suffering from a cold or from the effects of his accident, Bancroft launched into a paean to Minnesota that was a much briefer vote for the West than were his six historical volumes but was expressed in much the same terms: the place was beautiful, its valleys green, its bluffs verdant with vegetation, its soil fertile, its climate healthy. Indeed, "the half had not been told." He predicted that these western Democrats would soon become a state in the Union equal to, if not more distinguished than, eastern ones. (In fact, Minnesotans were reluctant to give up territorial status; Congress paid their territorial government's expenses, including the $32,500 cost of the Capitol; why exchange that just for an equal democratic voice in the nation's affairs?)[612]

Bancroft saved the best for his peroration: "[W]hen he concluded by bidding Minnesota be the North Star of the Union, shining forever in unquenchable luster, there was a general burst of applause throughout the crowded room."[613]

The crowd exited the Council Chamber and walked across the hall where the ball was to be held. Here a large band consisting of the five boats' musicians plus a St. Paul band was seated on a platform in the center of the room. Some who preferred dancing to eating went no farther while the rest entered the House of Representatives Chamber on the other side, where "tables of refreshments" beckoned them to "a great variety of delicacies": 200 pounds of assorted cakes, 950 sandwiches, thirty cooked hams, various cooked chickens, coffee, milk, almonds, and twenty-one pounds of fancy candies. Minnesotans and visitors conversed while eating, and some went "promenading the rooms of the immense building."[614]

Couples formed quadrilles for the dancing, for it was nearing ten o'clock, and the visitors would have to depart at eleven. Dancers gathered in the hall, decorated with evergreen branches and boughs in the form of garlands, stars, and other shapes; "a more brilliant looking ball room, the most gallant disciple of Terpsichore would not wish to worship in." The band played the "Prima Donna Waltz," among other numbers. A St. Paul paper reported, "[T]he acknowledged beauty of our St. Paul ladies never shone to better advantage than on this occasion; each seemed disposed to contribute her share to make our guests—*at home.*" A New York City paper emphasized that Minnesotans were now privileged to see "some of the beauty of the East." An upstate New York editor graciously praised "the manly and honest cordiality of Minnesota gentlemen, and . . . the beauty and grace of Minnesota ladies."[615]

(News of beauties led to a teasing letter from Syracuse, New York, to a Minnesota bachelor: "The monster excursion party created the grand sensation it seems among the *barbarians* of your far off western home. Did you dance with the fair pale damsels from the Orient? Judge [James R.] Lawrence and two daughters [Christine and Agnes] were there—didn't you see them—the daughters have staid at St. Anthony.")[616]

A few fireworks were set off for the entertainment of the crowd standing outside the building but unable to get in.[617]

Not all guests were satisfied with the ball and reception. Social activities were delayed by the politicians' speeches and cut short by the Sabbatarians' hurried schedule for reaching Chicago by Saturday night. Hiram Fuller complained, "The Ball was a regular squeeze . . . the dancing was about as hurried and satisfactory as a running dinner at a railroad station. . . . [T]he crowd was too thick for the display of the graces or the exhibition of the dignitaries." Bogart lamented that the "brilliant gathering of the ladies to the dance . . . was but brief; we were to leave at 11, and the festivities were forced to move on in locomotive style."[618]

Sure enough, around 11:00 p.m., the steamboats' whistles blew to signal departure. The dancing was "broken off, cinderella-like, at a fixed hour." Minnesotans "entreat us to remain longer," James Babcock reported,

"but the inexorable steamers demand the return of their flocks." Carriages took many ladies to the Lower Landing, but many gentlemen and some ladies had to pick their way down muddy paths to where they could board the five boats. Daniel Boone's latest biographer, William Bogart, seemed pleased to have a fur trader guide him and to note how twelve years earlier they might have been scalped on this path. Observers on the decks, who had not attended the ball, were surprised to see the same ladies who had left "looking 'pretty scrumptious'" come back with "their pretty feet and ankles" stained with black Minnesota mud.[619]

Shortly after midnight, with their bands playing the tune "Good Bye," the five steamboats pushed out into the channel and headed downriver. Excited by the day's events and by now being "homeward bound," many excursionists remained on deck for some time after the lights of St. Paul had disappeared behind the river bend: "the weather was charming and the scene again almost enchanting as the boats dashed along in the calm moonlight amid the splendid scenery." Catharine Sedgwick felt "[i]t was a day better than most lifetimes."[620]

Sitting down at tables to write up their reports, several editors felt that such a day ought not to have been marred by politics. Bogart criticized Gorman's and Fillmore's speeches: "It was an insult to that audience to drag in a review of past political action . . . it was not necessary to come unto St. Paul to have the dead bury their dead." Fuller seconded the motion. "For one, I am quite tired, not to say disgusted, at these constantly repeated addresses to our beflattered 'fellow citizens.'" Babcock objected to Fillmore "allud[ing] indirectly, and we think unfortunately, to the humbug Compromise of 1850," which paved the way for Kansas-Nebraska and the repudiation of the genuine Compromise of 1820.[621]

Dana praised Bancroft, who was not auditioning for any new political positions or defending his conduct in any former ones. His talk was "one of those brilliant and facile improvisations"; it was a "rapid and salient address, every sentence as clean cut as a finished statue, and delivered with admirable point and distinctness."[622]

Charles Weldon of the *New York Times*—perhaps the *Times* man who fell in the Mississippi, which might explain his curmudgeon's report—felt the day was longer than most lifetimes and Minnesotans greedier than most Yankees. At St. Paul, no cannon greeted them; no champagne was served to them; exorbitant prices were charged them for carriages, chewing tobacco, and brandy; land prices were outrageous; promotional pamphlets were "one huge lie from title-page to colophon." The Falls of St. Anthony were "a ripple on a river." Minnesota winters lasted for six months, covered the land with twelve feet of snow, and left inhabitants for seven months as isolated from civilization as were "the exiles of Siberia."[623] (Weldon's report sparked vigorous rebuttals from fellow *Times* correspondent "Excelsior" and the *St. Anthony Express*.)[624]

Despite a negative report, Minnesotans anticipated great promotional benefits. Goodrich admitted the excursion was meant to show investors the fruits of their confidence in the railroad. But the West too would benefit by such an assemblage of "Editors, Railroad men, Engineers, Geologists, Mineralogists, Artists, Divines, Statesmen, Poets, Historians, Literary men generally, Merchants, and . . . persons of Fashion" who would "become to us perpetual advertisements" to Minnesota's "future greatness." Such a company must have great influence with thousands of easterners. They would disseminate more information about Minnesota in the following ninety days than the normal means of publicity could spread in ten years. No wonder the *Minnesota Democrat* called it "the greatest epoch that has ever dawned upon our Territory."[625]

EXCURSUS

John Dean Caton and Antebellum American Law

LIKE MANY PIONEERS, Judge John Dean Caton was a jack-of-all-trades interested in most anything in an amateur way: an avid hunter, fisherman, camper, collector of Indian lore, naturalist, gentleman farmer, self-taught telegraphy expert, and telegraph company owner. With his massive head and thick neck, Caton looked more like a farmer or ox driver than a lawyer or judge. He had slight education in the law. It was hard to keep one's mind on replevin, nolo contendere, and precedent when Pottawatomie war dances, legendary sandstone bluffs, and a brash new railroad-and-telegraph economy seemed far more compelling.

His audience on the trains also wanted to hear of Starved Rock more than stare decisis, and some likely knew him, for they came from Utica and Rome, Oneida County, New York, where he spent his late teens studying law. Railroads brought specialization to Illinois, but pioneers like Caton preferred adventure, novelty, and variety to intense study of one topic:

Justice John Dean Caton.
(Album of Genealogy and Biography,
Calumet Book and Engraving Company)

[A]fter the mind had become weary with wrestling with some abstruse or difficult question of law, he would banish it entirely from his thoughts, and take up the subject of some telegraphic plan he was maturing, or why the prairies are not covered with trees, or some book he had in hand . . . or some work on navigation or hydraulic engineering, . . . or some literary work, as history or the classics. . . . His rule was never to pursue a study when the mind was wearied with it.[626]

As a generalist's generation gave way to the specialists, an excursion to see many sights in the company of many experts on many topics was a perfect entertainment, one unlikely to weary Caton's mind—even if it reminded him that trains brought eastern law professors like Harvard's Joel Parker, historians like George Bancroft, and geologists like Benjamin Silliman, any of whom might challenge his amateur opinions.

Judge Caton had freed himself from Illinois Supreme Court duties to go on the Grand Excursion by getting his fellow judges to postpone their June term one week. Chicago & Rock Island Railroad attorney Norman B. Judd, who would likely have business before the court, extended an invitation to the other four judges also—through Caton, for "you know just how the thing should be done"—but pressing business and poor health prevented them from accompanying Caton. None questioned the propriety of accepting a free vacation from one of the state's largest corporations. Nor, apparently, did Caton object when Judd offered to arrange for him to purchase shares in the Chicago & Milwaukee Railroad. He seemed unconcerned about the appearance of impropriety in his ties to his former law partner, Judd.[627]

The excursion also offered Caton an opportunity to benefit his telegraph company, which was erecting telegraph poles and setting up telegraph service for Joseph Sheffield and Henry Farnam's rail lines, and which was just then battling a rival to win the contract to provide telegraph service along the Michigan Southern route. Two Michigan Southern directors with a say in who won the contract were traveling on the excursion, and Caton would presumably have a chance to discuss it with them. (After the excursion ended, Caton's group won the contract.) However, he undoubtedly would have gone west even if the trip presented no such advantages.[628]

Presiding in Room 212 of the State House on the square at Springfield, Illinois, could grow wearisome, although the judges did not have to keep minutes of their conferences or print up their written opinions. "The first rule requiring anything printed in the record was in 1855," Caton later recalled. Next door to Room 212 was the State Law Library, Abraham Lincoln's home away from home, where he spent countless hours researching cases. Widely known for his circuit-court cases, Lincoln was actually more influential as a lawyer arguing before Caton's Supreme Court. Caton and his fellow judges would be hard at work in their conference late at night when they would hear "boisterous laughter" from the library. "We knew at once that Mr. Lincoln was telling some new story, for which he was so celebrated, and the temptation, to me at least, was very strong to go out and hear it."[629]

One of Lincoln's jokes was on them. It became known among the lawyers appearing before the Supreme Court that all three of its judges (the number changed over the years) were from Oneida County, New York. Caton entered the library after hearing laughter.

"Mr. Lincoln, who was seated on one of the tables, his feet hanging down nearly to the floor, said: 'Judge Caton, I want to know if it is true, as has been stated, that all three of you judges come from Oneida county, New York?'" Caton admitted that was true but wondered what possible meaning it could have. *"'Only this,'"* Lincoln replied. *"'I could never understand before why this was a One-i-dea court.'"* The room burst into laughter, and the other two judges came over from the conference room to have the pun repeated for their enjoyment.[630]

Spoofing the judges had its dangers for a lawyer who had to appear before this same tribunal in a day or two. (Here, Lincoln suffered no adverse consequences.) On the Eighth Circuit, where Lincoln practiced, and in other midwestern areas, lawyers sometimes held mock trials in private to vent their dissatisfaction with a judge. But it is noteworthy that the mock trial held onboard the *Sparhawk* included no lawyers or judges in any publicized role. Lawyers and judges did not mock their profession in public. In the 1840s and 1850s, they were in the process of establishing the law as a distinct profession that laymen could not practice (after some relaxation of standards during the Jackson years). Some bellwether states like New York laid down strict rules for admittance to the bar. The last thing they wanted was to lead public ridicule of the bench and bar.[631]

Beyond this, they were trying to insulate the law from theology and politics: (1) stressing practical and utilitarian—rather than moral or "natural law"—purposes for the common law; (2) defining justice more in terms of economic development and progress rather than a "fair" status quo; (3) ending juries' power to decide matters of law as well as matters of fact; and (4) using judicial review and the Constitution to minimize legislatures' ability to interfere with contracts and other legal matters. They raised the "banner of 'science'"—the law as a science—"to separate politics from law, subjectivity from objectivity, and laymen's reasoning from professional reasoning." The walls of separation were already mainly completed by 1854.[632] As the head of a telegraph company profiting from each mile of westward track-laying progress, as a judge who wanted to instruct juries, Caton was not opposed to these changes, even if he resisted the legal specialization implicit in the notion that law was a science.

The prevailing view was that law was a science, an organized, systematic body of knowledge that should use the Baconian, inductive method to arrive at its principles. The legal teacher James Wilson had summarized: "In all sciences, says my Lord Bacon, they are the soundest that keep close to particulars"; the human mind worked "from particular facts to general principles" and "common law, like natural philosophy [natural science], when properly studied, is a science founded on experiment."[633] A legal scientist started with actual cases, inductively reasoned some "specific low-level rules" from these cases, classified law (as if it were the animal kingdom) into various species and subspecies, and only then thought of identifying some higher principles. Even the process of filing pleas could be seen as scientific, as governed by rational principles, as long as science was not too narrowly defined.[634]

So lawyers were not one-idea men, nor Caton's court a one-idea court. The common law consisted of thousands of pieces of information, or "facts," that had to be diligently, humbly learned before a young man could consider himself an expert, a scientist, in the law. The data was not always put to a high scientific use. In one case, *People v. Thurber,* the Supreme Court could not affirm the lower court's ruling without "suspend[ing] the operations of all our election laws," Caton recalled, "and my duty was to hunt up shreds and scraps of statutes to sustain the decision" that the court already felt it must make.[635] The data being the decisions of many different judges, these facts might openly contradict one another. The law could not be a science exactly like geology or chemistry.

Caton and his cronies were already a bit outdated in 1854. In the more modern state of New York, a reform movement had partly succeeded in codifying state laws. Reformers were concerned "that common law judges exercised too much discretion when deciding cases." A systematized law would give clearer direction and limit judicial discretion just as lawyers and judges had earlier successfully limited jurors' discretion. Here the deductive method could be used to deduce correct applications of a simply stated law.[636]

A further specialization was also in the works that would prove distasteful to Caton. Antebellum legal scholars were specialists, but their Baconian method meant that they "roamed widely in their reading and writing—David Hoffman's *Course of Legal Study,* for instance, recommended passages ranging from the Bible to Aristotle to Bacon to Bentham." Later, their successors would concentrate "on the study of LAW, and law only."[637] That would not suit John Dean Caton, naturalist, collector of Indian lore, telegrapher, businessman, memoirist, hunter—and judge.

EXCURSUS

Cholera, C. B. Coventry, and Antebellum Medical Science

A MAJOR CHOLERA EPIDEMIC hit the East and the Mississippi River Valley in 1849. The Grand Excursionists were concerned about a recurrence, as were the organizers. Cholera was the most feared of all diseases. On June 1, George Mix assured Henry Farnam, "I hear of no sickness on the river and *I believe* that the present stage of water will render the Valley *perfectly healthy.*" Still, Mix advised Farnam that "emigrants and deck passengers" be kept off the excursion boats "to preserve health." Antebellum Americans believed lower-class persons were more susceptible to the disease.[638]

During the excursion, one steamboat captain told James Babcock of the *New Haven Palladium* that his experience confirmed this belief. In the summer of 1849, when the epidemic raged in St. Louis, 10 percent of his passengers succumbed to the disease, "but not one of them was a cabin passenger." He attributed this to lower-class deck passengers' neglect of the early symptoms of this rapid disease, especially diarrhea. Cabin passengers did not ignore this symptom, he asserted. He gave the example of a deckhand who carried "bags of salt, weighing over 200 pounds, from the boat to the shore at sundown on a certain day, yet he died of cholera before the next morning." He had taken only whiskey for his three-day-old diarrhea.[639]

Physician and cholera expert Charles Brodhead Coventry.

As it happened, one excursionist, Dr. Charles Brodhead Coventry, had written a book on cholera, *Epidemic Cholera,* published in 1849. Coventry served as professor of physiology and medical jurisprudence at the University of Buffalo, and held a similar position at Geneva College's Medical Institute.[640] Coventry's book illustrated how medical science, like the other sciences, relied upon traveling, gathering data, and making numerous observations that were then analyzed for cause-and-effect relationships in a manner similar to a historian's methods.

Cholera was rare in the United States until the early 1830s, when the increased use of steamships greatly speeded and simplified the Atlantic crossing that previously had hindered spread of the disease to North America. The city of Utica hired Coventry to go to Albany and New York City in 1832 to investigate the cholera epidemic there, and he wrote an initial report. The medical schools at Geneva and Buffalo sent him to Europe to investigate a reported outbreak, "but the destroyer had been temporarily arrested in its course in Russia," Coventry reported, and "he returned without having met the disease." Nevertheless, he did gather historical data and the observations of others while in Europe.[641]

He began his book with a history of cholera, its origins in India, its spread to Europe, and its transatlantic migration to North America, where "[i]ts general course was the same as it had been in Europe, following the course of navigable waters and principal highways, passing by many places without affecting them." This geographical pattern of diffusion did not establish a cause. In arguing that cholera was not contagious (not spread directly from infected persons to others), he relied on testimony from European authorities and on historical examples where people working with the sick had not been infected. He had no laboratory results pointing away from contagion. Instead, he had testimony that cholera epidemics ended after a storm or a change in the weather.[642]

Like a historian identifying background causes and triggering causes, he argued for an "epidemic cause" ("some peculiar condition of the atmosphere" that was enervating and "poisonous") and "sporadic causes" that affected the entire community ("bad air" from decomposing matter or stagnant water) or a single individual (exhaustion, an undernourished state, etcetera). Even fear could be a sporadic cause. "If we only look at a frightened person, we see that they present almost the first symptoms of cholera—the face is pale, the surface cold, the pulse feeble, the blood having retreated from the surface to the central organs."[643]

How could a person avoid cholera? "The best preventives are plenty of pure and wholesome air," good food, ample clothing, "moderate exercise in the open air, regular sleep at night, and, above all, a quiet mind." He or she should sleep in "upper rooms, or chambers," not lower ones. "No curtains should be admitted about the bed, and, if it can be avoided, several persons should not be crowded into the same room." Obviously, it would be hard for excursionists on crowded boats to follow that rule. "Wet feet, and night and damp air, should be as much as possible avoided, as well as over fatigue, and excesses of every description."[644] Excursionists found it impossible to avoid damp night air and fatigue; warnings such as these served to increase the fear that Coventry identified as itself a "sporadic cause."

This medical advice appeared in the newspapers. Little more than a week after the Grand Excursion, the *Galena* returned to St. Paul on its regular run with freight and passengers, five of whom had "symptoms of the Cholera. They were cabin passengers," contrary to the belief that it affected only poor deck passengers. Excesses were the cause, according to a St. Paul newspaper. Cholera "was probably brought on by over-eating, drinking large quantities of water, and keeping irregular hours." If that were true, then certainly some excursionists should have contracted the disease. "People who travel cannot be too careful as to diet. If they *will* gorge their stomachs with unhealthy food, they must suffer the consequences." The *Times* assured its readers, "These cases are not of an epidemic nature," but resulted from "over-indulgence in the good things to be found on board of the Upper Mississippi steamboats." The *Times* reported that two of the five had died the day before.[645]

Coventry's idea of epidemic and sporadic causes was based upon physicians' observations of patients and then inductive reasoning. This Baconian method enabled him to identify the stages of cholera: (1) white tongue,

fatigue, and "slight diarrhœa"; (2) "violent vomiting" and more severe diarrhea; (3) cold, clammy skin, slow breathing, and a very weak pulse; (4) "the tongue becomes brown or dark colored and parched . . . pulse weak and tremulous; great restlessness or muttering delirium; alternate chills and heat of surface" leading to death.[646] Such outward signs were observable, but the cause might not be. No laboratory work identified a causal agent. No doctor could accurately deduce the cause from a general principle of disease. No observation of stages could necessarily identify the right treatment. Baconian observation was the antebellum state of the art: "practically all of the significant work in American medicine lay in observational fields. Hardly any laboratory science came from America, probably because until very late in the century there were few laboratories."[647] A specific cause of the lack of medical laboratory work was religious opposition to dissecting the human body and to conducting autopsies. Thus, many American physicians relied on French sources "and the ready access to specimens that Paris afforded" to add to their "pathological museum" or cabinet of specimens of diseased organs.[648]

Of course, examining specimens in the laboratory might be only Baconian observation, absent scientific theories, equipment, and experiments that could reveal more than was visible to the naked eye or could reveal more of what the visible signified than could common sense or past experience.

Absent theories, equipment, and experiments, travel became a major means of gathering more cases from which to induce causes or cures. "Letters from abroad were a regular feature of medical journals in the 1820s and 1830s, and grew increasingly common with the proliferation of journals in the 1840s and 1850s."[649] Coventry's book was based on his travels.

The greatest example of the traveler gathering medical facts, "the supreme American attempt to use Baconian methods to fathom the natural environment for medical purposes," was Cincinnati physician Daniel Drake's massive two-volume *Systematic Treatise . . . on the Principal Diseases of the Interior Valley of North America . . .* (1850, 1854). After traveling some 15,000 miles on the Great Lakes, along the Mississippi River, and along the Gulf of Mexico, and after collecting facts and observations from physicians in these regions, Drake wrote a medical geography of more than 1,400 pages, "the most extensive antebellum American effort to . . . sort out the medical significance of the environment." He died two years before the excursion, but his magnum opus illustrates how the Baconian method linked science, medicine, and history. Because he believed that the environment helped to cause disease, he studied the "geology, zoology, botany, geography, vital statistics, and meteorology" of the Mississippi Valley. Because he relied on a study of actual cases, his book chronicled the medical history of the valley. It became "an invaluable historical source" after its medical value ceased.[650]

Drake's observations about Ottawa, Illinois, illustrated his methods. After describing the town and its surroundings, he summarized its state of health, as reported by local doctors: "I learned that autumnal fever is common in this locality, and that malignant intermittents are not unknown. The Irish laborers on the canal had suffered greatly." Drake reasoned, however, that digging the Illinois and Michigan Canal had not caused the fevers: "The two autumns in which the excavations were going forward, were the sickliest that Doctor Howland had known at this place; but, as the sickness prevailed in the adjoining country, it could not be said to depend on the excavation." A local physician "had also seen some proofs, that the first plowing up of the prairies is followed by fever."[651] Certain deductions could be made based on the many observations, but they were commonsensical ones that even a historian could make; in fact, they came close to the historian's fallacy of *post hoc ergo propter hoc.*

If the local environment played a large role in causing sickness, then it followed that the sick person might improve his or her condition by traveling to a new environment. Some excursionists—Charles Sedgwick, for example—undoubtedly took the trip partly for their health. Whether to avoid cholera or to aid his recovery from other ailments, Catharine Sedgwick tried to get Charles to follow commonsense advice such as Coventry's: plenty of sleep, no "fried potatoes," no unnecessary worrying. Despite his refusal to follow her recommendations, she was pleased with the trip's positive impact on his health.[652] This "travel therapy" was widespread in antebellum America, and patients saw it as their right. They were "sure that sea-voyaging, change of air, and avoidance of . . . inclement atmosphere will effect a cure, or at least prolong and alleviate existence." It might be travel to a health spa or springs, or to a different climate. "[T]here developed a tendency for northern physicians to send their patients to southern resorts and southern physicians to do the opposite."[653]

Of course, the Grand Excursion weakened and sickened some travelers instead of curing them. On Tuesday, June 6, the *Jenny Lind* returned from Dubuque with the fatigued and "several invalids."[654] That fact became just another medical observation. A physician like Coventry might attribute their illnesses to the overcrowding on the boats, the excitement of the occasion, the late nights and little sleep, the menu, the small staterooms, or the cold and rainy weather. There was no way of telling for sure, except, perhaps, by comparing it with a smaller excursion under warmer and drier conditions. Only collecting many such cases and analytically, inductively comparing them could enable the doctor or researcher to speculate about the causes of ill health. There would never be another excursion exactly like this one.

MISSISSIPPI RIVER WOODYARD *by Seth Eastman, pencil on paper, 1848. This "wooding up" place for steamboats on the west (Minnesota) bank of the Mississippi River was similar to the woodyard at Mount Vernon, Minnesota, where excursionist Reverend Duncan Kennedy gave his extemporaneous speech. (Minnesota Historical Society)*

CHAPTER EIGHT

"Going Down this Noblest of all Rivers"

FRIDAY, JUNE 9, 1854

THE TRIP DOWNRIVER was to be timed so that scenery that the Grand Excursionists passed at night on the way up would be seen in the daytime on the way down.[655] Accordingly, they entered Lake Pepin (which most saw by moonlight on Wednesday) at sunrise on Friday morning. The lake "was calm and placid as a mirror," reported Daniel Wager of Rome, New York, "and while the western side glittered in the brightness, on the east the grim shadows yet lay heavily." So mirrorlike was its calmness that "on the water one could trace the delicate outline of the cliffs— every chasm and indentation vividly mirrored. Even the branches of the trees and the interstices between the leaves seemed daguerreotyped on the faithful water" of Lake Pepin. As they pushed downstream "and as the swell from the paddle wheels reached the fairy line of shadow, the reflections" of cliff, branches, and leaves "rose and fell on the mimic wave and remained unbroken."[656]

As usual, Captain Daniel Smith Harris ran the *War Eagle* far ahead of the other steamboats (racing was forbidden, but no other boat tried to beat him, so he wasn't racing, apparently). Greatly helped by the current that ran about four miles per hour, the *War Eagle* averaged about twenty miles an hour on the return trip, according to Isaac Platt of the

Poughkeepsie Eagle. Harris stopped only to "wood up." They passed "many large rafts floating down," but Platt was surprised that they "hardly met a steamboat in the course of a day." It was good they didn't. The river twisted and turned among the islands "so that often one cannot see half a mile ahead." An oncoming steamboat half a mile away would meet them head-on in less than two minutes given their downstream speed. "The main channel is seldom half a mile wide," he estimated.[657]

The speed and ease of downstream travel seemed to remind him of the rapid westward advance of English-speaking peoples and of "the superior progressive character of the Anglo Saxon race." The country through which the *War Eagle* hurtled once belonged to France and would have had a different fate had Great Britain not acquired the east bank in 1763 and the United States the west bank in 1803. How fortunate, he concluded, that "the laws of progress and the Anglo Saxon spirit drove [France] out at every point, so that her language, arbitrary institutions and religion, scarcely found a foothold."[658]

So rapid was their descent that the supply of fish the *Sparhawk* had ordered on the way upriver was not yet ready when the boat arrived at the designated delivery point.[659]

The speed at which the Grand Excursion

was nearing its end, the beauty of the scenery, the fact that this portion of it was glimpsed with discomfort (if at all) through Wednesday's cold rain—all conspired to keep many excursionists out on deck nearly the entire day. Charles Sedgwick apologized to his wife, "But for looking all day at this glorious river I should have written you today." Catharine Sedgwick wrote to her niece, "Going down this noblest of all rivers I have seen, dearest Kate, like a bird of swiftest passage. . . . I cannot leave the deck long enough to describe one point of interest and beauty." The approaching end of the trip colored the view for John Munn: "A calm, subdued feeling possessed me, as I left behind such scenes, never again to look upon their like."[660]

Platt described it for his readers: numerous islands "covered with grass and tall forest trees" made it seem like traveling through "thick unbroken forest"; bluffs "frequently rise to high and continuous ridges from five to six hundred feet above the water, then they are divided by deep valleys through which streams descend"; but at other points there are no ridges, only "rock and isolated peaks of equal height lifting their heads boldly up against the sky" and forming a grand "panorama" that no other scenery could surpass "except the famous passage of the Highlands on the Hudson." He reported that he "gazed almost awe stricken throughout the day" at such scenic beauty.[661]

At two o'clock in the afternoon, the rapidly advancing Anglo-Saxons onboard the *War Eagle* were already steaming past Bad Axe, south of La Crosse, near the Minnesota-Iowa border.[662]

Far behind, the *Golden Era* stopped at La Crosse. A crowd gathered on shore and demanded to hear from the former president. Abby Fillmore told James Babcock of the *New Haven Palladium* to go out on deck and inform the "sovereigns" that "Mr. Fillmore is not well; has retired to his state-room for rest, and is unable to speak." Babcock did so.

"Can't we see him if we excuse him from speaking?" the assembled audience asked.

Abby went back to the "after-cabin" and returned with her father, who bowed to the crowd, apologized for his inability to give them a speech, and made a quick exit back to his resting place. Reverend Frederic Goodwin of Middletown, Connecticut, and Whig editor Charles Hudson of the *Boston Atlas,* said "a few clever things" that seemed to satisfy the citizens so that the *Golden Era* could proceed.[663]

At some time during the day, almost certainly south of La Crosse, the *Golden Era* met the steamboat *Royal Arch,* carrying the ex-president's brother Charles D. Fillmore and his wife up to St. Paul. "The two boats rounded to, for the purpose of allowing the brothers to meet for a moment."[664] Then the *Golden Era* continued its downstream journey.

At four o'clock that afternoon, its passengers held a meeting to decide on an appropriate way to thank the captain and crew and the excursion's organizers.[665] In a republic that valued classical Greek and Roman traditions and tried to perpetuate its founders' neoclassical stress on citizenship and the public good, these leaders would not be satisfied with sending individual "thank you" cards. The Chicago

& Rock Island Railroad's generosity must be collectively acknowledged and praised. They believed "that moral authority in a community is located in the public consensus of its members rather than in their individual private convictions." Despite their divisions over the Kansas-Nebraska Act and party politics, they retained sufficient consensus to meet, hear speeches, and vote their gratitude.[666] With five boats hurrying downstream to Rock Island to reach Chicago by Saturday night, it was impractical to lash all boats together to hold one meeting; however, citizens of a federal series of smaller and larger republics could easily constitute themselves the *Golden Era* republic—and meet.

No meeting could function without chair and secretary. John Granger of Canandaigua was chosen as chair. A brother of the Silver Gray leader Francis Granger, he represented the conservative Whigs. Babcock was selected as secretary. Forty-six years old, a Whig, Babcock had edited the *Palladium* for nearly a quarter-century; he was rapidly moving toward a more radical, free-soil position than the Silver Grays felt desirable. This was a balanced ticket. Fillmore was conspicuously absent—presumably because he was unwell—but Granger stood in for the Fillmore Whigs.[667]

After Granger spoke on the purpose of this gathering, Dr. David Rogers of Brooklyn read a set of proposed resolutions. Although it dealt with a nonpolitical, noncontroversial matter, this meeting functioned like a legislative body. The excursionists discussed and even amended Rogers's resolutions before adopting

them and signing their individual names to them. In this formal manner, they thanked Captain Hiram Bersie for "the order and neatness observed on board his boat" (Hiram Fuller observed, "No rowdyism, no drunkenness, no discords, no improprieties"); expressed their "entire satisfaction" with his crew's conduct; named clerk D. W. Dawley, steward Edward Wainey, and mate Paul Billinger as especially worthy of commendation; and offered the captain "a Silver Pitcher" as an expression of their thanks. To purchase and present this gift, they chose a committee consisting of one man from each of the nine states represented on the *Golden Era*. They contributed some three hundred dollars to purchase the gift, gave Bersie a copy of the resolutions as a sort of advance token of the pitcher, and heard his "very handsome and feeling response."[668]

Although women were allowed as a "courtesy" to vote on the proposed resolutions, only men spoke or were appointed to the committee. In a society that made even nonpolitical meetings into exercises in republican citizenship, in an era when women could not vote or hold public office, women could be excluded from nonpolitical leadership roles.[669]

Injecting humor into these formal proceedings, the *Golden Era*'s guests also decided to hold a ceremony to honor Henry Farnam's six-month-old son, Henry Walcott Farnam.

When Ann Sophia Farnam brought baby Henry (and his older brother George) on the excursion, some eyebrows were raised and some shoulders shrugged. A "crusty" bachelor warned, "We may look out for squalls now."

Tiny Henry "looked about" and "quietly entertained himself with sucking his fist" and did not cry once from Monday, June 5, to Friday, June 9. He showed no partiality when adults reached out to hold him. He went just as uncomplainingly to a rough western "sovereign" as to a pretty young miss like Hetty Hart Jarvis or Bessie Williams. Far from being a bother, Henry entertained them all. "It was frequently proposed to pinch him to see if he *could* cry; and in one instance the experiment was tried without success." By then, even the old bachelor delighted to hold him, and the company decided to gather donations and purchase a cup for him. "When they reflected how much a *crying* baby might have detracted from their enjoyment, [they] liberally opened their purses, and subscribed the handsome sum of $260."[670]

Since the passengers acted collectively in raising the money, there must be speeches and a public presentation (even though the cup was yet to be made). They came shortly after the general meeting. A former Connecticut congressman (1845–1849), fifty-two-year-old Whig attorney and specialist in Spanish and Mexican law John A. Rockwell was called on to give the speech of presentation.[671] In this oratorical society, a man had to be able to speak at a moment's notice on any occasion, and this topic was as far removed from Mexican law or James K. Polk's policies as it possibly could be. Yet Rockwell "address[ed] the baby" in fine style, "with due gravity and dignity," and with young Henry "jumping and chuckling" in Ann Farnam's arms at just the right times during the speech. The women were also highly amused at Rockwell's oratorical effort.[672]

Professor Alexander Twining was delegated to give the baby's reply.

"I, Henry W. Farnam, being young in years and wholly unaccustomed to public speaking, feel incompetent to discharge, in suitable terms, the duty imposed upon me on this interesting occasion. When I came on board this boat, it was the farthest from my expectation to make a speech. 'Man wants but little here below,' and babies still less. All my wants may be confined within this little cup which you propose to give me. . . . Some babies might cry for joy over my good fortune, but I am as unused to crying as to public speaking. I give you my best smile of thanks for your kindness, while I rely upon my interpreter for a further and more mature expression of the grateful emotions of my joyful and little heart."[673]

Mother and others rewarded Henry W. with kisses for his good behavior during the ceremony. Rockwell was given the task of buying a cup with the money donated, while Fillmore was to come up with a suitable inscription for it. Hiram Fuller felt rewarded just to hear pleasantries and jocularities and, thus, temporarily to escape "Nebraska Bills, Internal Improvements, Fugitive Slave Laws, and other stereotyped topics, with which everybody was surfeited" after spending five days with other regional and national leaders who naturally discussed such topics when thrown together.[674]

The Sparhawkians held a similar meeting at about the same time, to the dismay of twenty-three-year-old Charles Hale, reporter for his father Nathan's *Boston Daily Advertiser*. Charles Hale expressed a younger generation's preference for individuals' more private and presumably more sincere expressions of thanks instead of public, formal, communal ceremonies. He agreed that the excursionists ought to express their gratitude and that "it would doubtless have been worse taste for the *Sparhawk* to stand aloof" when passengers on other boats were holding such meetings. Yet, he argued, "[i]t would certainly be thought very singular if the guests at a gentleman's dinner party or a lady's ball should resolve themselves into a public meeting, with chairman and secretaries, to pass resolutions express[ing]" their thanks.[675]

Former governor and U.S. senator Roger Sherman Baldwin of Connecticut was chosen to chair the *Sparhawk* meeting, while Hale endured the duties of secretary (with W. E. P. Haskell). Baldwin set forth the purpose of the gathering. That sparked "a spicy discussion" involving Moses Kimball, William Bogart, and William Schouler—all of whom had been engaged in various spoofs and parodies that week, so that any meeting involving them could be predicted to be "spicy"—as well as Alderman Nathan C. Ely of New York City; Reverend E. P. Stimpson of Castleton, New York; Benjamin P. Johnson, the agricultural expert; and Reverend Dr. Thomas E. Vermilye, a Presbyterian minister in New York City. Vermilye suggested "that instead of resolutions, a brief letter, expressive of the feelings of the passengers, be prepared" by Baldwin

and sent to their hosts; however, the meeting followed more formal actions. Baldwin appointed only one of the week's jesters (Bogart) to the committee (Bogart, Vermilye, Johnson, and church historian Henry Boynton Smith of New York City) that drew up the resolutions—which, predictably, reflected the Sparhawkians' railroad interests.[676]

The resolutions thanked Joseph Sheffield and Farnam and the C&RI directors for generously "enabl[ing] us to inspect their road, . . . the last link of a continuous railroad from the Atlantic to the Mississippi"—but it also thanked other railroads and the steamboat lines that transported the excursionists free of charge. George Bliss of the Western Railroad and other Massachusetts railroad investors were on the *Sparhawk,* and they made it clear that this was not only a C&RI affair. Two New York State men were appointed to raise funds to buy a gift for the *Sparhawk*'s officers. In keeping with the formality, the "meeting then adjourned *sine die*"—a superfluous legislative gesture since they were to disperse the following day, "never all to meet together again," Hale noted. He disagreed with the gifts to the officers, which he compared to guests offering "a gratuity to the servants of your host at a private entertainment," which he felt would be "in bad taste." Many of his fellow excursionists, certainly the older ones, did not regard the Grand Excursion as "a private" affair but as an exceedingly public one, deserving public recognition.[677]

Sparhawk and *Lady Franklin* were not far apart as they rushed downriver, the Wisconsin shore on their left, the Minnesota on their right. *War Eagle* was far ahead of them; *Galena* and *Golden Era* were some distance behind them.

On the *Lady Franklin,* Charles Sedgwick tried to write to his wife, but "I have just been called out by a kind gentleman who has done the same thing several times to see the 'Wildcat's Bank' on the Minnesota shore." Near where Wildcat Creek flowed into the river, at Brownsville, this bluff was "an Exquisite place" that was "about one mile in length sparely covered with magnificent trees like a park with perpendicular monuments of rock to the summit." A French Canadian had a memorable scrape with a wildcat at the foot of this bluff, so the story went, and that gave it its name. Nearly 500 feet high, steamboat pilots used it as a landmark (Captain Legrand Morehouse may have been the "kind gentleman" who pointed it out). Wildcat Bluff ended "at a mountain which lies at right angles with the River & which seems to have been cleft to let the River pass perpendicularly thru the Rock," Sedgwick marveled. Below the bluff was "a group of islands with grand trees. The water is very high, in many places the trees at the base are covered by it 2 or 3 feet."[678]

At sunset, a "glorious" one, according to Charles Hale, the *G. W. Sparhawk* and *Lady Franklin* steamed past Prairie du Chien. The sight was grand. The Wisconsin town "lay on the level prairie, on the banks of the river, high steep bluffs forming the background— the whole illuminated by the setting sun." On the *Lady Franklin,* Catharine Sedgwick was

writing a letter at that moment and had just noted that Thursday, June 8, "was a day better than most lifetimes," when she added, "[H]ere I was stopped by our Commodore [George Mix] telling me I must not lose Prairie du Chien." She dropped her pen to see the sunset-lit scenery.[679]

Those aboard the *Lady Franklin* held a formal meeting. They chose Charles Sedgwick to preside and an editor (William E. McMaster of the *Syracuse Republican*) to serve as one secretary (a St. Louis man was the other). Sedgwick appointed himself as one of the members of the resolutions committee, along with Stephen A. Goodwin (the satirist at La Crosse) and E. Church Blackburn of St. Louis. In keeping with Sedgwick's enthusiasm over the Upper Mississippi Valley, the first resolution thanked the valley itself for its attributes and denied any eastern envy over its destiny as "the growing seat of empire and power . . . under the banner of Union . . . bound together by the triple chord of religious freedom, popular sovereignty and universal equality." They thanked the C&RI, Sheffield and Farnam, "all other railroad and steamboat companies," the crew of the *Lady Franklin*— especially Captain Legrand Morehouse and George Mix, "the admiral of the squadron and commander in chief." Somewhat impractically, they voted to appoint a five-member committee to consult with committees from the other boats to draft common resolutions, but rapidly scattering excursionists would be as hard to reunite as Atlantic and Mississippi waters. To Morehouse they offered "a silver service" (yet to be purchased). To Mix they offered merely a resolution that the other boats join with them in buying him "some token."[680]

Before these thanks were completed, "The Walker clique" left the room, Munn noted, "& added another link to the chain of events which has made them so notorious & so disagreeable."[681]

The women did not evidently protest the proceedings, but Secretary McMaster presented to them a separate resolution: "[t]hat the ladies, guests of the 'Lady Franklin,' heartily concur in the above resolutions." Of course, only ladies could vote on this question—its very wording granted them the franchise—and they passed it unanimously, apparently without speeches, discussion, or amendments. Catharine Sedgwick seems not to have made any public remarks here.[682]

Perhaps realizing that the reception and ball in St. Paul had been the last chance for all the excursionists to gather, that they would never catch the *War Eagle,* the captains of the *Galena* and the *Golden Era* lashed their boats together, and the citizens of these two small republics held a joint meeting in the *Galena's* cabin. For presiding officer, they selected Millard Fillmore. They honored several men with the title of vice president: Preston Blair, the anti-Nebraska agitator of the trip; Edward Bates, the auditioning Missourian; Fillmore's close friend and ally, ex-postmaster general Nathan Hall; and railroad investor cum clergyman William Jarvis of Middletown, Connecticut. Four newspaper editors (two

The War Eagle's *Captain Daniel S. Harris.*
(National Mississippi River Museum and Aquarium, Dubuque, Iowa)

Whigs, two Democrats) were chosen as secretaries: Charles Ray of Galena, John A. Bross of the *Chicago Daily Democratic Press,* Charles A. Dana of the *New York Tribune,* and H. H. Van Dyck of the *Albany Atlas.*

Nine men were appointed to a resolutions committee, including Leonard Bacon, John Granger, John Rockwell, and John Dix, currently the president of Farnam's Mississippi & Missouri Railroad Company.[683]

Reverend Bacon took the lead in writing the resolutions, as their contents revealed. And it was he who gave the speech introducing them to the assembled guests.[684] To illustrate the excursionists' dilemma of getting their friends back East to believe their tales of the glories of the Upper Mississippi Valley, he told a story about an Irishman "who got a friend to write for him a letter to the old country":

"Tell them," said he, "that I have meat twice a week."

"Why not tell them that you have it three times a day, which you know is true."

"Because," said Pat, "they will not believe it. Twice a week is as much as they will believe."

Bacon presented the resolutions, which began—as had those adopted on other boats—with thanks to Sheffield and Farnam, C&RI directors, and the other railroad and steamboat companies that had transported them. Bacon went on to give a theological, postmillennial exegesis of railroad completion: it was "the natural result of perfect civilization"; it assured a future transcontinental railroad; it demonstrated "the grandeur and destiny of our common country." Easterners were not envious of the new states, but filled "with gratitude to the God of our fathers, who endowed them with their foresight, and has rewarded their self-sacrifice by giving their

children so goodly a heritage." (His parents, David and Alice Bacon, were among the self-sacrificing pioneers.) The sight of westerners following their ancestors' love of liberty was especially welcome "in times like these when the question of man's capacity to govern himself, and of man's inalienable and sacred right to freedom, is assuming so great an importance." (The times of the Kansas-Nebraska debate, he implied.) The West would be "a safe and blessed asylum" for freedom-seeking immigrants and a "demonstration of what perfect liberty and perfect civil equality, under the light of Christianity, and aided by the inventions of science and the universal diffusion of knowledge can do for the elevation and advancement of the human race." Almost hidden in the final resolution was a reference to the "ample pecuniary results" of the C&RI railroad. More important, the Rock Island and similar lines would "rivet with iron bands the interests, the welfare and the union of this great Republic."[685]

Without questioning their theological tone, the appropriateness of a clergyman writing and presenting them, or their political implications, the excursionists unanimously adopted the resolutions and adjourned their joint meeting.[686]

The *Galena*'s passengers then held their own meeting. They had unfinished business. On Thursday evening, they chose a committee to draw up resolutions to thank captain and officers. Now they met "pursuant to adjournment"—John Dix presiding, several editors taking notes, and they all passing a resolution of thanks to captain and officers and promising to purchase "a fitting testimonial" for these men. Illinois Supreme Court judge John Dean Caton, Reverend Duncan Kennedy, and former New York senator James Cooley were charged with collecting funds and making the purchase. The two boats then separated.[687]

Perhaps the most telling blow for "Woman's Rights" came not in formal meetings and resolutions on the *Lady Franklin,* but when Sarah Morehouse went up to the pilot-house and took the wheel to steer the boat through rapids north of Dubuque. She "guided the boat under a full head of steam, for a distance of eleven miles." Cleveland editor Josiah Harris praised her highly as "one of the belles of the" excursion. "Agile as the fawn, joyous and musical as the mocking bird, sensible, educated and refined, free from the stiffness and formality of city manners, she was the life of the social circle, and equally at home in repartee, music, dance, or wheelhouse guiding the stately craft, which she occasionally did for miles with a skill and steadiness that brightened the eye" of her father, Captain Legrand Morehouse.[688]

By now it was night. The moon shone brightly. On the *Lady Franklin,* the band played music in the cabin; the "beautiful and accomplished" Miss Sarah undoubtedly took her turn on the dance floor, as the dancing continued until midnight. The inescapable reality that this was their last night together forced itself on excursionists' minds, and the moonlight must have heightened the bittersweet sentiments of farewell.[689]

On the *Galena,* sentiments of farewell stirred in Edward Prime's mind all day. "I have been seated with friends whose presence and converse has been a joy, and yet it has been a day of recollection." While they were on a river trip, his wife, Maria, had died of cholera onboard a Mississippi steamboat on May 13, 1851. "This river, apart from its wonderful and attractive features[,] has a strangely fascinating power over my heart. . . . Its dark stream rolls over the wrecks of joys which cannot revive. . . . And yet I have sought its shores and still linger around them as if in hope of a meeting which every thing but the heart tells me can never be on earth." Prime was not fully present while in his friends' company. "This day has been dream-like . . . memories have been coming in upon the heart, and now as the midnight is passing they come with still more absorbing power, and I seem almost conscious of another presence."[690]

Fittingly, the last speeches of the day came on the *Sparhawk,* home to the jesters, and the boat where oratory of all sorts was perhaps most highly valued (or, dancing less valued since so many of its men were without their wives). In the cabin that night, "some excellent speeches suggested by the approaching separation of the guests were made by [William C.] Prime," the twenty-eight-year-old author of *Owl Creek Letters* and brother of Edward Prime of the *New York Observer.* (William reported on the excursion for the *New York Journal of Commerce.*) The Reverend Dr. Thomas Vermilye also spoke. The *Sparhawk* wags resumed the Schouler case that had been postponed due to clearing weather on Wednesday. William Prime, the prosecutor, "stated his willingness to enter" a *nolle prosequi,* a prosecutor's notice that he would not continue his case against the accused. Moses Kimball, the defense attorney, agreed and so did Judge Bogart. Schouler "refused . . . to promise better behavior for the future," but he was released and his future traveling companions warned "to select the upper berth" to avoid felonious assaults upon their persons.[691]

Bogart "made a very happy parting speech, asking that the Committee on Entertainment and Amusement be discharged from further service." Editor Caleb Foote of the *Salem Gazette* thanked George Bliss, who had "performed good offices for the guests" and had secured invitations for the Massachusetts delegation. Despite his disapproval of formalities, young Charles Hale was chosen "to respond on behalf of the ladies" to the "three cheers" given in their honor. One of the young ladies was Elizabeth Colt, who (he informed his mother) "was on the Excursion with me, and I quite liked her." Then the meeting "broke up, and with half a dozen quadrilles to the lively music of our Sparhawk band, the social enjoyments of the company were closed."[692]

The speedy War Eagle, *ca. 1865, led the flotilla throughout the excursion's duration. (Minnesota Historical Society)*

Hale reported that a strong bond had formed between the excursionists on this boat, whose name had "seemed dull and meaningless to us as we went on board" on Monday evening, June 5—the name of some government functionary from St. Louis, he believed—but the name had become "a dear watchword—a permanent symbol of friendship. The cry *'I am a Sparhawkian,'* at least in the hearing of Sparhawkians, will prove as potent as was of old the cry 'I am a Roman citizen.'"[693]

Similar feelings of solidarity stirred on the other steamboats (John Munn felt "a sort of Free Masonry binds us together"), even if their guests turned sooner from communal meetings to the more individual farewells of the dance and the private conversation.[694] Far ahead of the *Sparhawk,* Benjamin Silliman did not report any dancing on the *War Eagle.* They held two meetings "to project and discuss and adopt resolutions"; Silliman served on the resolutions committee, gave a speech, and heard his son-in-law Professor Oliver Payson Hubbard deliver "some very happy remarks uttered in a modest & dignified manner." "Dubuque came into view with brilliant lights just as night came on," and they arrived at Galena around ten o'clock. Here, Silliman, his wife, Sarah, and a few others left the party to go and inspect a young college in Beloit, Wisconsin.[695] Far behind, on the *Galena,* Edward Prime stayed up all night with his thoughts and then disembarked at Dubuque.[696] The Grand Excursion was starting to disperse.

Antebellum renaissance man John A. Dix served as a figurehead railroad president whose political experience reassured investors.

CHAPTER NINE

"We Are on the Way to the Pacific"

SATURDAY, JUNE 10, 1854

THE GRAND EXCURSION steamboats continued moving downstream during the night. By 6:00 a.m., the *War Eagle* arrived at Rock Island. *Lady Franklin* was not far behind. There was no attempt to gather excursionists in Rock Island for a final ceremony, and the party was already dispersing "amid the turmoil attending the disembarkation of a large crowd" that mirrored the controlled chaos of embarking from Rock Island on Monday evening. When the regular Chicago & Rock Island train for Chicago left Rock Island depot at 8:00 a.m., many passengers from these two boats were onboard (a special excursion train was to leave at 1:00 p.m.).[697]

Not all of them were headed for Chicago. At Rock Island, the president of the Chicago & Mississippi Railroad invited them to go to St. Louis via the C&RI, Illinois Central, and C&M lines. Thus, a few excursionists got off at La Salle around noon to transfer to the Illinois Central train headed south for Bloomington, where they switched to the C&M, and went through Springfield on their way to St. Louis.[698]

The *Sparhawk* landed at Rock Island around 9:00 a.m. The C&RI directors had also issued an invitation to the excursionists to continue by steamboat down to St. Louis. Catharine and Charles Sedgwick, among many others, took them up on the offer. Arriving on *Lady Franklin* shortly after six, they transferred to the *Sparhawk* for the next stage but had to wait for the *Golden Era,* which was also continuing on to St. Louis. George Bancroft also transferred to the *Golden Era,* and blamed the hour wait on Millard Fillmore's indecision about whether he should go on to St. Louis. Despite his promise to his wife, Preston Blair decided to go on to St. Louis with son Frank: there he could visit Samuel Phillips Lee, his son-in-law, and both he and Frank were convinced that Missouri was a key state in the anti-Nebraska campaign in 1854.[699]

The *Golden Era* and *Galena* lagged about an hour behind the *Sparhawk.* Some of their passengers were still conducting the public, oratorical business that the other boats had finished the night before. That morning, on the *Golden Era,* the women held their own meeting—partly to thank their hosts and partly to blame their male fellow passengers for excluding them from voting or speaking roles at the previous night's discussions. The Seneca Falls Convention (1848) had placed women's rights on the national stage, but it is difficult to determine to what degree these women were serious about the issue. They chose leaders—Mrs. George R. Babcock and Miss Matelda Stuart of Buffalo, and Mrs. Thomas M. Howell of Canandaigua—from among the Fillmore faction, never known for its radicalism.[700]

Male newspaper correspondents did not take it seriously: "The excitement was tremendous; bright eyes flashed fire—soft cheeks burned with indignation—lily fingers, rose tipped, were clenched, as if to scratch." They appointed chair and secretary to lead what a reporter (but not necessarily the women) characterized as "this neat burlesque on Woman's Rights." He contrasted their good order to the informal frivolity of masculine meetings. They met in the ladies' cabin "with closed doors, all of the opposite 'sect' being" kept out. "They have shut their saloon doors," James Babcock confirmed (apparently writing while the events occurred), "and undoubtedly are in the midst of eloquent speeches. The doors are thrown open and the gentlemen have rushed in, giving three cheers for the ladies' meeting." The cheers may not have been sincere, and the women did not seem to want to entrust their handiwork to male eyes. They tried to keep their resolutions secret, or so Babcock said. It did seem odd to try to keep a public thanks private. Nevertheless, the investigative editor succeeded in obtaining a copy.[701]

They prefaced their one resolution with a more individualistic and less public-consensual statement (in effect, a "whereas" clause) proclaiming "every woman's legal privilege . . . to *express* whatever feeling may predominate in her mind." They collectively thanked Captain Hiram Bersie and crew but did so "independently of all masculine control," in protest at having been denied a voice at Friday night's

meeting.[702]

Not long after Babcock secured a copy of the resolution, the towns of Davenport and Rock Island came into "full view." It was about 10:00 a.m., four hours after the *War Eagle* finished her downstream run.[703] The grand flotilla had returned to its starting point in a geographical, though not a topical, sense. Monday's fireworks, bonfires, band music, and speeches hailed the past accomplishment, the first railroad to reach the Mississippi at Rock Island. Saturday's speeches looked to the future prospects of the new railroad heading west from Davenport. Iowa and the future took precedence over Illinois and the past. At Davenport, the *Golden Era* and *Galena* landed their passengers for an hour-long tour of the city (for which there had been no time on Monday). Davenport's citizens took the visitors, including Fillmore, in carriages back to the bluffs that overlooked the gradually sloping hillside.[704]

Babcock did not take the town boosters' carriage tour but walked around town and consulted a Davenport editor—"an Eastern [New England] man"—for the town's "statistics." Yet he too was impressed: "Davenport is much the pleasantest town that I have seen" during the excursion. "It lies on a hillside gently ascending from the banks of the river. There is nothing particularly attractive on the shore street" (First Street), he observed, but Second Street "contains blocks of fine stores," and two or three blocks farther from the river there were "several handsome dwelling houses and some neat cottages, around which are trees and shrubbery." The crowning pieces of architecture, to this New Englander, were "a noble school building, in which education is free," and "an imposing stone church" under construction.[705]

"I have returned from my stroll about town," he continued, "and find the Mayor of Davenport mounted on an empty hogshead addressing a welcome to the people on the boats." Forty-one years old, a native North Carolinian who moved to Illinois and Iowa to escape a slavery-based society, James Grant served as first president of the C&RI and accompanied its investors on the Grand Excursion. A small man, he climbed on the large barrel to be seen. His commanding voice could easily be heard. Possessing an excellent education from Chapel Hill, he uttered more classical allusions than hogsheads usually supported: Fillmore was destined to be another Jason leading a transcontinental rail excursion "to visit the golden fleece of California"; the "young Republic" of Iowa had been "born, like Pallas [Athena], from the brain of Jove, full grown in a day"; Illinois followed "no Eriean policy" but cooperated with Iowa in chartering and building the C&RI; now, the Mississippi & Missouri Railroad had "harnessed up" an iron horse "which, like the fabled steeds of Diomedes, vomiteth fire from his nostrils" and would be "the first train on the Pacific."[706]

Grant addressed various categories of excursionists in turn. He assured the "Fair Ladies" that Iowa's hills "long to be kissed by your feet." He praised the ex-president; welcomed former cabinet members and senators;

complimented Governor Joel Matteson and other Illinois politicians; urged Bancroft to add this "new chapter" to his history ("The author is worthy the subject, and the subject is not unworthy of the author"); invited Epes Sargent, "Poet of the Ocean Wave," to write a "new song" of the oceanlike prairies; bid scientists "come and explore this newly discovered country"; requested that clergymen "no longer tell our eastern brethren that we are heathens"; and boasted to all that here was the point of origin of a railroad to California. Visible to speaker and audience was the "first pier" of the railroad bridge (under construction) across the Mississippi and nearby, on Fifth Street, were the M&M tracks. "Our train is now ready to start through the Iowa prairies," Grant stated. "We have a Dix for a conductor and Flagg for a financier, Farnam for an Engineer and Sheffield for a fireman," and all the C&RI men to push things along. "Embark on this train and before our rivals are done talking of their projects, we shall have this train to California's golden sands half finished." He hinted at an excursion to "the summit of the Rocky Mountains" to mark completion of the new rail project.[707]

"Some Davenport man made a splendiloquent oration from the top of a hogshead," summarized Moore of Springfield.[708]

Two decades earlier, Alexis de Tocqueville observed a tendency for American orators "to use an inflated style." When dealing with mundane business matters, Americans spoke "in clear, plain language, devoid of all ornament." When they addressed larger concerns, he noted, "[t]hey then vent their pomposity from one end of a harangue to the other." He explained this tendency as a consequence of democracy. "In democratic communities, each citizen is habitually engaged in the contemplation of a very puny object, namely, himself." When he looks beyond himself, "he perceives only the immense form of society at large. . . . His ideas are all either extremely minute and clear, or extremely general and vague: what lies between is a void."[709] To be fair, Grant's speech did address grand themes, not puny ones that he inflated. The excursion was conducted on a grand scale. A Pacific railroad involved business matters but momentous ones on a gargantuan scale. How could Grant discuss it "devoid of all ornament"?

Perhaps taken aback by this florid oratorical welcome, Fillmore confessed, "I have no elegant words to return my acknowledgment." He fell back on his tried and true Grand Excursion speech: this reception "takes me by surprise"; he had "visited many beautiful scenes on the Mississippi River," but Davenport was the best; he was so preoccupied "with that which is beautiful and grand" that he would not "detain you longer."[710]

Fortunately, there was a prepared response to Grant's panegyric; the two were likely written and coordinated in advance. Conductor Dix—fifty-five-year-old John A. Dix, president of the M&M Railroad that began five blocks away—took the rhetorical baton from Grant. The crowd called for him to speak, but they would want to hear from

the head of *their* Iowa railroad, and their calls were likely prearranged.[711] A rather young veteran of the War of 1812 (he served at age fourteen), an ambitious man from rural New Hampshire who married a congressman's daughter and climbed up to the eastern elite, Dix was an antebellum Renaissance man: he rose to army major, practiced law, held state offices in New York, served in the U.S. Senate, edited a literary and scientific magazine, spent two years in southern Europe, wrote a book on that experience, and joined the New York City financial circle as financier and railroad lawyer. An expert chess player, he could converse in several languages and, like Grant, knew his classics. The previous winter Dix had spent significant time "preparing a series of papers on the history of Rome" for several family members who were going to visit there. Obviously, he did not handle day-to-day management of the M&M, but his connections, speaking ability, and reputation were useful in attracting eastern investors to its cause.[712]

More than railroads' profitability and their role in revolutionizing the U.S. economy caused this skilled leader to focus on pushing rail lines through Iowa rather than bills through Congress. The slavery issue had sidetracked Dix's political ambitions. Although a Democrat, he was on the outs with southern Democrats who controlled President Franklin Pierce's administration. A protégé of Martin Van Buren, Dix discovered a presidential mentor could be a hindrance as well as a help. Against his better judgment, Dix followed Van Buren and other Barnburners into the Free

Soil Party in 1848. Now southerners vetoed all suggestions of appointing him to any prominent position (the post of minister to France had been talked of).[713]

Dix evidently spoke from the deck of the *Galena* (the boat he was assigned to for the trip); at five feet eight inches he was not tall but did not need to stand on Grant's hogshead to be seen. Blue-eyed, his thin lips drawn tightly together and "expressive of firmness and decision," Dix was a bit of the man of the world after his two years in Spain and Italy. He was a gallant who seemed almost flirtatious in this speech: "I assure you ladies, I am not very greatly on the wrong side of fifty." He flattered them that "the encouraging smiles, which beam from gentle faces here" made his oratorical task easier.[714]

Dix's speech was clearly meant to be the peroration to a week of discussions and public addresses. On behalf of the collective "we" of the excursionists, he thanked all the river towns who had hosted them, Sheffield and Farnam for their endeavors, and the railroad and steamboat companies that gave them free transportation. "Indeed, there is no other quarter of the globe where such an excursion could have been made," Dix asserted with Democratic, Young America braggadocio. Africa and Asia were "the abode of barbarous and half civilized races." Europe was civilized but "split up into a multitude of independent States," each with its guarded borders. Why, "a party like ours, coming unexpected upon a custom house on the continent of Europe, with all its machinery for the scrutiny of per-

sons and passports and baggage, could not have got through it" in the forty-eight hours it took New York excursionists to reach Rock Island. They had traveled for "thousands of miles of country" where "there is no man authorized to question us as to our names, our business, our destinations, or what we carry with us." That liberty was not due to railroad technology but was "the fruit of the union of the States," which all should wish and pray "may be perpetual."[715]

Dix turned to the topic of the completed C&RI railroad, in which he was "a very small stockholder, but a larger bondholder—one of the very earliest." He expressed satisfaction with his investment and gave a detailed financial report, in effect, the report that investors on this traveling shareholders' meeting asked for on Tuesday but which C&RI president John B. Jervis stated was available only in New York City. C&RI revenues were estimated at $1.2 million annually and had been $109,000 for the month of May alone. The C&RI was indeed a good 10 percent investment. "This is the present prospect and nothing can well change it but some great improvement, which may leave railways in the rear, as railways have left turnpikes and common roads." No such superior technology was in sight. "There is the flying machine, it is true, but I think the stockholders may fairly calculate on getting their money back before" that was perfected enough to compete with trains.[716]

From the future, Dix turned back to the past and marveled at the progress made in his lifetime. He had traveled on the first steamboat to sail on Lake Huron in 1819, when there was no Chicago and when Detroit was a small village.[717]

Then he switched back to the future to reply to Grant's remarks about the iron horse chomping at the bit to get to California. "We have, as yet, gentlemen, only reached the Mississippi. But the tide of population has traveled far beyond it." And, the M&M had to follow that tide to the Missouri. "Let it not be supposed that we are to stop at the Missouri River." The trans-Missouri West "still invites us onward, and we shall go on. Our surveyors and engineers have been beyond Council Bluffs into Nebraska, as far as the Platte or Nebraska river; others have been several hundred miles farther west." Dix reported that Nebraska's soil fertility matched Iowa's. "Gentlemen, we may as well come to the point at once. We are on the way to the Pacific; and we intend to go there. It will require years of perseverance, but the work will be accomplished in good time! I may reasonably expect, with the ordinary chances of life, to live to see it." He appealed, indirectly and discreetly, for eastern investors to furnish the capital for the beginning stage through Iowa.[718]

Lest this all sound too mercenary and lest idealistic New Englanders think he was omitting the themes of advancing the Gospel and civilization, Dix added that Nebraska and other areas along this railroad-to-be "will continue to draw men and means from the East, and especially from New England, . . . sending out her legions, not for plunder or conquest, but to extend the arts of civiliza-

tion; to carry the hardy virtues of the Pilgrims, perpetuated in their descendants, into the pathless wilderness."[719]

It was not yet clear what pass this railroad would take through the Rockies. "The question is not an urgent one now." What was vital was for the northern states, at least, to agree on one railroad route through the Rockies to the Pacific. Here Dix suggested a negotiation of the regional and urban rivalries over a route that had defeated the land-grant bill in Congress. "A large view of this subject should extinguish all jealousy" and "narrowness of feeling."[720]

At this point, Babcock reported, "Mr. Farnam now holds up his watch to him, and he winds up his argument." A special 1:00 p.m. train awaited them at Rock Island, and they had to take lunch before that.[721] "The inexorable steam-whistle will sound in a few moments," Dix concluded, "and compel us to bid a reluctant farewell. . . . We have been together nearly a week; no untoward event, not even the slightest accident, has occurred to mar our enjoyment, and among the 1000 persons, who are about to part from each other, no unkind word has been spoken to cast a shadow on the memory of our friendly intercourse."[722]

The steamboats' bells rang, and the *Golden Era* and the *Galena* backed out into the channel, "amid cheers on shore and on board." On the *Golden Era,* Captain Hiram Bersie served them a quick lunch as they crossed over to Rock Island. On the way over, the passengers were "exchanging cards and expressing regrets that a separation is so soon to take place."[723]

Landed on the Illinois shore, the crew and passengers unloaded "an immense amount of baggage," which they hauled to the waiting railroad cars. They boarded the cars. Here, Joseph Sheffield joined the party, Babcock reported, "and gave us the first intelligence that we had received from New Haven for nearly a week." From the train, Moses Kimball declaimed one last campaign speech to the Rock Islanders, "soliciting their votes for the Presidency" with promises of government jobs, liquor, and money. He also promised he would "carry at least *four* of the Five Points!" The train pulled out of the station as the crowd waved handkerchiefs and shouted their farewells.[724]

The one train retraced the route the two excursion trains had taken on Monday. It dropped off passengers at the various towns along the C&RI track: Sheffield, Tiskilwa, Peru, La Salle, Ottawa. Someone pointed out Starved Rock to Andrew Aiken of the *New York Evening Post,* who told its readers about the siege that destroyed the Illinois Indians. "Gov. Matteson got out of the cars" at Joliet, "and upon leaving the company he was vociferously cheered by the distinguished visitors to which he appropriately responded. Cheers were also given for the Union and for Mr. Sheffield."[725]

At 9:00 p.m. Saturday, June 10, the special excursion train pulled into the La Salle Street station in Chicago.[726] Baggage was unloaded from the cars, but without a certain and common place to take it. The six days of common travel were at an end, and individuals or families were now on their own. "Our party found the same difficulty in obtaining lodgings at the Hotels that they experienced on their way West," Babcock complained. He "was fortunate in getting into the Matteson House with a few friends." It was cheaper than the Tremont, but the meals were every bit as luxurious. For "Dessert" he "counted no less than forty-three different articles, beginning with ice cream. Meats are in similar variety."[727]

Chicago was abuzz with reports that Senator Stephen A. Douglas was expected in the city that evening. People were "in a feverish state," the *Chicago Tribune* noted, "and scarcely anything else was talked of in the streets, in stores, shops and hotels. We have never seen so marked manifestations of indignation." More understatedly, the *Chicago Journal* detected "a very general disposition manifested, not to welcome him very cordially." Both papers blamed this agitated feeling on Douglas himself. Why would the author of the Kansas-Nebraska Act dare show his head in Chicago?[728] But Douglas did not show up, and Chicago's streets were quiet for the weekend, something the bachelors weary from the excursion were no doubt happy to see. Even the married John Munn, with his excellent stateroom and his prior steamboat experience, confessed to "great prostration of body" when he arrived in Chicago.[729]

A poster announces an upcoming voyage on the Golden Era, *which was Captain Hiram Bersie's boat on the excursion. (Murphy Library, University of Wisconsin–La Crosse)*

CHAPTER TEN

"An Angry, Turbid, Almost Frightful Looking Stream"

JUNE 11–14, 1854

THE *GOLDEN ERA* and *G. W. Sparhawk* left Rock Island Saturday afternoon to make the extended excursion down to St. Louis. It is hard to know with any certainty why the Chicago & Rock Island Railroad directors, Joseph Sheffield and Henry Farnam, decided to extend the trip to St. Louis, but several possibilities suggest themselves. That city, whose prosperity still rode upon Mississippi steamboat traffic (freight and passengers), opposed construction of the C&RI Bridge at Rock Island as a hindrance to navigation. The directors may have hoped to soften St. Louis opposition by bringing dignitaries there to say flattering words about Chicago's rival.[730] They may have been told by Missouri excursionists that bringing dignitaries to visit the Mississippi while snubbing its chief city would inflame that opposition. Of course, St. Louis was also a rival terminus for a Pacific railroad. Including that city might facilitate a compromise on that contentious issue. Missouri's anti-Nebraska politicians on the Grand Excursion—Frank Blair and Edward Bates—may have hoped that sailing into their city with a boatload of notables might increase their prestige and convert some Missourians to the anti-Nebraska cause. Finally, Millard Fillmore would be agreeable to a salute from this important city, which would bring his

year's travels full circle (he missed St. Louis on his March-to-May southern tour).

In any case, St. Louis would have to be satisfied with part of an excursion, an ex-president, and perhaps two or three hundred fellow travelers. Only three boats—the *Golden Era,* the *Sparhawk,* and the *Lady Franklin*—went to St. Louis; the *Lady Franklin* came down a day or two later than the others.[731] Some excursionists, including Isaac Platt of the *Poughkeepsie Eagle* and Daniel Wager of Rome, took the Illinois Central route to Alton and then crossed the river to St. Louis.

To his wife, George Bancroft implied some reluctance to leave "the clean & fast moving *War Eagle*" for the slower *Golden Era.* To her, he also hinted that young feminine company served to recompense him for the move to an older boat. "[H]aving persuaded the lovely Miss Hilton, the prettiest girl on the excursion, as well as the charming Miss Charlotte, to join [us], William [Bliss, his stepson] & I headed the party that removed to the *Golden Era*. There we found Mr. Fillmore bent on visiting St. Louis, Miss Fillmore[, etc.]."[732]

The persuasive historian also made a successful "suggestion" to New York City merchant and philanthropist Robert Bowne Minturn that he and "his party" take staterooms on the *Golden Era*. Nearly fifty, the wealthy Minturn led the family business— Grinnell, Minturn and Company—and gave away money to hospitals, poor-relief societies, and to aid emigrants arriving in New York (he served as an early commissioner of emigration for New York City). Raised a Quaker, he had switched to the Episcopal Church, which was less suspicious of moneymaking. Yet his philanthropy no doubt reflected his Quaker heritage. With him was "his party": his eighteen-year-old son Robert Bowne Minturn Jr., a student at Columbia University; John W. Minturn; and a Miss Minturn and a Miss Wendell (probably a niece). The whole party was decidedly Whig in wealth, politics, church, and culture.[733]

It amused the Democratic Bancroft to inquire into their politics—on Sunday, apparently. He struck up a conversation with "a charming young mother with her husband" who were traveling with the Minturns.[734]

"Is your husband a Democrat?" said Bancroft.

"No," said the young woman. "If he had been I never would have married him."

A "good shout followed" this exchange, and Bancroft assured his wife that the young woman's "sincerity made" he and she "the better friends."

For all his sociability—and despite a fog that slowed or halted their travel overnight— Bancroft had time to view the scenery south of Rock Island and to compare it ("less picturesque") with that of the Upper Mississippi. "This part of the Mississippi has not the bold bluffs & rocky bastions of the upper country,

but the river retains its grandeur & its banks are more thickly studded with farm houses and towns."[735]

They passed one site with historical associations: Nauvoo, Illinois, temporarily (1839–1847) the center of Joseph Smith's Mormon Church colony. Passing by a few days earlier, Thurlow Weed of the *Albany Evening Journal* reported that Smith's temple was built on an elevated location "and commands a view of the River for many miles up and down." Steamboat passengers had a view of it for many miles too, for it was situated at a point that marked a sharp bend in the river, and they could see it both coming and going. Though Smith was murdered ten years earlier and the temple wrecked, it was "still a magnificent Ruin, and reminds Travellers of the Temples of Greece and Rome."[736]

It was probably around church time, Sunday forenoon, that they passed Nauvoo. Onboard the *Sparhawk,* Catharine Sedgwick noted, "There is proverbially 'no Sunday on the river.'" No church services, no halt to the drinking at the bar, no relief from the annoying pleasantries of the barkeeper who urged her to visit his mother in St. Louis. No Sabbatarians on the steamboat, for they had taken the special C&RI train and were at church in Chicago that very hour. From time to time, the *Sparhawk* stopped to "wood up." "(Oh these trees, these leafy arches, these deep glades before me!)," she exclaimed parenthetically to her niece. The *Golden Era* stopped at Quincy, Illinois, and some passengers, including Bancroft, walked around the town.[737]

As the *Sparhawk* pushed south of Quincy, Sedgwick sat down near the door of her stateroom, "which opens on the deck with men of all aspects & conditions traversing between me & the guards," to write to Kate. "The shore is low & thickly wooded before us—with magnif[icen]t oaks & elms wreathed with luxuriant vines & now opening on to a wide prairie." On shore she saw "log huts—& unsightly framed houses" to match the unsightly manners of these Sabbath-breaking, drinking lower-class westerners who chatted with her and disturbed her letter writing.[738]

Later in the evening, the houses became more numerous, and Hannibal appeared on its bluff. Here the *Golden Era* was seen catching up to the *Sparhawk,* whose Captain Green told his passengers he would stop "half an hour—Will you go on shore?" They would, and were soon walking Hannibal's streets. Sedgwick had pocketed the bonbons served at supper, and they now came in handy. She "distributed them, Robin Hood fashion, among the black & white children & bo[ugh]t golden kisses from bright young lips" in exchange (not from Samuel Clemens, however, who had already left Hannibal). On a hill, they "took a wide survey of the beautiful surroundings," but "a violent gust of rain" sent them scurrying for the shelter of the boat.[739]

Robert Bennett Forbes, a friend of the Sedgwicks, boarded the *Sparhawk* at Hannibal and conversed with Charles Sedgwick. (Forbes was a director of the Hannibal & St. Joseph Railroad and was undoubtedly in Hannibal to try to raise money to construct this line.)

Catharine had wanted to go by boat, not by train, to St. Louis partly because she felt that would be "much less fatiguing" to Charles. That did not mean she was disappointed in how the excursion affected his health. He was enjoying the trip, the people ("were there ever affections so abounding! so plastic!"), and the scenery. "His health improves—and he has more spirits than any one on the boat," she exulted to his daughter. So much so that Charles told Forbes he was planning—"if I live another year"—to hire a boat to take a party up to St. Anthony Falls in the summer of 1855. Forbes replied, "I mean to do that thing in October next," and invited Charles to join his group. Whoever hosted it, Charles hoped wife Elizabeth, daughter Kate, son-in-law William Minot, and sister Catharine could all participate together in reliving the glories of the Grand Excursion.[740]

They were not eager to relive the glories of the cramped stateroom. Anticipating breakfast the next morning on dry land in St. Louis, Catharine rejoiced, "One night more only on the boat[.] Jubilate!" For the second time on the trip, Charles slept poorly as they passed Alton, Illinois, "by moonlight" and approached St. Louis. Unable to fall asleep, he "got up a little after one [a.m.] & sat in the wheel house" the rest of the night.[741]

Also finding it hard to sleep, no doubt, were "large numbers of foreign emigrants, nestled among their baggage, on the bank of the river" at Alton, "and passing the night in the open air." Platt pitied them as he walked from the train to catch a St.Louis–bound steamboat (possibly the *Sparhawk*) at 3:00 a.m. "Probably they had not enjoyed proper shelter or lodgings for weeks, as they are rarely treated like human beings in travelling in this part of the country." Such conditions were thought to lead to cholera among emigrants, and he noted, "We had heard that the cholera was in Alton."[742]

Heavy German immigration into Missouri did, however, lead to a stronger anti-slavery faction in what remained a slave state.[743]

Two miles below Alton, the Missouri River flowed into the Mississippi. Several excursionists were astonished by the change the former made in the latter. When dawn broke at St. Louis, Platt viewed the Mississippi and was "startled at the strange sight." The "clear, placid and beautiful river" of the past week had suddenly become "an angry, turbid, and almost frightful looking stream rushing past, containing successive masses of drift wood, in the shape of large trees, clumps of small trees, logs, bushes, stumps, and roots, in every variety, chasing each other in the rapid current." The river water was exceedingly muddy when he tried to use some in the washroom. Weed also noticed how the Missouri "immediately imparts its own color and character" to the mixture of rivers. "It is a dirty, dashing, impetuous torrent . . . , uprooting immense trees and madly breaking its bounds." A New York editor traveling with Platt thought he could see stretches of clear water still trying to maintain their character near St. Louis: "The purer waters of the Mississippi in their downward course

encounter and penetrate this bank of mud, and you may see large areas of mud and long strips of pure water side by side, apparently refusing to intermingle."[744]

It is perhaps not too conjectural to suggest that this "dirty, dashing, impetuous" Missouri struck excursionists (consciously or unconsciously) as a metaphor for the Slave Power, whose political aggressiveness, exhibited in the Kansas-Nebraska Act, seemed to overpower the pure, free North. Slavery ought to be only a tributary, a "peculiar institution" present in one section but subordinate to the more normal institutions of freedom that purified the main channel of the Union. Instead, the tributary forced its "color and character" upon the Union. Its impetuous, violent, uprooting character was seen in the filibustering expeditions of William Walker (into Mexico) and John A. Quitman (planned for that summer, against Cuba), in Pierre Soulé's dueling and threatening braggadocio aimed at forcing Spain to sell Cuba to the United States and making it a slaveholding state, in southern threats of secession (in 1850–1852), and in the violent talk on the House floor during the Kansas-Nebraska debate.[745] To anti-slavery northerners, including almost all excursionists, these events of President Franklin Pierce's administration represented an unnatural dominance of the tributary South over the North and the West.

Now some anti-slavery northerners were about to get their first close look at a slave state and its largest city—the slave state closest to disputed Kansas. During the past week, they had listened to Frank Blair, who argued against slavery on grounds that it weakened Missouri's economy and who tended (due to wishful thinking?) to downplay slavery's hold on the state.[746] Now they would see for themselves.

They had less than two days' notice of the excursionists' visit, but the citizens of St. Louis made quick preparations. They decided not to wait passively at the levee for the visitors to arrive, but at 7:00 a.m. sent their Committee of Arrangements, Colonel Thornton Grimsley commanding, and two militia companies onboard the steamboat *Michigan* "for the purpose of meeting Mr. Fillmore on his approach to the city." The St. Louis Grays wore light gray swallowtail coats with black collars, silver braid, and silver buttons "with a raised spread-eagle on each button," plus light gray trousers with a black stripe down each leg and black hats with a "tall plume of white feathers." The National Guards wore scarlet swallowtail coats, sky blue trousers, and a bearskin shako "with two gilt tassels hanging in front." St. Louis was well supplied with militia units and for good reason.[747]

Not long after eight o'clock, the cannons' roar signaled the approach of the *Golden Era* and *Michigan,* now "lashed together and proudly ploughing their way to the city." An "enthusiastic crowd" on the levee and on the decks of steamboats lying there yelled a "hearty welcome" as the cannon continued to fire. As if passing in review, the two boats did not stop but continued—with Fillmore "on the hurricane deck [of the *Golden Era*] all the

time—past the city downstream "a short distance" before turning around and coming back upstream. The crowd was not reviewing the excursionists on the *Golden Era;* Fillmore was inspecting the city.[748]

Quasi-military formalities multiplied when the steamboat *Minnesota,* going downstream, approached the *Michigan* and *Golden Era* going upstream. Just as the *Minnesota* came abreast, "there appeared upon her forecastle several of her deck hands, 'armed' with capstan bars, who went through all the military evolutions and came to a 'present arms' with their novel weapons as the boats met." This novel maneuver gratified and amused spectators on the lashed boats. A Mississippi River steamboat and its crew did not typically carry themselves with a military bearing.[749]

The two lashed boats pushed up on the levee, but instead of Fillmore and company simply disembarking, he, his party, and the Committee of Arrangements boarded "an adjoining boat," where Mayor John How and the city council formally received them. Mayor How gave a welcoming speech that could be heard by some of the immense crowd on the levee. Charles Sedgwick observed the proceedings from the deck of the *Sparhawk.* Platt of Poughkeepsie found "the display and ceremonies" a waste of time "as the movements were slow and tedious," but he watched to see how these westerners "would do things up on a great occasion."[750]

The scene was certainly a great one, and the "things" done up before a larger crowd than elsewhere on the excursion. Thousands of

Missourians stood on the levee or on the decks of steamboats by it. Paved with stone "rising obliquely from the water's edge," some "two hundred yards wide," the levee stretched for almost a mile. At times a hundred steamboats tied up here, "with Steam up and placarded for New Orleans, Louisville, Cincinnati, Pittsburgh, Council Bluffs, Galena, St. Paul's, &c., &c., while others *from* those places [were] discharging cargo." They lined up, "their bows butted up against the shore, as close as they can be crowded." The cargo lay piled on the levee, so that the crowds had to pick their way amid boxes and the wagons and carriages that came to fetch passengers and freight. Lining Front Street were blocks of warehouses.[751]

Mayor How and the city dignitaries likely received Fillmore on a boat to speak to him apart from the hubbub of the crowded levee. A Democrat from Pennsylvania, a businessman and free-soil ally of Frank Blair and Senator Thomas Hart Benton, How personified ex-northerners' dominance of St. Louis business—contrary to its image as southerners' bailiwick. Excursionists would find no shortage of like-minded Yankees among the city's elite. Yet, How assured Fillmore, "whatever political difference there may be amongst us lies dormant here to-day," and they greeted him "as citizens of that great confederacy over which you have with so much honor to yourself presided."[752]

Dormant was the right word; today only, the correct time. Feelings of political hostility seethed in St. Louis, not far beneath the surface. Two years earlier, a serious riot erupted on election day between German-Americans and Old Stock Americans, each mob numbering in the thousands, using pistols and stones against the other, and battling for control of the polling places. Nativists placed two cannons on Second Street and prepared to fire at hundreds of Germans before peace was gradually restored. Kansas-Nebraska and Know-Nothings were heating feelings toward the point of eruption, and the 1854 election day looked to be a repeat of 1852. Benton, the anti-Nebraska Democrat, fiercely campaigned for Congress against Know-Nothing Luther M. Kennett. Benton's aloof, imperious, vindictive personality created an anti-Benton Democratic faction; his emotional attack on Kansas-Nebraska added oil to the flames; "probably in no state did [the Kansas-Nebraska Act] create greater public excitement than in Missouri." Antagonism between Germans and Irish exacerbated the hostility. Anti-slavery Germans backed Benton while many anti-black Irish favored Kennett, who adroitly played to Irish and Know-Nothings. The latter stirred up nativist hatred toward both Irish and Germans. Military companies represented various groups—a German "Pioneer Corps," Irish "Washington Guards," and Old Stock St. Louis Grays and National Guards—but all cooperated under state command to suppress rioting.[753]

Fillmore's visit afforded the city's leaders a chance to stress unity. In a pacifying tone, the *St. Louis Republican* described the crowd on the levee: "Whig and Democrat—men of all shades and differences of principle—citizens of all kinds and from almost all countries, were grouped and crowded there, . . . to do honor to" Fillmore.[754] Who could better lower the city's political temperature than the president who fought for the Compromise of 1850 to end the agitation of the slavery issue and to preserve the Union?

Fillmore thanked the mayor for this reception and "was then conducted to the carriage" along with Nathan K. Hall, Bancroft, George Babcock, "and other distinguished gentlemen." The militia "form[ed] on the levee to keep back the immense throng." A parade began, led by Fillmore's carriage and its military escort, drawn from several militia companies, followed by a band and the St. Louis Grays. Next came the "Continentals" dressed in Revolutionary War uniforms and wearing white wigs; Light Guards; Washington Guards, a year-old Irish company—dressed in dark blue coats, sky blue trousers with yellow stripe, and combined American ("gilt spread-eagle") and Irish ("gilt harp entwined with shamrocks") insignia—that had introduced "the skirmish drill and sham battles" to St. Louis's military repertoire; National Guards; another band; the Union Riflemen; a fire-department unit; and St. Louis citizens on horseback and on foot. Conspicuously absent were two German outfits: a fierce axe-wielding Pioneer Corps and the St. Louis Mounted Rifles. "The procession traversed the various streets," where people gazed from the windows of houses and waved "white handkerchiefs and hats" from the sidewalks and streets.[755]

The parade ended in front of the Planter's House, a four-story luxury hotel in the neoclassical style, with columned sections in the center and on both wings (with penthouselike fifth floors above those sections), a cupola on the roof, and a wrought-iron balcony over the central entrance. "Its magnificent cuisine and splendid bar, where Planter's Punch was invented, provided a setting where the city's mercantile and political elite . . . planned, traded, and played." Many of the city's social elite and wealthiest guests were southerners, and the Planter's House flags flying from the roof indicated who set the tone for its high society.

After breakfast, Catharine Sedgwick witnessed this "great demon[stratio]n for the Pres[iden]t. The streets were crow[de]d before the hotel & colors fly[in]g, & drums beat[in]g & speechmaking." But, she continued, "poor Abby [Fillmore] O—not got a coach to come up from the boat—nor a basin of water to wash her face in." Abby Fillmore was apparently not included in the presidential procession, and Sedgwick did not feel these westerners displayed good manners in thus excluding her.[756]

Equal rights for different political views, not different genders, was the priority at the Planter's House speech-making. A pro-slavery Whig (to balance the anti-slavery Democrat How), Uriel Wright, gave the welcoming address here. A noted criminal lawyer who could eloquently argue the guilty free, Wright was a skilled orator adept at classical allusions, with a "clear and musical voice" but without great sincerity. After "a denunciation of gambling, so fierce and so pathetic that men trembled and wept as they listened to it, he might be seen at a card table." Yet there was no hypocrisy in his Unionist, pro-Compromise (1850), pro-commerce speech. "We cherish the Union of these States," Wright assured Fillmore, and those who acted to preserve it. "It was your fortune, Mr. Fillmore, to take the Presidential chair on one of the dark days of the Republic—when a black cloud hung with fearful portent over the union of these States." He did not mention the black cloud of hostility over Kansas-Nebraska but may have implied its presence. "You found our Union in peril—you left it consolidated and secured." He claimed, "We speak the bolder that we address a private citizen," but he issued only bold compliments to Fillmore, whose compromise policy had aided commerce, manufacturing, and investments. He praised Fillmore's approval of money for improving the less navigable stretches of the Mississippi River.[757]

Fillmore stood in his carriage to give his reply. "I confess, I am taken by surprise by this magnificent reception, so unexpected to me." Especially surprising was it, because "I am a private citizen, and come among you as such." He quickly passed by Wright's praise for his administration and came to St. Louis's commercial role. He used the very title the city's boosters were promoting, "Great Central City." He hinted that its centrality might gain it one Pacific railroad route. "We must have a railway across the continent" to preserve the Union in "one common brotherhood." He

flattered St. Louis by pointing to its rapid progress ahead of his home city, Buffalo. "[A]nd, what is more, from the vast throng that now surrounds me and the volunteers with their glittering uniforms, I see you have the spirit and the military power to defend and protect the city." After his talk, he was taken to his rooms at the Planter's House and the celebration ended.[758]

At noon, in the Planter's House lobby, Catharine Sedgwick and her hostess, Cornelia Carr, found Abby Fillmore, who had managed to make it to the hotel by then—apparently without the help of bands and militia companies. Abby had no room in which to formally receive them, Sedgwick complained, and so they had to converse in the lobby. Abby was an "old chum" of "Nelly" Carr; both had attended the boarding school for young women that Charles Sedgwick's wife, Elizabeth, operated in Lenox, Massachusetts.[759]

Through these school ties, Charles and Catharine connected to a small colony of New England–minded St. Louis Unitarians whom they found to be quite congenial hosts, so unlike some of the "cultivated & genteel vulgar" whom they met on the excursion. Cornelia, the daughter of prominent St. Louis merchant Wayman Crow, had recently married Lucien Carr. The Sedgwicks spent part of the morning with the Carrs, who were house-sitting for her absent father. Here they recuperated from the long trip, Catharine reported, by eating "a most comfortable family break[fas]t," taking a bath, and lying down for "a refreshing nap after break[fas]t." Lucien and

Charles walked through the downtown section of the city. Lucien introduced Charles, he noted, "to about 20 different persons from two of whom I have received invitations to tea in the Country this evening." Later in the day, while Cornelia took Catharine for a drive around town, Charles took his own bath and his own, less successful, nap: "I called for a bath & am washed for the first time in 14 days . . . I have been lying on the bed 1/2 an hour trying to go to sleep but in vain[—]I suppose, because, if a man feels clean here, he is not permitted to forget the strange sensation, while it lasts."[760]

While at the Carrs', Catharine visited with William Greenleaf Eliot—Unitarian minister, advocate of gradual emancipation of slaves, educator, and reformer in St. Louis. He exemplified what she fervently hoped to see: New England's moral influence in the West. Born in Massachusetts, educated at Harvard Divinity School, Eliot came to St. Louis in 1834 as the first Unitarian missionary west of the Mississippi River. With refined mouth, sensitive eyes, and longish hair over his ears and touching his collar, the forty-two-year-old Eliot appeared to Sedgwick "a very attractive person, with a spirituality and refinement that reminds you of Dr. [William Ellery] Channing, but with the freedom, frankness, and facility that belongs to a more practical, out-of-doors man." A busy speaker and author, Eliot was not merely a man of words, but in 1853–1854 was founding Washington Institute (later, Washington University) with the help of Wayman Crow, who was a leader

in his congregation, and Mayor John How and other of his members.[761]

"The day we were there," Catharine reported, "Colonel [John] O'Fallon, their Croesus (a man of a different faith from Eliot), gave him property to the amount of $30,000 for an industrial school." This school, later called O'Fallon Polytechnic Institute, was to hold evening courses for artisans and provide them with a library. It was a department within Washington Institute. Rougher-looking than Eliot and more of an out-of-doors man, O'Fallon was born to "an Irish gentleman-adventurer" and the sister of Revolutionary War hero George Rogers Clark and famed explorer William Clark. O'Fallon was severely wounded at Tippecanoe, fought in the War of 1812, and undertook long fur-trade trips for his Uncle William. O'Fallon made a fortune as a supplier to U.S. Army posts, bank president, real estate dealer, and investor-director in the Pacific Railroad Company, which hoped to reach California but had less than fifty miles of track in 1854. He stood at the pinnacle of financial and social power in St. Louis but was civic-minded. Such generosity helped Catharine Sedgwick to accept grudgingly the otherwise unacceptable money-grubbing in the West. "The insane avarice of our people is worse than the potato-rot," she wrote to Kate, but Eliot, Crow, and O'Fallon were exceptions to the western rule.[762]

O'Fallon was one of the two gentlemen who invited the Sedgwicks to tea, and that evening they were driven to his estate on the northwestern outskirts of St. Louis. "We were at this Col. O'Fallon's," Catharine noted, "& were drawn over his magnif[icen]t Park grounds—1200 acres in extent with a magnif[icen]t garden—with exotic decorations." She later described him as living "with the simplicity of a republican gentleman" amid his 1,200 acres, but republican simplicity did not ordinarily demand "exotic decorations."[763]

"From there we went to Mr. Yeatman's," she continued, "where we saw a very pretty hanging garden made in a sort of miniature crater. They are called by the *fanciful* name of *sink*." A native of Tennessee, James E. Yeatman also served as a public benefactor for cultural institutions, railroad investor, and banker. (Thomas Yeatman was an excursionist.) Balding, a peaceable-looking man with rounded shoulders, James Yeatman freed his slaves but was not a free-soil, Blair man. He favored compromise and conciliation. If unimpressed with his politics, the Sedgwicks were impressed with his house: "If ever they drank tea in the Alhambra it must have been at such a table as Mr. Yeatman's—such china— such silver—such flowers & fruits—& the host was a fit ideal of that embodiment of all virtues— in a travellers eye." Catharine thought she had never seen "a tea-table" in New England to match this one. Here was a cultured gentleman they could admire, if not a reformer of Eliot's high caliber.[764]

"[H]ospitality unbounded" at the Carrs', O'Fallons', and Yeatmans' did much to restore the Sedgwicks' equanimity after their long trip west. "Perhaps what most pleased us in St. Louis," Catharine observed, "was the absence of all obtrusive signs of what we consider the only misfortune of Missouri—the only obstacle to its future pre-eminence—slavery." Missouri was a slave state. Yet "this disease has made so little progress there" that she anticipated "the healthful young state will throw it off." Those were the oft-expressed opinions of Frank Blair, and she continued by praising "a '*young* man eloquent,' who is just entering, with sure promise, political life"—certainly, Blair—"who has the generous boldness to throw himself in the scale against it [slavery]—God speed him!"[765]

Taking tea and baths at the homes of St. Louis's elite—and listening to Blair—were not accurate means of gauging Missouri's economy or politics. Eliot and Blair stressed Missouri's ambivalence about slavery and its mildness there to convince the anti-slavery Sedgwicks to take a favorable view of their state and of their efforts. Eliot had been criticized by New England Unitarians as not sufficiently anti-slavery; he sought to explain his moderate stance to these Yankee cultural leaders.[766] The Sedgwicks did not question slavery's "little progress there," because that was exactly what they wanted to hear. Slaves made up only about 3 percent of the city's population (around 100,000), and manumissions were increasing; however, St. Louis was only a small part of Missouri. In Little Dixie, a string of counties along the Missouri River from Jefferson City to the Kansas border, farmers raised hemp and used slaves to grow, harvest, and process it. Tobacco farmers did likewise, but hemp was Missouri's most important slave-labor crop. Despite Blair's talk of unprofitable and unpopular slavery (likely, his attempt to avoid a moral abolitionistlike attack on slavery and to overstate his political chances), "the best evidence indicates that most Missourians considered slavery profitable and acted accordingly." The price of a male slave rose during the 1850s, a good sign of profitability.[767]

The Sedgwicks did not see this Missouri nor the slaves who worked as domestic servants inside St. Louis homes. They did not speak to the majority of Missourians who supported the Kansas-Nebraska Act or to masters worried lest a free Kansas on their western border become a refuge for runaway slaves. They did not seem to see the multitudes passing through St. Louis on the way to Kansas and Nebraska. "Each boat bound up the Missouri has on board more or less of them," a New York Times correspondent noted. "They seem generally of the sturdy farming population, and each is accompanied by his family, is provided with wagon and tent, and the ever present rifle." These pioneers were concerned about government surveys and land titles more than slavery's hypothetical possibilities in Kansas. Yet they were not the anti-slavery settlers sent out by northern emigration societies, who would not leave Boston until July 17. And border Missourians were concerned about slavery in Kansas.[768]

Alarmed by newspaper reports about these emigration societies, energized by Pierce's signing of the Kansas-Nebraska Act on May 30, and encouraged by their Senator David Atchison—who "warned his constituents that Boston's Faneuil Hall was coming to rule them," pro-slavery Missourians along the border had gotten the jump on northerners. They toasted Pierce, held rallies in several border towns, formed claims associations, staked out town sites in Kansas, and passed fiery resolutions. The first such meeting was held at Westport on June 3, the day the excursionists arrived in Chicago; on June 10, the day the Grand Excursion ended at Rock Island, Missourians rode on horseback some miles into Kansas, to Salt Creek Valley, to claim the territory for slavery with a formal proclamation.[769] The "Sovereigns" and "Squatter Sovereigns" whom New England excursionists gently ridiculed on the Upper Mississippi were already hard at work across the Missouri.

Andrew Aiken of the New York Evening Post reported a week after Fillmore's visit "that the feeling among a class of the Missouri frontier population is very intense against any attempt" by free-soil associations "to colonize" Kansas. Already, border Missourians had held a meeting "at Westport, near the Kansas line," to express these feelings. Aiken cautioned free-soil organizers that they might experience "some little difficulty in getting into the territory an emigration from the northern states." He was even advised not to reveal that he "was from 'that abolition paper, the Evening Post.'"[770]

Aiken continued on from St. Louis to Kansas Territory, but the other excursionists did not. The Sedgwicks, Bancroft, the Fillmores, and others left St. Louis—probably on Tuesday, June 13, and mostly by boat to Alton and by train from Alton to Chicago. At Springfield, Illinois, the Fillmores stopped briefly on Wednesday, June 14, for another public reception at the railroad depot. Fillmore "was received at the cars by a large concourse of citizens. A national salute was also fired"—presumably, by cannons. "He was introduced to the citizens by Hon. Abraham Lincoln, in reply to whom the ex-president made a brief speech."[771]

A former congressman but now largely retired from active politics, Lincoln was exceedingly busy that late spring with circuit court cases at Urbana, Danville, and Springfield. His legal practice was changing from one of "numerous cases with small fees and less consequence" to one "taken up with suits relating to the railroad network" in Illinois—many of them before Judge John Dean Caton and the Illinois Supreme Court; however, he still could not afford to turn down smaller cases or miss the circuit court sessions. He was undoubtedly not invited to the Grand Excursion but could not have accompanied his brother-in-law Ninian W. Edwards if he had been. Judge David Davis's Eighth Judicial District circuit court happened to be meeting in Springfield when Fillmore came through town, and so the forty-five-year-old lawyer was invited to give the introductory remarks.[772]

There is no record of what Lincoln said. Fillmore's "brief speech" aroused a newspaper controversy in Springfield, but the combatants did not refer to Lincoln's remarks. Kansas-Nebraska aroused Lincoln—along with many other northerners—to a renewed interest in and engagement with politics; however, he was busy with legal cases, saw no need as a private citizen to comment on the act, and was hesitant to speak too soon given the uncertainties in June and July about how the Kansas-Nebraska earthquake would reshape the political landscape. He had said nothing yet on the act and certainly did not on Wednesday, June 14.[773]

Neither did Fillmore, but the issue was so hot in Illinois his remarks were construed as a reference to it. The Democrats' *Illinois State Register* quoted Fillmore as praising Illinois as "a great State . . . because you love the Union, because you have always stood by the Union, and have never permitted yourselves to be blown about by the breath of faction, come in what shape it would." The *Register* parsed this sentence as a "scathing rebuke to those factionists" (including some excursionists) who were planning to establish a sectional, anti-Nebraska party. Moore of the Whigs' *Illinois State Journal* pooh-poohed this interpretation. Moore "heard Mr. Fillmore make some twenty little speeches last week, very similar to the one in Springfield," and in almost all of them he referred to "the Union," but he made it clear that he was referring "to those who stood by his administration and 'the Union' during the Compromise time of 1850." The ex-president was not rebuking anti-Nebraska men, for "the 'silver grey' men of New York are dead set against the Nebraska bill."[774]

Just as the "great national and centripetal

force" of the Kansas-Nebraska Act awakened Lincoln from political quiescence and gathered the political fragments into a new northern, anti-Nebraska party, so the centripetal force of the Grand Excursion was now ending, and the centrifugal power of domestic duties and attachments was breaking up the traveling party into dozens of smaller groups headed for dozens of destinations. Fillmore, his son Millard Powers, and Abby arrived in Chicago on Thursday evening, June 15. The next day father and daughter (the son went straight home to Buffalo) started on a voyage up Lakes Michigan and Huron to Sault St. Marie to view the canal under construction, a visible example of Fillmore's internal improvements. By June 27, "quite wearied out" from four months of travel, Fillmore (and Abby) returned to Buffalo, where they would stay "during the summer unless we shall be driven out by the cholera" afflicting the city—which Fillmore feared would become "an epidemic."[775]

From Chicago, Bancroft left for Detroit and Niagara Falls. Despite having told his wife that he would return this way and having twice strongly hinted to her that he expected to find a letter from her at each place, he found no letters at either stop. He journeyed more than 450 miles on Monday, June 19, he wrote her, "to get nearer you the sooner; but no word of love from my wife was at New York to greet my coming." She had gone to their summer home in Newport, and he was chagrined to find only two towels for his use at their New York City residence, "one for my feet & one for my hands." In a letter written

at 5:00 a.m., he complained, "I think this a very short allowance; & if I knew where to go I should buy a dozen." These were not "the sweetest offices of friendship & love" he had dreamed of on his trip. As he found out in 1823, when his studies in Europe ended, returning travelers sometimes encountered a chilly reception.[776]

Catharine Sedgwick enjoyed a much warmer reception. After stopping at Chicago, taking the Michigan Central to Detroit and the Canadian Great Western railroad to Niagara Falls and the New York Central to Albany, Charles and she returned to Lenox on Tuesday, June 20. Not to an empty house and no close relationships. There to greet her was Kate's daughter Alice. "My journey had its final crown & rejoicing when our precious little Alice sprang out of the dining-parlor door into my arms as I alighted from the last vehicle of our long travel." Her dreams of journey's end were realized. "Twenty times that day it had occurred to me 'what a delight it would be to find Alice at Lenox!' but with no expectation of finding that vision—that seemed to me like an *ignis fatuus* from my heart—realized." The trip, she reported to Kate, "was prosperous to its end" and accident-free. "Providence must think better of rail travel than William does." The West was prosperous and promising too. "I would not certainly give up one of our hearth-stones for it all—for my own life," she hastened to add. The West belonged to the future, to Alice's generation: "it is the soil for the young to take root & spread in; and if they will but take with them the elements of moral as well as of physical growth there need be no failure in this new world."[777]

They left the excursion around 10:00 p.m., Friday, June 9, and did not go to St. Louis, but Benjamin and Sarah Silliman returned by a route similar to the Sedgwicks' and Bancroft's. Yet there were differences in their views and their routes. From *Sparhawk,* the Sillimans traveled to Wisconsin's Beloit College, a young evangelical institution meant to compete against Catholics and Unitarians—and Eliot's new St. Louis school—for the minds and hearts of westerners. On Sunday June 11, they "passed a quiet Sabbath." The morning's sermon "on the character of God" Silliman praised; the afternoon's talk "on the origin of sin" he dismissed as "a discourse of speculative metaphysics." They delayed their drive around town and inspection of the college until Monday morning, and took the train to Chicago in the afternoon.[778]

At Chicago, after a walk around "the site of old Fort Dearborn," with old settler John Kinzie, Silliman's memories returned to the War of 1812. Kinzie was six years old when his father was captured by the British and their Indian allies in August 1812. As they toured the battlefield one-and-a-half miles east of the fort, Silliman undoubtedly saw a bit of his father and mother's wartime experiences in Kinzie's parents' ordeal. In Detroit, on June 15, he contemplated war and bloodshed again: "I looked over the history of Pontiac's war, and of his attempts at massacre here at

Detroit" in 1763 by reading Francis Parkman's *The History of the Conspiracy of Pontiac* (1851). He recalled General William Hull's tragic surrender of Detroit in 1812 and Americans' rashness, "boastful bravado," and inadequate preparations for the War of 1812. "On both sides the war was unnecessary and might have been prevented by good temper and a spirit of justice," he concluded.[779]

On Friday June 16, the Sillimans rode a steamboat across the Detroit River and boarded the Great Western train for the nine-hour trip to Niagara River. Early Saturday morning, they took "a pleasant carriage excursion—first up Lundy's Lane to the scene of the sanguinary battle of July 1814," just opposite Niagara Falls, on "the British side." Benjamin Silliman mused on war's futility and tragedy. Near the battlefield's center was a church cemetery. He pondered the juxtaposition, in July 1814, of the long dead "beneath the green turf" and the recently dead above it. The bloody affair was useless; like so "many more scenes of slaughter of that war [it] had no other result than to prove anew the indomitable energy & valor of the combatants, which none could doubt before. General [Winfield] Scott, wounded on that occasion, still survives," but hundreds of soldiers were buried in a mass grave. He climbed an eighty-foot-high tower with a British survivor of the battle, who pointed out "the position of the combatants." He was disgusted when the man told him he "thanked God" his captain died in the battle "as this gave him promotion! War in all its aspects is savage."[780]

Saturday afternoon, they toured Niagara Falls, Silliman's fifth visit there. His thoughts turned to "the overpowering grandeur[,] magnificence & richness of this wonderful display of the physical laws of God & their stupendous results." Yet he also saw the falls as an ongoing scientific experiment in Earth's chronology. The steady erosive progress of the Niagara River "affords a chronometer," or timepiece, for estimating the Earth's age, "but man has not discovered the scale nor when the initial digit was marked" and so could not read the timepiece. The rate of erosion might have changed. "Even if the amount of recess [in the Falls] had been marked since the French Explorers first saw the cataract it would not follow that the ratio has been the same ever since it began to wear away the rocks." He thought he detected a backward erosion of Horseshoe Falls since he first saw it in 1827 (but no estimates of erosion over the centuries could be extrapolated from so short an interval of time).[781]

At 4:15 p.m., they crossed the river to Lockport, New York, where excavations for a mill had unearthed Trilobita fossils and an Orthoceras. They had friends at Lockport, and the next day was Sunday, so they stayed here. "An earnest invitation" from a "young men's association" persuaded Silliman to lecture, without his usual experiments and illustrations, on the topic. "The powers that have produced the perfect condition of the globe preparatory to the introduction of life ending with man." He spoke to three hundred people for more than an hour.[782]

On Wednesday, June 21, they left Lockport; on June 22 they dined at Albany's Delavan House; by June 24, they were home in New Haven, "having been with all our late numerous companions on this most interesting tour of nearly 4,000 miles out and in, protected from every danger, & prospered in every particular! God's holy name be praised."[783]

Awaiting Silliman were letters to answer. On Friday, July 7, he wrote to Englishman John Taylor, briefly describing the Grand Excursion ("1000 people of both sexes were borne out & back almost 4000 miles without accident or alarm") and attacking Kansas-Nebraska ("this gigantic wrong"). Silliman agreed with Taylor that Europe had failed to set up moderate, constitutional liberty "in place of the hateful despotism of the bayonet & the cannon." Yet he seemed to include America in a prediction of dire consequences. "God reigns and we know that he will override all events for good, but at present we cannot discern any ground of hope for the masses except through scenes of bloodshed which it is fearful to contemplate." That might be true of America, he implied, because "the spirit of despotism under the form of the slave power is struggling for the mastery and has already advanced far toward attaining it."[784]

EXCURSUS
The Grand Excursion and Antebellum Travel Literature

IN A YOUNG NATION whose scientists, physicians, and historians indefatigably gathered specimens and documents, where the Baconian method, not theorizing, was the favored way to acquire knowledge, travel writing was a major literary genre. To travel was to gather characters, dialects, anecdotes, jokes, and impressions as a geologist gathers rocks. "To a striking extent, intellectual activity in antebellum America consisted of travel and writing or speaking about travel." For those who sought to understand America, these specimens could reveal much about this nation-in-the-making. Going right to the spot was perhaps the only way to understand such an assortment of regions, ethnic groups, denominations, and races. One could not know it from one's parlor in Boston—unless one read a travel book written by someone who had been there. "To travel, or to read about travel, was, after all, the appropriate way to learn about and to present knowledge about a nation on the move."[785]

It can hardly be surprising, then, that several literary accounts of the Grand Excursion appeared in print, in addition to the many newspaper reports. Some excursionists aspired to be more than mere chroniclers and attempted to interpret the excursion in an original and entertaining way. None wrote a full-length book. Most wrote sketches; one or two included the excursion as part of an essay. Yet that was typical of the times. Ever since Washington Irving's *The Sketch Book* (1819–1820) achieved "sensational" popularity, the sketch had become "the literary fashion in America." As a brief "verbal rendering of visualized scenes and characters," it was often based upon travels to novel scenes that featured unusual regional characters. The name itself suggests its connection to art, especially landscape painting. As John F. Kensett sketched scenes on the excursion, so a writer of prose presented his or her verbal renderings as sketches supposedly true to life because written down right on the spot.[786] Several accounts of the excursion fall into this category of the travel sketch. (Some newspaper correspondents' reports also displayed some of the literary qualities of a sketch.)

By 1854, travel sketches were so numerous that they had long been the target of satirists:

"I'll make a TOUR—*and then I'll* WRITE *IT.*
You well know what my pen can do,
And I'll employ me pencil too:—
I'll ride and write, *and* sketch *and* print,
And thus create a real mint;
I'll prose *it here, I'll* verse *it there,*
And picturesque *it everywhere.*[787]

The categories of the beautiful, the picturesque, and the sublime were only some of the conventions overused in the travel sketch.

Another convention was that a sketch represented antebellum America's dominant cultural perspective, that of "the disinterested (white, urban, Northeastern) gentleman" who could authoritatively interpret scenes and characters along the way. Even that man might have to bow to the more dominant perspective of the English gentleman, whom Nathaniel Hawthorne satirized in "The Canal-Boat": "Perceiving that the Englishman was taking notes in a memorandum-book, with occasional glances round the cabin, I presumed that we were to figure in a future volume of travels."[788] However, the two Englishmen listed as excursionists do not appear to have written a volume or even a sketch regarding the trip. The leisure to travel and the ability to sketch were both marks of social superiority, and that was usually communicated in the published piece.[789]

"THE ROCK ISLAND EXCURSION" BY A LADY. . . . BETSY BLAKE

Taking the Grand Excursion's eastern beginnings for a starting point, we come first to "The Rock Island Excursion," a lengthy and gently satirical sketch in Horace Greeley's *New York Tribune*. Allegedly "By a Lady," with the pseudonym Betsy Blake, this piece turned the conventions upside down, for its supposed author was a working-class young woman, and it was written in a disjointed and ungrammatical style, with an affected wide-eyed innocence and a naive bluntness appropriate to a Massachusetts nanny traveling with her wealthy boss, whose wife refused "to trust herself to all the lightning trains and high pressure boats" and so trusted her husband to go alone with her female servant.[790] Ironically it was the nanny who possessed upper-class leisure. Here, travel was a metaphor for life, and that was another convention. Packing luggage was like filling minds: we are "sure to make some mistake" and to leave behind "just the thoughts that will be the kind we'll want to use in a strange company."

On the train from Massachusetts to New York City, Betsy sketched the stock character of the newlywed. "I couldn't help knowing in a little while after we started, what people had been married that day and what had been married a great deal longer. The brides grew tired so soon, and had to lay their heads on the gentlemen's shoulders, which the gentlemen seemed to like very much. . . . The gentlemen that had been husbands so much longer, almost showed very plainly that they weren't so anxious to have anybody lean upon them, but thought reading the newspaper was full as pleasant." The same occurred from New York to Albany: "We had a new set of brides on the Hudson River Railroad, but they all were tired just the same before we got to the first station."

She poked fun at Americans who traveled only in Europe and regarded American scenery with snobbish disdain. They should pretend the Hudson was in Europe. "They would certainly write a book directly about their travels, besides not being seasick and spending much of their money."

Speaking in the character of an innocent working-class girl, the writer could place critical comments in Betsy's mouth that gentlemen would not say because they challenged social conventions. She mourned the fate of the Mohawk who used to inhabit this country and the fact "that strange people, with trunks and carpet-bags, should be looking out from the windows of railroad cars upon the wild, free places where they were born." Innocently, Betsy unmasked the pretense of totally disinterested railroad generosity by unconvincingly refuting other excursionists' critique that railroads treated them well to increase future passenger traffic: "But I couldn't feel that all the polite captains, and all the gentlemanly conductors, were treating us so, because they wanted to sell a great many tickets." No, "[i]t seemed to come so natural" to these men; she felt "they liked to be pleasant to strangers, especially such bright ones as there were in our party, from a great many editor's sanctums and such wise places." Railroads were least disinterested when they gave free passes to editors, when both sides implicitly understood that free publicity would be the result.

Betsy could ridicule boosters' rhetoric: "The next day we were at Monroe [Michigan], which I was told was a great deal prettier than it looked; but we didn't stop to know if it was true, as we went as fast as we could away to get to Chicago that night." At Chicago, unlike the newspapermen, she could be unimpressed by rapidly rising real estate values and boosters' braggadocio. "All the places West are so different from young ladies and gentlemen, that everybody knows want to be young as long as they can. Chicago is hurrying to be old, and can hardly stop to make things strong and well, because it wants to get on so quick." Streets and sidewalks were made of wood, "and it's very muddy when it storms." Chicago should build well, not fast. "But I suppose Chicago will not send for Betsy Blake to know how it's best to grow." She had enough to do "looking after Charlie's babies" and declined any feminist role in Chicago politics. Beside, she was a Yankee. "The 'Tremont House' sounded like Boston, and I felt quite at home in it, if I didn't look out the windows."

"Monday morning, two long trains, with engines looking as if their hearts were too hot and their bodies too hard to be covered with anything that looked like flowers, started with their wreaths and garlands for the great excursion." She poked fun at the collection of big egos leaving Chicago on June 5. "I don't suppose there will be so many such kind of heads on that road again, until we're all invited to the Pacific Ocean opening. If anything had happened to the trains, there would have been a great many large organs hurt."

They were off for Rock Island, admiring the prairie "that lay so broad and green along our way. The cattle, that we tried to fancy Buffaloes, had all the flowers, for the cars wouldn't stop to let little boys pick bouquets. . . . The cattle hadn't the least idea how much we would have thanked them for a little bit of their dinner." She used an oceanic metaphor for the prairie and tossed in free publicity for the Chicago & Rock Island Railroad, "if that's what they asked me for or not, in telling everybody that's got money enough and time to go over that road some day." She satirized the uneastern manners of easterners eating that picnic lunch west of Sheffield. "People that couldn't eat at home without napkins and silver forks, were pulling turkey dreadfully apart, and carrying great hand-loads of sandwiches to the ladies, who most always are taken care of, though they don't have their rights."

She objected to Rock Islanders' complaints that "our faces warn't anything extra to bring all the way from the East to show": "It was very muddy where we landed, and I had no idea that the people of Rock Island were standing there to look at our beauty, or I should have tried to look a great deal brighter as I picked my way down to our boat."

She heard Millard Fillmore's speech at Davenport that Monday evening and innocently wondered if his flattery won votes. The humble nanny with the shaky grammar put herself in the same class with the ex-president as future excursionists: "I was glad to hear him talk very certainly about the great Pacific Railroad . . . because I thought he and I might be invited again over that way." She modestly ended her piece at Davenport, for "a great many brighter people have begun their letters here, to tell about the going up to St. Paul and the Falls" and she feared that adding her words to these editors' letters would make readers *too* interested in the West. "Betsy Blake" was most likely an editor or correspondent who did not travel beyond Davenport or Dubuque. Her indirect critique of railroads seeking free publicity and her reference to editors writing their letters both point in that direction. Using this persona allowed the writer to depart from the clichés and stereotypical treatment of the excursion, which he had probably been forced to use in his newspaper accounts.

"THE GREAT WEST"
BY COUNT ADAM GUROWSKI

Travel writing, like speech-making, could be done for political purposes, however much it might try to conceal its true character by posing as a series of offhand objective observations. Count Adam Gurowski's article for the *New York Daily Tribune* was not a sketch but a public argument contrasting markedly with a private letter describing his brief participation in the Grand Excursion. Horace Greeley evidently encouraged several of his writers, including Gurowski and editor Charles Dana, to go on the excursion to "sound out and shape public opinion" on the Kansas-Nebraska Act. Greeley even sent a letter of introduction to Thurlow Weed, urged Weed to aid him on the trip, and commended Gurowski as "a very valuable expositor of the affairs of the Old World"—as if Weed wanted facts about Warsaw while he was eyeing the West. "I commend him to your good offices." The "mud, cold, and rain" of Monday and Tuesday, June 5 and 6, discouraged Gurowski. Also, his poor health, "the crowd on the steamers, and some other reasons peculiar to an old and spoiled European" caused him to go no farther than Rock Island or Davenport. Nevertheless, he "philosophized" about the West in an article headed "Chicago, June 11, 1854," but which he wrote at Niagara, not Chicago.[791]

Through his pen, the excursion became an editorial for free labor and democracy.

Adam Gurowski was an exiled Polish count, an ardent lover of liberty who joined in several Polish insurrections against Russian rule, suffered confiscation of his estates and exile, was sentenced to death, and acquired an eclectic education among émigré and literary circles in France and Germany. In 1835 he advocated Pan-Slavism (the unity of all Slavs under the czar), which restored him to the good graces of Russian officialdom. He made enemies at the Russian court, however, and in 1849 left for the United States, where he became the *Tribune*'s Russian expert, wrote *Russia As It Is* (1854), and interested himself in American politics, especially the slavery debate. An "odd little man, much bearded, and with a semi-military stride, in great boots outside his trousers," he could defend a strong opinion in eight different languages with "fiery independence" and a volcanic temper. A *Tribune* colleague noted, "His friendship is often exhibited very much" like "the tenderness of a bear is sometimes manifested, by a hug which seems almost fatal to the subject of it." He was "a man of great genius, great learning, and great fertility of mind."[792]

Such an opinionated, widely traveled man was unlikely to devote lengthy sentences to Indiana crops or oceanlike Illinois prairies. Gurowski wrote nothing about scenery, weather, or excursionists; he did not verbally render the scenes or the characters he saw. He acknowledged his topic—"the great Excursion, which, for the moment, attracts the attention of the American public"—but did not describe it. It was a platform that gave him public attention, and it also could be used as an exhibit in his case against European despotism and southern slavery. The C&RI's organizational work demonstrated "the combined action of liberty and association." Hundreds of guests transported "free of charge from different places, distant thousands of miles, invited by hosts to them unknown" were exhibits for freedom and against monarchy. "No sovereign could do anything on such an extensive scale. . . . This excursion offers a new illustration of how . . . freedom and free individual impulse are far more efficacious and successful than power, authority, and compulsive order."[793]

Newer, western societies must be places of more freedom and individuality, for progress favored later-settled regions "even over the highly advanced Eastern States" (New England, which he admired). Gurowski used a geological comparison. The new western settlements were

> ruled by the same law which is absolute in the geological formations of our planet. Since uncounted periods of time, the successively created and superposed strata are more perfect in matter as well as in animal life than the foregoing ones. In the same manner the younger societies and States, pouring as from the soil at the invocation of liberty, are molded by an organic principle broader, purer, more normal, more and more free from old rotten conventionalities, shams and other ragged relics transmitted by the past.

New England was more free than Poland or Russia; Iowa would be more free than New England. Not a Democrat, he still agreed with George Bancroft's faith in the West. A virgin environment and a lack of constraining traditions would liberate eastern settlers and European immigrants and, through them, the institutions they created. Why did European immigrants not go to Canada's virgin lands? "The reason is, that he finds there remains of what he shunned and detested in his primitive native country"—"Monarchy."[794]

Here Gurowski confronted a contradiction: the runaway American slave had to seek refuge in Canada. "[H]unted as a wild beast by his countrymen"—lovers of freedom and democracy—he became "a human being under the shelter of monarchy."[795]

"Why this contrast?" The free, democratic West did not produce runaways to monarchy. It was being rapidly built by free labor. Gurowski praised speculators who used freedom to "choose and trace out the spots for settlements and cities"; he praised their greatest creation, Chicago, growing with "lightning like speed." The stagnant South, not the West, was the source of the fugitive slaves. Nearly two centuries old, Charleston, South Carolina, "has scarcely 40,000 inhabitants"; its "streets are overgrown with moss and weeds"; while twenty-year-old Chicago had 70,000 people and street lots worth $250 per foot. "Let the apostles and admirers of Slavery—let the Nebrascals . . . look at facts like these." He described Chicago's railroads and its hopes to be a terminus for a Pacific railroad. But progress via liberty was threatened by the Kansas-Nebraska Act, which he condemned as "treason, the attempted assassination of Liberty, perpetrated by Douglas and Richardson, both from Illinois."[796]

This extended argument-by-travel did not reflect Gurowski's actual experiences, as related in a June 8 letter to a *Tribune* colleague. He noticed Chicago's "mud, cold, and rain" more than its lightning progress. His references to westerners' collective future may have signaled alert readers that he was dissatisfied with present, individual westerners. "In Iowa and here [Chicago] I mixed as much as possible with the thick-soled, rag-wearing part of the population, mostly strong Democrats," he noted. "We spoke about the Nebraska infamy. . . . I found, unhappily, a strong pro-Douglas feeling, based exclusively on the fallacious notion that the bill recognizes fully the squatter sovereignty and the absolute right of the people." He knew deceived westerners were "not to be talked out of this position"—despite their supposed freedom from rotten conventionalities—and so he advocated "several successive heavy shots fired in the Tribune" against this opinion before it took "deeper roots in the conviction of the people." The one point where his published account matched his private one was his anger at "the great traitor Richardson" (Douglas's ally in getting the bill through the House), whom he talked with and observed in the Chicago hotel.[797]

Then Gurowski was off to Niagara, where "I shall write out my impressions for the Tribune; Dana told me to do it." He sent in his "philosophical considerations of the excursion" and asked his colleague James Shepherd Pike to translate them into English (he undoubtedly wrote them in French), "before my return from the g-r-e-a-t excursion." His sketch appeared in the June 19 *Tribune.*[798]

"FORTY DAYS IN A WESTERN HOTEL"
AUTHOR UNKNOWN

Still another account based on a partial excursion to Chicago was "Forty Days in a Western Hotel," which appeared in *Putnam's Monthly Magazine* in December 1854. Published in New York City, *Putnam's* was "the first genuinely civilized magazine in America"; "it spoke with a New York voice as the nation's intellectual capital." This sketch followed the conventions. In keeping with *Putnam's* goal of being the authoritative voice on the nation's culture, the narrator was a gentleman from New York City who could judge the West authoritatively, who received his "complimentary ticket" to the Grand Excursion, and who, tired of city streets, decided to go West to be refreshed. The sketch began with a typical plot: the hardened city man left town "with a large supply of morning papers," but on viewing pastoral scenery from the railcar, he wrote, "I opened the window and threw out my newspapers. . . . these rural sights broke up the fountains of my heart . . . so did I seem to rise into a higher life." Beautiful scenery was supposed to have just this moral effect on the tourist.[799]

Though some tourists nostalgically recalled pre-railroad days and feared the train's speed marred their view of scenery, this narrator had no such qualms. There was "poetry" and "the element of sentiment" in the very swiftness with which the train sped him halfway across the continent.[800]

His trip began "pleasantly" along the Erie Railroad route through New York's southern tier. He described the scenery in terms of "the future picturesque": a wild landscape would one day become classically beautiful, with "lawns," "parks," and "vine-draped villas." A speculator in scenery, he had purchased a house here in anticipation of that future.[801] Beyond this spot, the tone changed drastically; he focused on the present not future, sights indoors not outdoors, persons not landscapes, and persons regionally, ethnically, and racially different from the urban eastern gentleman observer. Romantic expectations of travel encountered unpleasant realities, like hotel bedsheets: "when promise came to performance, there was a sad falling off." The gentleman straight from Broadway dissected and analyzed western society with condescension: a black waiter in Cleveland had none of the flair of a Virginia house slave; two Yankee emigrants were boringly taciturn; a hotel clerk in Chicago was impolite; a cook butchered the French language on his menu; "Connecticut men . . . will not eat of any dish that has not a plain Old Testament name to it"; Irish waiters in Chicago were insolent; westerners were busy, backslapping egalitarians who claimed acquaintance with U.S. senators, loved poker and steamboat races, and socialized at Young America clubs. Inside the railcars, westerners had created "lakes of tobacco juice," in which "strips of orange peels" were "sailing round like chips on a mill-pond" along with peanut shells and printed debris. His verdict was quickly and decisively rendered: "The higher arts which adorn human existence—elegant letters, divine philosophy—these have not yet reached the Mississippi."[802]

The future came to the rescue, however, and the American gentleman thereby nimbly avoided sounding only like a scolding Mrs. Trollope nagging Americans about their manners. "In good time, the western bottom lands will spontaneously grow poets." This present age of practicality and toil would produce "a republic of letters." He decided, "Niagara, the Mississippi, the Lakes, are not after all the great spectacle" for tourists to see. Emigrants headed for the prairie were the sublime scenery. Out his hotel window, he saw a German emigrant family passing by and foresaw an Iowa home, agricultural prosperity, and Americanization of their children. He himself never reached the Mississippi or left Chicago on June 5. He was glad to board the omnibus that took him to the Michigan Central train, "resolved not to stop until I had regained New York." Like Gurowski, he was dismayed by westerners in the flesh while hopeful of them as an abstract, future idea. "'All Western men and prairies are alike,' said I to myself, in stepping into the train; 'how I wish I were walking down Broadway.'"[803]

"ON LAKE PEPIN"
BY EPES SARGENT

In 1855, forty-eight contributors to the *Knickerbocker* magazine sent in sketches, essays, poems, and more for a book called *The Knickerbocker Gallery* to honor the magazine's editor, Lewis Gaylord Clark. Among them was "On Lake Pepin," a sketch by Epes Sargent.[804] Knickerbockers were "old-stock Anglo-Dutch or Huguenot bluebloods" of New York City and the Hudson Valley who opposed the Puritanism of Yankee transplants in Gotham and also the cultural democracy advocated by Young America. They "were Whigs, Episcopalians, anglophiles, and hostile to all political and literary radicalisms," and, in literature, "prosperous gentleman amateurs" . . . who dined well, told good stories at table, and wrote lightly ironical essays" for the

Knickerbocker, for no pay, for their literary leader, Clark.[805] Not exactly fitting into this circle, Sargent was a Yankee from Massachusetts who, in 1854, had just finished a six-year stint as editor of the *Boston Transcript.* Yet he was a noted magazine contributor and author of poems, sea stories, textbooks, and a biography of Henry Clay (1842). So his presence in the *Gallery* is not surprising.[806]

Sargent's contribution was a radically different retelling of the tale of Winona, the Dakota maiden who jumped to her death from the top of Maiden Rock, a bluff on the Wisconsin side of Lake Pepin. And yet he wrote a tale within a tale, for he made the Grand Excursion the outer narrative that framed and eventually distorted the inner, Dakota legend. The setting was onboard the *Golden Era* as it steamed down Lake Pepin. The time was Friday morning, June 9. "It was my fortune to be standing on the hurricane-deck, with my foot upon a life-preserving stool, and my elbow leaned upon my knee, when some of my lady acquaintances of the excursion broke in upon my contemplations." So his story went. And it could have happened that way; Hetty Hart Jarvis and Mary Jarvis of Middletown, Connecticut, could have been the two females, or Abby Fillmore and Matelda Stuart of Buffalo. They were all onboard the *Golden Era.*[807]

Before he told the *Gallery's* readers the story he had told the women, Sargent briefly narrated "[t]he excursion of June, 1854," which "was on a scale quite unparalleled in the history of similar celebrations"—thereby implying it deserved to be the subject of a sketch—and then he described the scenery in the standard terms. Bluffs, their vegetation, and their geology combined the picturesque— "precipitous" and "singular" and full of variety— with the beautiful—an "orchard-like appearance" and slopes "sweeping in curves of enchanting beauty." Geological formations of sandstone he compared to classical architecture. Vegetation on the hills he compared to "the outskirts of a nobleman's park, carefully kept free from under-brush . . . and rounded by some landscape gardener to satisfy the eye of taste," though there was "no sign of population" for forty miles or more. He carefully composed his description of Lake Pepin, as a painter might: in the foreground was the east bank, then a plateau in the middle ground, bluffs in the background, and on the bluffs "a single row of trees at a distance of several feet from one another, like warriors in Indian file."[808]

This skillful rearrangement of scenic details into a polished description ought to have alerted readers of the *Gallery* that Sargent could also rearrange a Dakota story. In quoting his dialogue with the ladies, however, he portrayed one of them as the revisionist and himself as the truthful narrator. The first lady asked "for the authentic version . . . and tell it like a faithful chronicler." The second one cited the existence of several versions to justify her insistence that Sargent give the Indian maiden a lover.[809]

"'Please to be seated ladies, and you shall hear the whole story; although it is many years since I received it from a Sister of Charity at Montreal.'"

"'But I insist upon it that a lover must be introduced,' said lady number two."

"'We can not promise,' said I; 'for the story will come to my recollection only by degrees, as I go along.'"

The story that slowly emerged was considerably altered in the recollecting and the telling. Perhaps the context in which Sargent recollected it—the excursion and Friday, June 9, 1854—helped to cause the alteration. As he told it, the story subverted Dakota culture and converted Winona to eastern, civilized norms that excursionists highly valued and wished to see the Dakota adopt. He did not give Winona a lover in the sense the second lady probably meant, a lover to compete against the unwanted suitor. He did give her a new culture and identity as, effectively, an antebellum Protestant American woman not too different from his two listeners.

His story was set in the late-seventeenth century, as was the traditional Dakota tale. Winona was the maiden whose parents wanted her to marry a man she hated. Lake Pepin was the site. There the similarities ended. Sargent's tale began with an aged Dakota man left to die in the winter cold when the band moved west to hunt buffalo, and he was unable to travel. Coming to his aid and prolonging his life, Winona acted as an antebellum social reformer protesting Dakota treatment of the aged. Conversing, Winona and he turned their reformers' anger on Dakota treatment of women. "Indian women are slaves," the old man complained. He urged

her to "go east, beyond the great lakes" (to upstate New York, where many excursionists came from)" . . . "where you will find the pale-faces . . . who will teach you much that will do your people good, should you ever return to them." After he died, Winona survived and flourished on her own, like a female Robinson Crusoe, demonstrating that a woman could do everything a man could.

At this point, Sargent addressed his two listeners directly and referred to the events of the excursion: Winona "ran along the shore as far as the point we are now skirting." And she gathered agates and carnelians much as the excursionists did, picking up "a handful," then, seeing "others more beautiful, she would throw aside those she had gathered, and replace them with new treasures."

As she was preparing to leave for the East, her parents and the hated suitor appeared. Now an independent woman, Winona told him, "Never will I be your wife! . . . Go vent your anger upon the poor slaves [his three wives] who are left to you, and be content!" When he pursued her, she shot an arrow into his arm, disabling him so that he could not beat his wives, reducing his status in the band so that he loses two wives and is reformed into monogamy, and changing him into a respectful husband.

But that was in the suitor's future, and Sargent returned to events at Maiden Rock. Contrary to "[a]lmost every version of the tradition" that accepted the pursuers' report that Winona leaped and drowned, he asserted that she leaped into the trees "and swung herself from bough to bough into the river," where she escaped by swimming away from her suitor and his companions. She headed East and, at Green Bay, met Jesuit missionaries who converted her to Christianity—but not exactly to their Catholicism, for she intelligently objected to "all its bewildering husks, forms, and wrappings" and only accepted "the pith of the matter . . . [t]he beauty and holiness of Christian morality." At Green Bay, she met La Crosse, a "young Parisian of education and refinement," nursed him back to health, and married him. Later, in Canada along the St. Lawrence, they play with their children "on their broad piazza amid roses and honeysuckle," attend church, educate their three children, and rejoice when one son "attained such proficiency on the bass-viol that he was employed by the priest to lead the choir in church."

Winona has become so Europeanized she weeps "passionately" when her husband dons Indian face paint, blanket, and tomahawk "to please some wandering Iroquois." Telling the story that his two listeners and their society wished to hear, Sargent transformed Winona into an educated, intelligent antebellum female reformer defending women's rights from the perspective of Protestant Christian morality stripped of Catholic "husks, forms, and wrappings."

Mary Henderson Eastman, wife of Captain Seth Eastman and a resident of Fort Snelling from 1841 to 1848, had published a traditional version of this tale in her 1849 book *Dahcotah; Life and Legends of the Sioux around Fort Snelling.* Sargent does not seem to have used this book as a source. Mary Eastman told the story as she heard it from Chequered Cloud, a Dakota "medicine woman and legend teller." Midway in her account, just after Winona has leaped and died, Eastman wrote, "Such is the story by the Dahcotahs; and why not apply to them for their own traditions?" She went on to interpret the story from an antebellum female American point of view and to tell another tale in which the suitor gets his comeuppance, but she apparently told Winona's tale as it was told to her before doing so.[810] Sargent's version is told by an excursionist to excursionists, both visiting Dakota country for three days and viewing it from the perspective of the eastern upper-class tourist who rendered an authoritative verdict on what he or she saw.

"THE GREAT EXCURSION TO THE FALLS OF ST. ANTHONY: A LETTER TO CHARLES BUTLER, ESQ."
BY ONE OF THE EXCURSIONISTS

In September 1854, *Putnam's Monthly Magazine* published the most straightforward sketch of the Grand Excursion, written by Catharine Sedgwick. This was not the magazine's first notice of the event. In the July 1854 issue appeared a brief, playful poem that could conceivably have been written by Sedgwick:

All ye excursionists going to see
The Falls of good St. Anthony,
How many falls pray had he?

Ask him please one thing to tell,
By what temptations first he fell.

This play on words could have been written by most any *Putnam's* writer.[811] It would hardly do for the nation's most authoritative cultural voice to let this bagatelle stand as its only reference to such an important event.

Interestingly, although she made authoritative judgments about the West and the excursion, Sedgwick couched them in the form of a letter to a New York City gentleman, Charles Butler. She opened with an apology for her "long letter," longer "than the customary space allotted to a woman's diffusive pen." She humbly thanked Butler for sending her the ticket to the excursion. Thus, she did not openly usurp the gentleman's traditional role as cultural arbiter. She presented her public judgments as private thoughts directed to a friend, a gentleman who could assess the West and its culture. Still, this letter sounded more like a sermon than a travel sketch. Nowhere in it did she suggest that women were marginalized and ought to assert their own authoritative voices on culture, the West, or the nation. That may have been because she tried to sound democratic—using anonymity instead of giving her famous name—and feared that her personal female voice was too linked to literary celebrity, her father's Federalism, and a bygone era of New England's dominance.[812]

Here was a sermon thinly disguised as a travel sketch thinly disguised as a private letter.

Sedgwick sounded authoritative from the start: the Grand Excursion "seems to me an illustration and proof of the advancement of true civilization." She began with public matters: a comparison of European and English festivals to this American one, which was far better ("Our munificent entertainers are our fellow-sovereigns. . . . They are productive laborers . . . not revellers in riches gained by war and rapine") because it was produced by free labor. The excursionists too were not idle nobility but people "whose holidays came between working-days." The time was long past when the public bowed to the opinions of traveling aristocrats who boasted of their leisure.[813] She described the sociable, festival atmosphere in Chicago on Saturday, June 3, but emphasized the excursion's public, patriotic purpose, to view the country and to intimate "its possible glorious future." To her, the West's future was clear: "First, must come our eastern people, with . . . their Puritan armor, the Bible and the school-book, and, in their track, to be taught and moulded by them, those who have been spoiled of their natural rights for ages." These were evidently to be freed slaves (although European emigrants were not excluded) whom New Englanders would teach "to stand erect, men among men"—and here she quoted part of the Declaration of Independence as their redeeming, liberating "creed."[814]

"I believe that the reflecting men and women of our excursion party felt, as they never felt before, the great mission of their children and their neighbors who are going West." That mission was not land speculation, but education for "intellectual and moral development." Sedgwick cited William Greenleaf Eliot's work in founding a school, John O'Fallon's in financing it, and Harriet Bishop's mission to St. Paul. Then she drew back from her sermonizing and apologized to Butler for "this long episode on a subject" that had to concern any objective, disinterested "observer."[815]

She switched topics and focused on a travel writer's more conventional topic, scenery. "You lost, my dear Mr. Butler, the most picturesque part of our travel, by turning back at Rock Island"—and she described it as picturesque scenery, with variety, strange rock formations, and solitude. Departing from the conventional assessment, Sedgwick denied that the Upper Mississippi bluffs "resemble[d] the romantic Highlands of our Hudson" or "the cliffs on the Rhine." "They are unique— they have no likeness—they daguerrotype new pictures on the mind." They did resemble the "foundations of ruined castles," so much so "that you unconsciously wonder what has become of the Titan race that built them!" But she turned from that unanswerable question to the marvels she had seen: the steamboats, Colonel George Mix's skillful leadership, Lake Pepin, the fantastic menus, the mixing-of-the-waters ceremony at St. Anthony Falls and the "troups and groups" scrambling on the rocks there, the sight of the six-oxen plow breaking sod, Minnehaha Falls, the ball at St. Paul, and the amazing sights at the St. Louis levee.[816]

She assessed slavery's progress in Missouri (probably inaccurately) as limited and temporary. She praised Frank Blair, but not by name.[817]

Sedgwick's conclusion mixed the personal and the public. "Do you ask me if I would live in the West? I answer without hesitation, no!" She preferred the Berkshires and was too old to migrate, but she did not deny New England's mission to civilize the West. Appropriately, this sermon ended with a benediction on those Yankees who undertook it: "Let the young go. They should. They do go in troops and caravans, and in the vast prairies of the Mississippi may they perfect an empire of which their Puritan Fathers sowed the seeds on the cold coast of the Atlantic." She blessed Joseph Sheffield and Henry Farnam for "this unprecedented hospitality." "Was ever a company so assembled and so blessed by heavenly and earthly Providence? Day unto day, and night, proclaimed their enjoyment from beginning to end, and no death—no illness— no disaster."[818]

MISCELLANEOUS ESSAYS AND EDITORIALS

The well-known literary critic, biographer, poet, and essayist Henry Tuckerman traveled on the Grand Excursion. Many of the party he knew well from the New York City literary salon of Anne Charlotte Lynch, soon to be the wife of excursionist Vincenzo Botta. At Lynch's weekly Saturday night conversazione, Tuckerman socialized with Sedgwick, Charles Butler, George Bancroft, Caroline Kirkland, and many others. The excursion was a week-long, round-the-clock traveling Lynch soiree without Lynch. The author of travel books on

Italy, Sicily, and England, Tuckerman did not choose to write one on Mount Vernon (Minnesota) and Monteville. Instead, he incorporated the June 1854 experience into an essay on "Holidays" that appeared in the *North American Review* of April 1857. This was not a sketch but an essay that logically and methodically developed a comparison between holidays in Europe and America. He wrote as the eastern gentlemen (who had traveled to Europe) entitled to render an objective and decisive judgment on the question.[819]

Tuckerman's was another antebellum attempt to establish America's cultural identity vis-à-vis Europe. The glass was half empty, he began: "no American festival . . . hallows the calendar to the imagination of our people" and there were "no saints' days for the Republic." The Fourth of July did not meet his exacting standards, being "a noisy carnival" of fireworks and "bombast" unworthy of "high civilization." The lack of "a national feast" might result in "sectional misunderstanding, hatred and barbarism culminating in a base and savage mutiny." He lamented the absence of the colorful public festivals of ancient Rome, medieval England, or present-day Spain. Such festivals could not thrive in a nation "devot[ed] to the immediate, the thrift, the enterprise, and the material activity which pertain to a new country." "Our festivals are chiefly on occasions of economic interest."[820]

The glass was also half full, Tuckerman said: economic festivals were "memorable." "One of the earliest" was the 1825 "celebration of the opening of the Erie Canal . . . and

one of the last was the grand excursion" of 1854. "To European eyes the sight of the thousand invited guests conveyed from New York to the Falls of St. Anthony would yield a thrilling impression of festal arrangements in this Republic." If Europeans thumbed through American newspapers for all economic occasions for all classes, trades, and industries, they would conclude "that we are the most social and holiday nation in the world." Therefore, American festivity was not typified by "rustics" celebrating May Day in the woods or subjects performing a state ceremony at a cathedral or soldiers changing the guard. Instead, "we should be most aptly represented by a fleet of steamers with crowded decks and gay pennons, sweeping through the lofty and wooded bluffs of the Upper Mississippi." The excursion here provided him with an (atypical) example that could raise America to near-equality with Europe.[821]

Tuckerman was idiosyncratic—as good essay writers were expected and allowed to be—in discussing the excursion under the category of "holidays." Editorialists placed it under the heading "Travel." The *New York Tribune* and *Illinois Journal* titled their reflections "Summer Travel." Charles Dana very possibly wrote the *Tribune* piece, which reported a "conversation a few days since," possibly on the *Golden Era,* in which elderly persons commented on the astounding increase in travel. One recalled that forty years earlier only two to four travelers took the U.S. mail coach from Philadelphia to New York on any given day. Now, the editorialist observed,

"We are ever on the move." Making the obligatory comparison with Europe, he added, "The immobility of Europeans is unknown to us." He remembered a few years earlier taking a meal at a hotel in Geneva, Switzerland, at which more than fifty of the sixty diners were Americans. He pointed to frequent and extensive travel as a sign of "the progress and grandeur of democracy" in America, and listed various sites worth seeing in the United States.[822]

The *Journal* largely agreed (but its editorial writer had evidently not made the European tour; his piece lacked the *Tribune's* authoritative tone of the eastern gentleman):

"Not to have traveled now-a-days, is reckoned next to being nobody. Formerly, it was reckoned the event of a life time, and rendered its performer a notable man in society, to make a European tour. Now it's a common event with thousands."

The Springfield newspaper focused more on travel to the West, which was "fast opening a wider view of the measureless wealth and resources of our Mississippi valley." The Grand Excursion contributed to that process. Travel nicely combined private pleasure with the public good. Tourists "will return with increased vigor of body, and elasticity of mind, while the west, the great west, pushes a bolder wing in the flight of Empire." Interestingly, the *Journal* advocated an exchange of visits between East and West but said nothing about the North visiting the South or vice versa, when the Mississippi would seem to facilitate and encourage North-South travel.[823]

Charles Brigham, editor of the *Troy*

(N.Y.) Daily Whig, did cite the excursion in a logically constructed argument for North-South travel. "Those who have returned from the great Excursion to the Lakes," praised "all they saw. Letter writers seem to 'realize the poverty of the dictionary' in describing" the sights. Travel brought more than private delight at indescribable scenery. Excursions, he reasoned, "tend to make men better acquainted with one another,—bring citizens of different and distant sections of the country to each other's doors." (That meeting was positive under festive circumstances of parades, fireworks, band music, and flattering speeches, but actual nose-to-nose debates on contentious issues might exacerbate tensions.) Brigham shared the antebellum faith in technology: "locomotive and steamboat are doing wonders in rooting up local prejudices and toppling over the walls which encircle narrow sectional jealousies,—walls as high and impregnable in many localities as those of the Chinese." (Opinions on slavery might prove more intractable than other "local prejudices.") Northerners should travel to the South to disabuse themselves of erroneous notions that demonized slavery, and southerners should visit the North. Excursions taught many lessons, but one was "the justice and beauty of the motto—'One Country—One Constitution—One Destiny.'"[824]

Brigham had not gone on the Grand Excursion. His armchair reasonings about what excursions logically must produce did not reflect actual observations of what occurred when the citizen of Utica landed on a St. Paul citizen's doorstep. And the excursion did not cross many "walls"; most excursionists followed the route of emigration from New England and upstate New York to Ohio and Michigan, then to Illinois, and upriver to Minnesota. The man from Utica or New Haven met ex-Uticans and ex-New Haveners as he went, and some in St. Paul too. His visit might confirm local prejudices: a western town was civilized because New Haveners built it. A new technology might simply extend an old tradition. Railroads perpetuated and strengthened the dominance of this New England–New York–Ohio–Illinois route; they did not uproot it. A visit to the Northwest did nothing to topple northeastern prejudices toward the South. It tended to confirm them: Yankees saw a prospering Northwest as further proof of slavery's debilitating effects. Brigham had evidently read newspaper reports of the "[l]etter writers," but these focused on scenery and socializing; some noted onboard discussions of Kansas-Nebraska but the sociable context and their status as the C&RI's all-expenses-paid guests inhibited editors from using the excursion as a political platform. Yet, in fact, the excursion served as a weeklong conversation among prominent northerners over how best to preserve the West they visited from the Slave Power's aggressions—a conversation across party lines that aided in the formation of a sectional party that would build a higher political wall between North and South.

Brigham's armchair thoughts were no further off the mark than the views of sketch writers, essayists, and editorialists who went on the excursion. All brought their own perspectives with them, and these colored their observations. Tuckerman cited the excursion to highlight the contrast with Europe, thereby largely evading the much more pressing (in 1857) North-South contrast. Concerned about slavery and not silent on it, Catharine Sedgwick chose to believe and emphasize what she was told at teatime in St. Louis. Epes Sargent turned a Dakota tale into an incredible dream of antebellum wish fulfillment, an escapist set piece that ignored the political tensions within his own society. Adam Gurowski constructed a Potemkin village of liberty and progress to conceal muddy, thick-soled western realities. The anonymous gentleman writer assumed the future and liberty would necessarily turn the caterpillar West into a butterfly without admitting that the liberty to bring slaves there threatened this transformation. Travel might have its limitations as a means to acquire knowledge of America if the view of the West from a Troy parlor was no more inaccurate than the view from a Mississippi steamboat's stateroom.

EPILOGUE

SO FAR AS CAN BE determined, all other passengers aboard the Grand Excursion returned home safely, albeit not always as quickly as their families wished. After going to St. Louis for a week, Charles Hale returned to Chicago and planned a brief trip to Cincinnati. "I am having an excellent time . . . I shall have a great deal to tell when I get home." Meanwhile, his family had a great deal to tell him but a great difficulty reaching him by mail or by telegraph. His father, Nathan, had suffered a slight stroke in State Street; his brother Edward rushed to Boston to edit the paper; his sister Lucretia wrote to him that Edward "said you would want to hurry directly home." A man Lucretia did not know had called at the house for Charles; "he had been with you on the Rock Island expedition, and was eloquent thereupon"; when he talked at length on the Hoosac Tunnel, "I guessed he was Mr. [Robert] Campbell" of Pittsfield.[825]

Despite his promise to his wife, despite his daughter Elizabeth's hope that her brother Frank would not consent to it, Preston Blair

Abby Fillmore served as her father's hostess during his presidency. A month after she joined him on the excursion, she contracted cholera and died.
(Picture History)

also went to St. Louis (with Frank). He visited E. T. Throop and Cornelia Martin at Willow Brook, in New York's Finger Lakes region, on his way back home. Throop Martin had time to visit his real estate agent in Mineral Point, Wisconsin, and still return home in time to see Preston Blair. Blair did not make it back to Silver Spring until June 24, "worn out with travel," Elizabeth reported, "& *put out* that Mother did not send for him at the [railroad] Cars on the strength" of one letter from his son-in-law. His wife and daughter were put out that he had not written to them, Elizabeth complained: "we have sent & sent for letters & telegraphs from him but none came, & I was really very troubled at not hearing from him." Elisha Riggs, the Washington banker and businessman, came back before Blair, and was also ill (with "the gout"). Riggs "gives droll acc[oun]ts of the quantity of brandy drank[,] segars smoked."[826]

Many home folks had to endure or enjoy lengthy accounts of the excursion. Noah Webster's daughter Julia, wife of excursionist

Chauncey A. Goodrich of New Haven, wrote to her daughter of "multitudinous conversations we have had about the same country [the Upper Mississippi] since your father's return." These talks must have been a pleasant escape from a bitter feud then raging among Webster's descendants over the rights to his dictionary. "I am curious to see some European comment upon the late trip," Julia added. "[N]o other nation but the 'universal Yankee nation' would ever have conceived just such a picnic at a distance of 2700 miles" and none "would have made it a free party, & nobody but a Yankee could have headed it."[827] Although he went only as far as Rock Island, Goodrich wrote a poem ("The Excursion") about the trip, and had it printed and distributed to excursionists.[828]

Joseph Sheffield could congratulate himself that "no accident" *had* occurred on the trip or immediately thereafter "to mar the pleasure of this beautiful and most important excursion—important to the whole western railroad interest."[829] However, the revelation on July 4, 1854, of a major railroad stock fraud served partially to undo its confidence-building effects. Robert Schuyler, president of the New York & New Haven Railroad, had fraudulently issued 19,000 shares worth $1.9 million. "All the false stock was signed by the President, who was the transfer agent of the Company, and the Secretary who is absent in Europe," the *New York Evening Post* reported, "but who left blanks signed for the President's use." Schuyler signed the stock certificates as president and, as transfer agent, transferred them to his brother and himself, and sold them or pledged them as security for loans (the Schuyler brothers were in financial trouble)—"most" of them, reportedly, to Cornelius Vanderbilt. Excursionists Richard M. Blatchford and (possibly) William Bliss were among those defrauded. George Bancroft had arranged for Bliss to purchase a bond that was part of Schuyler's offering; "Mr. Schuyler is by far the best person for the occasion," Bancroft wrote to his stepson. Wall Street "was thrown into consternation" by the news. Robert and George Schuyler were "regarded as the Railroad Kings of the city, and distinguished as the heaviest railroad operators in the United States." Over the holiday, the New York & New Haven directors stepped in to investigate, accepted Schuyler's resignation, suspended sales of NY&NH shares, and appointed excursionist William W. Boardman of New Haven as the temporary president.[830]

Robert Schuyler's fraud (his brother was innocent) was especially shocking in antebellum America, where business and politics and society were still linked together. He had a distinguished background: grandson of the Revolutionary War general Philip Schuyler, nephew of Alexander Hamilton, and a Harvard graduate (class of 1817, George Bancroft's class). He was no parvenu. People sought explanations. A story spread that Schuyler and his wife had "a secret marriage, and separate establishments in town," and "that his most intimate personal friends thought he was a bachelor."[831] Social deceptiveness could help to explain business fraud.

The Schuyler scandal shook investors' confidence in the railroad industry, but also in the fledgling New York Stock and Exchange Board on Wall Street, whose reputation for reliability rested on the soundness of the railroad stock that constituted the vast majority of the securities bought and sold there. The scandal could not help but hurt the efforts of Henry Farnam and Thomas Durant to persuade easterners to invest in their Mississippi & Missouri Railroad.

By mid-July, a concerned Reverend William Jarvis, the investor cum clergyman, wrote to his agent in Ohio: "The money market here is in a bad condition since the Schuyler fraud; and Rail Road securities are lower than ever before." He needed his real estate investments to come to his rescue. "Send all the money you can collect." (He need not have worried; he was doing quite well in the matrimonial market; his daughter Elizabeth was being courted at Newport by revolver inventor and manufacturer Samuel Colt; they would marry at the reverend's home in June 1856, thus guaranteeing the family's financial future.)[832] That month, a business agent reported to excursionist Simon Newton Dexter on the "close times" in Albany and the prospect of "no *'let up'* until all the Rail Road Kings were used up. How will *our friends* of the Southern (Michigan) Road stand it[?]." He felt the legislature ought to pass a law to protect the public from such frauds.[833] In early August, Alexander Twining wrote to his agent in Chicago, "Robt. Schuyler's fraud creates some feeling of insecurity in the doz[ens] of investments I should have formerly made," but he listed some that he could still afford and that he asked C. J. Salter to attend to—"and remember Kansas & Nebraska."[834]

By November 1854, the NY&NH was seeking the legal services of Roger S. Baldwin to defend it against lawsuits stemming from "the fraudulent certificates issued by R. Schuyler late Transfer Agent of the company." Baldwin agreed to help the company's New York lawyers, who likely wanted him to assist on any cases filed in Connecticut. (Jeffrey Orson Phelps of Simsbury may also have done legal work for the NY&NH in connection with the Schuyler fraud.)[835]

The month following the excursion was hard on railroad men near and far, but it was much more auspicious for those New Haveners—like Twining—who hoped for an all-party northern coalition to oppose the Kansas-Nebraska Act. Discussed by the Blairs and others on the steamboats, this fusion movement accelerated soon after the journey ended. Anti-Nebraska congressmen had already held an initial meeting on May 23, but the movement spread to the general public (albeit organized by political leaders) in late June and early July.[836] Efforts to control this movement from Washington largely failed; state-level leaders seized the initiative; the results varied widely from state to state, demonstrating again that a federal system of national, state, and local governments exerted a significant centrifugal force that placed much political power in the states and localities.

The Kansas-Nebraska Act was a "great national and centripetal force at Washington" whose pull was quickly felt at the state and local level.

On July 6, fifteen hundred delegates met in Jackson, Michigan, on the Michigan Central, to unite all anti-Nebraska groups in one new political party, which they named the Republican Party. To counter this move, the Democrats talked of nominating former Michigan governor John S. Barry, but he too was anti-Nebraska, and this proposed maneuver never materialized.[837]

On July 7, a much larger—if less formal—meeting was held at Ottawa, Illinois. "The gathering of people was large, from two to three thousand, and was composed mostly of the farmers and mechanics of the country." Although not a convention, they "passed a resolution in favor of the union of all parties [opposed to Kansas-Nebraska]."[838]

Other political forces at work that summer complicated and frustrated this anti-Nebraska drive. One was the magnetic attraction of that other "K-N" issue of 1854, the Know-Nothing movement. Success in harmonizing these competing forces varied from state to state. In Ohio, William Schouler of the *Cincinnati Gazette* sympathized with the Know-Nothings and helped to unite them and anti-Nebraska men in a People's party that "scored an astounding triumph" that fall.[839] In Illinois, despite Ottawa's enthusiasm, there was no union of anti-Nebraska men. Fragmentary nebula of old-style Whigs, anti-Nebraska Democrats, temperance advocates, and Know-Nothings resisted being gathered into one mass. Abraham Lincoln refused a position on a Republican state committee.[840] In Massachusetts, Know-Nothings gathered the scattered nebula into a resoundingly successful American party ticket for the fall election, despite the best efforts of Samuel Bowles of the *Springfield Republican* to create a Republican party that year.[841] In New York, editor Thurlow Weed of the *Albany Evening Journal* opposed an immediate anti-Nebraska union and sought to keep the Whig party alive temporarily to win William Seward's reelection to the U.S. Senate in 1855. Millard Fillmore's Silver Grays made common cause with the Know-Nothings, who showed surprising strength in the fall election, which left New York's politics as confused as ever.[842]

In this maneuvering, Know-Nothings were the swing vote in any anti-Nebraska fusion. "Wherever fusion had been victorious, the Know Nothings had supported its ticket. Where they opposed it . . . fusion went down to ignominious defeat."[843]

This key Know-Nothing role was a welcome development for Fillmore's presidential hopes. He could successfully appeal to nativist Know-Nothings, but could hardly hope to appeal to anti-Nebraska men; he could not sound more anti-Nebraska than did Seward and Weed. In the summer of 1854, "Fillmore was repeatedly informed by his closest advisers of the Know Nothings' astonishing power and of their likely support for his presidential candidacy in 1856." But he could afford to wait and watch this new movement's progress before deciding to join it officially.[844]

His political hopes for 1856 were not lost on his critics, and the debate over his excursion speech-making continued after the trip ended. After the *New York Times* (June 14) interpreted Reverend Duncan Kennedy's humorous speech at Mount Vernon, Minnesota, as a jab at Fillmore, the *Buffalo Express* tried to sort out the competing arguments. It expressed doubts that Kennedy "forgot the dignity of his grave profession for a moment" to satirize Fillmore, and it hoped that Fillmore had not been politicking so as to deserve that. But it called on Fillmore's defenders to explain his conduct.[845]

Reverend Kennedy felt he must explain his conduct. In a private, *"Confidential"* letter to Fillmore, he denied that his Mount Vernon speech was meant to be a parody of the former president's excursion talks, which he claimed not to have heard. Even if he had been critical of these talks, he would not have satirized them. "My profession & character as a clergyman would have forbidden it; & my common sense would have left the administration of rebuke to other hands."[846]

Responding, Fillmore admitted that he had heard of Kennedy's remarks being interpreted as a parody of himself but found Kennedy's explanation "quite satisfactory." However, a private explanation could not correct a public "slander." "I would respectfully suggest that if you desire to do me justice . . . this can only be done by giving publicity to your letter or the substance of it, through the public press."[847]

Kennedy equivocated. He sent a note that Fillmore was free to use and he revoked the confidential status of his earlier letter, but he was still eager to keep his name out of the newspapers and left the initiative up to Fillmore—who seems to have let the matter die.[848]

Kennedy was not the only excursionist to engage in a follow-up correspondence with Fillmore. Elizabeth Terry, who had also traveled on the *Golden Era,* responded to his note with a letter inviting Abby Fillmore to stop at her home on the Hudson to "renew our friendship so pleasantly begun on board of the Golden Era." Terry enclosed a brief quotation from the Bible, evidently meant for Fillmore the ambitious politician: "What shall it profit a man if he shall gain *the whole world* and lose his own soul?"[849]

Writing to his southern touring partner, John P. Kennedy, on June 30, Fillmore expressed concern about cholera in Buffalo. "Some few deaths have occurred but it does not yet appear as an epidemic, but I fear it may." He hoped "to remain in the city" during the summer, if possible.[850] Abby, however, went to visit her grandfather in East Aurora, New York, some thirty miles from Buffalo. There she contracted cholera and died within twenty-four hours, before her father or brother could reach her. A few hours later, on July 27, Millard's brother Charles died of dysentery (some reports said cholera) in St. Paul. Former Minnesota governor Alexander Ramsey's letter was sent downriver and then telegraphed to Buffalo, arriving only thirty minutes after the distraught father and his son had left for a week of rest in the country.[851]

Charles's widow requested that Millard Fillmore travel to St. Paul, but the bereaved father and former president refused (as Nathan K. Hall strongly recommended). "It would also be hazardous to perform so long a journey on the lakes and River where the cholera prevails to such an alarming extent." Besides, "the recent death of my daughter, has so overwhelmed Powers and myself with grief, that we were advised to leave Buffalo for a few days, where every thing reminds us of our irreparable loss."[852] A trip to Minnesota was not the restful escape that his friends had in mind.

Condolences poured in from his fellow excursionists. A critic of Fillmore's speechifying, Hiram Fuller still wrote a tribute to Abby for the *New York Weekly Mirror:* "It seems but yesterday that we saw her in the very flush and fullness of health, the centre of a happy circle, participating with all the enthusiasm of a true and simple-hearted girl in the pleasures of the late Western excursion, the rosiest rose in all that gay and graceful group of flowers." He reflected on death's suddenness, before recalling Abby's "modesty and grace," the "many virtues and accomplishments with which she adorned" the White House while serving as Fillmore's hostess.[853] Privately, Thomas M. Howell and John A. Granger of Canandaigua each expressed his sorrow, Granger as "your late happy fellow-traveler." Elizabeth Terry grieved "that she was the first of our delightful little band to be taken away."[854]

Actually, Abby Fillmore was not the first person onboard the five steamboats to die, although Terry would likely not have considered the crews as part of "our band." On June 27, "a fatal affray" that showed the rough life of steamboat workers "occured on the steamer G. W. Sparhawk." A boy was washing the cabin floor and "allowing water to run down through a hole in the cabin floor upon" second engineer C. D. Kelley, who was at work on the lower deck. Kelley asked the boy to stop washing, but he refused "and replied to Kelley in an impudent manner, whereupon he [Kelley] slapped his face a few times, and returned to his work." Steward Edward Augustus Dedieman, who had been praised along with the others by the resolution-passing excursionists, and a second steward then "attempted to punish Kelley for the injury done the boy." With an eighteen-inch piece of iron, Dedieman came after Kelley, while the other steward advanced with a loaded pistol. Kelley grabbed "a large carving knife" from the pantry and stabbed Dedieman in the heart, "killing him instantly." He seriously wounded the other steward in the same way. Kelley turned himself in to the police and pleaded the right of self-defense.[855]

Charles Sedgwick, who traveled on the *Sparhawk* to St. Louis, also faced a potential family tragedy. When he arrived home, his wife, Elizabeth, head of the school for girls, placed in his hands a letter she had received accusing him of adultery. A Louisville woman claimed, a shocked Charles wrote his son-in-law William Minot, that "I had been found *naked* with a fascinating woman also *naked*—that being surprised in that condition in her apartment at St. Louis & warning her with menaces not to betray me, I had subsequently gone off with this lady to another Hotel—that my guilty partner fainted & sobbed & I tried to comfort her with kisses." Charles wondered how his accuser had secured his name and address, why she wrote to Elizabeth, and why she gave her husband's name and address in Louisville. "Luckily," he added, "the letter was written at St. Louis" on June 11; Catharine and he did not arrive in St. Louis until Monday, June 12 (and he accompanied her to the O'Fallons, Yeatmans, and Crows); there-fore, the tale was clearly false, and he need not secure testimony from the steamboat officers or his "fellow travelers" on his behalf. Yet, he advised, "dear William let me caution you when you go up to St. Pauls to start with a fair character, & the confidence of your family & to keep a memo of your travels & complete *with dates.*"[856]

Charles evidently did not share this let-ter with his sister Catharine. To Minot, he noted, "Just before we got home my sister" made some comment about his grandson, "not dreaming of the surprise" that awaited her brother.[857] That was one advantage for Catharine of having a marriagelike relation-ship to her brother: it was not marriage, and she did not have to deal with issues such as accusations of adultery.

It was Minot who suggested that Catharine write her autobiography for her grandniece Alice. A little more than two months after the excursion, she sat down at noon "alone in my little parlor," to write another installment. Her subject was changes in travel since her youth: forty years earlier, a "turnpike through Stockbridge" and a stage-coach that made it from Boston to Albany "after driving the greater part of two nights." Her brother Theodore had been thought crazy for proposing a railroad from Boston to Albany. Theodore did not live "to witness the triumph of his opinion, but I have lived this very summer to travel to the Mississippi by rail!"[858]

Little more than a month after this entry, Catharine wrote in a letter, "Charles is not well, and I look on his pale face with a cowardly shrinking." He did not take the repeat trip to the Upper Mississippi that he dreamed of and died August 3, 1856. The fol-lowing day, Catharine wrote to Kate, "It is all done—my work is all done—with all the sweet and loving and kind faces around me the house is—oh how vacant—how cold—the love of my life is gone." Charles was buried in Stockbridge Cemetery in the large, circular family plot (known locally as the "Sedgwick Pie") with the graves of the parents, Theodore and Pamela Sedgwick, in the center, graves of their children (mainly) in the first circle around them, and graves of succeeding gener-ations in successive circles farther back. Part of the inscription on Charles's tombstone sounds as if it was written by Catharine: "To Charles Sedgwick, the beloved Benjamin of his father's flock, the central fount of light and warmth and joy in every sphere in which he moved."[859]

A wish-fulfilling genie continued to rest on the "eyes & lips & ears" of George Bancroft. His publishers complained that in his third volume on the American Revolution (his sixth volume in total) "no part of the American Revolution has even begun," but Bancroft blithely continued at his pace. To his wife, he worried whether he would live long enough to finish his *History of the United States*. "I feel a little as Fichte did, when taking out his loaf, he counted how many mouthfuls it contained, and asked himself anxiously if he would have enough of it to sustain him on his way." Yet he soldiered on. When he wrote her, he was reviewing 139 responses to an advertisement he had placed for someone to assist him. He continued to appreciate female beauty. "After I left you, the lines of my life fell in pleasant places: I reached the boat just in time and found there the belles of the season." His marriage remained intact with apparently no accusations of adultery. In November, he delivered an address to the New-York Historical Society, in which he compared the historian's analysis to those of a geologist sitting on a Mississippi bluff and trying to estimate the age of the earth.[860]

A wish-fulfilling genie did not rest on his Democratic party or his faith in western popular sovereignty. The election frauds committed in Kansas by Missouri's Border Ruffians discredited Stephen Douglas's popular sovereignty in northern eyes; then Douglas's opposition to the pro-slavery Lecompton Constitution for Kansas discredited it in southern eyes. Bleeding Kansas riveted the nation's attention for four years, as the West (this part of it, at least) became a source of disunity, not unity. The failure of Democratic presidents Franklin Pierce and James Buchanan to resolve the problem of Bleeding Kansas discredited and divided Bancroft's Democratic Party.[861] During this long descent, Bancroft kept making optimistic statements. "Having already assumed that the West would unify the country and fulfill manifest destiny, Bancroft regarded Douglas as the new Jackson who would save the party and the nation."[862] However, despite "Bancroft's propensity to put the best possible face on matters," even he could not deny that the 1860 split between northern and southern Democrats doomed Douglas's chances for the White House.[863]

Later, Bancroft met and advised President Abraham Lincoln, who "played rather well on Bancroft's vanity." He told an anecdote about Lincoln greeting him at a White House reception. "He took me by one of his hands, and trying to recall my name, he waved the other a foot and a half above his head, and cried out, greatly to the amusement of the bystanders: 'Hold on—I know you; you are—History, History of the United States—Mr.—Mr. Bancroft, Mr. George Bancroft.'" Most likely Lincoln knew his name from the start but wanted to have a laugh on Bancroft.[864]

With invaluable help from the Blairs, and after the failure of Fillmore's Know-Nothing (American Party) in 1856, the infant Republican Party succeeded in electing its first presidential candidate in 1860. And yet that election caused the Civil War that Silliman and many others had feared. During that war, Lincoln's Republican Party succeeded where Bancroft's and Douglas's Democrats failed—to get a transcontinental railroad bill through Congress. But Durant and Farnam were not to become its builders. After the panic of 1857 hit the stock exchange and most other markets, Farnam "discovered that [Durant] had been pledging the securities of their construction firm to underwrite Durant's personal dabbling in the stock market." Farnam only narrowly escaped bankruptcy and he never regained his trust in Durant. By June 1863, their partnership was ended. The Union Pacific had been organized, at least on paper, with excursionists Thomas Olcott as treasurer and Peter A. Dey as chief engineer. In October 1863, Thomas C. Durant seized control of the Union Pacific and had John A. Dix appointed its president. Dix was gone by May 10, 1869, when the last-spike ceremony was held at Promontory, Utah, but Durant was present, as the Union Pacific's vice president, to drive one of the last two spikes. Excursionists from the East were also present, but there was no steamboat ride this time.[865] Farnam was back in New Haven, living quietly with his family. But he was not left without a legacy. Young Henry W. Farnam became a famous economist and a professor at Yale.

Young Henry W. was, of course, far too young to fight in the Civil War, and his father was spared the anxious waiting endured by many excursionists whose sons did face cannon balls, bullets, and bayonets. Joseph Sheffield had a daughter who married a Yale professor but no sons who served in the war. These two fathers, who organized the Grand Excursion, undoubtedly would have been happy to trade away any role in the Union Pacific if that meant no role for their children in the tragic war. Their excursion, however, had done nothing to prevent or delay the war. Just by investing in an East-West railroad, and taking a pleasure trip up the Mississippi, the excursionists had not really bound the Union together with iron bands. They and their sons would have to reforge a new Union under much less pleasant circumstances, with different tools of iron.

ENDNOTES

CHAPTER 1: "Railroad Men from Near and Far"

1. *New York Weekly Mirror,* 24 June 1854, p. 2 (quoted); *New York Times,* 8 June 1854, p. 2 (quoted); *New York Tribune,* 7 June 1854, p. 5 (quoted); *Galena Daily Advertiser,* 7 June 1854, p. 2 (quoted).

2. *New York Weekly Mirror,* 24 June 1854, p. 2.

3. *New Haven Daily Register,* 12 June 1854, p. 2; Millard Fillmore to J. P. Kennedy, 30 June 1854, reel 42, microfilm edition of Millard Fillmore Papers, State Historical Society of Wisconsin Library, Madison.

4. The southerners I have discovered on the various lists of excursionists are William W. Howe, E. Church Blackburn, Francis P. (Frank) Blair Jr., and Edward Bates, all of St. Louis, Missouri; plus Francis P. Blair Sr. of the famous Blair family of Maryland and Virginia, and a few others.

5. *Rock Island Advertiser,* 1 March 1854, p. 1. For the *Virginia,* see William J. Petersen, *Steamboating on the Upper Mississippi* (Iowa City: State Historical Society of Iowa, 1968), 90–106.

6. Catharine Maria Sedgwick to "Dearest Kate," 1 June 1854, and CMS to William Minot, 30 May 1854 (quoted), reel 4, Catharine Maria Sedgwick Papers P-354, Massachusetts Historical Society, Boston; Mary E. Dewey, ed., *Life and Letters of Catharine Maria Sedgwick* (New York: Harper & Brothers, 1871), 352–53 (quoted).

7. Stephen Salisbury, *The State, the Investor, and the Railroad* (Cambridge: Harvard University Press, 1967), 60, 170–71, 242, 284 (quoted); J. E. A. Smith, compiler, *The History of Pittsfield, Massachusetts, from the Year 1800 to the Year 1876* (Springfield, Massachusetts: C. W. Bryan and Company, 1876), 411–12 and picture opposite page 411; Robert Campbell to Nathan Hale, 10 March 1854, item 2175, box 8, Hale Family Papers, Library of Congress.

8. Salisbury, *The State, the Investor, and the Railroad,* 178–79, 182; Alfred Chandler Jr., *The Visible Hand: The Managerial Revolution in American Business* (Cambridge: Harvard University Press, 1977), 96–97 (quoted).

9. Thomas C. Cochran, *Railroad Leaders 1845–1890: The Business Mind in Action* (Cambridge: Harvard University Press, 1953), 18–19; F. Daniel Larkin, *John B. Jervis: An American Engineering Pioneer* (Ames: Iowa State University Press, 1990), 124, 126; Mason A. Green, *Springfield, 1636–1886,* 385 (quoted); Salisbury, *The State, the Investor, and the Railroad,* 17, 182–84, 186–88, 223–44, 300, and picture opposite p. 11; Chandler, *Visible Hand,* 96–97; George Bliss, *Historical Memoir of the Western Railroad* (Springfield: Samuel Bowles and Company, 1863).

10. Entries for Nathan and Charles Hale in *Appleton's Cyclopaedia of American Biography;* entry for Charles Hale in *Dictionary of National Biography;* Arthur M. Johnson and Barry E. Supple, *Boston Capitalists and Western Railroads: A Study in the Nineteenth-Century Railroad Investment Process* (Cambridge: Harvard University Press, 1967), 34, 38, 43.

11. Charles Hale to Edward Everett Hale, 12 May (quoted), 18 May (quoted), and 22 May, all 1854, all in "Hale, Edward Everett, 1854 Jan–May" folder, box 18, and Charles Hale to Sarah Preston Hale, 1 June 1854 (quoted), in "Sarah Preston (Everett) Hale, 1854" folder, box 21, all in Outgoing Correspondence of Charles Hale, Hale Papers–Generation III, Smith College, Northampton, Massachusetts.

12. Salisbury, *The State, the Investor, and the Railroad,* 194–95; Catharine M. Sedgwick to William Minot, 30 May 1854 (quoted), reel 4, CMS Papers. Parts of this letter are printed in Dewey, ed., *Life and Letters,* 352–53. These references also explain their need to take a ferry across the Hudson at Albany.

13. Salisbury, *The State, the Investor, and the Railroad,* 276–77, map opposite p. 270.

14. M. M. Bagg, ed., *Memorial History of Utica, N.Y. from Its Settlement to the Present Time* (Syracuse: D. Mason and Company, 1892), 247. For the many Uticans leaving on that Tuesday, see John Munn Diary, Volume 22, p. 129, Chicago Historical Society.

15. Bagg, ed., *Memorial History of Utica,* 280; Biographical Sketch of John Munn in the finding aid to the John Munn Diary, Chicago Historical Society.

16. John Munn Diary, Vol. 22, p. 129–30 (quoted).

17. John Munn Diary, Vol. 22, p. 132 (quoted).

18. John Munn Diary, Vol. 22, p. 131; Catharine M. Sedgwick to Kate Sedgwick Minot, 1 June 1854, reel 4, CMS Papers, Massachusetts Historical Society.

19. Beth L. Lueck, *American Writers and the Picturesque Tour: The Search for National Identity, 1790–1860* (New York: Garland Publishing, 1997), 2 (map), 6 (quoted), 10–11, 16–18, 26n13 (quoted); James T. Callow, *Kindred Spirits: Knickerbocker Writers and American Artists, 1807–1855* (Chapel Hill: University of North Carolina Press), 125–26 (quoted).

20. Lueck, *Picturesque Tour,* 14, 17, 135–36, 194 (quoted).

21. *Springfield Daily Republican,* 6 June 1854, p. 2 (quoted); entry for Samuel Bowles in *Dictionary of National Biography;* George S. Merriam, *The Life and Times of Samuel Bowles* (New York: Century, 1885).

22. *Poughkeepsie Eagle,* 24 June 1854, p. 2 (quoted).

23. Here and above, *Cleveland Herald,* 2 June 1854, p. 3 (quoted); Bancroft to "My ever dear wife," 30 May and 4 June, and Bancroft to "Dear Wife," [31] May, all 1854, and Hillsdale County Real Estate Tax Certificate, 22 May 1854, all in reel 4, microfilm ed., Bancroft Papers, Collection #1262, Cornell University Library; M. A. DeWolfe Howe, *The Life and Letters of George Bancroft* (New York: Charles Scribner's Sons, 1908), 116; *Cleveland Daily Plain Dealer,* 8 June 1854, p. 2 (quoting the *New York Weekly Mirror*).

24. Howe, *Life and Letters,* 117.

25. Oscar Handlin and Mary Flug Handlin, "Origins of the American Business Corporation," *Journal of Economic History* 5, no. 1 (May 1945): 1–23; Handlin and Handlin, *Commonwealth: A Study of the Role of Government in the American Economy: Massachusetts: 1774–1861,* revised ed. (Cambridge: Belknap Press of Harvard University Press, 1969), 106–33; William G. Roy, *Socializing Capital: The Rise of the Large Industrializing Corporation in America* (Princeton: Princeton University Press, 1997), 41, 43, 46, 48, 51–55; L. Ray Gunn, *The Decline of Authority: Public Economic Policy and Political Development in New York, 1800–1860,* 48–51, 105–08; Ronald E. Seavoy, *The Origins of the American Business Corporation, 1784–1855* (Westport, Connecticut: Greenwood Press).

26. Roy, *Socializing Capital,* 72–96. This is a brief, oversimplified summary of Roy's interpretation.

27. Entry for Barry in *Dictionary of American Biography; Village of Constantine: Reflections of 150 Years* (Constantine, Michigan: 1978); *History of St. Joseph County, Michigan* (Philadelphia: L. H. Evarts and Company, 1877), 116; Robert J. Parks, *Democracy's Railroads: Public Enterprise in Jacksonian Michigan* (Port Washington, New York: Kennikat Press, 1972), 70–71, 82, 168 (quoted), 169–71, 174–77, 202–10.

28. John Lauritz Larson, *Bonds of Enterprise: John Murray Forbes and Western Development in America's Railway Age,* revised ed. (Iowa City: University of Iowa Press, 2001), 31–36, 45–46;

Larkin, *John B. Jervis,* 121–26; William Cronon, *Nature's Metropolis: Chicago and the Great West* (New York: W. W. Norton, 1991), 70, 76. Cronon states that the Michigan Southern entered Chicago first on February 20; I accept his account despite Larson's claim that the Central came first on May 21, 1852.

29. *Albany Daily Knickerbocker,* 2 June 1854, p. 2 (reporting on the *Southern Michigan* steamboat on Lake Erie); Johnson and Supple, *Boston's Capitalists,* 115–18; *Albany Morning Express,* 15 June 1854, p. 2.

30. *Albany Morning Express,* 15 June 1854, p. 2 (quoted).

31. "Memorandum of Excursion Tickets issued at the New York office of the Chicago & Rock Island Rail Road in May 1854," folder 667, box 53, Farnam Family Papers–Series I, Manuscripts and Archives, Yale. Note the line drawn through the names of people returning tickets unused.

32. John J. Palmer to Millard Fillmore, 5 July 1854, and attached statement "Millard Fillmore Esq. A/c with the Merchants Bank N.Y.," in reel 42, microfilm ed., Fillmore Papers, UW–Madison.

33. Charles Butler to "My dear Wife," 19 February 1853, reel 3, Charles Butler Papers, Library of Congress; Larkin, *John B. Jervis,* 122.

34. Larkin, *John B. Jervis,* 129–30 (quote from p. 130).

35. Howe, *Life and Letters,* 117–18 (quoted); Joseph Sheffield to George Bancroft, 22 May 1854, 1853–54 box, George Bancroft Papers, Massachusetts Historical Society, Boston; Lillian Handlin, *George Bancroft: the Intellectual as Democrat* (New York: Harper & Row, 1984), 250; Henry W. Farnam, *Memoir of Henry Farnam* (1889), 39 (quoted).

36. Sedgwick to "My dearest Kate," 1 and 4 June 1854, reel 4, CMS Papers, Massachusetts Historical Society.

37. [Chicago & Rock Island Railroad Co.] Committee to "Dear Sir," 1 May 1854, "C, RI RR Excursion—May 1, 1854" folder, box 38, Levi O. Leonard Railroad Collection, Special Collections, University of Iowa Library, Iowa City; Theodore C. Blegen, "The 'Fashionable Tour' on the Upper Mississippi," *Minnesota History* (December 1939), 385. For the view that promoting future rail traffic and not rewarding investors was the purpose, see *New York Daily Tribune,* 20 June 1854, p. 3.

38. Chandler, *Visible Hand,* 90–92.

39. May 1st letter, reprinted in Blegen, "'Fashionable Tour,'" 385.

40. George Sargent to Thomas C. Durant, 4 and 11 January 1854, "Sargent, George B. 1854–1875" folder, box 42, Leonard Railroad Collection.

41. Blegen, "'Fashionable Tour,'" 385; *Dictionary of National Biography* entry on Azariah C. Flagg; William Hyde, *Encyclopedia of the History of St. Louis* (New York: Southern History Company, 1899), 480 (quoted); "Cook, Ebenezer 1855–1863" folder, box 38, "Sargent, George B. 1854–1875" folder, box 42, and Statement of Interest Due Wm. Walcott 10th July 1854, "Stocks & Bonds—Chicago, Rock Island Railroad 1854–1857, 1922" folder, box 43, all in Levi Leonard Railroad Collection, Iowa City.

42. Sheffield to Farnam, 4 May 1854, "May 1–5" folder, box 10, Farnam Family Papers Series I, Yale.

43. *New Haven Morning Journal & Courier,* 19 June 1854, p. 2 (giving the initial plan for three hundred excursionists); Chauncey A. Goodrich, "The Excursion," printed poem (1854), Beinecke Rare Book and Manuscript Library, Yale.

44. Clark W. Durant to Thomas C. Durant, 21 and 23 November 1853, "Durant, Clark W. 1853–1858" folder, box 39; T. C. Durant to C. W. Durant, 22 May 1854 (quoted), "Durant, Thomas Clark Letter Press Book 1853–1869," box 39, all in Leonard Railroad Collection, Iowa City.

45. Sheffield to Farnam, 31 May 1854 (quoted), "May 27–31" folder, box 10, Farnam Family Papers Series I; Sheffield to Farnam, 1 June 1854 (quoted), "June 1–2" folder, box 10. For invitations to diplomats, see "Memorandum of Excursion Tickets issued at the New York office of the Chicago & Rock Island Rail Road in May 1854," in folder 667, Farnam Family Papers—Series I, Yale.

46. Sheffield to Farnam, 2 May 1854 (quoted), "May 1–5" folder, and Sheffield to John E. Henry, 5 June 1854 (quoted), both in box 10, Farnam Family Papers, Series I, Stirling Library, Yale. For Sheffield's anxieties, see Sheffield to Farnam, 17 August 1854, "Sheffield & Farnam 1852–1864" folder, box 42, Leonard Collection, Iowa City.

47. George Sargent to Thomas C. Durant, 4 and 11 January 1854, "Sargent, George B. 1854–1875" folder, box 42, and T. C. Durant to J. E. Sheffield, 30 May 1854, "Durant, Thomas Clark Letter Press Book 1853–1869," box 39, both in Levi Leonard Railroad Collection. The last letter deals with bonds of the related Peoria & Bureau Valley Railroad.

48. David Howard Bain, *Empire Express: Building the First Transcontinental Railroad* (New York: Penguin, 1999), 153. Bain is incorrect in stating that Farnam and Durant built the C&RI (it was Sheffield and Farnam) and that John A. Dix "nominally headed" the C&RI in 1854. See "Durant, Thomas Clark Letter Press Book 1853–1869" folder, letters in late May 1854, for Durant's role in the excursion promotion; see Farnam to Thomas C. Durant, 14 October 1854, in "Farnam, Henry Pres.—Chicago, Rock Island RR 1853–1856" folder, for Sheffield's concerns that Farnam was devoting too much attention to rail construction west of the Mississippi and not enough to the C&RI; see "Farnam & Durant Agreements 1850–1862" folder, for the partners' contract to build the M&M; see Sheffield to Farnam, 17 August 1854, in "Sheffield & Farnam 1852–1864" folder, for Sheffield's desire to retire and for his hopes for the C&RI.

49. Larkin, *John B. Jervis,* 129 (quoted).

50. Noah Porter, "A Discourse Commemorative of the Life and Character of Mr. Joseph Earl Sheffield, Delivered at Battell Chapel, June 26, 1882" (New Haven: Tuttle, Morehouse and Taylor, 1882), 4–7, 10–13; William Edward Hayes, *Iron Road to Empire: The History of 100 years of the Progress and Achievements of the Rock Island Lines,* picture opposite p. 18.

51. Joseph E. Sheffield to Henry Farnam, 17 August 1854, "Sheffield & Farnam 1852–1864" folder, box 42, Levi O. Leonard Railroad Collection, Iowa City.

52. Bain, *Empire Express,* 151–53 (quoted); Charles Edgar Ames, *Pioneering the Union Pacific: A Reappraisal of the Builders of the Railroad* (New York: Appleton-Century-Crofts, 1969), 20–22 (quoted).

53. Bain, *Empire Express,* 48–51; David M. Potter, *The Impending Crisis 1848–1861* (New York: Harper & Row, 1976), 147–51.

54. Sheffield to Farnam, 17 August 1854 (quoted), "Sheffield & Farnam 1852–1864" folder, box 42, Levi Leonard Railroad Collection.

55. Potter, *Impending Crisis,* 151 (quoted); Robert W. Johannsen, *Stephen A. Douglas* (New York: Oxford University Press, 1973), 390–96, 399–400 (quoted).

56. Potter, *Impending Crisis,* 151–71.

57. Charles Hale to "Dear Sir [Senator Edward Everett]," 27 January 1854, box 24, Nancy Hale Papers, Sophia Smith Collection, Smith College.

58. Johannsen, *Douglas,* 4–5, 429, 482 (quoted), 496 (quoted), 499 (quoted).

CHAPTER 2: "New England Finds Her Onward Movement at a Stand"

59. For a sample invitation card, see Committee to "Dear Sir," 1 May 1854, in "C,RI RR Excursion—May 1, 1854" folder, Levi O. Leonard Railroad Collection, University of Iowa Library, Iowa City. The card is reprinted in Theodore C. Blegen, "The 'Fashionable Tour' on the Upper Mississippi," *Minnesota History* (December 1939), p. 385.

60. Entry on James F. Babcock in *Appleton's Cyclopedia of American Biography;* Edward E. Atwater, ed., *History of the City of New Haven* (New York: W. W. Munsell and Company, 1887), 224 (quoted).

61. *New Haven Palladium,* 25 February 1854, p. 2 (quoted); B. I. Baker to Manton Marble, 2[5] February 1854, volume of correspondence 2 January 1852 to 13 March 1858, Manton Marble Papers, Library of Congress.

62. *New Haven Palladium,* 9, 10, and 11 March, all 1854, all p. 2.

63. See Chapter 7 ("A Railroad Promotion and Its Sequel") in David M. Potter, *The Impending Crisis 1848–1861* (New York: Harper and Row, 1976), 145–76. The quote is taken from p. 166. See also Roy F. Nichols, *Blueprints for Leviathan: American Style* (New York: Atheneum, 1963), 104–21.

64. *New Haven Palladium,* 27 May 1854, p. 2 (quoted).

65. *Albany Morning Express,* 25 May and 27 May (quoted), both 1854, both p. 2; Charles Butler to "My dear Wife," 26 May 1854, reel 2, Charles Butler Papers, Library of Congress; *Cleveland Weekly Plain Dealer,* 31 May 1854, p. 5 (reprinting a column written on Friday, May 26). I have used details of what occurred in Albany on the assumption that events in New Haven were very similar.

66. Potter, *Impending Crisis,* 166–67.

67. Rollin G. Osterweis, *Three Centuries of New Haven, 1638–1938* (New Haven: Yale University Press, 1953), 244–49.

68. *New Haven Morning Journal & Courier,* 12 June 1854, p. 2 (quoted); Henry W. Farnam, *Memoir of Henry Farnam* (1889), 18–22 (quote from p. 22).

69. Here and below, see Babcock's articles, clipped from the *Palladium* and pasted in a small notebook, Collection A/.B112 in MHS, St. Paul. His account has been edited and published as "Rails West: The Rock Island Excursion of 1854 as reported by Charles [sic] F. Babcock," *Minnesota History* (Winter 1954), 133–43. Silliman's account is on p. 191 of his journal [the entry for May 31, 1854], reel 4, Silliman Papers, microfilm 6463, University of Wisconsin–Madison. His apology for bad hand writing is on p. 205. See also George Bancroft to "My ever dear Wife," 30 May 1854, reel 4, Bancroft Papers, microfilm, Cornell University.

70. Alvin F. Harlow, *The Road of the Century: The Story of the New York Central* (New York: Creative Age Press), 267–74.

71. Silliman Journal, p. 192–93 (Tuesday, May 31); Benjamin Silliman Sr. to Benjamin Silliman Jr., 1 June 1854, in Silliman Family Papers, box 16B, Benjamin Silliman Jr. Series I, Mss. 450, Stirling Library, Yale.

72. *New York Observer* 32, no. 24 (15 June 1854), p. 190 (quoted); the correspondent ("Eusebius") was Edward Dorr Griffin Prime of New York.

73. D. W. Meinig, *Atlantic America, 1492–1800* (New Haven: Yale University Press, 1986), 234, 350–51, 356-57; R. Douglas Hurt, *The Ohio Frontier: Crucible of the Old Northwest, 1720–1830* (Bloomington: Indiana University Press, 1996), 164–66, 249–50; Silliman Journal, p. 193 (1 June 1854), microfilm ed., UW-Madison.

74. Hugh Davis, *Leonard Bacon: New England Reformer and Antislavery Moderate* (Baton Rouge: Louisiana State University Press, 1998), 1–5, 6, 9; *Proceedings in Commemoration of the Fiftieth Anniversary of the Settlement of Tallmadge; with the Historical Discourses of Hon. E. N. Sill, and Rev. L. Bacon* (Akron, Ohio: Beebe and Elkins, 1857), 50–51 (quoted).

75. Silliman's Journal, p. 196–97 (2 June 1854). For Noyes's story, see also Joy Day Buel and Richard Buel Jr., *The Way of Duty: A Woman and Her Family in Revolutionary America* (New York: W. W. Norton, 1984), 235–45. Hugh Davis, *Leonard Bacon: New England Reformer and Antislavery Moderate* (Baton Rouge: Louisiana State University Press, 1998), 1–5, 126–40, 156–58.

76. *New Haven Morning Journal & Courier,* 10 June 1854, p. 2 (quoted).

77. Lucius I. Barber, *A Record and Documentary History of Simsbury* (Simsbury, 1931), 400–01; Evan W. Woollacott, *The Gavel and the Book: The Simsbury Town Meeting 1670–1986* (Canaan, New Hampshire: Phoenix Publishing, 1987), 4447; "Ancestral chart of Jeffrey Orson Phelps with biographical notes," typescript in Connecticut State Library, Hartford; Volume 29 ("Jeffrey O. Phelps Notebook N.Y.N.H. Rail Road 1851–1857"), Volume 2 (1824–1860 Ledger), p. 212, and Volume 21 (Ledger 1852–1875), p. 58, 196, all in Jeffrey Orson Phelps Papers, Connecticut State Library. On August 22, 1854 (page 58 of Volume 21), Phelps charged—and Mather approved payment of—a legal fee of $1,750 to the FVRR. For the Connecticut temperance law of 1854, see *Norwich Examiner,* 1 July 1854, p. 2.

78. Osterweis, *Three Centuries of New Haven,* 303.

79. A. C. Twining to C. J. Salthe, 11 March 1854 and 22 May 1854, and T. P. Handy to "Dear Sir," 14 January 1854, all in Alexander C. Twining Papers, New Haven Colony Historical Society, New Haven. "Twining had also written a lengthy article"—[Alexander C. Twining], "The Nebraska Bill and Its Results," *New Englander* 12 (May 1854), 213–37; Davis, *Leonard Bacon,* 114–16. For the authorship and the reference, I am indebted to Richard J. Carwardine, *Evangelicals and Politics in Antebellum America* (New Haven: Yale University Press, 1993), 239, 407 note 12.

80. Here and below, see Twining, "The Nebraska Bill," 213–14 (quoted), 215 (quoted), 219 (geological metaphor), 221–22, 228, 236 (quoted, and with meteorological metaphor).

81. *New Haven Palladium,* 9 March 1854, p. 2.

82. Here and below, Babcock's letter dated 3 June 1854, written from Chicago, clippings from *Palladium,* MHS.

83. See Simeon Eben Baldwin, "Roger Sherman Baldwin, 1793–1863," in William Draper Lewis, ed., *Great American Lawyers,* Vol. 3 (Philadelphia: John C. Winston Company, 1908), 493–526.

84. William Curtis Noyes to Roger Sherman Baldwin, 10 November 1854, and Baldwin to Noyes, 14 November 1854, both in "1849–1854" folder, Roger S. Baldwin Legal Cases, box 134, Series VII, Baldwin Family Papers, Yale Stirling Library. Simeon Eben Baldwin, "Roger Sherman Baldwin. 1793–1863," in William Draper Lewis, ed., *Great American Lawyers,* Vol. 3 (Philadelphia: John C. Winston Company, 1908), 493–527, especially p. 526; portrait of RSB in Frederick Calvin Norton, *The Governors of Connecticut* (Hartford: Connecticut Magazine Company, 1905), 197. Holt, *American Whig Party,* 557, 811.

85. Here and above, this summary is based on Osterweis, *Three Centuries,* 297–302 (quotes from p. 300, 302); Baldwin, "Roger Sherman Baldwin," 498–506; and Iyunolu Folayan Osagie, *The Amistad Revolt: Memory, Slavery, and the Politics of Identity in the United States and Sierra Leone* (Athens: University of Georgia Press, 2000), 6–13 (quotes from p. 11). Steven Spielberg's movie *Amistad* replaced the distinguished Baldwin

with "a no-name property lawyer (Matthew McConaughey)" and thus distorted the events; Osagie, p. 121.

86. Noah Porter, "A Discourse Commemorative of the Life and Character of Mr. Joseph Earl Sheffield, Delivered at the Battell Chapel, June 26, 1882" (New Haven: Tuttle, Morehouse and Taylor, 1882), p. 5–8, 10 (quoted), 29–30, 31 (quoted), pamphlet at Connecticut State Library. Osterweis, *Three Centuries,* 251–52; Holt, *American Whig Party,* 639.

87. Osterweis, *Three Centuries,* 231, 251-52 (quoted), 260 (quoted), 261, 274, 278–79, 293, 318. See also the drawing of Brewster on p. 275.

88. Osterweis, *Three Centuries,* 274. Brewster participated in the May 26 anti-Nebraska meeting in New Haven; *New Haven Palladium,* 27 May 1854, p. 2. For Brewster's anti-liquor views, see the account of his March 1854 speech in *The Maine Law Advocate* (New Haven), 16 March 1854, p. 2.

89. See picture of Farnam following p. 18 in William Edward Hayes, *Iron Road to Empire: The History of 100 Years of the Progress and Achievements of the Rock Island Lines.*

90. *Poughkeepsie Eagle,* 24 June 1854, p. 2.

91. F. J. Nevins, "Seventy Years of Service: From Grant to Gorman," p. 8 (picture of the Tremont), in *Rock Island Magazine* (1922).

92. *Putnam's Monthly Magazine* (September 1854), p. 320–25 (quotes from p. 320, 321).

93. Catharine M. Sedgwick to "Dearest Kate," 4 June 1854, microfilm, reel 4, Catharine M. Sedgwick Papers P-354, Massachusetts Historical Society, Boston.

94. Here and below, "Forty Days in a Western Hotel," *Putnam's Monthly Magazine* 4, no. 24 (December 1854), p. 622, 626 (quoted). The first paragraph (p. 622) indicates that the writer was on the Grand Excursion, although he or she does not stress that fact.

95. *Chicago Journal,* 1 June 1854, p. 3 (quoted); Kristie Hamilton, *America's Sketchbook: The Cultural Life of a Nineteenth-Century Literary Genre* (Athens: Ohio University Press, 1998), 135–36. The panorama was to be at "Tremont Hall" on Friday evening, June 2, and Saturday evening, June 3. I interpret "Tremont Hall" to be the hotel, or a section of it.

96. Babcock letters to the *New Haven Palladium,* dated 3 June and 5 June 1854; William Cronon, *Nature's Metropolis: Chicago and the Great West* (New York: W. W. Norton, 1991), 64–72, 76–77; David M. Young, *Chicago Transit: An Illustrated History* (DeKalb: Northern Illinois University Press, 1998), 32–33; Harold M. Mayer and Richard C. Wade, *Chicago: Growth of a Metropolis* (Chicago: University of Chicago Press, 1969), 28–30, 35–43.

97. Babcock's letter to the *New Haven Palladium,* dated 5 June 1854.

98. *Albany Morning Express,* 16 June 1854, p. 2.

99. Here and below, see *Chicago Tribune,* 5 June 1854, p. 3.

100. *Chicago Journal,* 6 June 1854, p. 2 (quoted).

101. *Chicago Tribune,* 5 June 1854, p. 3 (quoted); *New York Weekly Mirror,* 17 June 1854, p. 2 (quoted); Hyde, *Encyclopedia of St. Louis,* 480; Timothy R. Mahoney, *Provincial Lives: Middle-class Experience in the Antebellum Middle West* (New York: Cambridge University Press, 1999), 249–51 (on the "frolic").

102. Hyde, *Encyclopedia of St. Louis,* 480 and photograph; *Albany Daily Knickerbocker,* 20 June 1854, p. 2 (quoted); *Kingston (N.Y.) Journal,* 14 June 1854, p. 2.

103. *New Haven Palladium,* 7 June 1854, p. 2 (quoted).

EXCURSUS: Catharine Sedgwick and Antebellum Gender Roles
104. Dion Boucicault to George Washington Riggs, 10 April 1861, Theatrical Manuscripts Collection, University of Rochester;

Springfield Republican, 9 June 1854, p. 2; Robert Hogan, *Dion Boucicault* (New York: Twayne Publishers), 34–36; Townsend Walsh, *The Career of Dion Boucicault* (New York: Dunlap Society, 1915), 48–49.

105. Catharine Maria Sedgwick to "My dear friend," 24 May 1854, reel 4, microfilm, Catharine Maria Sedgwick Papers P-354, Massachusetts Historical Society, Boston.

106. James A. Harrison, ed., *Complete Works of Edgar Allan Poe: Vol. 5, Literati and Autobiography* (New York: George D. Sproul, 1902), 108–13 (quote from p. 113).

107. Sarah Cabot Sedgwick and Christina Sedgwick Marquand, *Stockbridge 1739–1939: A Chronicle (1939),* 208–09, 213–16 (quote from p. 216); *America in the Fifties: Letters of Frederika Bremer,* 17 (quoted).

108. For biographies of Sedgwick, see, for example, Edward Halsey Foster, *Catharine Maria Sedgwick* (New York: Twayne, 1974) and Carolyn L. Karcher's "Introduction," in Catharine Maria Sedgwick, *Hope Leslie; or Early Times in the Massachusetts* (New York: Penguin Books, 1998); for "Lafayettism" see Mary Kelley's "Introduction," p. 33, in Kelley, ed., *The Power of Her Sympathy: The Autobiography and Journal of Catharine Maria Sedgwick* (Boston: Massachusetts Historical Society, 1993).

109. Catharine Maria Sedgwick to William Minot, 30 May 1854, Sedgwick to Kate Sedgwick Minot (KSM), 24 May 1854, and Sedgwick to KSM, 28 May 1854, all on reel 4, CSM Papers P-354, MHS, Boston.

110. Kelley, "Introduction," 17–31 (quote from p. 24) in Kelley, ed., *Power of Her Sympathy.* See also Karcher, ed., *Hope Leslie,* xiii–xiv.

111. Catharine Maria Sedgwick to Charles Butler, 25 May 1854 (quoted), reel 2, Charles Butler Papers, Library of Congress.

112. Kelley, ed., *Power of Her Sympathy,* 24–28, 29 (quoted), 30–31; Marshall Foletta, *Coming to Terms with Democracy: Federalist Intellectuals and the Shaping of an American Culture* (Charlottesville: University Press of Virginia, 2001), 105–07; Mary Kelley, "A Woman Alone: Catharine Maria Sedgwick's Spinsterhood in Nineteenth-Century America," *New England Quarterly* 51(June 1978), p. 215; Karcher, *Hope Leslie,* xiii–xiv.

113. Harriet Twining to Alexander C. Twining, 7 June 1854, box 10, folder D, Twining Papers, New Haven Colony Historical Society, New Haven.

114. Cornelia T. Martin to Francis Preston Blair, 30 May 1854 (quoted), folder 4, box 6, Throop and Martin Family Papers, II, Correspondence of Francis Preston Blair, Manuscripts and Special Collections, Firestone Library, Princeton University.

115. Kelley, "Introduction," 30, 36–37 (quoted), in *Power of Her Sympathy;* Karcher, "Introduction," xii, xiv–xvi (quoted), in *Hope Leslie.*

116. Kelley, "Introduction," 37–40, *Power of Her Sympathy;* Karcher, "Introduction," ix–xl, in *Hope Leslie;* Foster, *Sedgwick,* 114–15. See also the Sedgwick entry in *Dictionary of American Biography.*

117. Kelley, *Power of Her Sympathy,* 95–96 (the entry is dated August 31, 1854). Alice was the daughter of Sedgwick's beloved niece, Kate Sedgwick Minot, and the autobiographical journal was written for her.

118. For another perspective on Reverend Stephen West, see Donald Weber, *Rhetoric and History in Revolutionary New England* (New York: Oxford University Press, 1988), 91–112, 140–45.

119. Here and below, Catharine M. Sedgwick to "Dearest Kate," 1 and 4 June, both 1854, and CMS to William Minot, 20 May 1854, all in reel 4, CMS Papers P-354, Massachusetts Historical Society. Parts of these letters are printed in Dewey, ed., *Life and Letters,* p. 352–54.

120. Foletta, *Coming to Terms with Democracy,* 240 (quoted).

121. Entries for Theodore Sedgwick Sr. and Theodore Sedgwick Jr. in *Dictionary of National Biography;* Sedgwick and Marquand, Stockbridge, 218 (quoted); Foletta, *Coming to Terms,* 242–43; Kelley, "Introduction," p. 26–27, in *Power of Her Sympathy.* For Elizabeth's boarding school, see, for example, Cornelia Carr, *Harriet Hosmer: Letters and Memories* (New York: Moffat, Yard and Company, 1912).

122. George W. Curtis to Mrs. Bancroft, 9 August 1853, "General Correspondence 1852–1853" folder, box 8, Bancroft-Bliss Papers, Library of Congress.

CHAPTER 3: "All Under a Full Head of Steam"

123. *Poughkeepsie Eagle,* 1 July 1854, p. 2 (quoted).

124. *Albany Evening Journal,* 15 June 1854, p. 2 (reprinting article from *New York Courier & Enquirer*); *New Haven Daily Register,* 20 June 1854, p. 2.

125. Bessie Louise Pierce, comp. *As Others See Chicago: Impressions of Visitors, 1673–1933* (Chicago: University of Chicago Press), 164. This account, "Chicago in 1856," appeared in *Putnam's Monthly Magazine* 7 (June 1856), p. 606–13.

126. *Poughkeepsie Eagle,* 1 July 1854, p. 2; Massey Hamilton Shepherd Jr., *History of St. James' Church* (Chicago: privately printed, 1934), 26–27.

127. George Bancroft to "My ever dear wife," 4 June 1854, reel 4, microfilm edition, George Bancroft Papers, Carl Krech Library, Cornell University; McAdam et al., eds., *History of the Bench and Bar of New York,* vol. 1, p. 434.

128. Richard J. Carwardine, *Evangelicals and Politics in Antebellum America* (New Haven: Yale University Press, 1993), 4–5, 43–44.

129. Babcock letter, dated 5 June 1854, in *New Haven Palladium.*

130. Catharine Maria Sedgwick to "Dearest Kate" [Katherine Sedgwick Minot], 4 June 1854, and CMS to "dearest Jane," 4 June 1854, both in reel 4, CMS Papers P-354, Massachusetts Historical Society.

131. Foster, *Catharine Maria Sedgwick,* 116–17 (quoted), 118–22 (quote from p. 122); Daniel Walker Howe, *The Unitarian Conscience: Harvard Moral Philosophy, 1805–1861* (Cambridge: Harvard University Press, 1970), 83–91, 140, 146–48.

132. Here and above, Paul K. Conkin, *The Uneasy Center: Reformed Christianity in Antebellum America* (Chapel Hill: University of North Carolina Press, 1995), 211–20 (quote from p. 216); Vincent Harding, *A Certain Magnificence: Lyman Beecher and the Transformation of American Protestantism, 1775–1863* (Brooklyn: Carlson Publishing, 1991), 138–42, 155–58, 165–66, 177–82, 274–76; George M. Marsden, *The Evangelical Mind and the New School Presbyterian Experience: A Case Study of Thought and Theology in Nineteenth-Century America* (New Haven: Yale University Press, 1970), 45–52; Davis, *Leonard Bacon,* 101–06; Karcher, ed., *Power of Her Sympathy,* 96. See also Christopher Grasso's brief article on New Haven Theology in *Dictionary of Christianity in America* (InterVarsity Press, 1990), 815–16.

133. Here and below, see Davis, *Leonard Bacon,* 48 (quoted), 147, 154–55, 156–57, 182–83; Marsden, *Evangelical Mind,* 11. For Bacon's portrait, see Atwater, *History of New Haven,* opposite p. 136.

134. See Davis, *Leonard Bacon.* The term "fighting parson" is a quote from Daniel G. Reid's entry on Bacon in the *Dictionary of American Biography.* For the annual meetings, see, e.g., *New York Daily Tribune,* 13 May 1854, p. 6.

135. Entries for Sunday, May 28, and Sunday, June 4, both 1854, in Day Journals and Diaries, box 2, Bacon Family Collection Part III, August 1987 Addition, Manuscripts and Archives, Stirling Library, Yale.

136. Davis, *Leonard Bacon,* 45–46 (quoted), 99–104; 111 (quoted), 112; Louise L. Stevenson, *Scholarly Means to Evangelical Ends: The New Haven Scholars and the Transformation of Higher Learning in America, 1830–1890* (Baltimore: Johns Hopkins University Press, 1986), 19–20.

137. Stevenson, *Scholarly Means,* 24–27, 40–41, 74–75, 76 (quoted).

138. Stevenson, *Scholarly Means,* 9.

139. Entry for Robinson and von Jakob in *Appleton's Cyclopaedia of American Biography;* entry for Robinson in *Dictionary of American Biography;* Jerry Wayne Brown, *The Rise of Biblical Criticism in America, 1800–1870* (Middletown, Connecticut: Wesleyan University Press), 111–13, 115, 117–21; Henry Boynton Smith and Roswell D. Hitchcock, *The Life, Writings and Character of Edward Robinson,* reprint ed. (New York: Arno Press, 1977), 13 (quoted), 45–47.

140. Theodore Dwight Bozeman, *Protestants in an Age of Science: The Baconian Ideal and Antebellum American Religious Thought* (Chapel Hill: University of North Carolina Press, 1977).

141. *Brick Church Memorial Containing the Discourses Delivered by Dr. Spring on the Closing of the Old Church in Beekman St. and the Opening of the New Church on Murray Hill . . .* (New York: M. W. Dodd, 1861); Gardiner Spring, *Personal Reminiscences of the Life and Times of Gardiner Spring . . .* (New York: Charles Scribner and Company, 1866); Edwin G. Burrows and Mike Wallace, *Gotham: A History of New York City to 1898* (New York: Oxford University Press, 1999), 452–54; *Northwestern Christian Advocate* (Chicago), 14 June 1854, p. 3; *Chicago Daily Democratic Press,* 6 June 1854, p. 3.

142. Spring, *Personal Reminiscences,* Vol. II, p. 23, 38 (quoted); Marsden, *Evangelical Mind,* 82–86, 93–100.

143. Marsden, *Evangelical Mind,* 99–100.

144. Marsden, *Evangelical Mind,* 97 (quoted), 98–100.

145. *Boston Daily Evening Transcript,* 15 June 1854, p. 2; *Chicago Daily Tribune,* 12 June 1854, p. 2 (quoting *Buffalo Commercial Advertiser*); *Buffalo Commercial Advertiser,* 8 June 1854, p. 2.

146. John Frederick Lyons, *Centennial Sketch of the History of the Presbytery of Chicago* (Chicago, 1947), 11–12.

147. Howe, *Unitarian Conscience,* 270, 280–84, 287, 295–96, 297.

148. Cawardine, *Evangelicals and Politics,* 236–37; Robert W. Johannsen, ed., *The Letters of Stephen A. Douglas* (Urbana: University of Illinois Press, 1961), 300–01, 321; Johannsen, *Douglas,* 443–44 (quoted). For an excellent discussion of Douglas vs. the clergy, see Stewart Winger, *Lincoln, Religion, and Romantic Cultural Politics* (DeKalb: University of Northern Illinois Press, 2003), 29–34.

149. Here and above, Johannsen, ed., *Letters of Stephen A. Douglas,* 300-321 (quotes from p. 301, 303, 308, 311, 312); Johannsen, *Douglas,* 444 (quoted). Douglas's words are quoted from [Leonard Bacon], "Morality of the Nebraska Bill," *New Englander* (May 1854), p. 329.

150. [Bacon], "Morality of the Nebraska Bill," 312, 317, 328 (quoted), 329 (quoted), 330 (quoted), 333 (quoted), 334-35; Edward Beecher to Leonard Bacon, 16 February 1854, folder 103, box 6, Series I, Bacon Family Collection, Stirling Library, Yale. For Giddings' request, see Theodore Davenport Bacon, *Leonard Bacon: A Statesman in the Church* (New Haven: Yale University Press, 1931), 389–90.

151. [Bacon], "Morality," p. 328; [Bacon], "Morality," 331; Beecher to Leonard Bacon, 18 February 1854, folder 103, box 6, Series I, Bacon Family Collection, Yale.

152. [Bacon], "Morality," 334–35 (quoted).

153. *Chicago Daily Democratic Press,* 6 June 1854, p. 3; *The Christian Times* (Chicago), 8 June 1854, p. 2; *Northwestern Christian*

Advocate, 14 June 1854, p. 3.

154. *(Chicago) Christian Times,* 8 June 1854, p. 2; entry for Cutting in *Appleton's Cyclopaedia of American Biography; New York Recorder,* 21 June 1854, p. 4 (quoted).

155. *New York Observer* 32, no. 28 (13 July 1854), p. 218, quoted); Odd S. Lovoll, *The Promise of America: A History of the Norwegian–American People* (Minneapolis: University of Minnesota Press, 1984), 56; Odd S. Lovoll, *A Century of Urban Life: The Norwegians in Chicago before 1930* (Northfield, Minnesota: Norwegian-American Historical Association, 1988), 54–58 (picture on p. 56).

156. Here and above, Catharine Maria Sedgwick to Kate Sedgwick Minot, 4 June 1854, in Dewey, ed., *Life and Letters,* 353–54; and Sedgwick to "Dearest Jane," 4 June 1854, roll 18, CMS Papers, Massachusetts Historical Society.

157. *Poughkeepsie Eagle,* 1 July 1854, p. 2.

158. Leonard Bacon to "Dear Catherine," [sic] 4 June 1854, folder 104, box 6, Series I, Bacon Family Collection, mss. no. 46, Yale.

159. *New Haven Daily Register,* 12 June 1854, p. 2. This bound volume is at the Beinecke Rare Book and Manuscript Library at Yale University.

160. John Munn Diary, Vol. 22, p. 141 (quoted).

161. William Jarvis to [a grandnephew?] William Jarvis, 11 September 1853, and 1 February, 11 March, and 27 April, all 1854, in Box 1, William Jarvis Letters, Collection 70425, Connecticut Historical Society, Hartford. The younger Jarvis was his land agent in Hartsgrove, Ohio.

162. Joseph E. Sheffield to Henry Farnam, 2 May 1854, "May 1–5" folder, box 10, Series I, Henry Farnam 1803–83, Farnam Family Papers, Stirling Library, Yale.

EXCURSUS: Millard Fillmore and Antebellum Partisan Politics

163. Robert J. Rayback, *Millard Fillmore: Biography of a President* (Newtown, Connecticut: American Political Biography Press, 1959), 225–26, 231, 234-36; Holt, *American Whig Party,* 517–21, 534-37; Potter, *Impending Crisis,* 110.

164. Holt, *American Whig Party,* 432.

165. H. H. Green, quoted in Cawardine, *Evangelicals and Politics in Antebellum America,* 17–18.

166. Also unfair is Michael Holt's overly negative assessment of Fillmore (see, e.g., p. 521–22 of his *American Whig Party*); Holt admits that Fillmore was motivated by a desire to save the Union (p. 599); that he delivered "a political masterstroke" to save the Compromise of 1850 (p. 534–35); that he sought Whig party unity (p. 545); that he wrote a brilliant political analysis (p. 801); and that he would have made the best Whig presidential candidate in 1852 (p. 958). Taken together, these points would seem to negate his low view of Fillmore.

167. Charles M. Snyder, *The Lady and the President: The Letters of Dorothea Dix & Millard Fillmore* (Lexington: University Press of Kentucky, 1975), 27, 33 (quoted); Rayback, *Millard Fillmore,* 42-43 (quoted); Holt, *American Whig Party,* 431–32.

168. Rayback, *Millard Fillmore,* 45–46 (quoted); Henry Ward Beecher to Leonard Bacon, 18 February 1854, folder 103, box 6, Series I, Bacon Family Collection, Yale.

169. Daniel Walker Howe, *The Unitarian Conscience: Harvard Moral Philosophy, 1805–1861* (Cambridge: Harvard University Press, 1970), 300 (also quoting Emerson).

170. Rayback, *Millard Fillmore,* 36 (quoted); 43–44; Snyder, *Lady and the President,* 27.

171. Rayback, *Millard Fillmore,* 289–90.

172. Charles Sellers, *The Market Revolution: Jacksonian America, 1815–1846* (New York: Oxford University Press, 1991), 202–03

(quoted), 376–80 (describing Transcendentalism, a revolt against Unitarianism).

173. Rayback, *Millard Fillmore,* 195–204; Holt, *American Whig Party,* 396, 544–45.

174. Holt, *American Whig Party,* 801–02.

175. Holt, *American Whig Party,* 802.

176. Fillmore to Dorothea Dix, 9 and 18 February 1854, Snyder, ed., *Lady and the President,* 173, 182.

177. Rayback, *Millard Fillmore,* 386–87 (quoted). For Fillmore's promise (ca. December 1853) to go on the Grand Excursion, see Fillmore to Dix, 26 May 1854, reel 42, Fillmore Papers, SHSW; and in Snyder, ed., *Lady and the President,* 197.

178. Fillmore to Dix, 26 February 1854, in Snyder, ed., *Lady and the President,* 192–93; Robert J. Scarry, *Millard Fillmore* (Jefferson, North Carolina: McFarland and Company, 2001), 189, 199, 202, 265.

179. Fillmore to John P. Kennedy, 18 February 1854, reel 42, Fillmore Papers, SHSW.

180. Scarry, *Fillmore,* 199, 248; Rayback, *Millard Fillmore,* 365.

181. The best account of this trip is in Scarry, *Fillmore,* 248–53 (all quotes are from this account).

182. Holt, *American Whig Party,* 824.

183. John P. Kennedy to R. C. Winthrop, 4 June 1854, in Henry T. Tuckerman, *The Life of John Pendleton Kennedy* (New York: G. P. Putnam and Sons, 1871), 243–44.

184. N. K. Hall to Fillmore, 30 April 1854; Solomon G. Haven to Hall, 4 May 1854; and Haven to Fillmore, 5 May 1854, all on reel 42, Fillmore Papers; Scarry, *Fillmore,* 252–53.

185. Holt, *American Whig Party,* 806–21.

186. Holt, *American Whig Party,* 812.

187. Fillmore to Dix, 26 May 1854, in Snyder, ed., *Lady and the President,* 197–98.

188. Rayback, *Millard Fillmore,* 51–53; L. B. Proctor, *Bench and Bar of New York* (1870), 703–04; picture of Hall in Holt, *Rise and Fall of the American Whig Party,* after p. 556.

189. Rayback, *Millard Fillmore,* 245; Holt, *American Whig Party,* 430, 432, 527 (quoted).

190. N. K. Hall to Fillmore, 30 April 1854, reel 42, Fillmore Papers, SHSW.

191. Holt, *American Whig Party,* 805, 846 (quoted).

192. Holt, *American Whig Party,* 649–50, 653, 711, 721–22; Rayback, *Millard Fillmore,* 87–88, 333–34, 337; Holt, *American Whig Party,* 430, 432, 653 (quoted).

193. Holt, *American Whig Party,* 588–89.

194. Johannsen, *Douglas,* 11–15 (quotes from p. 11–12).

195. [John P. Kennedy], "Our Parties and Politics," *Putnam's Monthly* 4, no. 21 (September 1954), p. 233.

196. *Buffalo Commercial Advertiser,* 3 June 1854, p. 2.

197. William E. Gienapp, *The Origins of the Republican Party 1852–1856* (New York: Oxford University Press, 1987), 39–40.

198. Elbert B. Smith, *Francis Preston Blair* (New York: Free Press, 1980), 4, 229 (quoted). Halstead's description dates from 1856, not 1854.

199. Smith, *Francis Preston Blair,* 10 (quoted), 182 (quoted); 210; entries for the Blairs in *Appleton's Cyclopedia of American Biography.* For Elizabeth Blair Lee, see Virginia Jeans Laas, "Elizabeth Blair Lee: Union Counterpart of Mary Boykin Chestnut," *Journal of Southern History,* Vol. 50, No. 3 (August 1984), 385, 386–87; William Ernest Smith, *The Francis Preston Blair Family in Politics,* Vol. I (New York: Macmillan Company, 1933), 210–11.

200. Elizabeth Blair Lee to "Phil" [Samuel Phillips Lee], 25 May and 27 May, both 1854, both in folder 8, box 74, Papers of Samuel

Phillips Lee, Blair and Lee Family Papers; Francis Preston Blair to Cornelia T. Martin, 27 May 1854, folder 2, box 6, Throop and Martin Family Papers—all in Manuscripts and Special Collections, Firestone Library, Princeton University. I am indebted to Elbert B. Smith's notes, p. 453, for alerting me to the Blair-Lee correspondence at Princeton.

201. Frank Blair to Francis Preston Blair Sr., 1 May 1854, reel 2, Blair Papers, Library of Congress; and Francis Preston Blair Sr. to Frank Blair, 21 July 1854, reel 1, Blair Papers, Library of Congress.

202. Smith, *Francis Preston Blair,* 151–57, 163–68, 169–70, 175 (quoting Jackson's "deathbed letter"), 192, 216. On p. xii, Smith quotes Lincoln as saying, "The Blairs are . . . strong, tenacious men, having some peculiarities, among them the energy with which their feuds are carried on."

203. Smith, *Francis Preston Blair,* 1, 3, 4, 8.

204. Elizabeth Blair Lee to "Phil," 29 May 1854, folder 8, box 74, Blair-Lee Papers, Princeton; Smith, *Francis Preston Blair,* 215 (giving the departure date as May 28); E. T. Throop Martin to "My dear Wife," 4 June 1854 (two letters—an a.m. and a p.m. letter), folder 1, box 4, Throop and Martin Family Papers, Princeton.

205. Cornelia to "My Dear Children," 19 May 1887, Box 5, Throop and Martin Family Papers, Princeton; John S. Jenkins, *Lives of the Governors of the State of New York* (Auburn: Derby and Miller, 1851), 481, 516–17, 532–33, 541.

206. E. T. Throop Martin to "My dear Wife," 4 June 1854 (an a.m. and a p.m. letter), folder 1, box 4, Throop and Martin Family Papers, Princeton.

207. *New Haven Daily Register,* 9 June 1854, p. 2.

208. Kennedy to Fillmore, 28 May 1854, Reel 42, Fillmore Papers, SHSW.

CHAPTER 4: "Off She Goes!"

209. *Putnam's Monthly Magazine* 4, Issue 24 (December 1854), p. 627 (this excursionist turned back at Chicago, but it is clear from p. 622 that he or she started out on the excursion); this author quotes the porter as saying, "Omnibus ready for the Michigan Central cars!" but adds "or whatever road it may be"—so I have substituted "Chicago and Rock Island."

210. *Poughkeepsie Eagle,* 1 July 1854, p. 2; *Chicago Tribune,* 7 June 1854, p. 3.

211. Bessie Louise Pierce, comp., *As Others See Chicago: Impressions of Visitors, 1673–1933* (Chicago: University of Chicago Press), 157–58; Nevins, "Seventy Years of Service," 42 ("mud route").

212. *New York Times,* 12 June 1854, p. 2; *New York Evening Post,* 12 June 1854, p. 2.

212. *New York Times,* 12 June 1854, p. 2; *New York Evening Post,* 12 June 1854, p. 2.

213. David M. Young, *Chicago Transit: An Illustrated History* (DeKalb: Northern Illinois University Press, 1998), 33; F. J. Nevins, "Seventy Years of Service: From Grant to Gorman," reprint from *Rock Island Magazine* (1922), map on p. 10.

214. Nevins, "Seventy Years of Service," p. 11; *Poughkeepsie Eagle,* 1 July 1854, p. 2; *New York Times,* 12 June 1854, p. 2; *Illinois State Journal,* 7 June 1854, p. 2; *New York Evening Post,* 12 June 1854, p. 2 (using "garden City"); *Albany Evening Journal,* 10 June 1854, p. 2 (new cars); *Chicago Daily Democratic Press,* 6 June 1854, p. 3 ("clean as a parlor"); *Boston Daily Advertiser,* 19 June 1854. Accounts vary as to the number of cars; "Excelsior"'s report in the *New York Times,* which mentions baggage cars, seems the most accurate.

215. William Cronon, *Nature's Metropolis: Chicago and the Great West* (New York: W. W. Norton, 1991), 79; Charles Hale to "Dear Mother," 5 June 1854 (written from Rock Island), "Sarah Preston (Everett) Hale, 1854" Folder, Box 21, Hale Family Papers, Smith College.

216. *Poughkeepsie Eagle,* 1 July 1854, p. 2; *New York Evening Post,* 12 June 1854, p. 2; *New Haven Palladium,* 10 June 1854, p. 2 (whistle and "all aboard"). "Sheffield (probably Farnamtoo) was concerned"—Joseph E. Sheffield to John E. Henry, 5 June 1854, box 10, series I, Henry Farnam 1803-83, Farnam Family Papers, Yale. Sheffield referred to the train trip back to Chicago, but it is a reasonable inference that the same concerns applied to the trip from Chicago.

217. Arthur W. Large, "Ottawa, Illinois and the Rock Island Railroad," typescript in "Illinois—Rock Island R.R. in Ottawa, Illinois" folder, box 2, Arthur W. Large Papers, State Historical Society of Wisconsin, Madison. Part of Large's account is based on the *Chicago Journal,* 15 March 1853.

218. *Chicago Journal,* 7 June 1854, p. 2; *Illinois State Journal,* 7 June 1854, p. 2. For Farnam's "careful provision against accident," see *Chicago Journal,* 7 June 1854, p. 2.

219. *Chicago Democratic Press,* 8 June 1854, p. 2; *Poughkeepsie Eagle,* 1 July 1854, p. 2.

220. *Illinois State Journal,* 7 June 1854, p. 2; *Chicago Daily Democratic Press,* 8 June 1854, p. 2; Silliman Journal, 5 June 1854, p. 201, reel 4, microfilm 6463, Silliman Papers, microfilm edition, SHSW; *New York Observer* 32, no. 24 (15 June 1854), p. 190.

221. James T. Hickey, ed., "An Illinois First Family: The Reminiscences of Clara Matteson Doolittle," *Journal of the Illinois State Historical Society,* 69 (1976): 3–16 (quote from p. 7); *Dictionary of American Biography* entry; Nevins, "Seventy Years of Service," p. 12; Arthur Charles Cole, *The Era of the Civil War 1848–1870* (Freeport, New York: Books for Libraries Press, 1971 ed.), 44–45, 102-04; Mark W. Summers, *The Plundering Generation: Corruption and the Crisis of the Union, 1849–1861* (New York: Oxford University Press, 1987), 274–76.

222. Hickey, ed., "Illinois First Family," 3–4, 6, 8 (quoted); Mark W. Summers, *The Plundering Generation: Corruption and the Crisis of the Union, 1849–1861* (New York: Oxford University Press, 1987), xiii, 274–76.

223. William Bross, *Rock Island and Its Surroundings* (Chicago: Democratic Steam Press Print, 1854), 7.

224. *Silliman, Journal,* 5 June 1854, p. 201, reel 4, microfilm 6463, Silliman Papers, microfilm edition, SHSW; John F. Fulton and Elizabeth H. Thomason, *Benjamin Silliman 1779–1864: Pathfinder of American Science* (New York: Henry Schuman, 1947), 201–02.

225. *New York Times,* 8 June 1854, p. 2.

226. *New York Daily Times,* 12 June 1854, p. 2 (quoted); entry for David Magie in *Appleton's Cyclopaedia of American Biography;* Rev. D. Magie, "God's Voice, and the Lessons It Teaches," pamphlet (New York: John F. Trow, 1850), copy in SHSW Library, Madison.

227. *New York Daily Times,* 12 June 1854, p. 2; *Illinois State Journal* (Springfield), 7 June 1854, p. 2; *Boston Daily Advertiser,* 19 June 1854 ("Letter 11"), typescript at MHS, St. Paul.

228. *New York Daily Times,* 12 June 1854, p. 2; *New Haven Evening Register,* 12 June 1854, p. 2.

229. Entry for Redfield in James Grant Wilson and John Fiske, eds., *Appleton's Cyclopædia of American Biography* (New York: D. Appleton & Co., 1888); William C. Redfield, *Sketch of the Geographical Rout[sic] of a Great Railway . . . ,* 2nd ed. (New York: G. and C. and H. Carvill, 1830), 4–5, 7, 10–15, 15–17 (quote from p. 17), 25 (quoted), 25–26.

230. *New York Weekly Mirror,* 17 June 1854, p. 2; *Boston Daily Advertiser,* 19 June 1854 ("Letter 11"), typescript at MHS; Silliman journal, 5 May 1854, p. 200; Bessie Louise Pierce, *A History of Chicago,* Vol. II, *From Town to City 1848–1871* (New York: Alfred A. Knopf, 1940), 37–40; Kay J. Carr, *Belleville, Ottawa, and Galesburg: Community and Democracy on the Illinois Frontier* (Carbondale: Southern Illinois Press, 1996), 25–26, 79.

231. John Munn's Diary, Vol. 22, p. 145 (quoted), Chicago Historical Society.

232. Carr, *Community and Democracy,* 25 (quoted), 29, 31 (map).

233. *Ottawa Free Trader,* 10 June 1854, p. 2; *Ottawa Republican,* 10 June 1854, p. 2; Carr, *Community and Democracy,* 57–59 (quoted), 27, 82–83 (quoted), 96, 123 (quoted), 126–30; Cole, *Era of the Civil War,* 31 (quoted); Nevins, "Seventy Years of Service," p. 7; passenger list for the boats *Golden Era, Galena,* and *Sparhawk,* box 53, folder 667, Farnam Family Papers, Yale; Large, "Ottawa, Illinois and the Rock Island Railroad," typescript, box 2, Large Papers, SHSW.

234. Carr, *Community and Democracy,* 82–83; Pierce, *History of Chicago,* Vol. II, p. 35, 40–41 (quoted), 51; Larkin, *John B. Jervis,* 126; Large, "Ottawa, Illinois and the Rock Island Railroad," box 2, Large Papers, SHSW. The early Davenport–Rock Island promotional work is detailed—in a partly fictionalized style complete with dialogue—in Nevins, "Seventy Years of Service," p. 5–10. See Nevins, p. 7, for the freight-reimbursement rule. According to Large, eastern investors insisted on cancellation of the canal reimbursement clause before they would invest in the C&RI.

235. Carr, *Community and Democracy,* 74, 81.

236. Carr, *Community and Democracy,* 27–28, 56, 59, 62; *Ottawa Republican,* 10 June 1854, p. 2; *Ottawa Free Trader,* 10 June 1854, p. 2.

237. *Poughkeepsie Eagle,* 1 July 1854, p. 2; *New York Times,* 12 June 1854, p. 2; John Dean Caton, *Miscellanies* (Boston: Houghton, Osgood and Company, 1879), 119, 125–30 (quote from p. 125); Eaton G. Osman, *Starved Rock: A Chapter of Colonial History* (Chicago: A. Flanagan Company), 10–11, 174, 180. William Hickling also knew of the Starved Rock story (*Miscellanies,* p. 125); several others may have, too; but it seems reasonable to infer that the expert, Caton, told the story to the editors/reporters.

238. Silliman journal, p. 200, 5 June 1854, reel 4, Silliman Papers, SHSW.

239. Large, "Ottawa, Illinois and the Rock Island Railroad," box 2, Large Papers; *Kingston Journal,* 21 June 1854, p. 2; *Kingston Journal,* 21 June 1854, p. 2.

240. David Herbert Donald, *Lincoln* (New York: Touchstone, 1996), 84, 85–86, 139; *Illinois State Journal,* 7 June 1854, p. 2; *New York Weekly Mirror,* 17 June 1854, p. 2.

241. Bates entry in *Dictionary of National Biography;* Marvin R. Cain, *Lincoln's Attorney General: Edward Bates of Missouri* (Columbia: University of Missouri Press, 1965), 1 (quoted), 7, 68–78, 81; Holt, *American Whigs,* 525 (quoted), 527, 723–24.

242. *New York Weekly Mirror,* 17 June 1854, p. 2.

243. My interpretation of Edwards is taken directly from David Herbert Donald, *Lincoln* (New York: Simon & Schuster, 1995), 60, 84–85, although Donald does not give his source(s) for this characterization of Edwards.

244. Here and above, see *Cleveland Herald,* 9 June 1854, p. 2. For Fillmore's response and a confirmation of Harris's account, see *Albany Morning Express,* 16 June 1854, p. 2 (quoted).

245. *New York Times,* 12 June 1854, p. 2 ("magnificent rolling prairie"); *Illinois State Journal,* 7 June 1854, p. 2 ("the great land ocean"); *New Haven Palladium,* 10 June 1854, p. 2 ("like a sail in mid ocean"); *Rome Daily Sentinel,* 10 June 1854, p. 2 ("level as a house floor"); *Albany Evening Journal,* 10 June 1854, p. 2 ("Lake Huron"); *New York Weekly Mirror,* 17 June 1854, p. 2 ("graceful swells")—these last two quotes refer to the flat prairie south of Chicago.

246. *New York Weekly Mirror,* 17 June 1854, p. 2 (clearly referring, however, to the flat prairie south of Chicago, not the rolling prairie near Sheffield).

247. Lueck, *Picturesque Tour,* 26n13, 93–97 (discussing Washington Irving's *A Tour on the Prairies*), 108.

248. *New York Times,* 12 June 1854, p. 2.

249. *New York Times,* 12 June 1854, p. 2 (stories from "W." on the first train and "Excelsior" on the second); *Illinois State Journal,* 7 June 1854, p. 2; *Chicago Democratic Press,* 8 June 1854, p. 2; *New Haven Palladium,* 10 June 1854, p. 2 (reporting on the time of breakfast).

250. *Illinois State Journal,* 7 June 1854, p. 2; some excursionists did snack on sandwiches and some editors, at least, did consume alcohol—evidently before 2:00 p.m.—see *New York Weekly Mirror,* 17 June 1854, p. 2 (which also compares the women to black birds and morning glories).

251. *New York Weekly Mirror,* 17 June 1854, p. 2.

252. William Bross, *Rock Island and Its Surroundings* (Chicago: Democratic Press Steam Print, 1854), 34–35.

253. E. T. T. Martin to "My dear Wife," 11 June 1854 (quoted), folder 1, box 4, Throop and Martin Family Papers, Princeton.

254. Martin to "My dear Wife," 11 June 1854 (quoted), folder 1, box 4, Throop and Martin Family Papers, Princeton; *The Independent (N.Y.),* 22 June 1854, p. 196 (quoted; an article written by Leonard Bacon).

255. Charles Hale to "Dear Mother," 5 June 1854, "Sarah Preston (Everett) Hale, 1854" folder, box 21, Hale Family Papers, Smith College.

256. Here and above, *New York Times,* 12 June 1854, p. 2; *New York Weekly Mirror,* 17 June 1854, p. 2; *Poughkeepsie Eagle,* 1 July 1854, p. 1; *New Haven Evening Register,* 12 June 1854, p. 2; *New Haven Palladium,* 10 June 1854, p. 2; *New York Observer* 32, no. 24 (15 June 1854), p. 190.

257. John Munn Diary, Vol. 22, p. 149; Bagg, ed., *Memorial History of Utica,* 184–85; John J. Walsh, *Vignettes of Old Utica* (Utica: Utica Public Library, 1982), 81 (quoted). This account is based on Munn, of course, and he could be mistaken, but his story has the ring of authenticity.

258. Here and above, for the scene at Rock Island, see *New York Tribune,* 12 June 1854, p. 6; *Rome Daily Sentinel,* 10 June 1854, p. 2; *New York Weekly Mirror,* 17 June 1854, p. 2; *New York Times,* 12 June 1854, p. 2; *Illinois State Journal,* 7 June 1854, p. 2; *Poughkeepsie Eagle,* 1 July 1854, p. 2; *Albany Evening Journal;* 10 June 1854, p. 2; *Chicago Journal,* 7 June 1854, p. 2; *Chicago Tribune,* 7 June 1854, p. 2; *New York Post,* 12 June 1854, p. 2; *New Haven Morning Journal & Courier,* 19 June 1854, p. 2. For a denial of "confusion" at Rock Island, see William Schouler's account in *Cincinnati Gazette,* 15 June 1854, p. 2; for "Imposter," see "Chicago & Rock Island R.R. Co. Excursion Register. June 5, 1854," p. 2, ledger in folder 668, box 53, Series I, Farnam Family Papers, Yale. For the steamboat berths (or lack thereof) see John Munn Diary, Vol. 22, 147–48; Charles Hale to "Dear Mother," 5 June 1854, box 21, Hale Family Papers; E. T. T. Martin to "My dear Wife," 11 June 1854, Box 4, Throop and Martin Family Papers; *New Haven Morning Journal & Courier,* 12 June 1854, p. 2; Jeffrey O. Phelps to Mrs. Phelps, 7 June

1854, Simsbury Historical Society, Simsbury, Connecticut.

259. *Albany Evening Journal,* 12 June 1854, p. 2; *Rome Daily Sentinel,* 1 July 1854, p. 2; Thurlow Weed to William Schouler, 16 June 1854, in "1854" folder, "1840 to 1861" box, William Schouler Papers, Massachusetts Historical Society, Boston; William E. Gienapp, *The Origins of the Republican Party* (New York: Oxford University Press, 1987), 151 (quoted); John Stryker to Weed, 17 May, O. B. Matteson to Weed, 18 May, William H. Romeyn to Weed, 23 May, Washington Hunt to Weed, 25 May, Philo S. Shelton to Weed, 6 June, all 1854, all in Thurlow Weed Papers, University of Rochester.

260. *Rome Daily Sentinel,* 1 July 1854, p. 2 (quoted).

261. *New Haven Palladium,* 10 June 1854, p. 2; *Springfield Republican,* 13 June 1854, p. 2; *New York Post,* 12 June 1854, p. 2. For a photo of a cabin, see Frederick Way Jr., comp., *Way's Packet Directory 1848–1994* (Athens: Ohio University Press, 1994 paperback ed.), photos between p. 302 and 303.

262. *New Haven Palladium,* 10 June 1854, p. 2; *Springfield Republican,* 13 June 1854, p. 2; *Rock Island Advertiser,* 7 June 1854, p. 2; *Davenport Gazette,* 8 June 1854, p. 2; *Cincinnati Gazette,* 15 June 1854, p. 2

263. *Chicago Tribune,* 9 June 1854.

264. *Chicago Tribune,* 7 June 1854, p. 3 ("seven o'clock"); *Springfield Republican,* 13 June 1854, p. 2; G. A. Mix to Henry Farnam, 1 June, 2 June, and 3 June, all 1854, folder 127, box 10, Series I, Farnam Family Papers; *Way's Packet Directory,* 176, 191, 246, 275, 480; George Byron Merrick and William R. Tibbals, *Genesis of Steam Navigation on Western Rivers,* 117, 129 (and photo of Harris opposite), 138; William J. Petersen, *Steamboating on the Upper Mississippi* (Iowa City: State Historical Society of Iowa, 1968), 263; [Sedgwick], "Great Excursion to the Falls of St. Anthony," 322. Some sources give the sixth boat as the *J. McKee,* others as the *Jenny Lind;* the name of the sixth captain is also in doubt.

265. *Chicago Tribune,* 9 June 1854.

266. William Bross, *Rock Island and Its Surroundings* (Chicago: Democratic Press Steam Print, 1854), 31; David Buisseret, *Historic Illinois from the Air* (Chicago: University of Chicago Press), 66; William A. Meese, *Early Rock Island* (Moline: Desaulniers and Company, 1905), drawing opposite p. 31; Kathleen Seusy, "Rock Island History: A Companion to the Architectural Walking Tours," p. 5–7, pamphlet published by Rock Island Preservation Commission, revised ed., 1999.

267. *Chicago Tribune,* 9 June 1854 (quoted); "Rock Island History: A Companion to the Architectural Walking Tours," pamphlet (Rock Island Preservation Commission, 1999), 6; *Davenport Gazette,* 15 June (p. 2) and 22 June (p. 1), both 1854.

268. *Springfield Republican,* 13 June 1854, p. 2; *New Haven Palladium,* 10 June 1854, p. 2 (giving the population as "over 7,000"); *Davenport Gazette,* 8 June 1854, p. 2; Franc B. Wilkie, *Davenport Past and Present* (Davenport: Luse, Lane and Company, 1858), 120–21 (giving the population as 6,000).

269. *New Haven Palladium,* 10 June 1854, p. 2; *Cincinnati Gazette,* 15 June 1854, p. 2; *Springfield Republican,* 13 June 1854, p. 2; *Rock Island Advertiser,* 7 June 1854, p. 2; *Poughkeepsie Eagle,* 1 July 1854, p. 2; *Davenport Gazette,* 8 June 1854, p. 2; *Chicago Tribune,* 7 June 1854, p. 3.

270. *Cincinnati Gazette,* 15 June 1854, p. 2; *Chicago Journal,* 7 June 1854, p. 2; *Cleveland Herald,* 9 June 1854, p. 2; *New York Observer* 32, no. 24 (15 June 1854), p. 190.

271. *Chicago Journal,* 7 June 1854, p. 2 (quoted); *Cincinnati Gazette,* 15 June 1854, p. 2.

272. *Cleveland Herald,* 9 June 1854, p. 2.

273. *Cincinnati Gazette,* 15 June 1854, p. 2.

EXCURSUS: Antebellum America and the Mississippi Steamboat

274. *New Haven Palladium,* 19 June 1854, p. 2 (quoted); *Buffalo Commercial Advertiser,* 17 June 1854, p. 1 ("the guards").

275. Louis C. Hunter, *Steamboats on the Western Rivers: An Economic and Technological History* (Cambridge: Harvard University Press, 1949), 391 (quoted).

276. Hunter, *Steamboats on the Western Rivers,* 72, 390–99, 419, 481, 504-08 (quotes from p. 390, 398).

277. George A. Mix to Henry Farnam, 2 June 1854, Folder 127, Box 10, Farnam Family Papers, Stirling Library, Yale.

278. Hunter, *Steamboats on the Western Rivers,* 432–33.

279. Hunter, *Steamboats on the Western Rivers,* 391–97.

280. *Northwest Weekly Gazette,* 11 and 25 April 1854, both p. 2, and 7 April 1854, p. 1 (quoting the *Cincinnati Times*); Merrick, *Old Times,* 292.

281. Catharine Sedgwick to Dearest Kate, 11 June 1854, Reel 4, CMS Papers P-354, Massachusetts Historical Society; *New York Recorder,* 21 June 1854, p. 4 (quoted).

282. Hunter, *Steamboats on the Western Rivers,* 394 (quoted); Dewey, ed., *Life and Letters,* 355 (quoted).

283. Dewey, ed., *Life and Letters,* 355 (quoted). The Sedgwicks traveled on the *Lady Franklin* until the returning excursion reached Rock Island. Then they switched to the *Sparhawk* for the trip to St. Louis. However, this chapter describes the steamboats without regard to strict chronological order.

284. Hunter, *Steamboats on the Western Rivers,* 382–83.

285. Merrick, *Old Times,* 55 (quoted), 61; Merrick and Tibbals, *Genesis of Steam Navigation,* 125; *Weekly Northwestern Gazette* (*Galena*), 7 April 1854, p. 1.

286. *New Haven Daily Register,* 24 June 1854, p. 2.

287. *Harper's Monthly Magazine,* Vol. 9, No. 54 (November 1854), p. 851 (quoting the *Utica Telegraph*).

288. Merrick, *Old Times on the Upper Mississippi,* 59–61; *Kingston (N.Y.) Journal,* 5 July 1854, p. 1.

289. Hunter, *Steamboats on the Western Rivers,* 81 (quoted), 123 (quoted), 125–33, 260; Petersen, *Steamboating on the Upper Mississippi,* 261–62, 261, 411, 418–19; Merrick, *Old Times,* 292; Merrick and Tibbals, *Genesis of Steam Navigation,* 129; Dewey, ed., *Life and Letters,* 356; Silliman journal, 6 June 1854, p. 205, Microfilm ed., UW–Madison; George Bancroft to My Ever Dear Wife, 11 [June] 1854, Reel 4, Bancroft Papers–Cornell.

290. Hunter, *Steamboats on the Western Rivers,* 240–42; George Byron Merrick, *Old Times on the Upper Mississippi: The Recollections of a Steamboat Pilot from 1854 to 1863* (Cleveland: Arthur H. Clark Company, 1909), 78–79 (quoted); *Chicago Tribune,* 13 June 1854, p. 2.

291. John O. Anfinson, *The River We Have Wrought: A History of the Upper Mississippi* (Minneapolis: University of Minnesota Press, 2003), 9 (quoted),14, 16–20.

292. Merrick, *Old Times,* 71–74; Hunter, *Steamboats on the Western Rivers,* 238–39 (quoting Merrick); *Kingston* (N.Y.) *Journal,* 5 July 1854, p. 1 (quoted).

293. Merrick, *Old Times,* 143–48, 149, 150, 184–89; Hunter, *Steamboats on the Western Rivers,* 405, 506; George Byron Merrick and William R. Tibbals, *Genesis of Steam Navigation on Western Rivers,* photo of Harris after p. 128; Daniel Smith Harris file, Riverboat Museum, Dubuque, Iowa; William J. Petersen, *Steamboating on the Upper Mississippi* (Iowa City: State Historical Society of Iowa, 1968), 240–41, 406–30 (quotes from p. 407, 415, 423).

294. Petersen, *Steamboating on the Upper Mississippi,* 422–23.

295. *Northwest Weekly Gazette,* 11 and 25 April 1854, both p. 2, and 7 April 1854, p. 1; Merrick, *Old Times,* 270, 271, 276; Hunter, *Steamboats on the Western Rivers,* 86, 106, 112.

296. George A. Mix to Henry Farnam, 1 and 2 June 1854, Folder 127, "June 1–2," Box 10, Farnam Family Papers, Stirling Library, Yale.

297. Mix to Farnam, 3 June 1854 ("June 1–2 Folder") and 16 June 1854 ("June 15–19" Folder), Box 10, Farnam Family Papers, Yale; "Exhibit of the condition of the road supposing it to have been fully completed July 10, [']54," handwritten financial statement, "C,RI RR 1854–1933 Miscellaneous" Folder, Box 38, Levi O. Leonard Railroad Collection, Special Collections, University of Iowa Libraries, Iowa City.

298. *New Haven Palladium,* 19 June 1854, p. 2 (quoted).

299. *Chicago Democratic Press,* 13 June 1854, p. 2.

300. *Cleveland Evening Express,* 5 July 1854, p. 2 (quoting *Weekly Minnesotian* of June 14).

301. *Poughkeepsie Eagle,* 1 July 1854, p. 2 (quoted).

302. *Boston Daily Advertiser,* 19 June 1854.

303. Excursion Register for *Golden Era, Galena,* and *Sparhawk,* Folder 667, Box 53, Farnam Family Papers Series I, Stirling Library, Yale; James A. Harrison, ed., *The Complete Works of Edgar Allan Poe,* Vol. 15 (New York: George D. Sproul, 1912), 91–93 (quote from p. 93); Epes Sargent, "On Lake Pepin," in *The Knickerbocker Gallery* (New York: Samuel Hueston, 1855), picture facing p. 97.

304. Excursion Register for *Golden Era, Galena,* and *Sparhawk,* Folder 667, Box 53, Farnam Family Papers Series I, Stirling Library, Yale; Biographical Dictionary entries for Bartlett, Botta, Fitch; Robert V. Hine, *Bartlett's West: Drawing the Mexican Boundary* (New Haven: Yale University Press, 1968), 82–83, 91–92; William Jarvis Letters, Finding Aid, Box 1, Collection 70425, Connecticut Historical Society; Miss Jarvis to Mr. Kensett, 4 June [1855], John F. Kensett Papers, 1830–1872, in New York State Library, Albany; Charles Tyng, *Before the Wind: The Memoir of an American Sea Captain, 1808–1833* (New York: Viking), xv–xvi.

305. Excursion Register for *Golden Era, Galena,* and *Sparhawk,* Folder 667, Box 53, Farnam Family Papers Series I, Stirling Library, Yale; Claire McGlinchee, *The First Decade of the Boston Museum* (Boston: Bruce Humphries, 1940), 22, 46–50, 56; Bluford Adams, *E Pluribus Barnum: The Great Showman and the Making of U.S. Popular Culture* (Minneapolis: University of Minnesota Press, 1997), 21, 77, 116, 118–19, 121, 131; Lewis F. Stearns, *Henry Boynton Smith* (Boston: Houghton Mifflin, 1892), 148–50; F. Nicklason, "The Early Career of Henry L. Dawes, 1816–1871," (Ph.D. diss., 1967), 67, 75.

306. Excursion Register for *Golden Era, Galena,* and *Sparhawk,* Folder 667, Box 53, Farnam Family Papers Series I, Stirling Library, Yale; Craig Gilborn, *Durant: The Fortunes and Woodland Camps of a Family in the Adirondacks* (Sylvan Beach, New York: North Country Books), Chapter 2; Howard B. Furer, *William Frederick Havemeyer: A Political Biography* (New York: The American Press), 93–101; *Memoir of Robert Bowne Minturn* (privately printed in New York: Anson D. F. Randolph & Company, 1871) [copy in New York State Library, Albany]; Morgan Dix, comp., *Memoirs of John Adams Dix,* Vol. 1 (New York: Harper & Brothers, 1883), 284-85; Bain, *Empire Express,* 151–53, 156.

307. *Boston Daily Advertiser,* 19 June 1854 (quoted); *Rome Daily Sentinel,* 15 June 1854, p. 2; *Chicago Democratic Press,* 13 June 1854, p. 2.

308. *Galena Daily Advertiser,* 13 June 1854, p. 2. There is some doubt about which boat Shepard Knapp was on; the *Cleveland Herald* (9 June 1854, p. 2) reports him on the *Galena.*

CHAPTER 5: "Rain and Speaking, Words and Water"

309. *New York Times,* 12 June 1854, p. 2; Catharine Maria Sedgwick to "Dearest Kate," 6 June 1854, in Sedgwick Letters, Massachusetts Historical Society, Boston. The boat in question was probably the *Galena,* where George Jones, reporter for the *Times,* was assigned, per the register.

310. Catharine M. Sedgwick to Kate, Bess, and William, 6 June 1854, in CMS Papers, Massachusetts Historical Society.

311. *Boston Daily Advertiser,* 19 June 1854 (Hale's Letter No. 11 written 7 June). For the breakfast, see *Springfield Republican,* 13 June 1854, p. 2.

312. *Boston Daily Advertiser,* 19 June 1854 (Charles Hale [Carolus] Letter dated 7 June); *Galena Daily Advertiser,* 7 June 1854, p. 2; *Northwestern Weekly Gazette* (Galena), 11 April 1854, p. 2 (describing the *War Eagle,* newly arrived in Galena).

313. *Galena Daily Advertiser,* 7 June 1854, p. 2; *Illinois Daily Journal,* 9 June 1854, p. 2. For the water being "quite high," see *Chicago Journal,* 7 June 1854, p. 2.

314. Timothy R. Mahoney, *River Towns in the Great West: The Structure of Provincial Urbanization in the American Midwest, 1820–1870* (New York: Cambridge University Press, 1990), 65.

315. Here and below, *Illinois Daily Journal,* 9 June 1854, p. 2.

316. *Chicago Journal,* 7 June 1854, p. 2; *Albany Evening Journal,* 10 June 1854, p. 2; *New York Weekly Mirror,* 24 June 1854, p. 2; *Buffalo Commercial Advertiser,* 17 June 1854, p. 1; Rebecca Bedell, *The Anatomy of Nature: Geology & American Landscape Painting, 1825–1875* (Princeton: Princeton University Press, 2001), 85–107.

317. Bedell, *Anatomy of Nature,* 86, 91–93; James T. Callow, *Kindred Spirits: Knickerbocker Writers and American Artists, 1807–1855* (Chapel Hill: University of North Carolina Press), 124–26.

318. *Boston Daily Advertiser,* 19 June 1854 (Hale's Letter No. 11); *Buffalo Commercial Advertiser,* 17 June 1854, p. 1; *Appleton's Cyclopaedia* entry on Kensett; John Munn Diary, Vol. 22, p. 150. According to Munn, this stop occurred about one mile south of Galena on the Fever River. For New Year's Day visiting in Davenport, Dubuque, and Galena, see Timothy R. Mahoney, *Provincial Lives: Middle-class Experience in the Antebellum Middle West* (New York: Cambridge University Press, 1999), 148–52.

319. *Boston Daily Advertiser,* 19 June 1854; *Buffalo Commercial Advertiser,* 17 June 1854, p. 1; *New York Weekly Mirror,* 24 June 1854, p. 2; *Galena Daily Advertiser,* 7 June 1854, p. 2; *New York Evening Post,* 13 June 1854, p. 2.

320. *Weekly Northwestern Gazette,* 6 June 1854, p. 1; *Buffalo Commercial Advertiser,* 17 June 1854, p. 1; *Boston Daily Advertiser,* 19 June 1854; *Poughkeepsie Eagle,* 8 July 1854, p. 2; *Springfield Republican,* 13 June 1854, p. 2; *Rome Daily Sentinel,* 10 June 1854, p. 2; *New Haven Morning Journal & Courier,* 20 June 1854, p. 2. The observer was Mrs. Elizabeth F. Ellet, in 1852; Petersen, *Steamboating on the Upper Mississippi,* 224.

321. Silliman journal, 6 June 1854, p. 204, microfilm edition, UW–Madison; *Boston Evening Transcript,* 16 June 1854, p. 2.

322. *Galena Daily Advertiser,* 6 June 1854, p. 2; Petersen, *Steamboating on the Upper Mississippi,* 210–14.

323. Augustus L. Chetlain, *Recollections of Seventy Years* (Galena: Gazette Publishing, 1899), 7, 45; Petersen, *Steamboating,* 215–26.

324. Sedgwick to Kate, Bess, William, 6 June 1854, Sedgwick Papers, microfilm, Massachusetts Historical Society; *Albany Evening Journal,* 10 June 1854, p. 2; *Illinois Daily Journal,* 9 June 1854, p. 2; *New York Times,* 12 June 1854, p. 2.

325. Mahoney, *River Towns,* 114, 126.

326. *Chicago Journal,* 7 June 1854, p. 2. For Galena's wholesale trade and its decline, see Chetlain, *Recollections,* 46; and Timothy R. Mahoney, *River Towns in the Great West: The Structure of Provincial Urbanization in the American Midwest, 1820–1870*

(New York: Cambridge University Press, 1990), 218–19, 264–65. The best account of the war over a western terminus for the Galena and Chicago Union Railroad (and northern terminus of the Illinois Central) is Mahoney, *Provincial Lives,* 232–33.

327. *Albany Morning Express,* 12 June 1854, p. 2.

328. *New York Times,* 12 June 1854, p. 2; *Albany Morning Express,* 19 June 1854, p. 2; John Munn Diary, Vol. 22, p. 152.

329. Here and above, see *New Haven Palladium,* 17 June 1854, p. 2.

330. *New York Times,* 14 June 1854, p. 2; *Boston Daily Advertiser,* 19 June 1854; *New York Times,* 14 June 1854, p. 2; Silliman, *Journal,* 6 June 1854, p. 203.

331. Charles Sedgwick to Lizzie (Elizabeth Sedgwick), 7 June 1854, Folder 12.8, Sedgwick IV Papers, Massachusetts Historical Society, Boston.

332. Silliman journal, 6 June 1854, p. 203; *New York Weekly Mirror,* 24 June 1854, p. 2; observations made by the author on a trip to the site, July 2002; *Cincinnati Gazette,* 22 June 1822, p. 2.

333. *New Haven Morning Journal & Courier,* 20 June 1854, p. 2 (quoted).

334. Chetlain, *Recollections,* 11–12; *Poughkeepsie Eagle,* 8 July 1854, p. 2; *New York Tribune,* 14 June 1854, p. 4; *New Haven Palladium,* 17 June 1854, p. 2.

335. *New York Tribune,* 14 June 1854, p. 4; *Galena Daily Advertiser,* 8 June 1854, p. 2; Silliman journal, 6 June 1854, p. 203–04, microfilm edition, UW–Madison.

336. *Poughkeepsie Eagle,* 8 July 1854, p. 2; *New York Tribune,* 14 June 1854, p. 4 (Charles Dana reported that Silliman spoke first, then Geer replied); *New Haven Palladium,* 17 June 1854, p. 2.

337. Mahoney, *Provincial Lives,* 113–67.

338. *Poughkeepsie Eagle,* 8 July 1854, p. 2; *New Haven Palladium,* 17 June 1854, p. 2; *New York Tribune,* 14 June 1854, p. 4; *New York Weekly Mirror,* 24 June 1854, p. 2.

339. *New York Tribune,* 14 June 1854, p. 4; *New York Evening Post,* 13 June 1854, p. 2; *Poughkeepsie Eagle,* 8 July 1854, p. 2; *New Haven Palladium,* 17 June 1854, p. 2. It is not clear whether Gear's and Silliman's speeches came before or after the lunch; most likely, some guests were down in the mine and some up eating and drinking—all at the same time.

340. *New York Tribune,* 14 June 1854, p. 4; *Poughkeepsie Eagle,* 8 July 1854, p. 2; Silliman journal, 6 June 1854, p. 204-05, microfilm ed.; *New Haven Palladium,* 17 June 1854, p. 2; McAdam, et al., eds., *History of the Bench and Bar of New York,* 440–41.

341. *Buffalo Commercial Advertiser,* 17 June 1854, p. 1 (reprinting a report from the *St. Louis Republican*).

342. *New York Times,* 14 June 1854, p. 2; *New Haven Morning Journal & Courier,* 20 June 1854, p. 2.

343. John Munn Diary, Vol. 22, p. 151, 152; *New York Observer* 32, no. 25 (22 June 1854), p. 198).

344. *Albany Evening Journal,* 10 June 1854, p. 2; *Springfield Republican,* 15 June 1854, p. 2; *New York Tribune,* 14 June 1854, p. 4; *Cincinnati Gazette,* 22 June 1854, p. 2; *Rome Daily Sentinel,* 10 June 1854, p. 2; *Illinois Daily Journal,* 9 June 1854, p. 2.

345. *New York Evening Post,* 13 June 1854, p. 2.

346. *Springfield Republican,* 15 June 1854, p. 2; *Galena Daily Advertiser,* 7 June 1854, p. 2; *New York Tribune,* 14 June 1854, p. 4; *Cincinnati Gazette,* 22 June 1854, p. 2.

347. Holt, *Rise and Fall of the American Whig Party,* 525, 527, 723–24, 923; *New York Tribune,* 14 June 1854, p. 4. In five years, Dana's boss Greeley would be championing Bates for the 1860 Republican presidential nomination; Potter, *Impending Crisis,* 420–21.

348. *Buffalo Commercial Advertiser,* 17 June 1854, p. 1 (quoting the *St. Louis Republican* correspondent).

349. *Springfield Republican,* 15 June 1854, p. 2 (quoted); *Galena Daily Advertiser,* 7 June 1854, p. 2 (reporting a 3:00 p.m. departure); *Illinois Daily Journal,* 14 June 1854, p. 2 (3:00 p.m. departure); *New York Times,* 14 June 1854, p. 2 (2:00 p.m.); Silliman, *Journal,* p. 205 (an impossibly early departure "about noon").

350. *Galena Daily Advertiser,* 7 June 1854, p. 2.

351. *Illinois Daily Journal,* 14 June 1854, p. 2; *Kingston (N.Y.) Journal,* 28 June 1854, p. 1 (quoted); U.S. Army Corps of Engineers, *The Middle and Upper Mississippi River: Ohio River to Minneapolis, 1935* (Washington, D.C.: GPO, 1935), Chart No. 37. Then or later, this slough was named Harris Slough.

352. Merrick, *Old Times on the Upper Mississippi,* 74–76; Hunter, *Steamboats on the Western Rivers,* 250–55.

353. *New York Times,* 14 June 1854, p. 2; William J. Petersen, *Iowa: The Rivers of Her Valleys* (Iowa City: State Historical Society of Iowa, 1941), 90–92; U.S. Army Corps of Engineers, *Middle and Upper Mississippi,* chart 37 and map.

354. *New Haven Palladium,* 17 June 1854, p. 2; *Poughkeepsie Eagle,* 8 July 1854, p. 2; *New Haven Morning Journal & Courier,* 20 June 1854, p. 2. It is unclear how far south of Dubuque they stopped.

355. *New Haven Palladium,* 17 June 1854, p. 2.

356. *Poughkeepsie Eagle,* 8 July 1854, p. 2 (the quote is Editor Platt's description of "the captain observing").

357. Petersen, *Rivers of Her Valleys,* 82-87; *Buffalo Commercial Advertiser,* 17 June 1854, p. 1 (quoting the *St. Louis Republican*); "Galena–Franklin" register, folder 667, box 53, Farnam Family Papers Series I, Yale; Callow, *Kindred Spirits,* 125, 126-28, 130-32; *Rome Daily Sentinel,* 10 June 1854, p. 2.

358. Bedell, *Anatomy of Nature,* 3-4, 5 (quoted), 91, 99–103.

359. *Poughkeepsie Eagle,* 8 July 1854, p. 2; *New York Times,* 14 June 1854, p. 2 (quoted); *New Haven Palladium,* 17 June 1854, p. 2; *New York Tribune,* 14 June 1854, p. 4; Silliman journal, p. 205; *Dubuque Miners' Express,* 13 June 1854, p. 2.

360. *Dubuque Miners' Express,* 1 and 5 and 13 June, all 1854, all p. 2.

361. *New Haven Daily Register,* 16 June 1854, p. 2 (quoted); *Cincinnati Gazette,* 22 June 1854, p. 2 (quoted); *New Haven Palladium,* 17 June 1854, p. 2 (quoted); *New York Times,* 14 June 1854, p. 2; *Dubuque Miners' Express,* 7 June 1854, p. 2; *New York Tribune,* 14 June 1854, p. 4; *New York Observer* 32, no. 25 (22 June 1854), p. 198, quoted; *New Haven Morning Journal & Courier,* 20 June 1854, p. 2 (quoted); Morton M. Rosenberg, *Iowa on the Eve of the Civil War: A Decade of Frontier Politics* (Norman: University of Oklahoma Press, 1972), 38, 86–87, 149.

362. *Dubuque Miners' Express,* 7 and 13 June 1854, both p. 2; *New York Evening Post,* 13 June 1854, p. 2 (quoted); Silliman journal, p. 205.

363. *Dubuque Miners' Express,* 7 and 13 June both 1854, both p. 2; *Cincinnati Gazette,* 22 June 1854, p. 2; Morgan Dix, comp., *Memoirs of John Adams Dix* (New York: Harper and Brothers, 1883), Vol. I, p. 271–77, and Vol. II, p. 264; entries on John A. Dix in *Dictionary of National Biography* and *Appleton's Cyclopaedia of American Biography.*

364. Robert F. Klein, *Dubuque: Frontier River City* (Dubuque: Research Center for Dubuque Area History, 1984), 76–78, 110–11, 118–19 (quote from footnote 4, p. 111); Mahoney, *Provincial Lives,* 220 (quoted), 232–33.

365. *Dubuque Miners' Express,* 7 June 1854, p. 2; *Cincinnati Gazette,* 22 June 1854, p. 2; *New York Times,* 14 June 1854, p. 2; *Chicago Journal,* 12 June 1854, p. 2; *Springfield Republican,* 15 June 1854, p. 2; *Buffalo Commercial Advertiser,* 17 June 1854, p. 1 (quoting the *St. Louis Republican*); *New Haven Palladium,* 17 June 1854, p. 2.

366. *Dubuque Miners' Express,* 13 June 1854, p. 2 (quoting Ray from

the *Galena Jeffersonian*).

367. *Dubuque Miners' Express,* 13 June 1854, p. 2. For the estimate of three hours at Galena, see Bacon's report in the *(N.Y.) Independent,* 22 June 1854 (Vol. 6, No. 290, p. 196).

368. *New Haven Palladium,* 17 June 1854, p. 2; *Illinois Daily Journal,* 14 June 1854, p. 2.

369. Jay [James] Monaghan, *The Man Who Elected Lincoln* (Indianapolis: Bobbs-Merrill, 1956), 13, 14–21, 38–40; Augustus L. Chetlain, *Recollections of Seventy Years* (Galena: Gazette Publishing Co., 1899), 56. Monaghan's style is imaginative, but he is persuasive on Ray's wandering editorial and political eye, and Chetlain partly confirms his account.

370. The *(N.Y.) Independent* 6, no. 290 (22 June 1854), p. 196 (quoted).

371. *Poughkeepsie Eagle,* 8 July 1854, p. 2 (quoted); *New Haven Palladium,* 17 June 1854, p. 2 (reporting they had been in Dubuque for "an hour and a half").

372. *Illinois Daily Journal,* 14 June 1854, p. 2.

373. John Munn Diary, Vol. 22, p. 149, 155 (quoted), 160.

374. *New Haven Palladium,* 17 June 1854, p. 2 (quoted); *Boston Daily Advertiser,* 19 June 1854; *New York Evening Post,* 13 June 1854, p. 2; *Chicago Journal,* 12 June 1854, p. 2 (quoted); *Illinois Daily Journal,* 14 June 1854, p. 2 (quoted); *New York Times,* 14 June 1854, p. 2; *Buffalo Commercial Advertiser,* 17 June 1854, p. 1 (quoting the *St. Louis Republican*).

375. *New Haven Palladium,* 17 June 1854, p. 2; *New York Evening Post,* 13 June 1854, p. 2.

376. *Illinois Daily Journal,* 14 June 1854, p. 2.

377. Sheffield to Farnam, 27 May 1854, in May 27–31 Folder, Box 10, Correspondence, Farnam Family Papers, Series I, Yale.

378. *Boston Daily Advertiser,* 19 June 1854; *New York Evening Post,* 13 June 1854, p. 2; *New York Times,* 8 June 1854, p. 2; *Cleveland Herald,* 14 June 1854, p. 2 (quoted).

379. *New York Times,* 14 June 1854, p. 2 (quoted); *Chicago Journal,* 12 June 1854, p. 2.

EXCURSUS: Benjamin Silliman and Antebellum American Science

380. Silliman journal, p. 202, 5 June 1854, microfilm edition, reel 4, UW–Madison.

381. Silliman journal, "Remarks on the great expedition to the W[est] & N[orth] W[est] & its results," p. 245–46, microfilm edition, roll 4.

382. Chandos Michael Brown, *Benjamin Silliman: A Life in the Young Republic* (Princeton: Princeton University Press, 1989), 3–4 (quoted), 5 (quoted), 6, 10–17.

383. Brown, *Life in the Young Republic,* 3–4, 5 (quoted).

384. Brown, *Life in the Young Republic,* 12, 25.

385. George P. Fisher, *Life of Benjamin Silliman, M.D., LL.D.: Late Professor of Chemistry, Mineralogy, and Geology in Yale College,* Vol. I (New York: Charles Scribner, 1866), 44 (quoted).

386. *New Haven Palladium,* 10 March 1854, p. 2 (giving Silliman's speech).

387. Brown, *Life in the Young Republic,* 69–70; Fisher, *Life of Benjamin Silliman,* Vol. I, 91–93 (quoted); Leonard G. Wilson, ed., *Benjamin Silliman and His Circle: Studies on the Influence of Benjamin Silliman on Science in America* (New York: Science History Publications, 1979), 2–6.

388. Brown, *A Life in the Young Republic,* 62–63. The Noyes tragedy is best described in Joy Day Buel and Richard Buel Jr., *The Way of Duty: A Woman and Her Family in Revolutionary America* (New York: W. W. Norton, 1984).

389. Perhaps the clearest analysis of this dimension to his work is found in John C. Greene, "Protestantism, Science, and American Enterprise: Benjamin Silliman's Moral Universe," in Wilson, ed.,

Benjamin Silliman and His Circle, 11–27. For Dwight's views, see Brown, *Life in the Young Republic,* 83–84.

390. Robert V. Bruce, *The Launching of Modern American Science 1846–1876* (New York: Alfred A. Knopf, 1987), 15 (quoted); Fulton and Thompson, *Benjamin Silliman,* 173–95, 196–203; Brown, *Life in the Young Republic,* xiii; Wilson, ed., *Benjamin Silliman and His Circle,* 1–10.

391. Quoted in Gloria Robinson, "Charles Upham Shepard," p. 87, in Wilson, ed., *Benjamin Silliman and His Circle.*

392. Silliman journal, p. 189, 28 May 1854, microfilm edition, reel 4, UW–Madison.

393. Bruce, *Launching of American Science,* 140–41; Wilson, ed., *Benjamin Silliman and His Circle,* 195; Fulton and Thomson, *Benjamin Silliman,* 239–40.

394. Robinson, "Charles Upham Shepard," 85–103 (quote from p. 86).

395. Robinson, "Charles Upham Shepard," 87–88; Fulton and Thomson, *Benjamin Silliman,* 158, 203; Bruce, *Launching of American Science,* 99–100.

396. Bruce, *Launching of American Science,* 100; entry in *Appleton's Cyclopedia of American Biography* on William C. Redfield.

397. Bruce, *Launching of American Science,* 94–106 (quotes from p. 96, 103).

398. Bruce, *Launching,* 64 (quoted), 69 (quoted). The best single treatment of the Baconian method and evangelicals like Silliman is Bozeman, *Protestants in an Age of Science.*

399. I have taken this simile from David Hackett Fisher, *Historians' Fallacies.* See also Brown, *Life in the Young Republic,* 203.

400. Benjamin Silliman, "Outline of the Course of Geological Lectures, Given in Yale College," 9–10 (quoted), printed at the back of Robert Bakewell, An *Introduction to Geology: Comprising the Elements of the Science . . . ,* 1st American ed. (New Haven: Hezekiah Howe, 1829).

401. George Bancroft, "Oration, Delivered before the New York Historical Society, at its Semi-Centennial Celebration, November 20, 1854," in Bancroft, *Occasional Addresses,* 481–82 (quoted).

402. Bruce, *Launching of American Science,* 121 (quoted).

403. Brown, *Life in the Young Republic,* 84.

404. Fisher, *Life of Benjamin Silliman,* Vol. I, p. 133 (quoted), 139.

405. Fisher, *Life of Benjamin Silliman,* Vol. I, p. 286-88; Fulton and Thomson, *Benjamin Silliman,* 136-39; Brown, *Life in the Young Republic,* 225.

406. I have reconstructed this interview based on Benjamin Silliman to Gardiner Spring, 24 July and 10 September, both 1854, Benjamin Silliman Papers, 1984 Addition, box 55, Yale; Fisher, *Life of Benjamin Silliman,* Vol. II, p. 147–50 (reprinting these two letters). For Silliman's acceptance of the "day-age" theory, see Greene, "Protestantism, Science and American Enterprise," p. 16–17.

407. Fisher, *Life of Benjamin Silliman,* Vol. II, p. 144 (quoting Silliman to Hitchcock, 17 March 1837).

408. Silliman to Spring, 24 July 1854, quoted in Fisher, *Life of Benjamin Silliman,* Vol. II, p. 148.

409. Fisher, *Life of Benjamin Silliman,* Vol. II, p. 149 (Fisher's interpretation is that Silliman's reference in his September 10 letter to Spring refers to the "Outline"); Silliman, "Outline," 7 (quoted), 126 (quoted), an appendix to Bakewell, *Introduction to Geology,* 1st American ed. (1829).

410. Fisher, *Life of Benjamin Silliman,* Vol. II, p. 372; Fulton and Thomson, *Benjamin Silliman,* 173–79. The term *"philosophy of geology"* is Silliman's own, from his "Outline of the Course of Geological Lectures," p. 3, in Bakewell, *Introduction,* 1st American ed. (1829).

411. Laura Hadley Moseley, ed., *Diary (1843–1852) of James Hadley*

Tutor and Professor of Greek in Yale College, 1845–1872 (New Haven: Yale University Press), 97.

412. Mosely, ed., *Diary of James Hadley,* 97-98. For an analysis of how Yale scholars who came after Silliman, including James Dwight Dana, used German idealism in their reconciliation of science and religion, see Stevenson, *Scholarly Means to Evangelical Ends,* 67–77.

413. Bruce, *Launching of American Science,* 123-24. The *Vestiges* may have been "the speculations" mentioned by Spring during their conversation onboard the *War Eagle;* in his July 24 letter to Spring, Silliman writes, "I have no sympathy with the speculations to which you then alluded."

CHAPTER 6: "Bluffs Like Gigantic Sentinels"

414. *New York Evening Post,* 13 June 1854, p. 2 (quoted); *New York Times,* 14 June 1854, p. 2 (quoted).

415. *New York Times,* 14 June 1854, p. 2.

416. *New York Times,* 14 June 1854, p. 2 (quoted).

417. *Rome Daily Sentinel,* 20 June 1854, p. 2 (quoted); Clement Eaton, *Jefferson Davis* (New York: Free Press, 1977), 16–18, 21–22, 82.

418. Peter Lawrence Scanlan, *Prairie du Chien: French, British, American* (Menasha, Wisconsin: George Banta Publishing Company, 1937), 137–41.

419. *Rome Daily Sentinel,* 20 June 1854, p. 2 (quoted).

420. *New Haven Palladium,* 17 June 1854, p. 2.

421. *New York Times,* 14 June 1854, p. 2; John Munn Diary, Vol. 22, p. 162 (quoted). A State Historical Society of Wisconsin Web site has Black Hawk and General Atkinson's accounts, but the latter doesn't mention killing women or children; www.wisconsinhistory.org/oss/lessons/secondary/bh_badaxe.htm.

422. Here and below, see *Rome Daily Sentinel,* 15 June 1854, p. 2; *Poughkeepsie Eagle,* 8 July 1854, p. 2; *Illinois State Journal,* 14 June 1854, p. 2; *Cincinnati Gazette,* 22 June 1854, p. 2; *New York Evening Post,* 13 June 1854, p. 2; *New Haven Palladium,* 17 June 1854, p. 2. Editors' estimates of the number varied from a dozen to forty; I take two dozen as a reasonable compromise. Babcock reported this encounter as occurring at 9:00 a.m., while Moore reported it "[a]bout noon"; apart from a misprint or other error, the best explanation would be that Moore's boat trailed Babcock's by several hours.

423. *Illinois State Journal,* 14 June 1854, p. 2 (quoted); *New Haven Morning Journal & Courier,* 19 June 1854, p. 2 (quoted). Woodward's comments applied to the entire trip, not just to the Wednesday discussions.

424. Silliman journal, Wednesday June 7, p. 206; *Poughkeepsie Eagle,* 8 July 1854, p. 2.

425. Charles Sedgwick to Lizzie, 7 June 1854, box 12, folder 12.8, Sedgwick IV Papers, Massachusetts Historical Society.

426. *Boston Daily Advertiser,* Letter No. 11, 19 June 1854, p. 2. For the concept of a male "frolic" I am indebted to Mahoney, *Provincial Lives,* 98–103, 249–51.

427. *Cleveland Herald,* 15 June 1854, p. 2. This report was written on June 7, but it is possible the conversation occurred on June 6. The two Ottawa men were Theophilus L. Dickey and William Reddick.

428. *Rome Daily Sentinel,* 20 June 1854, p. 2.

429. *New York Times,* 14 June 1854, p. 2.

430. Rev. Spencer Carr, "A Brief Sketch of La Crosse, Wisc'n, Showing the Location of the Place" (La Crosse: W. C. Rogers Printer, 1854), pamphlet reprinted by La Crosse County Historical Society (1977), 5–10; *Springfield Republican,* 15 June 1854, p. 2 ("large wooden cross"); Sanford and Hirshheimer, *History of La Crosse,* 9, 51–56, 136–37; Benjamin F. Bryant, ed., *Memoirs of La Crosse County* (Madison: Western Historical Association, 1907), 34–38 (on p. 35, quoting the jest from a *New York Tribune* report of 1853).

431. *New York Times,* 14 June 1854, p. 2; *Chicago Daily Democratic Press,* 13 June 1854, p. 2; *Rock Island Republican,* 27 June 1854, p. 2 (quoted, on the willow levee); *Kingston (N.Y.) Journal,* 12 July 1854, p. 1 (quoted).

432. This description is a composite of several accounts, as given in Albert H. Sanford and H. J. Hirshheimer, *A History of La Crosse, Wisconsin 1841–1900* (La Crosse: La Crosse County Historical Society, 1951), 32–38; and *La Crosse Democrat,* 25 April 1854, p. 2.

433. *Chicago Daily Democratic Press,* 13 June 1854, p. 2 (quoted).

434. *New York Times,* 14 June 1854, p. 2.

435. *New York Tribune,* 14 June 1854, p. 4; Carr, "Brief Sketch," p. 6.

436. *New York Tribune,* 23 June (p. 5) and 12 July (p. 7), both 1854.

437. Register of Steamboat Passengers, Grand Excursion, Farnam Papers; Sanford and Hirshheimer, *History of La Crosse,* 69, 155; La Crosse Democrat, 25 April (p. 2) and 1 May (p. 3), both 1854; Carr, "Brief Sketch," p. 21, 23.

438. *New Haven Palladium,* 16 June 1854, p. 2.

439. *Kingston (N.Y.) Journal,* 12 July 1854, p. 1 (quoted).

440. Here and below, this composite account is taken from the following sources: *Boston Evening Transcript,* 14 June 1854, p. 2; *Boston Daily Advertiser,* 29 June 1854; *New York Tribune,* 14 June 1854, p. 4; *New York Weekly Mirror,* 1 July 1854, p. 2 (quoting the *Journal of Commerce*); *Chicago Tribune,* 13 June 1854, p. 2; and *New York Evening Post,* 13 June 1854, p. 2. For mock courts in general, see Mahoney, *Provincial Lives,* 209-11. Most likely, this mock trial was held at intervals (between stops and meals) during the day; it may have begun on June 6.

441. *Boston Daily Advertiser,* 29 June 1854.

442. *Rome Daily Sentinel,* 15 June 1854, p. 2; Sedgwick to Lizzie, 7 June 1854, Sedgwick IV Papers.

443. Here and below, *Rome Daily Sentinel,* 15 June 1854, p. 2. Reverend Dr. Samuel Osgood of Springfield, Massachusetts, also spoke (it is unclear what toast he responded to); *New York Times,* 14 June 1854, p. 2.

444. Elbert B. Smith, *Francis Preston Blair* (New York: Free Press, 1980); William E. Parrish, *Frank Blair: Lincoln's Conservative* (Columbia: University of Missouri Press, 1998), 37–38, 48, 54.

445. The sources for his speech are *Rome Daily Sentinel,* 15 June 1854, p. 2 and *New York Evening Post,* 19 June 1854, p. 2 (quoting *Galena Jeffersonian* of June 15); the source for Benton's battle is Smith, *Francis Preston Blair,* 216, and Holt, *American Whig Party,* 850–51.

446. Smith, *Francis Preston Blair,* 214 (quoted), 215 (quoted), 216; Parrish, *Frank Blair,* 11, 14, 15–16, 54–55. Not all lists of excursionists show both Blairs; one that does is *St. Paul Daily Times,* 9 June 1854, p. 2; and Smith's book is clear on the presence of both.

447. *Rome Daily Sentinel,* 15 June 1854, p. 2.

448. *Rome Daily Sentinel,* 15 June 1854, p. 2; Sedgwick to Kate, Bess & William, 6 June 1854 [but with added sheets clearly written after that], CMS Papers, microfilm, Massachusetts Historical Society.

449. *New York Recorder,* 21 June 1854, p. 4 (quoted).

450. *New Haven Palladium,* 16 June 1854, p. 2; *Albany Evening Journal,* 13 June 1854, p. 2.

451. *New Haven Palladium,* 16 June 1854, p. 2.

452. *New Haven Palladium,* 16 June 1854, p. 2; *Boston Daily Advertiser,* 15 June 1854, p. 2; *New Haven Daily Register,* 16 June 1854, p. 2; John Munn Diary, Vol. 22, p. 163–64 (quoted). Estimates of the numbers varied from four or five to seven or

453. *Boston Daily Advertiser,* 15 June 1854, p. 2.

454. *New Haven Palladium,* 16 June 1854, p. 2. For Williams, see D. Hamilton Hurd, comp., *History of New London County, Connecticut,* Vol. 2, p. 682, 701–02.

455. *New Haven Palladium,* 16 June 1854, p. 2.

456. *Chicago Daily Democratic Press,* 13 June 1854, p. 2; *Boston Daily Advertiser,* 15 June 1854, p. 2.

457. *New York Observer* 32, no. 25 (22 June 1854), p. 198 (quoted).

458. *New York Observer* 32, no.26 (29 June 1854), p. 206 (quoted); *Chicago Daily Democratic Press,* 13 June 1854, p. 2; *New Haven Daily Register,* 16 June 1854, p. 2; *Albany Evening Journal,* 13 June 1854, p. 2.

459. Jeffrey O. Phelps to "Wife," 7 June 1854, Phelps Papers, Simsbury Historical Society.

460. Here and below is a composite account based on different versions in the following newspapers: *New Haven Palladium,* 16 June 1854, p. 2; *Albany Evening Journal,* 13 June 1854, p. 2; *Buffalo Commercial Advertiser,* 17 June 1854, p. 1; *New York Times,* 14 June 1854, p. 2; *Illinois State Journal,* 15 June 1854, p. 2; and *New Haven Daily Register,* 16 June 1854, p. 2.

461. *Galena Daily Advertiser,* 13 June 1854, p. 2; Silliman journal, 7 June 1854, p. 206.

462. *New Haven Palladium,* 16 June 1854, p. 2; *Galena Daily Advertiser,* 13 June 1854, p. 2; Silliman journal, June 7, p. 206.

463. Silliman's account of this lecture is in his journal, Wednesday June 7 [1854], p. 206-07, microfilm edition, UW–Madison.

464. Here and below, this composite account is based on the following sources: *Chicago Journal,* 13 June 1854, p. 2; *Chicago Daily Democratic Press,* 13 June 1854, p. 2; *Rock Island Republican,* 27 June 1854, p. 2 (quoting and paraphrasing the *Democratic Press*); *Albany Evening Journal,* 15 June 1854, p. 2; and *New York Times,* 14 June 1854, p. 2. The sources vary on whether this place was Mount Vernon, Winona, or Minneowah; I choose the former based on a description of Mount Vernon in Franklin Curtiss-Wedge, ed., *History of Winona County, Minnesota* (1913), 206–07. The journal's statement that this occurred at 6:00 a.m. is impossible to credit; just what time it occurred is impossible to determine. Some editors are quoting and others paraphrasing Kennedy. For Kennedy's insistence that he did not intend to mock Fillmore, see Kennedy to Fillmore, 27 June 1854, in Fillmore Papers, microfilm edition, roll 42, SHSW.

465. John Munn Diary, Vol. 22, p. 165 (quoted).

466. John Munn Diary, Vol. 22, p. 164–65 (quoted).

467. John Munn Diary, Vol. 22, p. 167 (quoted), 168.

468. *Poughkeepsie Eagle,* 8 July 1854, p. 2; Silliman journal, Wednesday June 7, p. 207.

469. *New York Times,* 14 June 1854, p. 2; *Albany Morning Express,* 19 June 1854, p. 2.

470. *Poughkeepsie Eagle,* 8 July 1854, p. 2; *New York Times,* 14 June 1854, p. 2; *Albany Morning Express,* 19 June 1854, p. 2.

471. Silliman journal, Wednesday June 7, p. 207, microfilm edition, Silliman Papers.

472. *Chicago Tribune,* 13 June 1854, p. 2; *Boston Daily Advertiser,* 15 June 1854, p. 2.

473. *New Haven Palladium,* 16 June 1854, p. 2; *Chicago Tribune,* 13 June 1854, p. 2.

474. *New York Times,* 14 June 1854, p. 2.

475. John Munn Diary, Vol. 22, p. 168 (quoted); Mason A. Green, Springfield, 1636-1886, 490; Mason A. Green, *Springfield Memories: Odds and Ends of Anecdote and Early Doings* (Springfield: Whitney & Adams, 1876), 76–79.

EXCURSUS: George Bancroft and Antebellum American Historians

476. Joseph Sheffield to George Bancroft, 22 May 1854, Bancroft Papers, 1853–1854 box, Massachusetts Historical Society, Boston; George Bancroft, *History of the United States from the Discovery of the American Continent,* Vol. VI (Boston: Little, Brown and Company, 1854), x. Sheffield refers to "your Nephew (I believe it is) or a cousin"—but stepson William Bliss was the only relative to accompany Bancroft on the trip.

477. Lillian Handlin, *George Bancroft: the Intellectual as Democrat* (New York: Harper and Row, 1984), 97, 121, 164, 168, 170, 182–83, 245–46, 250.

478. George Bancroft to Charles Butler, 29 December 1856, "Addition: Correspondence (original) 1854–1929, No date" folder, box 5, Charles Butler Papers, Library of Congress. Although this letter was written two years after the excursion, it shows Bancroft's keen interest in investments, and that was present in 1854.

479. See the frontispiece portrait ("George Bancroft about 1854") in M. A. DeWolfe Howe, *The Life and Letters of George Bancroft,* Vol. II (New York: Charles Scribner's Sons, 1908).

480. Bancroft to "My ever dear wife," 30 May and 4 June, both 1854; and Bancroft to "Dear Wife," [31] May 1854, all in reel 4, microfilm edition, Bancroft Papers, Collection #1262, Cornell University Library.

481. Handlin, *Intellectual as Democrat,* 5, 8–10, 17, 18; Russel B. Nye, *George Bancroft: Brahmin Rebel* (New York: Alfred A. Knopf, 1945), 18–19, 28–29.

482. Nye, *Brahmin Rebel,* 32, 33–57; Handlin, *Intellectual as Democrat,* 53–80.

483. Nye, *Brahmin Rebel,* 58.

484. Nye, *Brahmin Rebel,* 96–98, 102–03; Handlin, *Intellectual as Democrat,* 126–29; Robert H. Canary, *George Bancroft* (New York: Twayne, 1974), "Chronology" before p. 1; Charles T. Congdon, *Reminiscences of a Journalist* (Boston: James R. Osgood and Company, 1880), 63 (quoted).

485. Alexis de Tocqueville, *Democracy in America,* "Some Characteristics of Historians in Democratic Times" (page numbers vary in different translations and editions).

486. Nye, *Brahmin Rebel,* 167–68, 170.

487. Nye, *Brahmin Rebel,* 190–91; Bancroft, *History,* Vol. VI, p. iii-ix; Handlin, *Intellectual as Democrat,* 235.

488. Peter Novick, *That Noble Dream: The "Objectivity Question" and the American Historical Profession* (New York: Cambridge University Press, 1988), 24–25, 34–37; Nye, Brahmin Rebel, 99–100.

489. Bancroft, *History,* Vol. VI, p. x. See also Vitzthum, *The American Compromise,* 34.

490. Nye, *Brahmin Rebel,* 185, 186 (quoted), 187 (quoted); Hildreth quoted in Ernst Breisach, *Historiography: Ancient, Medieval, & Modern* (Chicago: University of Chicago Press, 1983), 258.

491. Nye, *Brahmin Rebel,* 187–88.

492. Novick, *That Noble Dream,* 45–46.

493. Vitzthum, *American Compromise,* 25 (quoted), 26, 28–29; Noble, *Historians Against History,* 19–23, 30–31; Winger, *Romantic Cultural Politics,* 62–70.

494. Charles C. Little & James Brown to George Bancroft, 25 May 1854; and Richard Bentley to George Bancroft, 26 May 1854, both on reel 4, Bancroft Papers, Cornell.

495. Bancroft to C. C. Little and James Brown, 30 May 1854, reel 4, Bancroft Papers, Cornell.

496. Bancroft to "My ever dear wife," 31 May and 4 June, both 1854, reel 4, Bancroft Papers, Cornell.

497. George Bancroft, *History of the United States, from the Discovery of the American Continent,* Vol. VI (Boston:

Little, Brown and Company, 1854), 33–34 (quoted); Bancroft, *History*, Vol. V, 12th ed. (Boston: Little, Brown, 1858), 163–64.

498. Richard C. Vitzthum, *The American Compromise: Theme and Method in the Histories of Bancroft, Parkman, and Adams* (Norman: University of Oklahoma Press, 1974), 15–17, 29, 37; Nye, *Brahmin Rebel*, 100–01.

499. Bancroft, *History of the United States, Vol. VI*, p. 471–72 (quoted).

500. Nye, *Brahmin Rebel*, 119–20; Handlin, *Intellectual as Democrat*, 246.

501. Smith, *Francis Preston Blair*, 175–76.

502. Handlin, *Intellectual as Democrat*, 262–63; Stewart Winger, *Lincoln, Religion, and Romantic Cultural Politics* (DeKalb: Northern Illinois University Press, 2003), 116, 146–48; David W. Noble, *Historians Against History: The Frontier Thesis and the National Covenant in American Historical Writing Since 1830* (Minneapolis: University of Minnesota Press, 1965), 32–36.

503. Bancroft, *History of the United States, from the Discovery of the American Continent*, Vol. V (Boston: Little, Brown and Company, 1852), 285–94.

504. Nye, *Brahmin Rebel*, 105.

505. Winger, *Romantic Cultural Politics*, 76–77.

506. Bancroft, *Literary and Historical Miscellanies*, 516.

507. Bancroft, *Literary and Historical Miscellanies*, 491, 492-93 (quoted).

508. Bancroft, "The Necessity, the Reality, and the Promise of the Progress of the Human Race," in *Literary and Historical Miscellanies*, 481–517 (quotes from p. 483, 493, 498).

509. For Agassiz the polygenist, see Louis Menand, *The Metaphysical Club: A Story of Ideas in America* (New York: Farrar, Straus and Giroux, 2001), 104–06.

510. Bancroft, *Literary and Historical Miscellanies*, 506–08 (quoted), 511. The quote about Christianity comes from Bancroft, *History*, Vol. IV, p. 7.

511. Bancroft, *Literary and Historical Miscellanies*, 513 (quoted), 515 (quoted), 517 (quoted).

512. George Bancroft to "My ever dear Wife," 9 June 1854, "Photostats—Geo. Bancroft to wife 1854-55" folder, box 5, Bancroft-Bliss Family Papers, Library of Congress.

513. Bancroft to "My ever dear wife," 11 June 1854, reel 4, Bancroft Papers, Cornell.

CHAPTER 7: "The Greatest Epoch That Has Ever Dawned"

514. *New York Weekly Mirror*, 24 June 1854, p. 2 (quoted); *Boston Daily Advertiser*, 15 June 1854; *New York Times*, 14 June 1854, p. 2 (quoted); *Poughkeepsie Eagle*, 8 July 1854, p. 2 (quoted); *Salem Gazette*, 16 June 1854, p. 2.

515. *New York Times*, 14 June 1854, p. 2 (quoted); William Watts Folwell, *A History of Minnesota*, Vol. I, 1956 reprint edition (St. Paul: Minnesota Historical Society, 1956), 353; Gary Clayton Anderson, *Little Crow: Spokesman for the Sioux* (St. Paul: Minnesota Historical Society Press, 1986), 67–75.

516. *Cincinnati Gazette*, 22 June 1854, p. 2 (quoted); *New York Times*, 14 June 1854, p. 2 (confirming Schouler's account). For the identification of these birds as cliff swallows, I am indebted to naturalist David Berg, phone conversation with the author, April 28, 2003.

517. *Minnesotian*, 9 June 1854, p. 3; *St. Paul Daily Times*, 9 June 1854, p. 2; *Minnesota Pioneer*, 9 June 1854, p. 2; Silliman journal, 8 June Thursday, p. 207, microfilm edition, UW-Madison; *New York Recorder*, 21 June 1854, p. 4 (quoted). Some accounts say 9:00 a.m., but the majority give the time as close to 8:00 a.m.

518. *Minnesotian*, 9 June 1854, p. 3; *St. Paul Daily Times*, 9 June 1854, p. 2; *Minnesota Pioneer*, 9 June 1854, p. 2; *Albany Evening Journal*, 15 June 1854, p. 2 (quoted); *New Haven Daily Register*, 20 June 1854, p. 2.

519. *Minnesota Democrat* (St. Paul), 14 June 1854, p. 2.

520. *Boston Daily Journal*, 20 June 1854 (quoted); *Minnesota Democrat*, 14 June 1854, p. 2; *Illinois State Journal*, 14 June 1854, p. 2.

521. *Chicago Journal*, 13 June 1854, p. 2 (quoted); *New York Times*, 14 June 1854, p. 2 (quoted, both "W" and "Excelsior"); *Chicago Daily Tribune*, 13 June 1854, p. 2; *New York Tribune*, 14 June 1854, p. 4; *St. Anthony Express*, 8 July 1854, p. 2 (quoting Bogart's report ["Sentinel"] in the *New York Courier & Enquirer* of June 14); *Illinois State Journal*, 15 June 1854, p. 2 (quoted); J. Fletcher Williams, *A History of the City of Saint Paul to 1875*, Borealis reprint edition (St. Paul: Minnesota Historical Society Press, 1983), 349.

522. *Chicago Daily Tribune*, 13 June 1854, p. 2 (quoted); *Minnesota Democrat*, 14 June 1854, p. 2 (quoted); *Rome Daily Sentinel*, 20 June 1854, p. 2; *Minnesota Weekly Times*, 20 June 1854, p. 2; *Boston Daily Journal*, 20 June 1854.

523. *Kingston (N.Y.) Journal*, 5 July 1854, p. 1 (quoted).

524. Ray's report in the *Galena Jeffersonian* quoted in *Minnesota Weekly Times*, 20 June 1854, p. 2. Gorman and Ramsey's presence is recorded in *New York Tribune*, 14 June 1854, p. 4.

525. *New York Weekly Mirror*, 24 June 1854, p. 2.

526. *Albany Evening Journal*, 15 June 1854, p. 2 (quoting Bogart in *New York Courier & Enquirer*); *St. Anthony Express*, 8 July 1854, p. 2 (a more complete quote from Bogart's report); *Hartford Courant*, 20 June 1854, p. 2; *Chicago Tribune*, 13 June 1854, p. 2 (reprinting the City Council resolutions); (St. Paul) *Minnesotian*, 9 June 1854, p. 3 (reprinting the resolutions).

527. *Illinois State Journal*, 14 June 1854, p. 2 (quoted); *New York Weekly Mirror*, 24 June 1854, p. 2; *Rome Daily Sentinel*, 20 June 1854, p. 2 (quoted); *St. Anthony Express*, 3 June 1854, p. 2; *Cincinnati Gazette*, 22 June 1854, p. 2; *Poughkeepsie Eagle*, 8 July 1854, p. 2; *Buffalo Commercial Advertiser*, 17 June 1854, p. 1.

528. Here and below, see *New Haven Palladium*, 19 June 1854, p. 2.

529. *New York Tribune*, 14 June 1854, p. 4; Theodore C. Blegen, *Minnesota: A History of the State*, 1975 edition (Minneapolis: University of Minnesota Press, 1975), 181; William G. Le Duc, *Recollections of a Civil War Quartermaster*, 42-53.

530. *New York Evening Post*, 15 June 1854, p. 1.

531. *Cleveland Herald*, 19 June 1854, p. 2.

532. *Poughkeepsie Eagle*, 8 July 1854, p. 2; *Boston Daily Advertiser*, 15 June 1854.

533. *New York Weekly Mirror*, 24 June 1854, p. 2; *Minnesota Historical Society Collections*, Vol. 14, p. 243; clipping from *New York Evening Mirror*, 16 February 1855, in box 2, Abby Abbe Fuller and Family Papers, MHS, St. Paul. Jane Gay Fuller later published *The Grahams* (New York: M. W. Dodd, 1864) and *Bending Willow: A Tale of Missionary Life in the Northwest* (New York: R. Carter, 1872), as well as many magazine articles and other works.

534. *St. Paul Daily Times*, 10 June 1854, p. 2 (quoted); *Chicago Daily Tribune*, 13 June 1854, p. 2 (quoted).

535. *Poughkeepsie Eagle*, 8 July 1854, p. 2.

536. *Minnesota Weekly Times*, 20 June 1854, p. 2 (quoting the *Galena Jeffersonian* of June 13).

537. John Munn Diary, Vol. 22, p. 172-73, 175 (quoted).

538. *Buffalo Commercial Advertiser*, 17 June 1854, p. 1; *New York Evening Post*, 15 June 1854, p. 1; *Chicago Daily Tribune*, 13 June 1854, p. 2; *Cincinnati Gazette*, 22 June 1854, p. 2; *Rome Daily Sentinel*, 20 June 1854, p. 2; *Chicago Journal*, 13 June 1854, p. 2.

539. *Buffalo Express,* 14 June 1854, p. 2; *New York Tribune,* 14 June 1854, p. 4.

540. *Illinois State Journal,* 15 June 1854, p. 2; *Chicago Daily Tribune,* 13 June 1854, p. 2.

541. *New York Tribune,* 14 June 1854, p. 4.

542. *Cincinnati Gazette,* 22 June 1854, p. 2 (quoted).

543. *Cincinnati Gazette,* 22 June 1854, p. 2 (quoted); *St. Anthony Express,* 8 July 1854, p. 2 (quoting the *New York Courier & Enquirer* of June 14); *Albany Evening Journal,* 13 June 1854, p. 2; *Rome Daily Sentinel,* 20 June 1854, p. 2. A similar plow was at work on the west side of the river; John Munn Diary, Vol. 22, p. 177–78.

544. *Cincinnati Gazette,* 22 June 1854, p. 2.

545. *Illinois State Journal,* 15 June 1854, p. 2 (quoted).

546. *Davenport Gazette,* 6 July 1854, p. 1 (quoting the Galena Jeffersonian); *New Haven Palladium,* 19 June 1854, p. 2. Babcock confirms the accident, but his version is less dramatic: he does not mention Dante's *Inferno,* and Bancroft fell because he "lost his balance" when digging in his coat pocket. The two accounts are not necessarily contradictory: reading the book and the rut in the road could have contributed to his loss of balance.

547. *New Haven Palladium,* 19 June 1854, p. 2; Harriet E. Bishop, *Floral Home; or, First Years of Minnesota* (New York: Sheldon, Blakeman and Company, 1857), 153; Lucy Leavenworth Wilder Morris, ed., *Old Rail Fence Corners,* reprint edition (St. Paul: Minnesota Historical Society Press, 1976), 183 (placing it on University hill); "Description of Cheever House" by Kate Hunt, typescript, collection P1189-13, MHS, St. Paul; *Chicago Daily Tribune,* 13 June 1854, p. 2 (quoted); *Boston Daily Advertiser,* 15 June 1854; Francis Wilkinson, "Here and There in America: Adventures and Observations of a Craven Lad," *Minnesota History,* 27 (December 1946), p. 287.

548. *Chicago Daily Tribune,* 13 June 1854, p. 2; *New Haven Daily Register,* 20 June 1854, p. 2; *Springfield Republican,* 15 June 1854, p. 2; *Minnesota Weekly Times,* 20 June 1854, p. 2 (quoting *Galena Jeffersonian* of June 13); John Munn Diary, Vol. 22, p. 176-77.

549. Blegen, *Minnesota: A History,* 48–49; *New York Times,* 17 June 1854, p. 2.

550. *Chicago Daily Tribune,* 13 June 1854, p. 2 (quoted). See also Jane Fuller's lament about man's "utilitarian finger" marring St. Anthony Falls; *New York Weekly Mirror,* 3 June 1854, p. 3.

551. *Northwestern Democrat* (St. Anthony), 14 June 1854, p. 2; *Springfield Republican,* 15 June 1854, p. 2; *Cincinnati Gazette,* 22 June 1854, p. 2; *New Haven Palladium,* 19 June 1854, p. 2.

552. *New York Weekly Mirror,* 24 June 1854, p. 2. See also *Springfield Republican,* 15 June 1854, p. 2. There is a map of the Falls district in Folwell, *Minnesota,* Vol. III, p. 345.

553. Silliman journal, 8 June 1854, p. 209, microfilm edition, UW-Madison.

554. *New York Commercial Advertiser,* 13 June 1854, p. 2 (quoted); *Chicago Daily Tribune,* 13 June 1854, p. 2; *New Haven Daily Register,* 24 June 1854, p. 2 (quoted); *New Haven Palladium,* 19 June 1854, p. 2. These footbridges probably only went from the east bank to Nicollet Island.

555. Silliman journal, 8 June 1854, p. 209-10, microfilm edition, UW-Madison.

556. *New Haven Palladium,* 19 June 1854, p. 2 (quoted).

557. *New York Times,* 17 June 1854, p. 2; *St. Anthony Express,* 8 July 1854, p. 2 (quoting the *New York Courier & Enquirer* of June 14); *Albany Evening Journal,* 13 and 14 June 1854, both p. 2; *Chicago Journal,* 13 June 1854, p. 2 (quoting Hudson); *Chicago Daily Tribune,* 13 June 1854, p. 2; *Boston Daily Advertiser,* 15 June 1854.

558. *New York Times,* 17 June 1854, p. 2; *Chicago Tribune,* 13 June 1854, p. 2; *Albany Evening Journal,* 14 June 1854, p. 2 (giving what is clearly Johnson's own text of the speech).

559. *Springfield Republican,* 15 June 1854, p. 2 (quoted); *Buffalo Commercial Advertiser,* 17 June 1854, p. 1 (quoted); *Boston Daily Advertiser,* 15 June 1854. See also *Chicago Journal,* 13 June 1854, p. 2; *Minnesota Weekly Times,* 20 June 1854, p. 2 (quoting *Galena Jeffersonian* of June 13). Longfellow's *Song of Hiawatha* was not published until 1855, so the excursionists were unfamiliar with the tale of Hiawatha and Minnehaha. Most likely whites suggested the name Minnehaha Falls, and not the Dakota; Warren Upham, *Minnesota Geographic Names: Their Origin and Historic Significance,* reprint edition (St. Paul: Minnesota Historical Society, 1969), 230–31.

560. *Rome Daily Sentinel,* 23 June 1854, p. 2 (quoted); and *Minnesota Weekly Times,* 20 June 1854, p. 2—both quoting the *Galena Jeffersonian.*

561. Here and below, *Albany Evening Journal,* 14 June 1854, p. 2.

562. *Hartford Courant,* 20 June 1854, p. 2; *New York Recorder,* 21 June 1854, p. 4; Catharine Sedgwick to K. S. Minot, 11 June 1854, in Dewey, ed., *Life and Letters,* 356; Sedgwick, "Great Excursion to the Falls of St. Anthony," p. 322.

563. Zylpha S. Morton, "Harriet Bishop, Frontier Teacher," *Minnesota History,* Vol. 28, No. 2 (June 1947), 132–41; Winifred D. Wandersee Bolin, "Harriet E. Bishop: Moralist and Reformer," in *Women of Minnesota,* 7–19; Harriet E. Bishop, *Floral Home,* 52-55, 56, 83-89; Foster, *Sedgwick,* 114-15.

564. *New York Recorder,* 21 June 1854, p. 4 (quoted).

565. Sedgwick to Mrs. K.S. Minot, in Dewey, ed., *Life and Letters,* 356 (quoted); Sedgwick, "Great Excursion," 322 (quoted).

566. *Poughkeepsie Eagle,* 15 July 1854, p. 2; Folwell, *History of Minnesota,* Vol. I, picture of Capitol opposite page 382; "Specifications of the Capitol Building at St. Paul Minnesota," in Box 113.C.2.2 F), Commissioner of Public Buildings Records, Territorial Records, State Archives, MHS, St. Paul.

567. *Chicago Daily Tribune,* 13 June 1854, p. 2.

568. *Chicago Daily Tribune,* 13 June 1854, p. 2 (quoted). It appears that he made this tour after going to St. Anthony Falls, but it may have been before.

569. George S. Hage, *Newspapers on the Minnesota Frontier 1849–1860* (St. Paul: Minnesota Historical Society, 1967), 46–49, 60–62.

570. *Chicago Daily Tribune,* 13 June 1854, p. 2.

571. *Buffalo Express,* 14 June 1854, p. 2 (this correspondent came to Minnesota before the weekend before the excursion).

572. *Minnesota Pioneer,* 9 June 1854, p. 2; *Minnesotian,* 9 June 1854, p. 3 (quoted).

573. *Minnesota Democrat,* 14 June 1854, p. 2; Hage, *Newspapers,* 48.

574. *St. Paul Daily Times,* 9 June 1854, p. 2; *Minnesotian,* 9 June 1854, p. 3; Hage, *Newspapers,* 48–49.

575. *New Haven Palladium,* 19 June 1854, p. 2; Boston Daily Advertiser, 15 June 1854.

576. *St. Anthony Express,* 10 June 1854, p. 2 (quoted).

577. *Boston Daily Advertiser,* 15 June 1854; *St. Anthony Express,* 10 June 1854, p. 2 (quoted); Silliman journal, 8 June 1854, p. 210 (quoted). These accounts do not agree on all details of the accident. H. L. Tobey reported another accident, caused by an aggressive driver; *Kingston (N.Y.) Journal,* 5 July 1854, p. 1.

578. *Buffalo Commercial Advertiser,* 17 June 1854, p. 1.

579. *St. Paul Daily Times,* 9 June 1854, p. 2.

580. *Chicago Democratic Press,* 13 June 1854, p. 2 (quoted); *New Haven Daily Register,* 24 June 1854, p. 2.

581. *Poughkeepsie Eagle,* 15 July 1854, p. 2 (quoted). Confirming the

sentry's presence was Bogart of the *New York Courier & Enquirer*, quoted in *St. Anthony Express*, 8 July 1854, p. 2.

582. *St. Anthony Express*, 8 July 1854, p. 2 (reprinting Bogart's article in the *New York Courier & Enquirer* of June 14); *New Haven Palladium*, 19 June 1854, p. 2; *Poughkeepsie Eagle*, 15 July 1854, p. 2; *New York Times*, 17 June 1854, p. 2 (watering horses); *Chicago Daily Tribune*, 13 June 1854, p. 2 (reporting on the two companies present, but omitting the artillery); *New York Times*, 14 June 1854, p. 2 (reporting the 4th Artillery).

583. *Rome Daily Sentinel*, 20 June 1854, p. 2 (quoted).

584. *New York Times*, 14 June 1854, p. 2 (quoted).

585. *Buffalo Commercial Advertiser*, 17 June 1854, p. 1; *Poughkeepsie Eagle*, 15 July 1854, p. 2.

586. *Chicago Daily Tribune*, 13 June 1854, p. 2 (quoted). For the officers giving the tour, see *Minnesota Democrat*, 14 June 1854, p. 2. For guests poking their heads into rooms, see *Chicago Journal*, 13 June 1854, p. 2 (quoted).

587. *St. Anthony Express*, 8 July 1854, p. 2 (reprinting *New York Courier & Enquirer* article of June 14).

588. E. T. Throop Martin to Cornelia Martin, 11 June 1854, folder 1, box 4, Throop and Martin Family Papers, Princeton.

589. *Chicago Democratic Press*, 13 June 1854, p. 2; *New Haven Daily Register*, 24 June 1854, p. 2.

590. *New Haven Daily Register*, 20 June 1854, p. 2; *Springfield Republican*, 15 June 1854, p. 2; *Minnesota Democrat*, 14 June 1854, p. 2; *New York Observer* 32, no. 26 (29 June 1854), p. 206; *New York Recorder*, 21 June 1854, p. 4 (quoted).

591. Silliman journal, 8 June 1854, p. 211, microfilm edition, UW-Madison.

592. *Minnesota Democrat*, 14 June 1854, p. 2; *New Haven Palladium*, 19 June 1854, p. 2.

593. *Buffalo Commercial Advertiser*, 17 June 1854, p. 1 (quoted); *Chicago Daily Tribune*, 13 June 1854, p. 2.

594. *Rome Daily Sentinel*, 20 June 1854, p. 2.

595. *New Haven Palladium*, 19 June 1854, p. 2; *Chicago Daily Tribune*, 13 June 1854, p. 2; *St. Paul Daily Times*, 9 June 1854, p. 2.

596. *Kingston (N.Y.) Journal*, 5 July 1854, p. 1 (quoted).

597. Here and below, see *Boston Daily Journal*, 20 June 1854; *Cleveland Herald*, 24 June 1854, p. 2; *New York Times*, 14 June 1854, p. 2 (Excelsior); and *Rock Island Republican*, 27 June 1854, p. 2; and *Albany Morning Express*, 16 June 1854, p. 2. The *Express* has by far the most complete version of Schouler's speech. Schouler may have been also ridiculing Mayor David Olmstead's speaking deficiencies. For Olmstead's defects, see J. W. Bass to Henry Farnam, 16 June 1854, "June 15–19" folder, box 10, Farnam Family Papers, Series I, Stirling Library, Yale.

598. *Albany Morning Express*, 16 June 1854, p. 2 (quoted).

599. *Poughkeepsie Eagle*, 15 July 1854, p. 2; *New Haven Palladium*, 19 June 1854, p. 2; *Rome Daily Sentinel*, 20 June 1854, p. 2.

600. *Minnesota Democrat*, 14 June 1854, p. 2; *New York Times*, 17 June 1854, p. 2; *Chicago Daily Tribune*, 13 June 1854, p. 2; *New Haven Palladium*, 19 June 1854, p. 2.

601. *New Haven Palladium*, 19 June 1854, p. 2; *Minnesota Democrat*, 14 June 1854, p. 2.

602. *Minnesota Pioneer*, 10 June 1854, p. 2; *Minnesota Democrat*, 14 June 1854, p. 2; *Boston Daily Advertiser*, 15 June 1854 (on Gorman's lack of popularity compared to Ramsey).

603. *Minnesota Pioneer*, 10 June 1854, p. 2; *New Haven Palladium*, 19 June 1854, p. 2; *New York Tribune*, 14 June 1854, p. 4 (quoted); *Minnesota Democrat*, 14 June 1854, p. 2; *St. Paul Daily Times*, 9 June 1854, p. 2; *New York Times*, 14 June 1854 (quoting Gorman "about as follows").

604. *New York Tribune*, 14 June 1854, p. 4 (quoted); *Minnesota Pioneer*, 19 June 1854, p. 2; *New Haven Palladium*, 19 June 1854, p. 2.

605. *New York Tribune*, 14 June 1854, p. 4 (quoted); *Minnesota Pioneer*, 10 June 1854, p. 2.

606. Henry H. Sibley to I. I. Stevens, 6 June 1854, roll 31, microfilm edition, Sibley Papers, MHS, St. Paul; David Haward Bain, *Empire Express: Building the First Transcontinental Railroad* (New York: Penguin, 1999), 49, 51.

607. *Boston Daily Journal*, 20 June 1854; *Minnesota Democrat*, 14 June 1854, p. 2 (quoted); *Chicago Democratic Press*, 13 June 1854, p. 2 (quoted). These are the editors' paraphrases, not exact quotes.

608. *Minnesota Pioneer*, 10 June 1854, p. 2.

609. *Buffalo Commercial Advertiser*, 17 June 1854, p. 1; George Bancroft to "My ever dear Wife," 9 June 1854, "Photostats—Geo. Bancroft to wife 1854-55" folder, box 5, Bancroft-Bliss Family Papers, Library of Congress.

610. *New York Tribune*, 14 June 1854, p. 2 (quoted); *Minnesota Democrat*, 14 June 1854, p. 2 (quoted); *St. Paul Daily Times*, 9 June 1854, p. 2 (quoted).

611. *Minnesota Democrat*, 14 June 1854, p. 2; *New York Times*, 17 June 1854, p. 2 (quoted).

612. *Minnesota Democrat*, 14 June 1854, p. 2 (quoted); *Springfield Republican*, 15 June 1854, p. 2 (on Bancroft's voice); *Boston Daily Advertiser*, 15 June 1854 (on reluctance to become a state); *Collections*, Vol. 12 (St. Paul: Minnesota Historical Society, 1908), p. 8.

613. *New York Tribune*, 14 June 1854, p. 4 (quoted); *St. Paul Daily Times*, 9 June 1854, p. 2; *Minnesota Democrat*, 14 June 1854, p. 2. Dana's version is a paraphrase.

614. *Minnesota Democrat*, 14 June 1854, p. 2; *Chicago Daily Tribune*, 13 June 1854, p. 2; *New Haven Palladium*, 19 June 1854, p. 2 (quoted); William Le Duc to Committee of Arrangements, Statement dated 9 June 1854, in William Le Duc Papers, Box 144.6.1.8(F), MHS, St. Paul.

615. *New Haven Palladium*, 19 June 1854, p. 2; *New York Tribune*, 14 June 1854, p. 4; *Minnesota Democrat*, 14 June 1854, p. 2 (quoted); *Springfield Republican*, 15 June 1854, p. 2 (quoted); *Boston Daily Advertiser*, 15 June 1854 (naming the Prima Donna Waltz); *St. Anthony Express*, 8 July 1854, p. 2 (reprinting *New York Courier & Enquirer* of June 14); *Rome Daily Sentinel*, 20 June 1854, p. 2 (quoted).

616. Frank A. Thayer to "My Dear ____ [?]," 22 June 1854, Box 144.G.1.8(F), Le Duc Papers, MHS. For confirmation of the Lawrences' presence, see Merlin Stonehouse, *John Wesley North and the Reform Frontier* (Minneapolis: University of Minnesota Press, 1965), 77.

617. *New York Times*, 17 June 1854, p. 2.

618. *New York Weekly Mirror*, 24 June 1854, p. 2 (quoted); *St. Anthony Express*, 8 July 1854, p. 2 (reprinting *New York Courier & Enquirer* of June 14).

619. *St. Anthony Express*, 8 July 1854, p. 2 (reprinting *New York Courier & Enquirer* of June 14); *New York Tribune*, 14 June 1854, p. 4; *New Haven Palladium*, 19 June 1854, p. 2 (quoted); *Poughkeepsie Eagle*, 15 July 1854, p. 2 (quoted).

620. *Minnesota Democrat*, 14 June 1854, p. 2; *Poughkeepsie Eagle*, 15 July 1854, p. 2 (quoted); Catharine Sedgwick to Kate Sedgwick Minot, 9 June 1854, in Dewey, ed., *Life and Letters*, 354.

621. *St. Anthony Express*, 8 July 1854, p. 2 (reprinting *New York Courier & Enquirer* of June 14) (quoted); *New York Weekly Mirror*, 24 June 1854, p. 2 (quoted); *New Haven Palladium*, 19 June 1854, p. 2 (quoted).

622. *New York Tribune,* 14 June 1854, p. 4 (quoted).

623. *New York Times,* 14 and 17 June 1854, both p. 2, both signed "W" (who, I assume, was Weldon, while the other *Times* correspondent who signed his articles "Excelsior" was probably George Jones). For another report that confirmed the price-gouging, see *Albany Morning Express,* 20 June 1854, p. 2.

624. *New York Times,* 29 June 1854, p. 2; *New York Tribune,* 17 July 1854, p. 3; *St. Anthony Express,* 22 July 1854, p. 4. At the end of his report in the June 17 issue of the *Times,* "W" promises another article; however, a search of the *Times* through July 4, 1854, failed to turn up any more from "W." Most likely, the editors did not want to alienate Minnesotans and their friends any further.

625. *Minnesota Pioneer,* 10 June 1854, p. 2 (quoted).

EXCURSUS: John Dean Caton and Antebellum American Law

626. Caton, *Miscellanies,* 117, 141; *Dictionary of American Biography* entry; Robert Fergus, *Biographical Sketch of John Dean Caton, Ex-Chief-Justice of Illinois* (Chicago: Fergus Printing Company, 1882), 9–10, 12, 13 (quoted), 22, 23.

627. Norman B. Judd to "My dear Judge" [John Dean Caton], 24 April 1854 (quoted); Samuel H. Treat to Caton, 27 April and 1 May, both 1854; Walter B. Scates to Caton, 28 April 1854; Lyman Trumbull to Caton, 9 and 29 May 1854, all in box 5, John Dean Caton Papers, Library of Congress.

628. William P. Caton to John Dean Caton, 2 June 1854; E. Cornell to Caton, 3 June, 6 June, and 14 June, all 1854, all in Caton Papers, Library of Congress.

629. John J. Duff, *A. Lincoln: Prairie Lawyer* (New York: Rinehart and Company, 1960), 243, 247; John Dean Caton, *Early Bench and Bar of Illinois* (Chicago: Chicago Legal News Company, 1893), 185 (quoted).

630. Caton, *Bench and Bar,* 185 (quoted). Italics in the original.

631. Lawrence M. Friedman, *A History of American Law* (New York: Simon and Schuster, 1973), 276–78.

632. Morton J. Horwitz, *The Transformation of American Law* (Cambridge: Harvard University Press, 1977), 253, 254–56, 257 (quoted), 262, 264. Horwitz's thesis has been disputed by, among others, William J. Novak, *The People's Welfare: Law and Regulation in Nineteenth-Century America* (Chapel Hill: University of North Carolina Press, 1996).

633. Stephen M. Feldman, *American Legal Thought from Premodernism to Postmodernism* (New York: Oxford University Press, 2000), 53 (quoting Wilson).

634. Feldman, *American Legal Thought,* 52–54, 56–57 (this is Feldman's analysis, except for my analogy to the Animal Kingdom).

635. Caton, *Bench and Bar,* 186 (quoted).

636. Feldman, *American Legal Thought,* 70–71.

637. Feldman, *American Legal Thought,* 92 (quoted).

EXCURSUS: Cholera, C. B. Coventry, and Antebellum Medical Science

638. George A. Mix to Henry Farnam, 1 June 1854, "June 1–2" folder, and Mix to Farnam, 3 June 1854, both in box 10, Farnam Papers, Yale.

639. *New Haven Palladium,* 6 July 1854, p. 2 (quoted).

640. C. B. Coventry, M.D., *Epidemic Cholera* (Buffalo: Geo. H. Darby and Company, 1849), title page; Francis R. Packard, M.D., *History of Medicine in the United States* (New York: Hafner Publishing Company, 1963), 740–41, 754.

641. Coventry, *Epidemic Cholera,* v, vi. Coventry gives the year as 1831, but other sources state that 1832 saw the first significant number of cases in New York and the United States; Burrows

642. and Wallace, *History of New York City,* 589–93.

643. Coventry, *Epidemic Cholera,* 9–29 (quote from p. 27), 38–50.

644. Coventry, *Epidemic Cholera,* 51–57 (quote from p. 57).

645. Coventry, *Epidemic Cholera,* 103–04 (quoted).

646. *Minnesota Weekly Times,* 20 June 1854, p. 2 (quoted).

647. Coventry, *Epidemic Cholera,* 58–65 (quoted).

648. Phyllis Allen Richmond, "The Nineteenth Century American Physician as a Research Scientist," in Felix Marti-Ibañez, M.D., ed., *History of American Medicine* (New York: MD Publications, 1958), 142 (quoted).

649. Richard Harrison Shryock, *Medicine in America: Historical Essays* (Baltimore: The Johns Hopkins Press, 1966), 78; John Harley Warner, *Against the Spirit of System: The French Impulse in Nineteenth-Century American Medicine* (Princeton: Princeton University Press, 1998), 138–40 (quotes from p. 138, 139).

650. Warner, *Against the Spirit of System,* 136 (quoted).

651. Daniel Drake, *A Systematic Treatise, Historical, Etiological and Practical, on the Principal Diseases of the Interior Valley of North America, as They Appear in the Caucasian, African, Indian and Esquimaux Populations* (Cincinnati: Winthrop B. Smith and Company, 1850, 1854); James H. Cassedy, *Medicine and American Growth, 1800-1860* (Madison: University of Wisconsin Press, 1986), 50–54, 82–83 (quotes from p. 50, 51); John Duffy, *From Humors to Medical Science: A History of American Medicine,* 2nd ed. (Urbana: University of Illinois Press, 1993), 121–24 (quote from p. 124).

652. Drake, *Systematic Treatise,* Vol. I, 325 (quoted).

653. Sedgwick to "My dearest Kate," 4 June 1854 (quoted) and to "Dearest Kate," 1 June 1854, both in CMS Papers, microfilm edition, Massachusetts Historical Society.

654. Cassedy, *Medicine,* 56–57 (quoted).

655. *Poughkeepsie Eagle,* 8 July 1854, p. 2 (quoted).

CHAPTER 8: "Going Down This Noblest of All Rivers"

655. *Buffalo Commercial Advertiser,* 17 June 1854, p. 1.

656. *Rome Daily Sentinel,* 20 June 1854, p. 2 (quoted). Wager writes that "at sunrise we entered it," but he seems to place this account with his description of Wednesday's trip, so it is possible (but unlikely) that he means sunset of Wednesday.

657. *Poughkeepsie Eagle,* 15 July 1854, p. 2 (quoted).

658. *Poughkeepsie Eagle,* 15 July 1854, p. 2 (quoted).

659. *Boston Daily Advertiser,* 1 July 1854, Letter No. VII, dated June 12, 1854.

660. Charles Sedgwick to "Dearest Bess," 9 June 1854, folder 12.8, box 12, Sedgwick IV Papers, Massachusetts Historical Society, Boston; Dewey, ed., *Life and Letters,* 354; John Munn Diary, Vol. 22, p. 182–83 (quoted).

661. *Poughkeepsie Eagle,* 15 July 1854, p. 2 (quoted).

662. *Poughkeepsie Eagle,* 15 July 1854, p. 2 (quoted). This estimate of the time seems too early in the afternoon (the did not reach Galena until 10 p.m.), but that is what Platt reported.

663. *New Haven Palladium,* 20 June 1854, p. 2.

664. Clipping (n.d.) reprinting *New Haven Journal and Courier* article (n.d. but late July or early August 1854), in reel 42, Fillmore Papers, microfilm edition, SHSW; *Minnesota Weekly Times,* 13 June 1854, p. 2.

665. *Buffalo Commercial Advertiser,* 17 June 1854, p. 1; *Chicago Journal,* 13 June 1854, p. 2.

666. Gregory Clark and S. Michael Halloran, eds., *Oratorical Culture in Nineteenth-Century America: Transformations in the Theory and Practice of Rhetoric* (Carbondale: Southern Illinois University Press, 1993), 2 (quoted), 3, 6, 8.

667. *New Haven Palladium,* 20 June 1854, p. 2; Francis Granger to

Benjamin Silliman, 16 September 1850, box 5, Silliman Papers, microfilm ed. Silliman Papers, UW-Madison; James F. Babcock entry in *Cyclopedia of American Biography*.

668. *New Haven Palladium*, 20 June 1854, p. 2 (quoted); *Buffalo Commercial Advertiser*, 17 June 1854, p. 1; *New York Weekly Mirror*, 24 June 1854, p. 2 (quoted); *Chicago Journal*, 13 June 1854, p. 2.

669. *Buffalo Commercial Advertiser*, 17 June 1854, p. 1; *Oratorical Culture*, 8.

670. Henry W. Farnam, *Memoir of Henry Farnam*; Passenger Register, *Golden Era*, folder 667, box 53, Farnam Family Papers Series I, Sterling Library, Yale; *Boston Evening Transcript*, 28 June 1854, p. 2 (quoted). The *Transcript* mentions "the beautiful Miss W. or Miss J."; based on the register, I have assumed these to be Miss Jarvis and Miss Williams, both from Connecticut, both on that boat.

671. *Boston Evening Transcript*, 28 June 1854, p. 2; John A. Rockwell, *A Compilation of Spanish and Mexican Law* (New York: John S. Voorhies, 1851); Dwight Loomis and J. Gilbert Calhoun, eds., *The Judicial and Civil History of Connecticut* (Boston: Boston History Company, 1895), 327–28; D. Hamilton Hurd, comp., *History of New London County, Connecticut* (1882), 39.

672. *Oratorical Culture*, 7; *Boston Evening Transcript*, 28 June 1854, p. 2 (quoted); *New York Weekly Mirror*, 24 June 1854, p. 2; *New Haven Palladium*, 20 June 1854, p. 2.

673. *New Haven Palladium*, 20 June 1854, p. 2 (quoted). I have used Babcock's quote despite his (overly modest?) admission: "I may not have given you a very correct report of this excellent speech on behalf of the baby."

674. *New Haven Palladium*, 20 June 1854, p. 2; *Boston Evening Transcript*, 28 June 1854, p. 2; *New York Weekly Mirror*, 24 June 1854, p. 2 (quoted).

675. *Boston Daily Advertiser*, 4 July 1854 (quoted); Nathan and Charles Hale entries, *Appleton's Cyclopaedia of American Biography*; Albert P. Langtry, ed., *Metropolitan Boston: A Modern History*, Vol. II (New York: Lewis Historical Publishing Company, 1929), 510.

676. *Albany Evening Journal*, 16 June 1854, p. 2 (quoted); *Chicago Tribune*, 13 June 1854, p. 2; *Boston Daily Advertiser*, 15 June 1854; Vermilye entry in *Cyclopaedia of American Biography*.

677. *Chicago Tribune*, 13 June 1854, p. 2; *Albany Evening Journal*, 16 June 1854, p. 2; *Boston Daily Advertiser*, 15 June, 29 June (quoted), and 4 July (quoted), all 1854; Thomas C. Cochran, *Railroad Leaders 1845–1890: The Business Mind in Action* (Cambridge: Harvard University Press, 1953), 18-19.

678. Charles Sedgwick to "Dearest Bess," 9 June 1854, folder 12.8, box 12, Sedgwick IV Papers, Massachusetts Historical Society; Carol Walhovd and Fern Heiller, *The Brownsville Story* (Winona: St. Mary's College Press, 1976), 3, 8–9, 13.

679. *Boston Daily Advertiser*, 1 July 1854 (quoted); *New York Times*, 14 June 1854, p. 2 (quoted); Catharine Sedgwick to Kate Sedgwick Minot, 9 June 1854, reel 4, microfilm ed., CMS Papers P-354, Massachusetts Historical Society.

680. *Chicago Democratic Press*, 13 June 1854, p. 2 (quoted).

681. John Munn Diary, Vol. 22, p. 185 (quoted).

682. *Democratic Press*, 13 June 1854, p. 2 (quoted).

683. *New Haven Palladium*, 20 June 1854, p. 2; *Dubuque Miners' Express*, 16 June 1854, p. 2.

684. Here and below, *New York Daily Tribune*, 14 June 1854, p. 5; *New Haven Palladium*, 20 June 1854, p. 2 (quoted—the story of the Irishman).

685. *New Haven Palladium*, 20 June 1854, p. 2; *Chicago Journal*, 12 June 1854, p. 2 (quoted); *Dubuque Miners' Express*, 16 June

1854, p. 2 (reprinting the *Journal* report).

686. *Dubuque Miners' Express*, 16 June 1854, p. 2.

687. *Chicago Journal*, 12 June 1854, p. 2 (quoted); *New Haven Palladium*, 20 June 1854, p. 2 (quoted). Cooley sent to Morehouse "a pair of large Silver Pitchers and a small silver pitcher for one of the Pilots and a gold signet ring and gold chain for the other [pilot], with a California Gold Ring for the Steward," the entire cost of $361.75 coming from the collection taken; J. E. Cooley to John Dean Caton, 3 July 1854 (quoted) and receipts dated 30 June and 3 July 1854, box 6, Caton Papers, Library of Congress.

688. *Chicago Journal*, 13 June 1854, p. 2 (quoted); *Cleveland Herald*, 24 June 1854, p. 2 (quoted). The *Journal* states that Sarah piloted the *Galena*—and that is possible, for it was captained by her uncle, D. B. Morehouse—but it was more likely the *Lady Franklin* (commanded by her father) that she piloted.

689. *Chicago Democratic Press*, 13 June 1854, p. 2.

690. *New York Observer* 32, no. 26 (29 June 1854), p. 206 (quoted); E. D. G. Prime, *Notes Genealogical, Biographical and Bibliographical of the Prime Family* (privately printed, 1888), 92; a copy of this book is at the library of the State Historical Society of Wisconsin.

691. *Boston Daily Advertiser*, 29 June 1854 (quoted); Excursion Register for *Golden Era, Galena*, and *Sparhawk*, Farnam Papers, Stirling Library, Yale (showing that William Prime was onboard, whereas his brother Edward D. G. Prime traveled on the *Galena*; also, that Thomas Vermilye was onboard while Ashbel G. Vermilye was not on the *Sparhawk*).

692. *Boston Daily Advertiser*, 29 June 1854 (quoted); Charles Hale to "Dear Mother," 5 July 1854, "Sarah Preston (Everett) Hale, 1854" folder, box 21, Hale Family Papers, Smith College.

693. *Boston Daily Advertiser*, 29 June 1854 (quoted).

694. John Munn Diary, Vol. 22, p. 192.

695. Silliman journal, Friday 9 June 1854, p. 212–213, microfilm edition, UW–Madison.

696. *New York Observer* 32, no. 27 (6 July 1854), p. 215.

CHAPTER 9: "We Are on the Way to the Pacific"

697. *Boston Daily Advertiser*, 1 July 1854, p. 2; *Boston Transcript*, 16 June 1854, p. 2 (quoted).

698. *Poughkeepsie Eagle*, 15 and 22 July 1854, both p. 2.

699. *Boston Daily Advertiser*, 1 July 1854, p. 2; Catharine M. Sedgwick to "Dearest Kate [S. Minot]," 9 June 1854, (part printed in Dewey, *Life and Letters*, 354), reel 4, CMS Papers, Massachusetts Historical Society; George Bancroft to "My ever dear wife," 13 June 1854, "Photostats—Geo. Bancroft to wife 1854–55" folder, box 5, Bancroft–Bliss Family Papers, Library of Congress; Elizabeth Blair Lee to "Phil," 13, 15, and 18 June, all 1854, all in Folder 8, Box 74, Blair and Lee Family Papers, Princeton.

700. *New Haven Palladium*, 20 June 1854, p. 2; *Buffalo Commercial Advertiser*, 17 June 1854, p. 1.

701. *Buffalo Commercial Advertiser*, 17 June 1854, p. 1; *New Haven Palladium*, 20 June 1854, p. 2.

702. *Buffalo Commercial Advertiser*, 17 June 1854, p. 1 (quoted); *New Haven Palladium*, 20 June 1854, p. 2.

703. *New Haven Palladium*, 20 June 1854, p. 2 (quoted).

704. *Davenport Gazette*, 15 June 1854, p. 1, 2; *New Haven Palladium*, 22 June 1854, p. 2; *Illinois State Journal*, 15 June 1854, p. 2 (giving the arrival at 10:00 a.m. and the start of speechmaking at 11:00 a.m.).

705. *New Haven Palladium*, 22 June 1854, p. 2 (quoted).

706. *New Haven Palladium*, 22 June 1854, p. 2 (quoted); *History of*

Scott County, Iowa (Chicago: Inter-State Publishing Co., 1882), 318–29; *Illinois State Journal,* 15 June 1854, p. 2 (confirming he spoke "from the top of a hogshead"); *Davenport Gazette,* 15 June 1854, p. 2 (quoted). Presumably, by "no Eriean policy," Grant meant Illinois did not fight against Iowa on the C&RI project; Eris was the Greek goddess of strife and discord.

707. *Davenport Gazette,* 15 June 1854, p. 2 (quoted); typed transcript of *Gazette* article, Davenport Public Library; Morgan Dix, comp., *Memoirs of John Adams Dix* Vol. 1 (New York: Harpers and Brothers, 1883), 302–03 (quoted).

708. *Illinois State Journal,* 15 June 1854, p. 2 (quoted).

709. Tocqueville, *Democracy in America,* "Why American Writers and Orators Often Use an Inflated Style."

710. *Davenport Gazette,* 15 June 1854, p. 2 (quoted); typed transcript of *Gazette* article, Davenport Public Library.

711. *Davenport Gazette,* 15 June 1854, p. 2 (Dix thanks the crowd for "calling on me to address you").

712. Dix entries in *Dictionary of National Biography,* and *Appleton's Cyclopaedia of American Biography;* Bain, *Empire Express,* 152–53; Dix, comp., *Memoirs,* Vol. I, 282-83 (quoted), and Vol. II, 264-65.

713. Dix entries in *Dictionary of National Biography,* and *Appleton's Cyclopaedia of American Biography;* Dix, comp., *Memoirs,* Vol. I, 260–64, 271–78, 285, and Vol. II, 328–35.

714. Register of Steamboat Passengers, Grand Excursion, Farnam Family Papers, Yale; Dix, comp., *Memoirs,* Vol. II, 264 (quoted); *Davenport Gazette,* 15 June 1854, p. 2; transcript of *Gazette* article in Davenport Public Library (quoted).

715. *Davenport Gazette,* 15 June 1854, p. 2; transcript of *Gazette* article in Davenport Public Library (quoted).

716. *Davenport Gazette,* 15 June 1854, p. 2; transcript of Gazette article in Davenport Public Library, p. 8 (quoted).

717. *Davenport Gazette,* 15 June 1854, p. 2; transcript of *Gazette* article in Davenport Public Library, p. 9–10.

718. *Davenport Gazette,* 15 June 1854, p. 2; transcript of *Gazette* article in Davenport Public Library, p. 11 (quoted); *New York Weekly Mirror,* 1 July 1854, p. 2 (quoted, giving a lengthy excerpt from Dix's speech).

719. *Davenport Gazette,* 15 June 1854, p. 2; transcript of *Gazette* article in Davenport Public Library, p. 12 (quoted); *New York Weekly Mirror,* 1 July 1854, p. 2 (quoted).

720. *Davenport Gazette,* 15 June 1854, p. 2; transcript of *Gazette* article in Davenport Public Library, p. 12 (quoted); *New York Weekly Mirror,* 1 July 1854, p. 2 (quoted).

721. *New Haven Palladium,* 22 June 1854, p. 2 (quoted); *Boston Daily Advertiser,* 1 July 1854, p. 2. Based on the wording of the first sentence of Dix's last paragraph, I have assumed Farnam's move came just before that sentence.

722. *Davenport Gazette,* 15 June 1854, p. 2; transcript of *Gazette* article in Davenport Public Library, p. 13 (quoted).

723. *New Haven Palladium,* 22 June 1854, p. 2 (quoted).

724. *New Haven Palladium,* 22 June 1854, p. 2 (quoted); Babcock, Letter No. 13 (quoted), in *Palladium,* typescript in James F. Babcock Papers, A.-B112., MHS, St. Paul.

725. *Albany Evening Journal,* 16 June 1854, p. 2; *New York Evening Post,* 19 June 1854, p. 2; Joliet Signal, 13 June 1854, p. 2 (quoted); Babcock, Letter No. 13 for the *Palladium,* typescript, MHS.

726. *Albany Evening Journal,* 16 June 1854, p. 2; *Boston Daily Advertiser,* 1 July 1854, p. 2.

727. Babcock, Letter No. 13 (quoted) for the *Palladium,* typescript, MHS.

728. *Daily Chicago Journal,* 12 June 1854, p. 2; *Chicago Journal,* 12

June 1854, p. 2.

729. John Munn Diary, Vol. 22, p. 187 (quoted).

CHAPTER 10: "An Angry, Turbid, Almost Frightful Looking Stream"

730. *Rock Island Advertiser,* 5 July 1854, p. 2 (quoting *St. Louis Republican*). But for a persuasive refutation of the common view that St. Louis's leaders "ignore[d] railroads because of the rivers," see James Neal Primm, *Lion of the Valley: St. Louis, Missouri, 1764–1980,* 3rd edition (St. Louis: Missouri Historical Society Press, 1998), 223–26 (quote from p. 224).

731. Catharine Sedgwick to "Dearest Kate," 11 June 1854, reel 4, Sedgwick Papers P-354.

732. George Bancroft to "My ever dear Wife," 11 June 1854, reel 4, Bancroft Papers, Cornell.

733. Bancroft to "My ever dear Wife," 11 June 1854, reel 4, Bancroft Papers, Cornell; *Memoir of Robert Bowne Minturn* (New York: Anson D. F. Randolph and Company, 1871), 41, 54–55, 57–63; entry for Minturn and son in *Appleton's Cyclopaedia of American Biography;* "Excursion Register," p. 9, Farnam Family Papers, Stirling Library, Yale.

734. Here and below, Bancroft to "My ever dear Wife," 11 June 1854, reel 4, Bancroft Papers, Cornell.

735. Bancroft to "My ever dear Wife," 13 June 1854, "Photostats— Geo. Bancroft to wife 1854–55" folder, box 5, Bancroft-Bliss Family Papers, Library of Congress; Bancroft to "My ever dear Wife," 11 June 1854, reel 4, Bancroft Papers, Cornell. He writes the second letter "On the Mississippi below Hannibal M[issouri]," but much of it describes events north of there, so it is unclear to what section of the river this description applies. For the fog, see Catharine Sedgwick to "Dearest Kate," 11 June 1854, reel 4, Sedgwick Papers.

736. Bancroft to "My ever dear Wife," 11 June 1854, reel 4, Bancroft Papers, Cornell; *Albany Evening Journal,* 12 June 1854, p. 2 (quoted).

737. Catharine Sedgwick to Kate Sedgwick Minot, 11 June 1854, in Dewey, ed., *Life and Letters,* 355; and reel 4, microfilm ed., Sedgwick Papers P-354, Massachusetts Historical Society; Bancroft to "My ever dear Wife," 11 June 1854, reel 4, Bancroft Papers, Cornell.

738. Sedgwick to "Dearest Kate," "On the Mississippi just below Quincy," 11 June 1854, reel 4, microfilm ed., Sedgwick Papers P-354, Massachusetts Historical Society (partly printed in Dewey, ed., *Life and Letters,* 355–56).

739. Sedgwick to "Dearest Kate," "On the Mississippi just below Quincy," 11 June 1854, reel 4, microfilm ed., Sedgwick Papers P-354, Massachusetts Historical Society; Dewey, ed., *Life and Letters,* 356.

740. Sedgwick to "Dearest Kate," 9 June 1854, reel 4, microfilm ed., Sedgwick Papers P-354, Massachusetts Historical Society (partly printed in Dewey, ed., *Life and Letters,* 354); Arthur M. Johnson and Barry E. Supple, *Boston Capitalists and Western Railroads: A Study in the Nineteenth-Century Railroad Investment Process* (Cambridge: Harvard University Press, 1967), 163–65; Charles Sedgwick to Kate, 12 June 1854, Folder 12.8, Box 12, Sedgwick IV Papers, Massachusetts Historical Society.

741. Catharine Sedgwick to "Dearest Kate," 11 June 1854, reel 4, Sedgwick Papers P-354; Charles Sedgwick to Kate, 12 June 1854, folder 12.8, box 12, Sedgwick IV Papers, Massachusetts Historical Society.

742. *Poughkeepsie Eagle,* 22 July 1854, p. 2 (quoted).

743. Perry McCandless, *A History of Missouri: Vol. 11, 1820 to 1860* (Columbia: University of Missouri Press, 1972), 38; Primm, *Lion of the Valley,* 169, 229–30.

744. *Poughkeepsie Eagle,* 22 July 1854, p. 2 (quoted); *Albany Evening Journal,* 12 June 1854, p. 2 (quoted); *New York Commercial Advertiser,* 19 June 1854, p. 2 (quoted). But see also the rather different description of George Bancroft, who wrote that the Missouri joined the Mississippi in an "unpretending" and almost unnoticed manner; Bancroft to "My ever dear Wife," 13 June 1854, "Photostats—Geo. Bancroft to wife 1854–55" folder, box 5, Bancroft-Bliss Family Papers, Library of Congress.

745. Potter, *Impending Crisis,* 124–26, 143–44, 166, 177–80, 183–89.

746. Primm, *Lion of the Valley,* 179, 229–30; McCandless, *History of Missouri: Vol. II,* 277; *New Haven Palladium,* 21 June 1854, p. 2 (quoting a Democrat who could very well be Frank Blair Jr.).

747. *Buffalo Commercial Advertiser,* 16 June 1854, p. 2 (quoting the *St. Louis Republican* of 13 June 1854); Primm, *Lion of the Valley,*172; William Hyde, *Encyclopedia of the History of St. Louis, a Compendium of History and Biography* (New York and Louisville: The Southern History Company, 1899), 1490 (quoted), 1498 (quoted).

748. *Buffalo Commercial Advertiser,* 16 June 1854, p. 2 (quoting *St. Louis Republican* of 13 June 1854).

749. *Buffalo Commercial Advertiser,* 16 June 1854, p. 2 (quoting *St. Louis Republican* of 13 June 1854).

750. *Buffalo Commercial Advertiser,* 16 June 1854, p. 2 (quoting *St. Louis Republican* of 13 June 1854); Charles Sedgwick to Kate Sedgwick Minot, 12 June 1854, Folder 12.8, Box 12, Sedgwick IV Papers; *Poughkeepsie Eagle,* 22 July 1854, p. 2 (also quoted).

751. *Buffalo Commercial Advertiser,* 16 June 1854, p. 2 (quoting *St. Louis Republican* of 13 June 1854); *Albany Evening Journal,* 12 June 1854, p. 2 (quoted); *Poughkeepsie Eagle,* 22 July 1854, p. 2 (quoted); *New York Times,* 15 June 1854, p. 2 (quoted); Primm, *Lion of the Valley,* 158-59 (with photo of the levee in 1853).

752. *Buffalo Commercial Advertiser,* 16 June 1854, p. 2 (quoting *St. Louis Republican* of 13 June 1854); Primm, *Lion of the Valley,* 151, 170, 191, 198, 224–25, 226, 227.

753. Primm, *Lion of the Valley,* 167–70, 172; J. Thomas Scharf, *History of Saint Louis City and County,* Vol. II (Philadelphia: Louis H. Everts & Co., 1883), 1837–38; McCandless, *History of Missouri: Vol. II,* 68–69, 265 (quoted); Holt, *American Whig Party,* 850–52.

754. *Buffalo Commercial Advertiser,* 16 June 1854, p. 2 (quoting *St. Louis Republican* of June 13).

755. Here and below, *Buffalo Commercial Advertiser,* 16 June 1854, p. 2 (quoting *St. Louis Republican* of 13 June 1854); Primm, *Lion of the Valley,* 181 (quoted); Hyde, *Encyclopedia of St. Louis,* 1502, 1503-04 (quoted).

756. Catharine Sedgwick to ___?, St. Louis, Tuesday [13 June 1854], Reel 4, CMS Papers, Massachusetts Historical Society.

757. *Buffalo Commercial Advertiser,* 16 June 1854, p. 2 (quoting *St. Louis Republican* of 13 June 1854); Hyde, *Encyclopedia of St. Louis,* 2553–54 (quoted); Primm, *Lion of the Valley,* 226.

758. *Buffalo Commercial Advertiser,* 16 June 1854, p. 2 (quoting St. *Louis Republican* of 13 June 1854); *New York Times,* 15 June 1854, p. 2 (for "Great Central City" title).

759. Catharine Sedgwick to ___?, St. Louis, Tuesday [13 June 1854], Reel 4, CMS Papers, Massachusetts Historical Society; Sarah Cabot Sedgwick and Christina Sedgwick Marquand, *Stockbridge 1739–1939: A Chronicle* (1939), 218 (regarding Elizabeth Sedgwick's boarding school); Snyder, *Lady and the President,* 36; Hyde, *Encyclopedia of St. Louis,* 531–32; Scharf, *History of Saint Louis,* Vol. I, p. 873.

760. Catharine Sedgwick to ___?, St. Louis, Tuesday [13 June 1854], Reel 4, CMS Papers; Charles Sedgwick to Kate Sedgwick Minot, 12 June 1854, Folder 12.8, Box 12, Sedgwick IV Papers, both in

Massachusetts Historical Society; Scharf, *History of Saint Louis,* 873. Lucien Carr wrote the history of Missouri for the "American Commonwealths" series; Lucien Carr, *Missouri: A Bone of Contention* (Boston: Houghton, Mifflin and Company, 1888).

761. Catharine Sedgwick to Kate Sedgwick Minot, 25 June 1854 (partly reprinted in Dewey, ed., *Life and Letters,* 357–58, as a June 24th letter); Primm, *Lion of the Valley,* 179, 250, 251 (photo), 492; entry for Eliot in *Appleton's Cyclopedia of American Biography;* Charlotte C. Eliot, *William Greenleaf Eliot: Minister, Educator, Philanthropist* (Boston: Houghton, Mifflin & Co., 1904), 82–84; information for the Sesquicentennial of Washington University of St. Louis at www.library.wustl.edu (website); Scharf, *History of Saint Louis,* 873. W. G. Eliot was a grandfather of the famous writer T.S. Eliot.

762. Catharine Sedgwick to Kate Sedgwick Minot, 25 June 1854 (partly reprinted in Dewey, ed., *Life and Letters,* 357–58, as a June 24th letter); Primm, *Lion of the Valley,* 111, 133, 136–37, 144, 183, 186, 188, 198, 200, 203–8, 218, 222 (photo), 225 (quoted); Eliot, *William Greenleaf Eliot,* 85–86; Hyde, *Encyclopedia of St. Louis,* 1662–63.

763. Catharine Sedgwick to Kate Sedgwick Minot, 25 June 1854 (partly reprinted in Dewey, ed., *Life and Letters,* 357–58, as a June 24th letter); Primm, *Lion of the Valley,* 344; *Putnam's Monthly Magazine,* September 1854, p. 324 (quoted).

764. Catharine Sedgwick to Kate Sedgwick Minot, 25 June 1854 (partly reprinted in Dewey, ed., *Life and Letters,* 357-358, as a June 24th letter); Primm, *Lion of the Valley,* 186, 205, 226, 252 (photo); *Putnam's Monthly Magazine,* September 1854, p. 324 (quoted). Sedgwick spells his name "Yateman"; I changed that to the generally accepted Yeatman.

765. Catharine Sedgwick to Will, 18 June 1854, Reel 4, CMS Papers; *Putnam's Monthly Magazine,* September 1854, p. 325 (quoted).

766. Eliot, *William Greenleaf Eliot,* 130, 131–32, 149.

767. Primm, *Lion of the Valley,* 178–79; McCandless, *History of Missouri: Vol. II,* 59–61 (quote from p. 61).

768. McCandless, *History of Missouri: Vol. II,* 265, 270–71; *New York Evening Post,* 24 June 1854, p. 2; *New York Times,* 15 June 1854, p. 2 (quoted).

769. Alice Nichols, *Bleeding Kansas* (New York: Oxford University Press, 1954), 9–11; Charles H. Robinson, *The Kansas Conflict* (n.p., n.d.), 76–77; Jay Monaghan, *Civil War on the Western Border 1854–1865* (Boston: Little, Brown and Company), 8 (quoted), 9; *National Intelligencer,* 22 June 1854, p. 3.

770. Potter, *Impending Crisis,* 199–203. Potter dates the meeting at Weston as July 29, 1854, but Aiken's report in the *Post* established that Missourians' opposition began earlier than that.

771. *Illinois State Register,* 15 June 1854, as quoted in William E. Baringer, *Lincoln Day by Day: A Chronology 1809–1865: Vol. II: 1849–1860* (Washington: U.S. Lincoln Sesquicentennial Commission, 1960), 123–24. Catharine Sedgwick wrote, "We came in two days to Chicago" (from St. Louis); Sedgwick to Will, 18 June 1854, Reel 4, CMS Papers, Massachusetts Historical Society.

772. Baringer, *Lincoln Day by Day: Vol. II,* 122–24; David Herbert Donald, *Lincoln* (New York: Touchstone, 1995), 145–56 (quote from p. 154).

773. Donald, *Lincoln,* 168–71.

774. *Illinois State Journal,* 16 June 1854, p. 2 (quoted, refuting the *Register*) and 20 June 1854, p. 2 (quoted).

775. *Chicago Daily Democratic Press,* 16 June 1854, p. 3; Scarry, *Millard Fillmore,* 261–62; Millard Fillmore to Edward Everett, 27 June 1854 (quoted), and Fillmore to John P. Kennedy, 30

June 1854 (quoted), both in Reel 42, Fillmore Papers, SHSW.

776. Bancroft to "My ever dear wife," 4 and 11 June 1854, and to "My very dear wife," 20 June 1854 (quoted), all in Reel 4, microfilm ed., Bancroft Papers, Cornell University Library.

777. Sedgwick to Will, 18 June 1854, and Sedgwick to "My dearest Kate," 25 June 1854 (quoted), both in Reel 4, microfilm ed., Sedgwick Papers, Massachusetts Historical Society.

778. Silliman journal, 9 June to 13 June 1854, p. 213–16, microfilm ed., UW–Madison.

779. Silliman journal, p. 217–18, 220 (quoted), 221 (quoted), microfilm ed., UW–Madison.

780. Silliman journal, p. 223–24, 226, 227, 228-29 (quoted), microfilm ed., UW–Madison.

781. Silliman journal, p. 233–34 (quote on p. 234), microfilm ed., UW–Madison.

782. Silliman journal, p. 234–36 (quote from p. 235-36), microfilm ed., UW–Madison. There are two pages numbered 235.

783. Silliman journal, p. 236, 238–39 (quote from p. 239), microfilm ed., UW–Madison.

784. Benjamin Silliman to John Taylor, 7 July 1854, handwritten copy in microfilm ed, Reel 6, UW-Madison. See also Silliman's September 19, 1854 letter to Taylor on the same reel.

EXCURSUS: The Grand Excursion and Antebellum Travel Literature

785. Lewis Perry, *Boats against the Current: American Culture between Revolution and Modernity, 1820–1860* (New York: Oxford University Press), 129 (quoted). See also Kristie Hamilton, *America's Sketchbook: The Cultural Life of a Nineteenth-Century Literary Genre* (Athens: Ohio University Press, 1998), 39–40; and Lueck, *Picturesque Tour,* 3–4, 18.

786. Hamilton, *America's Sketchbook,* 14, 15 (quoted), 21, 35 (quoting Fred Lewis Pattee).

787. Lueck, *Picturesque Tour,* 15 (quoting William Combe's character Doctor Syntax).

788. Hamilton, *America's Sketchbook,* 16 (quoted), 21 (quoting Hawthorne).

789. Hamilton, *America's Sketchbook,* 21, 38–40.

790. Here and below, see *New York Tribune,* 7 July 1854, p. 3.

791. *New York Daily Tribune,* 19 June 1854, p. 5; Gurowski to James Shepherd Pike, 8 June 1854 (quoted), reprinted in Pike, *First Blows of the Civil War* (1879), microfiche copy at University of Minnesota Wilson Library; LeRoy H. Fischer, *Lincoln's Gadfly: Adam Gurowski* (Norman: University of Oklahoma Press), 57 (quoted); Horace Greeley to Thurlow Weed, 28 May 1854 (quoted), Thurlow Weed Papers, University of Rochester. Fischer writes that "Greeley sent Gurowski" and Dana West, but the June 8 letter that he cites does not explicitly state that.

792. Entry for Gurowski in *Appleton's Cyclopedia of American Biography;* Fischer, *Lincoln's Gadfly,* vii, 56, 58–59; Pike, *First Blows,* 252 (quoted); Congdon, *Reminiscences,* 237 (quoted).

793. *New York Daily Tribune,* 19 June 1854, p. 5 (quoted).

794. *New York Daily Tribune,* 19 June 1854, p. 5 (quoted).

795. *New York Daily Tribune,* 19 June 1854, p. 5 (quoted).

796. *New York Daily Tribune,* 19 June 1854, p. 5 (quoted).

797. *New York Daily Tribune,* 19 June 1854, p. 5 (quoted).

798. Gurowski to Pike, 8 and 14 June and 30 July, all 1854, all in Pike, *First Blows.* Greeley sometimes edited and altered Gurowski's work, so we cannot be sure the article appeared exactly as written, but these were Gurowski's views, generally speaking.

799. "Forty Days in a Western Hotel," *Putnam's Monthly Magazine* 4, no. 24 (December 1854), 622–32 (quotes from p. 622); Lueck, *Picturesque Tour,* 12–14; Thomas Bender, *New York Intellect: A History of Intellectual Life in New York City, from 1750 to the*

Beginnings of Our Own Time (Baltimore: The Johns Hopkins University Press, 1988), 163–65 (the first quote from p. 164 represents Frank Luther Mott's words; the second one, from p. 165 represents Bender's words).

800. Hamilton, *America's Sketchbook,* 135; "Forty Days," 623 (quoted).

801. "Forty Days," 623 (quoted).

802. "Forty Days," 623 (quoted), 624, 625 (quoted), 626–27, 628 (quoted), 629 (quoted), 630–31.

803. "Forty Days," 629 (quoted), 630 (quoted), 631–32 (quoted).

804. *The Knickerbocker Gallery: A Testimonial to the Editor of the Knickerbocker Magazine from its Contributors* (New York: Samuel Hueston, 1855).

805. Burrows and Wallace, *Gotham,* 42 (quoted), 729 (quoted), 730.

806. Entries for Sargent in *Appleton's Cyclopaedia of American Biography* and *American National Biography.*

807. "On Lake Pepin," 99 (quoted); "Steamer 'Golden Era,'" passenger list in Farnam Family Papers, Yale.

808. "On Lake Pepin," 97–99 (quoted). For "picturesque composition," see Lueck, *Picturesque Tour,* 93–96.

809. "On Lake Pepin," 99–100 (quoted). Here and below, see the tale itself on p. 100–11. For the traditional Dakota version, I rely on Mary Henderson Eastman, *Dahcotah, or Life and Legends of the Sioux around Fort Snelling,* reprint ed. (Afton, Minnesota: Afton Historical Society Press, 1995), 123–29. Dacotah "was first published by John Wiley, New York, in 1849."

810. Rena Neumann Coen, "Preface: Mary Henderson Eastman: A Biographical Essay," ix, x, xii-xvii (quote from p. xvi), xxvii, and "The Maiden's Rock; or, Wenona's Leap," 126 (quoted), 127–29, all in Eastman, *Dahcotah,* reprint edition.

811. *Putnam's Monthly Magazine* (July 1854), p. 35.

812. "Great Excursion," 320 (quoted).

813. "Great Excursion," 320 (quoted).

814. "Great Excursion," 321 (quoted).

815. "Great Excursion," 321 (quoted), 322.

816. "Great Excursion," 323–24 (quoted).

817. "Great Excursion," 325.

818. "Great Excursion,' 325 (quoted).

819. Entry on Tuckerman in *American National Biography;* Carl Bode, *The Anatomy of American Popular Culture 1840–1861* (Berkeley: University of California Press, 1959), 208–10; Henry T. Tuckerman, *The Criterion; or the Test of Talk about Familiar Things* (New York: Hurd and Houghton, 1866), 132–59; *North American Review* 84, no. 175 (April 1857); Handlin, *George Bancroft,* 249; *Memoirs of Anne C. L. Botta Written by Her Friends* (New York: J. Selwin Tait and Sons, 1894), 13, 16 note 1.

820. Tuckerman, *Criterion,* 132–33 (quote from p. 133), 134–42, 146 (quoted), 156–57 (quoted).

821. Tuckerman, *Criterion,* 146–47 (quoted), 148–49 (quoted).

822. *New York Daily Tribune,* 20 June 1854, p. 4 (quoted).

823. "The *Journal* largely agreed," 29 June 1854, p. 2 (quoted).

824. *Troy Daily Whig,* 19 June 1854, p. 2.

EPILOGUE

825. Charles Hale to "Dear Mother," 21 June 1854 (quoted), "Sarah Preston (Everett) Hale, 1854" folder, box 21; Sarah P. Hale to "My dear Charlie," 18 June 1854, "Hale, Charles, 1854–56" folder, box 11; Lucretia Hale to "My dear Charlie," 19 June 1854 (quoted), "Hale, Charles, 1848–56: typescripts" folder, box 49, all in Hale Family Papers, Sophia Smith Collection, Smith College.

826. Elizabeth Blair Lee to Phil, 15 June and 24 June (quoted), both 1854, folder 8, box 74; Francis Preston Blair to "My Dear Daughter," 15 June [1854], folder 6, box 233, all in Blair and

Lee Family Papers, Princeton; Cornelia T. Martin to Mrs. Francis P. Blair, 21 June 1854, folder 2, box 6; and E. T. Throop Martin to "My dear Wife," 11 June 1854, folder 1, box 4, both in Throop and Martin Family Papers.

827. Julia Goodrich to Fanny, 28 June 1854 (quoted); "Mother [Julia] to My dearest child," 8 May 1854; W. C. Fowler to C. A. Goodrich, 29 May 1854; Julia Goodrich to Fowler, 29 May 1854; Goodrich to Fowler, 24 June 1854, all in folder 29, box 3, Goodrich Family Papers Series I, Manuscripts and Archives, Sterling Library, Yale; David Micklethwait, *Noah Webster and the American Dictionary* (Jefferson, North Carolina: McFarland and Company), 201–03, 242–43, 256–57, 264–71.

828. Chauncey A. Goodrich, *The Excursion* (New Haven?: n.p., 1854 or 1855), copy in Beinecke Rare Book and Manuscript Library, Yale.

829. Sheffield to John E. Henry, 5 June 1854, Folder 127, Box 10, Farnam Family Papers, Series I, Stirling Memorial Library, Yale.

830. *New York Evening Post,* 5 July 1854, p. 3 (quoted); *New Haven Palladium,* 6 July 1854, p. 2, and 8 July 1854, p. 2 (quoting *New York Mirror*); *Poughkeepsie Eagle,* 8 July 1854, p. 2 (quoted); *Rome Daily Sentinel,* 6 July 1854, p. 2; *Boston Evening Transcript,* 8 July 1854, p. 2; Arthur M. Johnson and Barry E. Supple, *Boston Capitalists and Western Railroads: A Study in the Nineteenth-Century Railroad Investment Process* (Cambridge: Harvard University Press, 1967), 140; George Bancroft to "Dear William" [Bliss], 9 June 1853, "Family Correspondence 1853-1854" folder, box 2, Bancroft-Bliss Family Papers, Library of Congress (Bancroft could be referring to George Schuyler, but more likely to his Harvard classmate Robert Schuyler).

831. *Boston Evening Transcript,* 8 July 1854, p. 2; *New Haven Palladium,* 8 July 1854, p. 2 (quoting *New York Mirror*). I have not tried to confirm this story from other sources.

832. Rev. William Jarvis to William Jarvis, 14 July 1854, box 1, William Jarvis Letters, Connecticut Historical Society; William Hosley, *Colt: The Making of an American Legend* (Amherst: University of Massachusetts Press, 1996), 28–29.

833. Andrew White to Simon Newton Dexter, 10 July 1854, Box 3, Simon Newton Dexter Papers, Special Collections, Carl Kroch Library, Cornell University.

834. Twining to C. J. Salter, 4 August 1854, folder D, box 10, Twining Papers, New Haven Colony Historical Society.

835. William Curtis Noyes to Roger Sherman Baldwin, 10 November 1854, and Baldwin to Noyes, 14 November 1854, both in "1849–54" folder, Baldwin Legal Cases, box 134, Series VII, Baldwin Family Papers, Manuscripts and Archives, Sterling Library, Yale; "Ancestral Chart of Jeffrey Orson Phelps," typescript, p. 4, Connecticut State Library.

836. William E. Gienapp, *The Origins of the Republican Party 1852–1856* (New York: Oxford University Press, 1987), 89 and note 80 on p. 89. There is some debate over the date of the meeting, but Gienapp appears to settle on May 23.

837. Gienapp, *Republican Party,* 104-05; *New York Evening Post,* 14 July 1854, p. 1.

838. *New York Evening Post,* 14 July 1854, p. 2 (quoted).

839. Gienapp, *Origins,* 113–19 (quote from p. 119).

840. Gienapp, *Origins,* 122–25.

841. Gienapp, *Origins,* 133–38; George S. Merriam, *The Life and Times of Samuel Bowles,* Vol. I (New York: Century, 1885), 116–21.

842. Gienapp, *Origins,* 147–57.

843. Gienapp, *Origins,* 158 (quoted). See also the discussion in Holt, *Rise and Fall of the American Whig Party,* 830–78.

844. Holt, *Rise and Fall of the American Whig Party,* 898 (quoted), 899, 908. Holt writes that Fillmore was informed "[d]uring the spring" of the Know Nothings' rise, but his sources (p. 1161,

note 80) only support a midsummer date.

845. *New York Times,* 14 June 1854, p. 2; *Buffalo Express,* 19 June 1854, p. 2 (quoted). The *Express* also quoted the *New York Courier and Enquirer* in criticism of Fillmore's speech at St. Paul's Capitol ball.

846. Duncan Kennedy to M. Fillmore, 27 June 1854, reel 42, microfilm edition, Fillmore Papers.

847. Fillmore to Kennedy, 28 June 1854, reel 42, microfilm edition, Fillmore Papers.

848. D. Kennedy to M. Fillmore, 3 July 1854, reel 42, microfilm edition, Fillmore Papers.

849. Elisabeth Terry to Fillmore, 30 June 1854, reel 42, microfilm edition, Fillmore Papers.

850. Fillmore to J. P. Kennedy, 30 June 1854, reel 42, microfilm edition, Fillmore Papers.

851. Alexander Ramsey to Millard Fillmore, 27 July 1854, and N. K. Hall to Fillmore, 29 July 1854, late July 1854 clipping quoting the *New Haven Journal and Courier* (and attributing Charles's death to cholera), and Fillmore to Mrs. Charles D. Fillmore, 31 July 1854, all in reel 42, microfilm edition, Fillmore Papers. Ramsey reports Charles Fillmore's death as occurring at 6:00 a.m. on the 27th; Abby Fuller dates his death on the 25th (but misdates her letter as the 26th when it must have been the 27th); Abby Fuller to "Dear Lizzie," 26 July 1854, box 1, Abby Abbe Fuller and Family Papers, Minnesota Historical Society, St. Paul.

852. Millard Fillmore to Mrs. Charles D. Fillmore, 31 July 1854, and Ramsey to Fillmore, 27 July 1854, both on reel 42, microfilm edition, Fillmore Papers.

853. *New York Weekly Mirror,* 24 June 1854, p. 2 (criticizing Fillmore's speeches); *National Intelligencer,* 1 August 1854, p. 1 (quoting the *Mirror*).

854. John A. Granger to Fillmore, 28 July 1854 (quoted); T. M. Howell to Fillmore, 30 July 1854; Elisabeth Terry to Fillmore, 31 July 1854 (quoted); and John T. Terry to Fillmore, 1 August 1854, all on reel 42, microfilm edition, Fillmore Papers.

855. *Rock Island Advertiser,* 5 July 1854, p. 2 (quoted, reprinting the *Missouri [St. Louis] Republican* of June 28); *Chicago Journal,* 13 June 1854, p. 2 (listing Dedieman as one of the *Sparhawk* crew); *Albany Evening Journal,* 16 June 1854, p. 2 (printing the *Sparhawk* resolutions).

856. Charles Sedgwick to William [Minot], 21 June 1854, box 12, Sedgwick IV Papers, Massachusetts Historical Society, Boston.

857. Charles Sedgwick to William [Minot], 21 June 1854, box 12, Sedgwick IV Papers, Massachusetts Historical Society, Boston.

858. Kelley, ed., *Power of Her Sympathy,* 3, 94-95 (quoted), and note 61 on p. 95.

859. Dewey, ed., *Life and Letters,* 360 (quoted); Kelley, "A Woman Alone," 220 (quoted); author's visit to Stockbridge Cemetery, 2 August 2003.

860. Charles Little and James Brown to George Bancroft, 16 June 1854; Bancroft to Little and Brown, 21 June 1854; Richard Bentley to George Bancroft, 21 July 1854 (quoted); Bancroft to "Dear Wife," 4 September 1854 (quoted), all in microfilm edition, Bancroft Papers, Cornell.

861. Potter, *Impending Crisis,* 199–224, 297–327 (Potter used the term "descent" to describe the crisis).

862. Handlin, *Intellectual as Democrat,* 262–63 (quoted).

863. Winger, *Lincoln, Religion, and Romantic Cultural Politics,* 70.

864. Winger, *Lincoln, Religion, and Romantic Cultural Politics,* 151 (quoted).

865. David Bain, *Empire Express,* 124-25, 154 (quoted), 155–56, 658–63, 666.

INDEX